CAMBRIDGE
UNIVERSITY PRESS

International History, 1870-1945

for Cambridge International AS Level History

COURSEBOOK

Phil Wadsworth

Series editor: Patrick Walsh-Atkins

CAMBRIDGE
UNIVERSITY PRESS

University Printing House, Cambridge CB2 8BS, United Kingdom

One Liberty Plaza, 20th Floor, New York, NY 10006, USA

477 Williamstown Road, Port Melbourne, VIC 3207, Australia

4843/24, 2nd Floor, Ansari Road, Daryaganj, Delhi – 110002, India

79 Anson Road, #06–04/06, Singapore 079906

Cambridge University Press is part of the University of Cambridge.

It furthers the University's mission by disseminating knowledge in the pursuit of education, learning and research at the highest international levels of excellence.

Information on this title: www.cambridge.org/ 9781108459327

First published 2019

20 19 18 17 16 15 14 13 12 11 10 9 8 7 6 5 4 3 2 1

Printed in Malaysia by Vivar Printing

A catalogue record for this publication is available from the British Library

ISBN 978-1-108-45932-7 Paperback

Contents

iii

How to use this book

This book contains a number of features to help you in your study.

Each chapter begins with a set of **Learning objectives** that briefly set out the points you should understand once you have completed the chapter.

Learning Objectives:

In this chapter, you will:

- understand the economic, social and cultural background to European imperialism in the late 19th century
- learn how, when and why various countries developed empires in Africa and China
- find out how the empire-building process affected relations between European countries

Before You Start

1 Look again at Chapter 1.1 and 1.2 regarding the impact of imperialism on China in the late 19th century.

Identify appropriate evidence to support each of the following statements:

a 'In the 19th century, China lacked a government that was capable of maintaining control over the country.'

Before you start activities are designed to activate the prior knowledge you need for each chapter.

The **Timeline** provides a visual guide to the key events which happened during the years covered by the topic.

Timeline

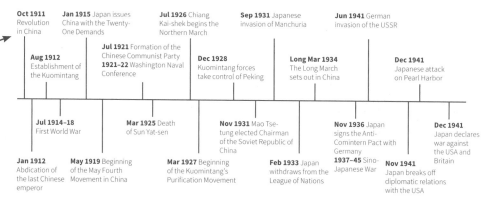

Each chapter contains multiple **Activities**. These are a mixture of individual and group tasks to help you develop your skills and practise applying your understanding of a topic.

ACTIVITY 1.12

a Look carefully at the extracts from President Fillmore's letter to the Japanese.

i How would you describe the tone of the letter? Note down the phrases you would use as examples in your answer

Reflection boxes are included throughout the book so that you have the chance to think about how your skills are developing and how you can enhance your independent learning skills.

Reflection: Review your answer to this activity. What evidence would you expect to see if the League of Nations was successfully achieving its aims?

Key terms are important terms in the topic you are learning. They are highlighted in black bold and defined where they first appear in the text.

 KEY TERMS

Monopoly: a market structure characterised by a single seller facing no competition.

SUN YAT-SEN (1866–1925)

Sun Yat-sen was educated abroad and graduated as a doctor of medicine. He became a professional revolutionary, touring Europe and the USA to raise funds for the Save China League. Risking imprisonment and possible execution, he returned to China several times to campaign for a revolution against the Manchu dynasty, but he was in the USA when the revolution finally took place in 1911.

Key Figure boxes highlight important historical figures that you need to remember.

Key Concepts boxes contain questions that help you develop a conceptual understanding of History, and how the different topics you study are connected.

KEY CONCEPT

Interpretation

Look at the alternative ways in which historians have interpreted the Japanese government's willingness to make concessions at the Washington Naval Conference. Which interpretation do you find most convincing, and why?

Think Like a Historian boxes contain prompts and questions requiring that you apply your skills in evaluation and analysis. They go beyond the syllabus to help you understand how these skills apply in the real world.

●●● THINK LIKE A HISTORIAN

As we have seen, public support for European imperialism in the late 19th century owed much to nationalism and racism. Consider the ways in which both nationalism and racism continue to affect our lives today.

Summary

After working through this chapter, make sure you understand the following key points:

- what imperialism is and the reasons why it became a major element in the policies of certain late-19th century European nations
- the reasons for, and impact of, European imperialism, particularly in Africa and China

Each chapter ends with a summary, Exam-style questions and a Sample answer. The **Summary** is a brief review of the main points in the chapter to help you revise.

Exam-Style Questions provide an opportunity to relate your learning to formal assessment and practise writing longer answers.

1 a Compare and contrast the views expressed in Sources A and B regarding the agreement which emerged from the Munich Conference.

b 'In October 1938, the British people believed that the risk of war with Germany was over.' How far do Sources A to D support this view?

The two senators agree that the USA should play a role in helping to maintain future world peace. Harding says that 'America will not fail civilisation in the advancement of peace'. Cox says that the USA should work together with other nations to 'avoid war in the future'.
However, they disagree on the issue of whether the USA should join the League of Nations. Harding is clearly opposed to the USA joining the League. He argues that joining the League would lead to 'foreign interference' in American affairs and the USA being forced into 'menacing involvement'. He says that the USA should remain 'free agents', rather than being 'shackled' to an agreement which would force the USA to take action against its will. In particular, he is concerned that the USA might be forced to take part in war on the instructions of the League. Cox takes the opposite view. He argues that the League of Nations would make 'another war impossible'. Joining the League would enable the USA to 'participate in the advancement of peace'. The sentence 'shall we unite with our former allies to make the League effective' implies that the League would be likely to fail without American involvement. Cox claims that, if the USA did not join the League, it would need to enhance its army and navy in order to guarantee its own protection – this would not only mean increased taxation, but could also lead to the kind of arms race with other countries which led to the First World War.
Therefore, the two senators agree that it is important for the USA to help preserve world peace, but disagree about the best way to achieve this.

The **Sample answer** to one of the exam-style questions is a realistic student response, annotated with explanations about what makes it successful and commentary on how it could be improved.

This answer is based on sound understanding of the arguments put forward by the two senators. It accurately identifies areas of agreement and disagreement, backed up by well-selected supporting evidence.

However, there is very little evaluation. This aspect could have been improved in two ways.

Further reading

Hall, K., Brown, D. and Williams, B. (2015). *Nationalism, Dictatorship and Democracy in 20th Century Europe.* **Pearson.** The section on Germany contains a useful analysis of the extent to which Hitler was responsible for the Second World War. The section on Spain provides a good account of the Spanish Civil War.

Henig, R. (2005). *The Origins of the Second World War 1933–1941.* **Routledge.** A short book which analyses the short- and long-term causes of the Second World War.

The **Further Reading** section suggests additional resources where you can explore the topic in more detail.

v

Introduction

Aims of the coursebook

Cambridge International AS Level History is a revised series of three books that offer complete and thorough coverage of the Cambridge International AS Level History syllabus (9489). Each book covers one of the three AS Level options in the Cambridge International syllabus for first examination in 2021. These books may also prove useful for students following other AS and A Level courses covering similar topics. Written in clear and accessible language, *Cambridge International AS Level History-International History, 1870–1945* enables students to gain the knowledge, understanding and skills to succeed in their AS Level course (and ultimately in further study and examination).

Syllabus

Students wishing to take just the AS Level take two separate papers at the end of a one year course. If they wish to take the full A Level there are two possible routes. The first is to take the two AS papers at the end of the first year of the course and a further two A Level papers at the end of the following year. The second is to take the two AS papers as well as the two A Level papers at the end of a two year course. For the full A Level, all four papers must be taken.

There are four topics available to be studied within the International option:

- Empire and the emergence of world powers 1870–1919
- The League of Nations and international relations in the 1920s
- The League of Nations and international relations in the 1930s
- China and Japan 1912–1945

The two AS Level papers are outlined below.

Paper 1

This is a source based paper which lasts for one hour and 15 minutes and is based on one of the four topics listed above. Your school/college will be notified in advance which topic it will be. The paper will contain at least three sources and students will have to answer two questions based on them. The questions will be based on one of the four key questions set out in the syllabus. **There is no choice of question**. Students will be expected to have the ability to understand, evaluate and utilise those sources in their answers, as well as having sound knowledge of the topic. In the first question, (a), students are required to consider the sources and answer a question based on one aspect of them. There is a particular emphasis on source comprehension and evaluation skills in this question, but contextual knowledge is important as well. In the second question, (b), students must use the sources as well as their own knowledge and understanding to address how far the sources support a given statement. The relevant knowledge is provided in the appropriate chapter in this book.

Paper 2

This paper lasts for one hour and 45 minutes. This paper contains **three** questions, and students must answer **two** of them. There will be one question on each of the three remaining topics which have **not** been examined for Paper 1. So for example, if the topic covered in Paper 1 is China and Japan, Paper 2 will contain a question on each of the following three topics:

- Empire and the emergence of world powers 1870–1919
- The League of Nations and international relations in the 1920s
- The League of Nations and international relations in the 1930s

Each question has two parts: part (a) requires a causal explanation; and part (b) requires analysis. All the questions will be based on one of the four key questions set out in the syllabus. The focus of this paper is on assessing the candidates' knowledge and understanding of the specified topics and also assessing their analytical skills. The syllabus makes it clear what specific skills are being assessed in each paper, and how marks are allocated.

Acknowledgements

The authors and publishers acknowledge the following sources of copyright material and are grateful for the permissions granted. While every effort has been made, it has not always been possible to identify the sources of all the material used, or to trace all copyright holders. If any omissions are brought to our notice, we will be happy to include the appropriate acknowledgements on reprinting.

Thanks to the following for permission to reproduce images:

Cover Image: Design Pics Inc/GI

Chapter 1: Universal History Archive/GI; De Agostini Picture Library/GI; Ann Ronan Pictures/GI; Hulton Archive/GI; Stock Montage/GI; Fotosearch/GI; German illustration from the book itself: Satirical caricature of Germany's civilizing mission: Simplicissimus (3 May 1904), vol. ix, no. 6, p. 58, drawing by Wilhelm Schulz; a postcard from the website genocide.leadr. msu.ed; Chris Hellier/GI; Ann Ronan Pictures/GI; Punch Cartoon Library/TopFoto; Leemage/GI; Universal History Archive/ GI; Hulton Archive/GI; Bettmann/GI; Hulton Archive/GI; **Chapter 2:** Harald Wenzel-Orf/GI; Cartoon 'European Baby Show' by Burt Randolph Thomas, The Detroit News in Review of Reviews, Vol. 59, No. 6, pp. 570; OFF/GI; Historical/GI; Hulton Archive/GI; Walter Sanders/GI; John Frost Newspapers/Alamy; BIPS/GI; Three Lions/GI; AFP/GI; David Low/Solo Syndication; Hulton-Deutsch/GI; Hulton Archive/GI; Cartoon 'The Gap in the Bridge' by Leonard Raven-Hill from Punch Magazine, 10 December 1919; CARTOON: VERSAILLES TREATY. The Accuser. An American cartoon of 1920 by Rollin Kirby after the U.S. Senate returned the Versailles Treaty unratified to President Woodrow Wilson © The Granger Collection Ltd.; **Chapter 3:** Historical/GI; AFP/GI; Keystone/GI; Hulton Archive/GI; Michael Nicholson/Getty Images; Ullstein Bild Dtl./GI; Bettmann/ GI; Bettmann/GI; Associated Newspapers Ltd/Solo Syndication; A 1939 Herblock Cartoon, © The Herb Block Foundation; **Chapter 4:** Zhang Peng/GI; Fotosearch/GI; Charles Chusseau-Flaviens/GI; A poster published by the Chinese government in 1959, reproduced with the permission of Chinese Poster Shop; Hulton Archive/GI; Hulton Archive/GI; Bettmann/GI; Granger Historical Picture Archive/Alamy; Historical/GI; Time Life Pictures/GI; **Chapter 5:** Caiaimage/Sam Edwards/GI; Universal History Archive/GI; STF/GI; The political cartoon 'Rendezvous' by David Low from British Cartoon Archive at the University of Kent.

Key: GI = Getty Images

Chapter 1
Empire and the emergence of world powers 1870–1919

Learning Objectives:

In this chapter, you will:

- understand the economic, social and cultural background to European imperialism in the late 19th century
- learn how, when and why various countries developed empires in Africa and China
- find out how the empire-building process affected relations between European countries
- understand the circumstances of Japan and the USA at the beginning of this period, and how they both developed rapidly to become world powers.

Timeline

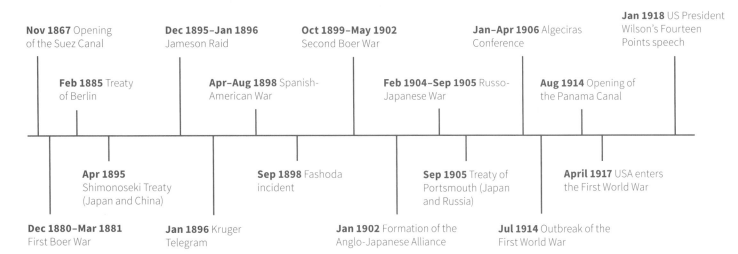

Nov 1867 Opening of the Suez Canal

Dec 1895–Jan 1896 Jameson Raid

Oct 1899–May 1902 Second Boer War

Jan–Apr 1906 Algeciras Conference

Jan 1918 US President Wilson's Fourteen Points speech

Feb 1885 Treaty of Berlin

Apr–Aug 1898 Spanish-American War

Feb 1904–Sep 1905 Russo-Japanese War

Aug 1914 Opening of the Panama Canal

Apr 1895 Shimonoseki Treaty (Japan and China)

Sep 1898 Fashoda incident

Sep 1905 Treaty of Portsmouth (Japan and Russia)

April 1917 USA enters the First World War

Dec 1880–Mar 1881 First Boer War

Jan 1896 Kruger Telegram

Jan 1902 Formation of the Anglo-Japanese Alliance

Jul 1914 Outbreak of the First World War

Before You Start

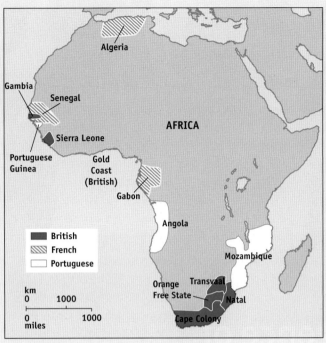

Figure 1.1: European African possessions in 1870

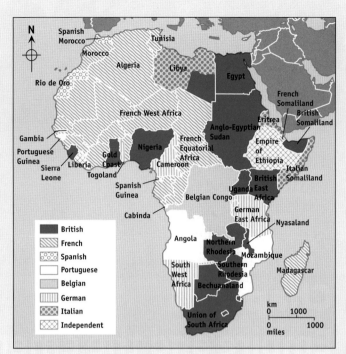

Figure 1.2: European African possessions in 1914

Look carefully at Figures 1.1 and 1.2, maps showing European African possessions in 1870 and 1914. Working in pairs, answer the following questions:

1 a What did the African territories controlled by European nations in 1870 have in common?

   b What factors might explain this?

2 a In what ways had the situation changed by 1914?

   b What factors do you think might explain these changes?

   c Which parts of Africa remained independent of European control by 1914?

3 Why do you think European nations were able to gain such a powerful influence in Africa in such a short period of time?

4 Make a list of factors that you think might explain why European nations were so keen to gain territory in Africa.

5 How do you think the desire to gain African territory might have affected relations between European countries?

Introduction

European nations had a long tradition of increasing their wealth, prestige and power by seeking overseas possessions. As early as the 16th century, Spain had taken control of large parts of South America. In the 18th century, Britain and France had competed for territory in North America and India. In the early 19th century, Britain already controlled an empire stretching from New Zealand to Canada. Portugal had been exploring the African coast as far as modern Mozambique from the 15th century, with Dutch competition from the 17th century.

By the early 19th century, European involvement in overseas expansion had unquestionably declined. The costs involved in maintaining control over their overseas possessions, which frequently involved expensive wars, proved too great for Europe's **imperial** nations. Britain had lost control over its 13 colonies in North America following the American War of Independence (1775–1883), while Spain no longer had extensive influence in South America. Nevertheless, the desire to identify and exploit profitable ventures overseas remained. As their interests in the Americas declined, European nations began to look elsewhere, such as Africa and Asia. This was to lead to a new wave of imperialism in the period from 1871 to 1914.

KEY TERM

Imperialism: the policy of extending a nation's power by gaining political and economic control over more territory. This is sometimes referred to as colonialism and the territories taken under control are known as colonies.

1.1 Why was imperialism a significant force for late 19th-century Europe?

Economic and political motives for imperial expansion

The desire to find and exploit new trading opportunities had been one of the main reasons for imperial expansion in the 16th, 17th and 18th centuries. Following a policy of **mercantilism**, the most powerful European nations aimed to increase their wealth through trade. Their governments established firm control over all aspects of trade with the aim of limiting the cost of imports and increasing the value of exports. This would enable nations to accumulate large quantities of gold and silver. Gaining overseas possessions provided a cheap source of raw materials and labour, and valuable products, such as spices and silks, which were not available in Europe. At the same time, the overseas possessions provided a guaranteed and lucrative market for European goods.

KEY TERM

Mercantilism: an economic policy based on the belief that there was only a limited amount of wealth in the world. European nations aimed to increase their share of that wealth at the expense of their rivals, a situation that encouraged imperialism and led to frequent wars.

Many European businessmen and private companies were able to become extremely wealthy by exploiting this favourable, government-supported trading situation. The most obvious example of this exploitation is the slave trade. From as early as the 16th century, ships had sailed from European ports to the coast of Africa. There the Europeans would acquire slaves, either by bartering with local chieftains or simply by capturing local people. The human cargo was then shipped across the Atlantic Ocean and sold to plantation owners in the USA and Caribbean islands to work as slaves picking cotton, or harvesting

tobacco or sugar. The ships would then return to Europe carrying these profitable commodities.

Empires were neither stable nor permanent constructs. Belief in mercantilism began to decline during the 18th century. Maintaining control over overseas possessions and protecting vital trade routes from rival nations was expensive and often led to wars. In the second half of the 18th century, for example, Britain fought hugely expensive wars in an attempt to maintain control over its territorial possessions in North America. While Britain was able to retain Canada, it was finally forced to accept the independence of the United States of America. At the same time, the Spanish Empire in Latin America was collapsing; once Brazil declared full independence from Portugal in 1827 very little remained of the Latin American empires of Spain and Portugal.

Moreover, new economic theories were suggesting that a nation's wealth should not be judged by the amount of gold and silver it possessed, but by its ability to produce goods and services. The most influential of these theories was put forward by the Scottish economist Adam Smith in *An Inquiry into the Nature and Causes of the Wealth of Nations*, published in 1776. Smith suggested that, in many respects, imperialism was far from profitable. Writing at a time when Britain was beginning to undergo its industrial revolution, Smith argued that a nation's ability to increase its production of goods and services depended on investment in new methods. Government control over a nation's economy, he concluded, was neither necessary nor desirable. Wealthy individuals would be more likely to invest if they could reap the financial rewards without government interference. In line with these new economic theories, the incentive for government-sponsored imperial expansion declined.

Economic motives for imperial expansion: industrialisation

During the 19th century, however, a new economic motive for imperial expansion developed. The industrial revolution, based on mechanisation, meant that European industry expanded rapidly. Goods were mass-produced on such a scale that it became essential to find new sources of raw materials with which to make them and new markets in which to sell them. Moreover, **entrepreneurs**, who had made rapid profits from industrialisation, sought new places in which to invest their wealth.

KEY TERM

Entrepreneurs: people who invest their money (known as capital) in business ventures. They are prepared to take this financial risk in the hope of making large profits.

3

As the first country to undergo an industrial revolution, Britain enjoyed enormous economic advantages during the first half of the 19th century. The development of steam-powered machinery revolutionised Britain's textiles industries, while new techniques were introduced for the production of iron and steel. Railways and steamships enabled Britain to transport its products more efficiently. Britain was 'The Workshop of the World', able to produce goods more quickly and more cheaply than any other country.

As the industrial revolution spread across Europe, Britain's advantageous economic situation ended. In the second half of the 19th century, Britain began to face growing competition from its European rivals and also from the USA, which was rapidly emerging as an economic power in its own right. By 1850, the economies of the German states had been transformed by the development of railways and the formation of a customs union (the *Zollverein*), which enabled greater trade between them. By the time of its unification in 1871, Germany had emerged as a serious industrial and commercial challenger to Britain. Though much slower to industrialise than Germany, France too was making a concerted effort to extend its international trade. With a well-established trading outpost in Senegal, France increased its commercial interests in Africa with the conquest of Algeria (1830–47). Between 1850 and 1870, France developed the second most powerful navy in the world, surpassed only by Britain, and established naval bases in the Indian Ocean (in the Seychelles) and Indo-China (Cambodia and Vietnam) to enhance and protect French trade with Asia.

Economic motives for imperial expansion: the 'Long Depression'

This competition was enhanced by what became known as the 'Long Depression', a period of price **deflation** that lasted from 1873 to 1896. As a result of rapid industrialisation across Europe and the USA, principally in Germany and Britain, the production of goods was outstripping demand. Businessmen and industrialists were forced to lower their prices, which, in turn, led to declining wages and job losses. Governments were put under enormous pressure to protect and promote their nations' economies. European countries, therefore, began competing for new overseas possessions that would provide guaranteed markets for their industrial products.

KEY TERM

Deflation: Falling prices caused by a drop in demand. This leads to falling wages and unemployment, which, in turn, further reduces demand as less people can afford to buy goods.

Economic motives for imperial expansion: competition for raw materials

Just as Europe's industrialised nations needed to find new markets for the huge increase in their output of manufactured products, so they also needed to identify and exploit new sources of raw materials, such as cotton, copper, rubber and tin. Large quantities of these materials could be found in Africa and Asia. For example, raw cotton in Mozambique and India, copper in Southern Africa, rubber in the Congo and tin in British Malaya (modern Malaysia). At the same time, Africa and Asia offered other products that were highly valued in Europe – tea and silk (China), gold and diamonds (the Transvaal), and palm oil (West Africa).

Writing in 1902, the British economist John Hobson summarised the economic reasons for imperial expansion in the last quarter of the 19th century:

> Imperialists argue that we must have new markets for our growing manufactures and new outlets for the investment of our surplus capital. Imperial expansion is a necessity for a nation with our great and growing powers of production. An ever large share of our population is devoted to manufacturing and commerce, and is therefore dependent for life and work upon food and raw materials from foreign lands. In order to buy and pay for these things, we must sell our goods abroad. During the first three-quarters of the 19th century Britain could do so without difficulty by a natural expansion of commerce with European nations and our overseas lands, all of which were far behind us in the main arts of manufacture and trade. So long as Britain held a virtual **monopoly** of the world markets for manufactured goods, imperialism was unnecessary.
>
> **John A. Hobson, 'The Economic Taproot of *Imperialism*'; from Imperialism a Study (1902)**

 KEY TERM

Monopoly: a market structure characterised by a single seller facing no competition.

Political motives for imperial expansion: growth of nationalism

By 1871, the political map of Europe had been settled. New nation states were declared in Germany and Italy, and borders within Europe had been agreed. Only war could change these borders, and war was something that all nations were keen to avoid. Although Russia and Austria continued to eye possibilities in the Balkans following local uprisings against the ruling Ottoman Empire, there was little possibility of expansion within Europe itself. Countries needed to look overseas in order to enhance their own industrialisation and increase their wealth, power, prestige and influence.

> **KEY TERM**
>
> **Nationalism:** a sense of belonging to a nation and supporting its interests above those of other nations. The belief that your country is superior ethnically, culturally, politically and historically to all other countries.

The late 19th century witnessed an increase in **nationalism** throughout Europe. Germany and Italy were keen to establish themselves as newly unified nation states. France was determined to recover from its humiliating defeat in the Franco-Prussian War (1870–71). Confronted by increasing economic competition from its European neighbours, Britain proudly boasted about the size of its empire and the power of its navy.

Addressing the British parliament in February 1870, for example, the Earl of Carnarvon said:

> We have an Empire such as no other people ever possessed. Spain had a great empire, but it has almost disappeared. France had considerable possessions across the seas, but it has seen them gradually absorbed by other nations. Britain alone has built up a vast Empire. It is an Empire of which we have reason to be proud.

In the Naval Defence Act, 1889, the British government formally adopted the 'two power standard'. This aimed to ensure that the British navy remained at least as powerful as the combined strength of the next two largest navies (French and Russian at the time).

European governments increasingly portrayed overseas possessions as symbols of national pride and power. French governments, for example, argued that it was France's destiny to be superior to other nations and to spread its language, culture and beliefs to other parts of the world through overseas expansion.

The French politician Paul Doumer argued:

> Just as Rome civilised the barbarians beyond its borders, we too have a duty to extend French culture and religion to the backwards people of the world.

French missionaries in Indo-China, however, did rather more than simply spread Christianity and French culture. Their leaders, such as Bishops Lefèbvre, Pellerin and Puginier actively helped French military forces take control over parts of Vietnam.

Political motives for imperial expansion: imperialism as social policy

By 1870, political power in Europe remained largely in the hands of wealthy landowners, businessmen and entrepreneurs. Many of them stood to gain from overseas expansion. However, their political control was being threatened. Industrialisation had led to the emergence of a large and increasingly organised working class, which demanded social, economic and political reform.

In an effort to reduce this threat, governments portrayed overseas expansion as beneficial to everyone. Senior politicians, such as the long-serving French Prime Minister Jules Ferry and Britain's Joseph Chamberlain, viewed imperialism as a way of diverting popular attention away from social, economic and political inequalities. They argued that imperialism would provide their countries with the finance required to pay for social reform, and improve the condition of the working classes by ensuring steady employment. Governments, therefore, used imperialism as a way of uniting their peoples, regardless of wealth or class, behind a common aim – the development of the economic and political power of their country through overseas expansion.

Political motives for imperial expansion: strategic control of key regions

Prior to 1869, trading with India and the Far East had involved Europeans in a lengthy and hazardous voyage around the southern tip of Africa. To supply and protect its ships on this vital trade route, Britain had established a port in Cape Colony in southern Africa. Between 1859 and 1869, the Suez Canal Company, financed largely by British and French entrepreneurs, constructed a canal linking the Mediterranean Sea and the Red Sea across Egyptian territory. This enabled European ships to travel to and from India and the Far East more quickly and more cost-effectively. However, the instability of the Egyptian government threatened this new trading route and so, in 1882, Britain reluctantly took over the administration of Egypt. Many historians believe that it was the establishment of British power in Egypt that encouraged other European nations to gain territory in Africa. What originated as a strategy to facilitate commercial activity became a political motive for seeking overseas possessions.

Figure 1.3: The opening of the Suez Canal greatly shortened the journey from Europe to India and the Far East.

ACTIVITY 1.1

The policy of imperial expansion is a political and economic system. In the area of economics, there is a need, felt more and more urgently by the industrialised population of Europe, and especially the people of our rich and hard-working country of France – the need for outlets for exports. What our major industries lack more and more are outlets. Germany and the USA are setting up trade barriers. Not only are these great markets becoming more and more difficult to access, but these great states are

ACTIVITY 1.1 (CONTINUED)

beginning to pour into our own markets. Our navy needs safe harbours and supply centres on the high seas. That is why we need imperial expansion. If we do not expand into Africa and the Far East, in less time than you think, France will sink from the first rank of nations to the third or fourth.

Jules François Camille Ferry, speech before the French Chamber of Deputies, 28 March 1884

Should Germany begin on the road to imperialism? I believe we should. We are an industrial nation. In order to maintain our factories and produce our goods we need access to natural resources which can be found in Africa and Asia. Obtaining overseas possessions will open up new markets to trade our goods, and provide our bankers with new projects to invest money in. Imperialism will strengthen our military and defend our nation. By engaging in imperialism we can limit the power of our competitors, Britain and France. We can prevent territory falling into their hands. Taking part in imperialism would increase national pride in Germany. We will show the world that we are a strong nation. We can restore Germany's position as the most prestigious, important and influential nation in Europe.

Friedrich Fabri, *Does Germany Need Colonies?* (1879)

Working in pairs, discuss the following questions and prepare detailed notes:

a Compare and contrast the arguments used by Ferry and Fabri to justify imperial expansion by their respective countries.

b What economic factors encouraged European nations to seek overseas possessions in the late 19th century?

c What political factors encouraged European nations to seek overseas possessions in the late 19th century?

Make sure that your notes include both the economic and the political factors which led to imperialism.

The emergence of 'New Imperialism'

The period from 1871 to 1914 witnessed a new wave of imperialism that is referred to as 'New Imperialism'. There is some disagreement between historians regarding just how 'new' this 'New Imperialism' actually was. Some argue that it was simply a continuation of earlier overseas expansion by European nations, while others suggest that it was fundamentally different in character.

Nature of 'New Imperialism'

What is referred to as 'New Imperialism' by historians had three main characteristics:

1. **Geographic scope:** whereas previous imperialism had been largely focused on the 'New World' (North and South America), 'New Imperialism' centred on Africa and Asia. Explorers had shown that the African interior contained an abundant supply of valuable minerals and other raw materials including rubber and tin. One of the most famous explorers was David Livingstone, a Scottish missionary, who discovered the source of the River Nile. His African expeditions were heavily funded by the British government, which realised the potential value of his discoveries. Meanwhile, the crumbling Chinese Empire offered opportunities to increase vital trade links with the Far East. The French explorer Henri Mouhot led several expeditions to Siam, Cambodia and Laos, his discoveries paving the way for subsequent French imperial control over large areas of Indo-China.

2. **Maintaining peaceful relations:** although the rush to acquire new overseas possessions inevitably involved rivalry between European nations, there was a very real attempt to prevent this leading to the constant warfare that had characterised earlier imperialism. The Treaty of Berlin (1885), for example, effectively laid down rules by which European nations should carry out their plans for expansion in Africa – a clear attempt to avoid possible confrontation. In China, imperial nations occupied their own discrete areas of influence, and, indeed, were prepared to collaborate against the Chinese.

3. **New imperial countries:** earlier imperialism had been carried out by the main European powers – Britain, France, Spain, Portugal and the Netherlands. With 'New Imperialism', the desire for overseas expansion was no longer confined to the great powers of Europe. Massive industrial growth led the USA to seek greater control over Central and South America, together with access to trading rights in Asia. This required the development of a strong navy and the acquisition of overseas bases from which it could operate. Meanwhile, Japan embarked on its own industrial and military revolutions, enabling it to seek greater power and influence within Asia. This was to bring Japan into immediate conflict with one of the major European powers, Russia, and made subsequent rivalry with the USA more likely.

Factors enabling 'New Imperialism'

If 'New Imperialism' was motivated by political, economic and strategic issues, social and technological factors made it possible:

1. **Medical advancement**: in the late 18th century, Africa was known as 'the white man's grave' because of the dangers of diseases such as malaria. The medicine quinine, discovered by French scientists in 1817, proved to be an effective treatment for malaria. As fears of contracting and dying of diseases gradually faded, the African interior and the jungles of Asia became more accessible to Europeans.

2. **Technological advancement**: the industrial revolution had led to the introduction of new methods of producing iron and steel both cheaply and in large quantities. For example, Henry Bessemer's system for the mass production of high-quality steel became widely used after 1856. This facilitated developments in railways and steamships, which made transport both quicker and safer. Iron-hulled, steam-driven ships (which, unlike sailing ships, did not need deep hulls for stability and did not depend on wind power) were able to navigate rivers such as the Congo, the Zambezi and the Niger, offering easier access to the African interior. Similarly, communications systems were greatly improved. A telegraph network was established, and by 1891 its cables reached from London to North and South America, India and New Zealand. This made it far easier for imperial nations to administer and control their overseas possessions.

At the same time, the development of fast-firing rifles, machine guns and heavy artillery gave Europeans a distinct advantage over poorly armed Africans. For example, although vastly outnumbered by their African opponents, the possession of machine guns enabled British soldiers to gain rapid victory in the Matabele War of 1893. With such effective weaponry, territory in both Africa and Asia could be taken with little effective resistance from the local people.

Opposition to slavery

By 1820, most European governments had banned the slave trade, arguing that slavery was 'repugnant to the principles of natural justice' (P. E. Lovejoy, *Transformations in Slavery: A History of Slavery in Africa*, Cambridge University Press, 2000, 290). It was known that slavery remained common in Africa and that many African chieftains continued to barter in human beings. Many Europeans believed that they had a moral duty to put an end to this practice.

The theory of racial superiority

In the early 19th century, scientists such as Johann Friedrich Blumenbach and Joseph Arthur Comte de Gobineau developed theories regarding the classification of races. White people were classified as racially superior to other groups, such as Asians and Africans. The publication in 1859 of Charles Darwin's influential book *On The Origins of Species* was widely, if mistakenly, interpreted as providing further scientific justification for such theories. It appeared to imply that certain races were inferior, being less evolved and thus less human than others. These views, presented through poor science and consciously or unconsciously motivated by political and ideological factors, were widely accepted both in Europe and in the USA. Convinced of their racial superiority, many Europeans believed that they had a duty to bring order, stability and civilisation to the lives of 'pagan' Africans and Asians. The missionary-explorer David Livingstone, for example, argued that it was essential to introduce Africans and Asians to the three 'Cs' – commerce, Christianity and civilisation.

> The French economist, Paul Leroy Beaulieu, writing in 1891, suggested that:
>
> > The great part of the world is inhabited by barbarian tribes or savages who participate in wars without end and brutal customs. They do not know how to work, invent, or exploit their land and its natural resources. The civilised people of the west have a duty to spread knowledge of medicine, law and Christian religion.
> >
> > **Paul Leroy-Beaulieu, *On the Desirability of Imperialism* (1891)**

The claim that European nations were gaining overseas possessions in order to improve the lives of local people provided convenient justification for actions that were, in reality, motivated by self-interest and characterised by exploitation. Lord Lugard, a British soldier and explorer who was later governor of the British colony of Nigeria.

While recognising that Africans may have benefitted from the British presence on their continent, Lord Lugard, a British soldier and explorer who was later governor of the British colony of Nigeria, openly accepted that

Britain's main motive was to 'serve our own interest as a nation' by enhancing trade. It is interesting to note that he clearly saw nothing wrong in this, claiming that it was Britain's 'right' to take such action, quickly dismissing the views of those who argued that Africa 'belongs to the native'. In asserting that Britain had every right to take possession of African land in order to address its own national interests, Lord Lugard was clearly implying that the rights and needs of Europeans outweighed those of Africans. In this, he was conforming to the widespread belief in European racial superiority.

In Germany, Social Democrat politician August Bebel addressed the Reichstag in 1906 pledging SPD support for German imperialism as 'a great cultural mission', even though he had in 1899 told the same assembly that 'the substance of all colonisation is to exploit a foreign population to the utmost degree':

As Sebastian Conrad comments in his *German Colonialism: A Short History* (Cambridge University Press, 2012, 35) 'there was no question of even the SPD actually opposing colonisation as such'.

ACTIVITY 1.2

> It is well to realise that it is for our advantage – and not alone at the dictates of duty – that we have undertaken responsibilities in East Africa. It is in order to foster the growth of the trade of this country, and to find an outlet for our manufactures that our far-seeing statesmen and our commercial men advocate colonial expansion . . . There are some who say we have no right in Africa at all, that it 'belongs to the native'. I hold that our right is the necessity that is upon us to provide for our ever-growing population and to stimulate trade by finding new markets, since we know what misery trade depression brings at home. While thus serving our own interest as a nation, we may bring at the same time many advantages to Africa.
>
> **F. D. Lugard, *The Rise of Our East African Empire* (1893)**

Answer the following questions and then discuss your answers in pairs or small groups.

a In your own words, explain why the opening of the Suez Canal was so important to European nations.

b What did Lord Lugard say were the reasons for British imperialism in the late 19th century?

c How did European nations attempt to justify their takeover of African territory in the late 19th century? List the three most important factors.

d Put into an order of significance the various reasons why European countries began to seek territory in Africa during the late 19th century. Put what you consider to be the most important factor at the top, and the least important at the bottom. Hold a group discussion on the reasons. Each student should make the case for their most important factor. Remember you must provide evidence for your reason.

Nature and purpose of the 'scramble for Africa'

In 1870, only 10% of Africa was under direct European control, most of it in the coastal regions. Europeans knew little about the African interior, other than that it seemed to be a mysterious, inhospitable and dangerous place. As medical advancements reduced the health risks and steam ships made river transport more accessible, explorers began to venture into Africa. Some, such as David Livingstone, were missionaries, determined to bring Christianity to the 'uncivilised' African natives. Others were financed by wealthy entrepreneurs, keen to find new resources and trading opportunities. One of the most famous explorers, Henry Morton Stanley, was hired by **Leopold II, King of Belgium**, to secure treaties with local chieftains along the course of the Congo River.

KING LEOPOLD II OF BELGIUM (1835–1909)

Leopold was King of Belgium from 1865 to 1909. He financed the colonisation of the Congo Free State (now the Democratic Republic of the Congo), which he exploited in order to make money from ivory and rubber. Leopold's regime in Africa was characterised by cruelty towards the native inhabitants, and he was eventually forced to hand control of the Congo to the Belgian government in 1908.

As increasing exploration reduced European fears of Africa, the opportunities it offered became increasingly apparent. The last quarter of the 19th century witnessed what contemporary journalists labelled the 'scramble for Africa' – a rush by European nations to take control of African territory. By 1900, over 90% of the African continent was under the control of European nations.

Britain

Britain's original concern had been to protect its vital Indian Ocean trading routes, and this explains its interest in Egypt and South Africa. The discovery of gold, diamonds and other valuable minerals in the Boers' independent republic in the Transvaal (South Africa) alerted Britain to the economic rewards that might be gained by acquiring further land in Africa. Determined to prevent other European countries, particularly France and Germany, from gaining these potentially mineral-rich areas for themselves, Britain moved quickly to secure as much of Africa as possible. Encouraged by the success of imperialist adventurers such as Cecil Rhodes, Britain took possession of most of southern and East Africa in the last 20 years of the 19th century. By 1900, British possessions in Africa included Egypt, the Sudan, British East Africa (Kenya and Uganda), British Somaliland, Southern and Northern Rhodesia (Zimbabwe and Zambia), Bechuanaland (Botswana), Orange Free State and the Transvaal (South Africa), Gambia, Sierra Leone, Nigeria, British Gold Coast (Ghana) and Nyasaland (Malawi). These countries accounted for more than 30% of Africa's population. Rhodes's ambition was to build a railway and telegraph line from Cairo in the north to the Cape in the south, thus reinforcing Britain's commercial gain from its African possessions. The British magazine *Punch* published a cartoon of Rhodes in 1892 (Figure 1.4).

Given the USA's own history of having to fight for independence from Britain, it is perhaps not surprising that many Americans were heavily critical of European imperialism. An American cartoon, published around 1900, reflects a rather different impression of Britain's activities in Africa. Britain is shown in the form of a wild-eyed man eating Africa in order to fuel an insatiable hunger (Figure 1.5).

Figure 1.4: Imperialist, explorer and businessman Rhodes as a colossus bestriding Africa. Caption reads: 'The Rhodes Colossus Striding from Cape Town to Cairo.'

Figure 1.5: An American view of Britain's relationship with Africa. The image caption reads: 'Don't bite off more than you can chew, John'.

ACTIVITY 1.3

a Comment on the British cartoon depicting Cecil Rhodes (Figure 1.4), making reference to:
- where he is standing (both feet)
- cable
- gun
- facial expression
- size
- cartoonist's message.

b In what ways does the American cartoon (Figure 1.5) give a contrasting impression of Britain's activities in Africa? What does this suggest about the American attitude towards imperialism? Discuss your answers in pairs or small groups.

France

While Britain concentrated on East Africa, France was more active in the west and north-west of the continent. Earlier in the 19th century, economic and diplomatic disputes, and the desire for a popular military success, had led France to invade what is now Algeria. Partly as a result of involvement in the slave trade, France controlled the coastal regions of Senegal. In the late 19th century, the French then moved inland in search of raw materials, such as palm oil and timber, and new markets for France's industrial output. French politicians, determined to enhance their country's wealth, prestige and power following defeat in the Franco-Prussian war, saw the development of a large overseas empire as essential.

Belgium

Belgium itself had only been independent since 1830, but King Leopold II of Belgium was determined to enhance his country's prestige and his own wealth by claiming the enormous Congo basin. Leopold was prepared to use his own money to pay for African territory that was considerably larger than Belgium itself. He saw the enormous financial advantages to be gained by exploiting the Congo's large quantities of raw rubber, a commodity much in demand in Europe.

Portugal

Building on long-standing contacts with the African coast from the first wave of western exploration in the 16th century, and determined not to be left behind in the race to acquire African land, Portugal extended its long-established claims to Angola and Mozambique.

Germany

Germany entered the 'scramble' later than its European rivals. Germany had only become a unified nation following the Franco-Prussian War in 1871. Germany's location in the centre of Europe, surrounded by potential enemies, led its chancellor, Otto von Bismarck, to concentrate on national security by forming alliances and avoiding unnecessary rivalry with other countries. By 1881, however, pressure from German businessmen and industrialists forced the government to change its previous policy of resistance to gaining territory in Africa. A frenzy of activity left Germany in control of Kamerun (an area now divided between Cameroon and a part of Nigeria), German East Africa (an area now divided between Rwanda, Burundi and most of Tanzania), German South-West Africa (now Namibia) and Togoland (an area now divided between Togo and part of Ghana). By the time of Germany's entry in the race for African possessions, most of the profitable areas had already been taken by other nations, and Germany's colonies in East Africa cost her considerably more than they were worth.

The 'scramble for Africa' may have begun for logical strategic and commercial reasons, but it rapidly descended into a mad rush for overseas possessions. European countries seemed determined to seize as much African land as possible, regardless of its potential value, simply to prevent it falling into the hands of their rivals. More than ever before it had become an issue of national pride and prestige.

ACTIVITY 1.4

a Why did Germany enter the race for African territory later than other European nations?

b Why would German industrialists and businessmen want Germany to seek territorial possessions in Africa? List the three most important factors.

c In pairs, discuss whether national pride was the main reason why European nations became involved in the scramble for Africa. Complete the table below with evidence which suggests that national pride was the main reason, such as Germany's determination to gain African territory, even if it was of no economic value. Now complete the right side of the table with other factors that encouraged European nations to seek possessions in Africa. How do the two lists balance?

Evidence for national pride	Evidence for other factors

ACTIVITY 1.4 (CONTINUED)

d Africa was clearly of great interest to the major European nations, yet it was not until the last quarter of the 19th century that they began to seek territorial possessions there. In small groups, consider the reasons why the 'scramble for Africa' took place in the late 19th century rather than earlier. Make a bullet point list of the reasons your group has decided on.

The impact of European imperialism on Africa

European imperialism had an enormous effect on Africa and its people. The European imperialists might point to benefits they had brought to the African people during the period of colonisation as a whole.

- They developed states with administrative and governmental systems.
- They provided education for the native inhabitants.
- They created new systems of transport and communications, building roads, railways and running telegraph wires across the continent.
- They engineered water and sanitation systems, and provided medical care and hospitals.
- They introduced more efficient methods of farming and new, more productive crops, such as maize, pear, cassava, cotton, sisal and plantain.

However, these benefits came at a price.

- Africa was randomly partitioned according to the needs and wishes of Europeans who took no account of existing boundaries. With little knowledge of the local geography, no understanding of the tribal/ethnic groupings of the local people and a steadfast refusal to take the opinions of local chiefs into account, boundaries were arbitrarily drawn.

As the British prime minister, Lord Salisbury, admitted:

> We have been engaged in drawing lines upon maps where no white man's feet have ever trod; we have been giving away mountains and rivers and lakes to each other, only hindered by the small impediment that we never knew exactly where the mountains and rivers and lakes were.
>
> **Lord Salisbury, reported in *The Times*, 7 August 1890**

- Many African chiefs or kings were killed or sent into exile for resisting attempts by Europeans to take over their land. Chief Mkwawa of the Hehe, for example, was beheaded for opposing German colonial rule in Tanganyika.
- While in many of its African possessions, such as Northern Nigeria, Britain adopted a form of indirect control, governing through local chiefs, other European nations preferred more direct rule. In both cases, however, government was based on a clear administrative hierarchy, with Europeans at the top and Africans below. This power structure partly reflected the European assumption that Africans were inferior to them. Stanley expressed this when he said of Africans, 'In order to rule them and keep one's life amongst them, it is necessary to regard them as children' (H. M. Stanley, *The Autobiography of Sir Henry Morton Stanley*, 1909, 377).
- Traditional African cultures were undermined as the Europeans introduced Western-style education, clothes, buildings and religion.
- The introduction of money completely changed the nature of the African economy.
- As ownership of land shifted to Europeans, many Africans were no longer able to farm their former land, leaving them little choice but to take jobs as cheap labour on public works, such as building roads and railways.
- There was large-scale exploitation of African resources. Raw materials were taken to support European industrial expansion, preventing Africa from developing industries of its own. European businessmen were able to enhance their own wealth through investment in African copper, gold, diamonds, ivory and cash crops such as cotton and coffee.
- At times, this exploitation caused alarming levels of inhumanity. King Leopold II of Belgium, for example, amassed a huge fortune from rubber plantations in the Congo basin. He used forced labour, effectively a form of slavery. Workers who failed to meet their quotas were beaten, mutilated or killed.

The missionary, John Hobbis Harris, was so shocked by what he saw in the Congo that he wrote to Leopold's representative in the area:

> I have just returned from a journey inland to the village of Insongo Mboyo . . . The abject misery and utter abandon is positively indescribable . . . I was so moved, Your Excellency, by the people's stories that I took the liberty of promising them that in future you will only kill them for crimes they commit.
>
> **Quoted in Congo Reform Association,** *Evidence laid before the Congo Commission of Inquiry* (1905)

These views are in stark contrast to King Leopold's own claims that Belgium was involved in a civilising mission in the Congo

- African resistance to European rule sometimes led to harsh retribution. Between 1904 and 1907, for example, the Herero and Nama peoples rebelled against German colonial rule in German South-West Africa (modern Namibia). The Germans drove them out into the Kalahari Desert, where most were to die of thirst or starvation. The allegation that German soldiers poisoned desert wells has led to charges of **genocide**.

KEY TERM

Genocide: the deliberate and systematic destruction of an ethnic, racial, religious or national group. In 1985, the United Nations labelled the German action against the Herero and Nama peoples as genocide.

ACTIVITY 1.5

a Look carefully at King Leopold II's public letter of 1897. In what ways did he claim that Belgian occupation of the Congo was benefitting the native people? Note down the main points.

b Look carefully at the British cartoon published in 1906. In what ways does this cartoon contradict King Leopold's public letter? Note down the main points next to your list from the answer above.

The task which Belgian agents have to accomplish in the Congo is noble. We have to carry on the work of civilisation in Africa. The aim is to improve races whose misfortune is hard to realise. This is already lessening, little by little, through our intervention. Each step forward by our people should mark an improvement in the condition of the natives. In those huge regions of land, mostly uncultivated and unproductive, where the natives hardly knew how to get their own daily food, European experience, knowledge, resources and enterprise have brought to life unimaginable wealth. Exploration of new lands goes on, communications are established, highways are opened and trade is established.

Public letter by King Leopold II of Belgium, June 1897

Figure 1.6: A cartoon from the British magazine *Punch*, 1906, shows an African caught in King Leopold's coils. Image text reads: 'In the Rubber Coils. Scene–The Congo "Free" State.'

Figure 1.7: Herero survivors, frail and emaciated. What do think the photographer's intentions were in taking the photograph?

Reasons for, and extent of, domestic support for overseas expansion in Britain, France and Germany

While there was some opposition to 'New Imperialism', many British, French and German people appeared to enthusiastically support their countries' involvement in overseas expansion in the late 19th century. While the reasons for this varied in each of the three countries, they all reflected the increase in nationalism that characterised the late 19th century.

Britain

Even before the emergence of 'New Imperialism', Britain possessed a vast overseas empire, far larger than that of any other European nation. The British people were accustomed to the fact that their country had influence in, and control over, distant foreign lands. That the empire was a symbol of national pride, power and prestige was heavily stressed in numerous ways during the late 19th century.

Popular support for British imperialism was encouraged from a young age through the introduction of compulsory state education. In addition to teaching the basics of reading and writing, schools aimed to encourage national pride and loyalty. Maps of the British Empire were proudly displayed on classroom walls. As literacy levels increased and new technology reduced printing costs, more people had access to newspapers. Owned and controlled by wealthy pro-imperialists (such as Lord Northcliffe, who co-founded the *Daily Mail*), newspapers aimed to shape public opinion in favour of overseas expansion. Stories about mysterious foreign lands, and their strange inhabitants seen as 'barbaric', were hugely popular.

13

So, too, were exciting accounts of how British heroes were fighting against 'savages' in order to 'civilise' them. These newspaper articles, usually exaggerated and often untrue, reinforced belief in European racial superiority and encouraged nationalistic feelings in their readers.

Popular literature also helped to shape public opinion in favour of imperialism. The novel *Kim* by English writer Rudyard Kipling, for example, justified British rule in India by implying that the Indian people were fortunate Britain was willing to help them, and emphasising Indian people cooperating and participating in British activities. Much of the literature produced for children, and particularly boys, was even more blatant in encouraging support for imperialism and patriotism. In Britain, for example, magazines such as *Wizard* and *Union Jack* published stories of British 'heroes' fighting to defend parts of the British Empire against barbaric local inhabitants and other Europeans determined to steal territory that 'rightly' belonged to Britain.

Common items, such as tea packets and biscuit tins, were adorned with pictures of exotic foreign lands and heroic images of soldiers defending Britain's imperial possessions. At a time when there was little in the way of public entertainment, music halls became extremely popular in Britain. Performers, often dressed in colourful military uniforms, sang songs that justified imperialism as a means of civilising the 'savage' populations of foreign lands.

In various ways, therefore, the positive aspects of imperialism were stressed while evidence of maltreatment and exploitation of native peoples was ignored. This was particularly evident on the issue of slavery. Having banned slavery in 1807, Britain now had a duty to free slaves and end the practice of slavery in Africa. Britain was carrying out its moral responsibility to bring civilisation to other races, a responsibility that Rudyard Kipling described as 'the white man's burden' in a poem published in 1889.

France

Unlike in Britain, it was the government that played the leading role in encouraging popular support for imperialism in France. French pride had been severely damaged by the humiliating defeat in the Franco-Prussian War (1870–71). Gaining overseas possessions was seen as a way of restoring French prestige. **Patriotism** was fostered through the introduction of a state education system. French children were encouraged to be proud of their country's achievements, its navy and its growing empire. They were taught that they had a duty to their country, which was unique, superior to all others, and had both the right and the responsibility to spread its culture across the world.

KEY TERM

Patriotism: love for and pride in your country. A less extreme form of nationalism.

Working closely with a number of missionary societies, whose agents were spread across Asia and Africa, the French government formally adopted a policy known as the 'Mission Civilisatrice' (Civilising Mission). The Roman Catholic Church stressed the civilising aspects of French imperialism in publications such as *La Croix*. This painted French imperialism in a positive light – it was helping people rather than exploiting them. It was bringing Christianity, civilisation and French culture to people in distant lands whose customs included human sacrifice, slavery and other forms of brutality.

At the same time, the government was proclaiming the social, political and economic advantages that France would gain from its overseas possessions. Imperialism, it was argued, would enhance the wealth of France enabling it to address the social and economic hardships of the lower classes. The main beneficiaries of French imperialism, businesses, banks and entrepreneurs, paid newspapers to carry stories demonstrating how their overseas activities were benefitting the French people.

In justifying French imperialism in the late 19th century, the influential politician Jules Ferry argued, 'the superior races have a right regarding the inferior races because they have a responsibility to civilise them'. Such views, echoing those of Rudyard Kipling, were, of course, based on the prevailing belief in the racial superiority of white people. They provided a reason for French people to feel proud of their country's activities in distant lands, such as Africa and Asia.

Germany

The situation in Germany was rather different to that in Britain and France. Germany had only become a unified country in 1871, and its Chancellor, Bismarck, was initially reluctant to become involved in imperial expansion. He feared that seeking overseas possessions would bring Germany into conflict with other European nations, threatening the newly formed country's security and development. Under pressure from German businessmen, who noted that their counterparts in other European nations were gaining benefits from access to new sources of raw materials and new markets, Bismarck began to take a greater interest in imperialism.

In addition to the potential economic advantages that Germany might achieve through gaining overseas possessions, the German government was also keenly aware of its usefulness in promoting nationalism. As a country formed of people from different social, political, religious and cultural backgrounds, something was needed to unite them – to give them a genuine sense of German nationality. Imperialism provided this uniting factor and, as in France, the government was keen to stress the enormous social and economic advantages it would bring to the German people. The establishment of organisations such as the Colonial Society and the Navy League were clear attempts by the German government to encourage public support for German imperialism.

German missionaries, just like their French counterparts in Asia and Africa, were at the forefront of Germany's imperial growth. With the justification of bringing Christianity to 'heathen' populations, they provided the government with information and connections that facilitated Germany's acquisition of new territories. The point is clearly made in a cartoon from 1904, which shows priests and troops advancing together while non-Europeans flee (Figure 1.8).

Figure 1.8: A German satire of imperialism. What can you infer about the artist's intentions by making the religious figures large and the army small?

German nationalism, and the country's right and responsibility to extend its influence into foreign lands, were promoted in newspapers, literature, art and even postcards. Postcards were an effective way of communicating a message, being cheap and widely distributed. The German postcard in Figure 1.9 represents the Herero as robbing the home of a German colonist whom the raiders have tied up. The justification for the war against the Herero is not difficult to see.

Opposition to imperialism

In all three countries and in a variety of ways, therefore, the positive aspects of imperialism were heavily stressed. Some historians argue that this inevitably meant that the majority of Europeans genuinely supported their countries' involvement in imperialism. Other historians disagree, suggesting that most European people had little real interest in imperialism in this period, and no significant opinions about it.

What is clear, however, is that some people remained steadfastly opposed to imperialism, albeit for a variety of different reasons. A number of religious leaders, intellectuals and writers argued that it was morally wrong to seize control of territory that rightly belonged to the local inhabitants. For example, in his short novel *Heart of Darkness*, published in 1899, the Polish-British author Joseph Conrad raised major issues about imperialism and **racism**. The novel challenged the widely accepted view that the imperial nations were 'civilised' while native peoples were 'savages'. Marlow, one of the characters in the book, concludes that 'imperialism is not a pretty thing when one looks into it too much'.

 KEY TERM

Racism: a belief in the superiority of one race over another, based on prejudice and leading to discrimination.

Arguably the most wide-ranging criticism of imperialism came from the British economist, John Hobson. In his 1902 book *Imperialism: A Study* he concluded that involvement in 'New Imperialism' had harmed Britain economically, politically and socially. It had not been cost effective – while some wealthy businessmen and entrepreneurs had clearly benefitted from it, there had been little increase in Britain's trade, and the advantages derived from having overseas possessions were outweighed by the expense of maintaining control over them. It had increased tensions with other imperial nations, tensions that were only increased by Britain's

15

Der Herero-Aufstand in Deutsch Süd-West-Afrika.
Omanbonbe: Plünderung der Farm des Herrn Gamisch.

Aecht Franck

Figure 1.9: A German postcard shows an imperialist version of events in South West Africa. The postcard caption reads: *'The uprising in German South-West Africa: The pillaging of Herrn Gamisch's farm.'* Would you describe the postcard as showing a biased view? Why or why not?

involvement in costly and embarrassing wars. The Boer Wars, the second of which ended in the same year as the publication of Hobson's book, was a clear example of this, especially in view of criticism of Britain's involvement from other European nations. Moreover, Hobson claimed, the high expenditure needed to maintain the Empire made it impossible for the British government to carry out much needed social reform to alleviate the conditions of the lower classes.

Hobson's arguments regarding the economic impact of 'New Imperialism' reflected the views of other European economists, politicians and writers who are collectively referred to as 'Liberals'. For example, the German politician Eugen Richter, the French economist Gustave de Molinari and the British historian/politician Lord Acton all criticised the economic policies associated with imperialism as short-sighted. European governments concentrated on developing trade with their overseas possessions. At the same time, they were trying to protect their domestic industries by imposing taxes on imports from rival European nations. These Liberals campaigned for greater and tax-free trading links between European

countries, which, they claimed, would be of economic benefit to all of them. They also argued that governments should reduce taxation and expenditure, and that, therefore, the high costs involved in maintaining overseas possessions was unsustainable.

Hobson's view that imperialism enhanced tensions between the major European countries and increased the potential of war between them is reflected in Bismarck's initial reluctance to involve Germany in the quest for overseas possessions. His priority was the security of the newly unified Germany. He did not want this threatened by conflict with other nations, which he believed would inevitably occur if Germany adopted imperial policies.

Anti-imperialistic sentiments grew stronger in Britain after it became necessary to mount a long and expensive campaign to maintain control of South Africa in the period from 1880 to 1902, with wars against the Zulus, Boers, Matabele and others. Organisations such as the Stop The War Committee campaigned against the British government's involvement in the Boer Wars, arguing that it was merely supporting the greed of entrepreneurs for gold and diamonds. Liberal politicians, such as Campbell-

Bannerman and Lloyd George accused the government of using barbaric strategies in order to preserve and extend British influence in South Africa. Despite this, however, the overwhelming majority of British newspapers supported the government's imperial policy in general, and involvement in the Boer Wars in particular. Moreover, that the British public continued to perceive imperialism in a positive light is reflected in the election successes of pro-imperial politicians.

In France, in particular, governments continued to promote imperialism as a means of encouraging national unity and to deflect attention away from domestic issues, such as poor living and working conditions. Once Germany embarked on the quest for overseas possessions, Bismarck was careful to ensure that government expenditure was balanced between welfare provision and the development of the country's armed forces. This ensured that he retained the support of the German working classes.

While there were frequent challenges to specific aspects of imperial policies, therefore, the fundamental principles of imperialism appear to have been accepted, if not necessarily enthusiastically supported, by most Europeans.

ACTIVITY 1.6

Working in pairs, discuss and make notes on the following questions:

a   How did European governments justify taking possession of overseas territories in the late 19th century?

b   Why did some Europeans oppose imperialism in the late 19th century?

Reflection: Look back at the answers you gave to the questions in the Before You Start activity at the beginning of this chapter. How would you amend those answers in the light of your subsequent reading?

●●● THINK LIKE A HISTORIAN

As we have seen, public support for European imperialism in the late 19th century owed much to nationalism and racism. Consider the ways in which both nationalism and racism continue to affect our lives today.

1.2 What was the impact of imperial expansion on international relations?

The impact of growth of overseas empires on relations between European nations

In the late 19th century, European nations were rivals, competing for raw materials, markets, trade and territory. In a period of intense nationalism, European governments were determined to protect their own rights and interests, to gain as much overseas territory as possible and to defend their empires. Moreover, public opinion demanded that they did so. National pride was at stake and, increasingly, countries were prepared to adopt aggressive foreign policies to preserve this pride. This naturally opened up the risk of direct conflict breaking out between European nations.

Fashoda Incident

In 1898, for example, a clash between the rival African ambitions of Britain and France almost led to war. While France was expanding rapidly eastwards from French West Africa, the British were expanding southwards from Egypt towards the Cape. Their paths crossed in Sudan – a French expedition under Major Marchand met a British force, led by Lord Kitchener, in the village of Fashoda. Both claimed Sudan for their respective countries. The 'Fashoda Incident', as it has become known, led to widespread outrage in both Britain and France, with each country accusing the other of unjustified aggression. Both nations began the process of mobilising their fleets in preparation for war before a compromise was eventually reached. France recognised British possession of Egypt and Sudan, while Britain formally acknowledged the French presence in Morocco.

Germany's 'place in the sun'

In fact, despite the obvious risks created by rival imperialism and rising nationalism, there were no wars between any of the major European powers in the period from 1871 to 1914. Incidents, such as that at Fashoda, undoubtedly raised tensions, but peace was maintained as nations were eventually prepared to compromise. Nevertheless, imperial rivalry helped to instigate an arms race, as countries began to enhance their military capabilities in order to defend their empires.

This was particularly evident after Wilhelm II became Kaiser of Germany in 1888. Wilhelm embarked on a policy of *Weltpolitik* (World Policy), which involved actively seeking overseas possessions, or, as Kaiser Wilhelm termed it, 'a place in the sun'. Germany's relatively late entry into the race for African possessions only added to the existing tensions. Britain, in particular, saw German acquisitions in Africa as a threat to its own strategic and commercial interests. Moreover, in 1906, Germany embarked on a naval development programme, arguing that this was necessary to protect its overseas trade and empire.

Kaiser Wilhelm explained the reasons for Germany's naval expansion in an interview with a British journalist in 1908:

> Germany is a young and growing empire. It has a world-wide commerce which is rapidly expanding and to which the legitimate ambition of patriotic Germans refuses to assign any bounds. Germany must have a powerful fleet to protect that commerce and its many interests in even the most distant seas. Germany expects those interests to go on growing, and it must be able to champion them manfully in any quarter of the globe. Germany's horizons stretch far away and it must be prepared for any eventualities. Only those powers that have great navies will be listened to with respect and, if for that reason only, Germany must have a powerful fleet.

> *Daily Telegraph*, 28 October 1908

Entente Cordiale

German naval development caused alarm in Britain, which argued that Germany's overseas possessions were not sufficient to warrant such a large navy. Britain was concerned that, while its own navy was dispersed around the world to protect its empire, the German navy would be concentrated in the North Sea, posing a threat to British security. This led to a naval arms race that greatly increased tensions between Britain and Germany.

The French, still incensed by their humiliating defeat in the Franco-Prussian War, also had reason to feel threatened by Germany's newly aggressive foreign policy under Kaiser Wilhelm II. For example, France claimed possession of Morocco, a region in which both France and Britain had extensive trading interests. In 1904, Britain and France signed an agreement known as the 'Entente Cordiale', which settled the long-standing imperial rivalries between the two countries in North Africa. In line with this agreement, Britain supported France's claims in Morocco. The Kaiser believed that the new friendship between Britain and France posed a threat to Germany's international prestige and influence. He viewed French claims over Morocco as an opportunity to weaken the improved relationship between Britain and France.

Tangiers, Algeciras and Agadir

In March 1905, Kaiser Wilhelm made an aggressive speech in the Moroccan city of Tangiers, making it clear that Germany favoured an independent Morocco. Rather than causing a split between Britain and France, his warlike speech had the opposite effect. Britain continued to support French claims over Morocco, and these were largely upheld at an international conference in Algeciras in early 1906. Increasingly suspicious of German intentions, Britain and France developed an even closer relationship. In 1911 Kaiser Wilhelm sent a gunboat (the *Panther*) to the Moroccan port of Agadir, with the intention of undermining French power in the region. Britain sided with France and the kaiser backed down, although many German politicians and generals had urged him to go to war over the issue. This has become known as the 'Algeciras Crisis'.

ACTIVITY 1.7

In pairs, discuss and make notes on the following questions:

a   What reasons did Kaiser Wilhelm II give to explain his decision to expand the German navy?

b   Why would the expansion of the German navy cause concern in Britain?

c   Both the Fashoda Incident and Kaiser Wilhelm's actions in Morocco threatened to lead to war between major European countries. In both cases, war was avoided. How might this be explained?

d   Britain and France had been traditional enemies and their rival imperial ambitions had almost led to war between them. However, by the end of the 19th century, relations between Britain and France were becoming more friendly. What do you consider were the two main reasons for this?

Disputes with China over imperial expansion: the Boxer Rebellion

Although there were no wars between the major European nations in the period from 1871 to 1914, their quest to seize, and maintain control of, overseas territories was neither peaceful nor without far-reaching consequences.

With a civilisation dating back thousands of years, the Chinese considered themselves superior to people from other countries, and the authorities tended to be convinced that they had little to learn or gain from contact with foreigners. China's internal economy was well organised and efficient, with merchants dealing in the products of agriculture and highly skilled craftsmen.

China was self-contained, with no need or desire to trade with other countries. However, what looked like stability and continuity to the government was increasingly revealed during the 19th century as an inability to adapt as circumstances began to change.

By the beginning of the 19th century, Britain, France, Spain, the Netherlands and Portugal had all established trade links with Asia. Their contact with China was initially confined to the area surrounding the port of Macau on the south-east coast. The Chinese government's attempts to restrict and control foreign trade were largely unsuccessful, and European traders began encroaching into other parts of the country. The industrial revolution in Western Europe brought with it an ever-increasing need for raw materials and new markets. There was huge potential for these in China, and European merchants and businessmen found China's reluctance to trade both mystifying and irritating. What the Europeans could not get by agreement, they achieved by force.

Britain quickly established itself as China's largest foreign trading partner, purchasing Chinese tea and products such as silks and porcelain. Towards the end of the 18th century, Britain began importing vast quantities of opium into China. The Chinese government, realising the potential social and economic impact that such an addictive drug could have, attempted to ban its importation. Such restrictions were difficult to enforce, and British merchants largely ignored them.

Defeated by Britain in the First Opium War of 1839–42 and the Second Opium War in 1856, China granted Britain control over Hong Kong and preferential trading status. In the Treaty of Tientsin in 1860, China legalised the importation of opium and opened its ports to foreign traders.

With restrictions now lifted, foreign diplomats, traders and missionaries poured into China. Major cities, such as Shanghai, Canton, Foochow and Ningpo (Guangdong, Fuzhou and Ningbo) were internationalised. Britain, France, Russia, Germany and Japan all established spheres of influence, in which they built railways and factories, ignored Chinese laws and took political control. The Chinese government's weakness was further exposed by the Taiping Rebellion of 1850–64. Some historians estimate that as many as 20 million people died during the rebellion, through fighting, executions, famine and disease. The government only put down the rebellion with the support of British and French forces.

The situation worsened in 1894, when China faced war against Japan following disputes regarding control over the Korean Peninsula. The First Sino-Japanese War, as it has become known, was a disaster for China. Chinese troops, poorly led and relying on outdated equipment, were no match for Japan's well-organised forces, equipped with modern weaponry. As a result of its crushing defeat, China was forced to sign the Treaty of Shimonoseki (1895), ceding Korea, Formosa (Taiwan) and the strategic military harbour known as Port Arthur to Japan.

In 1899, the Chinese government was undermined by yet another foreign power. Concerned that European and Japanese involvement in China posed a threat to its own economic interests, the USA negotiated an 'open door policy'. The policy aimed to ensure that all foreign nations could enjoy the benefits of Chinese trade on an equal basis, and to avoid the possibility that one nation might take full control of China. These negotiations were undertaken with the other imperial nations and not with the Chinese government, which was merely informed of the outcome.

ACTIVITY 1.8

Look carefully at Figure 1.10. What points do you think the cartoonist is trying to make?

In order to begin analysing it, make sure you can identify each figure, take account of how they are drawn (their appearance), and understand the narrative (what is taking place).

Figure 1.10: A French cartoon published in 1898

The Boxer Rebellion

Chinese nationalists, angered by their government's failure to prevent foreigners gaining increasing influence within China, took up arms in what became known as the Boxer Rebellion (1898–1901). The Chinese government, initially hesitant, eventually supported the rebellion and declared war on the foreign powers. An eight-nation alliance involving Britain, Russia, Japan, France, the USA, Germany, Italy and Austria-Hungary took Peking (now Beijing) and defeated the rebellion. The Chinese government was forced to pay £67 million in compensation (over a period of 39 years) for the damage that had been done to foreign-owned property during the rebellion. The humiliation of China was complete.

By the beginning of the 20th century, therefore, much of China was effectively under the control of foreigners. Several European nations, together with Japan and the USA, had established their individual areas of influence, and had been prepared to cooperate with each other in order to maintain their dominance over the Chinese. Clearly, however, this situation created the potential for growing rivalry between these nations as they each endeavoured to enhance their own interests in China.

ACTIVITY 1.9

In pairs, consider the following questions:

a Why do you think China, with its huge population, was unable to offer effective resistance to European imperialism?

b Which two non-European countries were also seeking to exploit China's weakness?

c Make a list of evidence which suggests that foreign nations were prepared to work together, rather than in direct opposition to each other, in order to exploit China.

d What were the aims of the 'open door' policy, and why do you think all of the European nations seeking to exploit China were willing to support it?

Tension between Britain and Germany over South Africa

As the British experience in South Africa demonstrated, ownership of African territory was often far from peaceful. Originally a Dutch colony, Britain took control of the colony (known as Cape Colony or the Cape of Good Hope) following the end of the Napoleonic Wars in 1814.

British immigration began in 1820, and shortly afterwards English became the official administrative language in the colony and a new tax system was imposed. This created tensions with farmers of Dutch descent (known as Boers), which came to a head following the abolition of slavery in the colony in 1834. Most Boers were dependent on slave labour to maintain their farms, and although compensation for freed slaves was offered by the British government, the amount was seen by the Boers as inadequate. Fuelled by resentment towards British rule, many Boers left Cape Colony between 1835 and 1840 and moved east in what became known as the 'Great Trek', settling in areas that later became the autonomous republics of Transvaal and the Orange Free State.

Maintaining control of Cape Colony involved constant border wars with native tribes during the 19th century. Conflict with the Xhosa had occurred during Dutch control of the colony and lasted until 1879. The Anglo-Zulu War of 1879 was the most notable conflict. The British were eventually victorious, but only after a series of bloody battles, including an opening victory for the Zulus at Isandlwana.

In 1877, following a failed attempt to persuade the gold and diamond-rich Transvaal and Free Orange State to join Cape Colony in a federation, Britain claimed possession of the republics. Despite the alarm this caused the Boers, the threat of war with the neighbouring Zulu kingdom prevented the Boers from opposing British rule. Once assured that the Zulu threat had been removed, the Transvaal Boers rebelled and claimed independence. The First Boer War (1880-81) was little more than a series of skirmishes, in which the ill-prepared British troops were defeated. Under the terms of the Pretoria Convention (1881), Transvaal and Orange Free State were given self-governing status under British oversight. In particular, Britain retained the right to maintain a military presence within the region, and to protect it from foreign intervention.

Further discoveries of gold deposits in Transvaal in 1886 brought many new settlers, mostly British. These newcomers were denied political and economic rights by the Transvaal president **Paul Kruger**. British expansionist ambitions, encouraged mainly by Cecil Rhodes, Prime Minister of Cape Colony, led to the failed Jameson Raid of 1895. Rhodes hoped that the settlers in the region would rebel against the Transvaal government, providing justification for an invasion. The intention was for pro-British forces – led by Leander Starr Jameson – to go to the assistance of the rebelling settlers. However, when the rebellion failed to materialise,

Jameson led his forces into the Transvaal anyway. They were swiftly driven back by the Boers.

Other European nations resented this attempted British invasion of what they regarded as a small, independent nation. In particular, this was to lead to increased tension between Britain and Germany. Kaiser Wilhelm II sent a telegram to Kruger, congratulating him on defeating the raiders.

The kaiser's interference in British African affairs caused great indignation in Britain, not least because the telegram seemed to imply that Germany was prepared to support the Boers in any future conflict with Britain. This resulted in a deterioration in Anglo-German relations.

I express to you my sincere congratulations that you and your people, without appealing to the help of friendly powers, have succeeded, by your own energetic action against the armed bands which invaded your country as disturbers of the peace, in restoring peace and in maintaining the independence of the country against attack from without.

Telegram from Wilhelm II to Paul Kruger, 3 January 1896

The kaiser's motives for sending a telegram that would obviously lead to increased tension between Britain and Germany have been hotly debated by historians. While some claim that it is further evidence of Wilhelm's impetuous personality, others suggest that he was, somewhat reluctantly, acting at the insistence of senior members of the German government. In his memoirs, published in 1922, the kaiser himself claimed that he was pressured into signing the telegram, most notably by the foreign secretary, Baron Marschall von Bieberstein. While the kaiser's memoirs are seen as highly unreliable, there is other, more trustworthy evidence to support his claim. Marschall himself stated that it was important to 'teach Britain a lesson'. The German Foreign Office did indeed have good reasons to justify sending the telegram. First, it would enhance Germany's international prestige by placing it at the forefront of European criticism of British conduct in South Africa. This, in turn, would enhance Germany's policy of seeking to isolate Britain. Second, there is considerable evidence to suggest that Marschall planned for Germany to replace Britain as the most influential foreign power in the Transvaal. Britain's belief that this was Germany's intention goes far in explaining why the telegram aroused such anger.

21

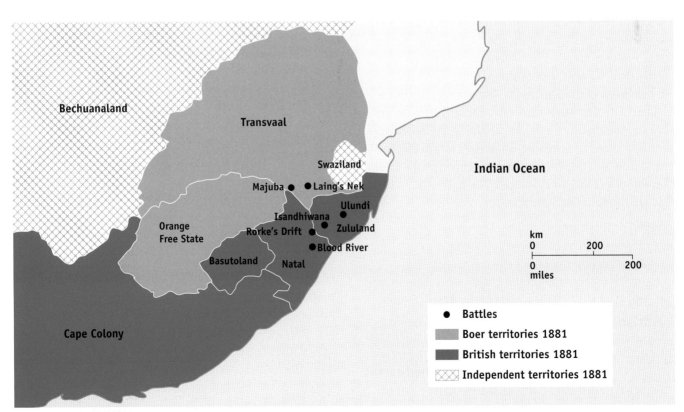

Figure 1.11: South Africa during the Boer Wars in 1880–81

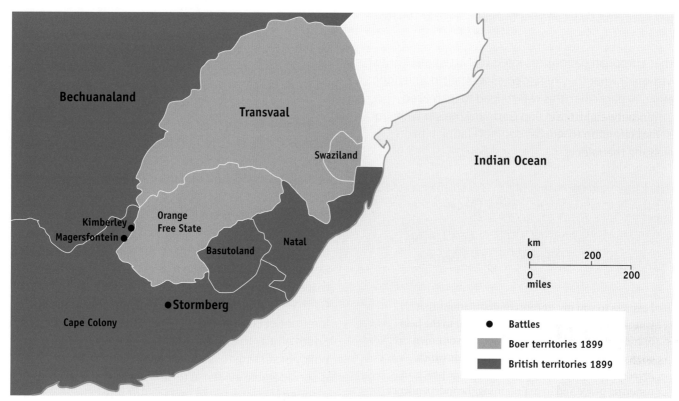

Figure 1.12: South Africa during the Boer Wars 1899–1902

In 1899, Kruger demanded the withdrawal of British troops and full independence for the Transvaal. When Britain refused to grant this, Kruger declared war. After a series of early victories by the Boers, Britain dramatically increased its forces in South Africa. British troops were successful in relieving several besieged cities, and captured the Transvaal capital, Pretoria, in June 1900. After this, the Boers adopted guerrilla tactics, carrying out surprise raids on British-held railways and storage depots. The fact that they were equipped with German Mauser rifles caused further anger in Britain. After two further years of fighting, the Boers were eventually forced to surrender. Britain's victory in this, the Second Boer War (1899–1902), was confirmed by the Treaty of Vereeniging (1902), which placed Orange Free State and Transvaal firmly under British control.

However, victory came at a price. The power of the British Empire had been severely challenged by a relatively small number of Boer farmers, revealing fundamental weaknesses in the British army. The Second Boer War, in which 22 000 soldiers of the British Empire were killed, cost the British taxpayer more than £200 million, a huge amount of money at the beginning of the 20th century. In addition, Britain was condemned by the international community for deploying **'scorched earth'** strategies during the war, and for the establishment of

PAUL KRUGER 1825–1904

Kruger was president of the South African Republic (Transvaal) 1883–1900. After the First Boer War, Kruger played a role in negotiations with Britain to restore self-government to the region. He later led the Boers in their struggle against Britain during the Second Boer War.

concentration camps in which the wives and children of Boer fighters were imprisoned. These camps were originally intended to be refugee centres for civilians left homeless by the fighting, but conditions there were poor and they were administered harshly in the hope that this would force the Boers to surrender. With bad hygiene and little food, suffering and death were commonplace in the camps, and 30 000 civilians died during the war.

22

Emily Hobhouse, a British woman who opposed the Boer Wars and was concerned about the suffering of South African women and children, described conditions in one such concentration camp in Bloemfontein in 1901:

> When the eight, ten or twelve people who lived in the bell tent were squeezed into it to find shelter against the heat of the sun, the dust or the rain, there was no room to stir and the air in the tent was beyond description. Soap was an article that was not dispensed. The water supply was inadequate. No bedsteads or mattresses were available. The rations were extremely poor and when, as I frequently experienced, the actual quantity dispensed fell short of the amount prescribed, it simply meant famine.

KEY TERM

'Scorched earth': a battle tactic in which an army deliberately burns crops and property in an area to deny the enemy food and shelter.

The Boer Wars highlighted the problems that Britain would increasingly face in defending its large empire. British politicians – and public opinion in general – grew divided over whether Britain should continue its imperialist policies. Other European nations, particularly Germany, had openly condemned British actions in South Africa, leaving Britain feeling both isolated and vulnerable. It had become clear that Britain would need to do two things if it wanted to maintain control over its empire – increase its own military capabilities and end its isolation by seeking allies elsewhere in the world.

ACTIVITY 1.10

Prepare notes on the key points for the following questions:

a What factors might explain why Britain found it so difficult to defeat a relatively small number of Boer farmers?

b Why did other European countries object to the methods that Britain used in order to defeat the Boers?

c Why did so many people die in British concentration camps during the Boer Wars?

d What were the implications of the Boer Wars for British foreign policy?

Make sure that your notes contain details of the problems which Britain faced in defeating the Boers and the implications of the Boer Wars for British foreign policy.

Attempts to resolve tensions between imperial nations

The leading European nations were competing for as much overseas territory as possible in order to enhance their national wealth and prestige. The 'New Imperialism' that characterised the last quarter of the 19th century inevitably carried the risk of war between them. That no such wars occurred is due to the fact that European statesmen did everything possible to avoid them.

The Berlin Conference (1884–85)

The fact that countries were prepared to negotiate and compromise rather than going to war is most clearly demonstrated by the Berlin Conference of 1884–85. Organised by the German Chancellor, Otto von Bismarck, the conference was designed to regulate European imperialism and trade in Africa in order to prevent direct conflict breaking out between European nations competing in the 'scramble for Africa'. Representatives of 13 European nations met in Berlin between 15 November 1884 and 26 February 1885, their negotiations resulting in the Treaty of Berlin (1885). The main articles of the treaty stated that:

- free passage should be given to all ships on the Niger and Congo rivers, both of which provided access to the African interior
- slavery should be abolished throughout the African continent. This was included in the treaty to satisfy those who had doubts about the right of European countries simply to take land in Africa. Abolishing slavery provided a suitable justification for imperialism in Africa.

In order to take possession of an African territory, a European nation would have to inform other governments of its claim immediately, and demonstrate that the territory was 'effectively occupied'. This meant that the territory was genuinely under the control of the European nation – it could be properly administered and defended. This was intended to prevent a country claiming an area over which it had no real control simply to prevent rival countries attempting to gain it. Article XII of the treaty specified that any disputes regarding control over a particular African territory should be settled by negotiation rather than war. In many ways, the outcome of the Berlin Conference added further impetus to the 'scramble for Africa'. European nations rushed to 'effectively occupy' as much African territory as possible, secure in the knowledge that this could be achieved without the risk of a major war. Important as African possessions were to national pride and prestige, European nations were not prepared to fight each other over them. This was clearly demonstrated by the willingness of Britain and France to settle the Fashoda Incident by compromise rather than war.

The Berlin Conference established rules by which imperial nations could gain possession of African territory, dividing the continent between them without consulting the Africans themselves. This arrogant imperialism was also evident in China, where each foreign nation established its own areas of influence and control, ignoring Chinese laws and the authority of the Chinese government. In 1899, for example, when the USA sought to establish its own trading rights in China through the 'open door policy', negotiations took place between the imperial powers without consultation with the Chinese government. Similarly, during the Boxer Rebellion (1898–1901), the imperial nations fought side by side to defend their own interests from the threat posed by a Chinese nationalist uprising.

Despite these carefully laid plans to avoid armed conflict between rival imperial nations, tensions inevitably remained. These intensified, for example, when Germany entered the race for African possessions. Britain, in particular, saw German acquisitions in Africa as a threat to its own commercial and strategic interests. Similarly, Japan's rapid development as an industrialised nation, and its growing imperial ambitions in China, threatened the existing interests of European nations.

The Treaty of Shimonoseki (1895)

The Treaty of Shimonoseki (1895), which followed Japan's crushing victory in the First Sino-Japanese War, caused considerable alarm in Russia. Under the terms of the treaty, Japan took control of Port Arthur (modern-day Lüshunkou), a district of Dailan in north-eastern China. Port Arthur was originally a small fishing village sited on

an excellent natural harbour. The village was fortified during the 1880s by the Chinese government due to its strategic location, and was subsequently seized by the Japanese during the First Sino-Japanese War. Japan occupied both the port and the whole of the surrounding Liaodong Peninsula during the war. Russia had itself been seeking to gain control over Port Arthur, since it would provide a warm-water (ice-free) port on the Pacific Coast from which to expand its own trading interests in the Far East. Russia argued that the terms of the Treaty of Shimonoseki would undermine the existing interests of European nations and cause instability in China. With the support of France and Germany, Russia put diplomatic pressure on Japan to return Port Arthur to Chinese control. This has become known as the 'Triple Intervention'. Although their own interests were not directly affected by the Japanese acquisition of Port Arthur, France and Germany each had their own reasons for supporting Russia. Fearing being diplomatically isolated, and therefore vulnerable, in Europe, France felt compelled to honour the alliance it had formed with Russia in 1894. Germany became involved in exchange for Russian support for its own imperial ambitions elsewhere in the world.

Japan was in no position to resist the military force of three major European powers, which had a combined force of 38 warships in the region. After unsuccessful attempts to gain support from Britain and the USA, the Japanese government reluctantly agreed to remove its troops from Port Arthur in exchange for financial compensation. Almost immediately, Russia occupied the Liaodong peninsula and established control over Port Arthur, while France, Germany and Britain all took the opportunity to exploit China's weakened position by extending their own interests in the country. War between the imperial nations had been avoided, but Japanese resentment of the Triple Intervention was to have far-reaching consequences.

ACTIVITY 1.11

In pairs, complete the sentences started in List A by adding the most appropriate endings from List B.

List A	List B
The main aims of the Treaty of Berlin (1885) were to	settle any disputes between them by negotiation rather than war.
Russia wanted to gain control over Port Arthur because	it wanted Russian support for its own imperial ambitions.
Countries that signed the Treaty of Berlin (1885) agreed to	France joined the 'Triple Intervention', which forced Japan to give up its rights to Port Arthur.
Russia claimed that the Treaty of Shimonoseki (1895) would	abolishing slavery throughout the African continent.
Because it did not want to become isolated, and because it had entered into an alliance with Russia in 1894,	it could not compete with the combined military power of Russia, France and Germany.
Germany joined the 'Triple Intervention' because	regulate imperialism in Africa and prevent conflict between rival European nations.
Japan had no choice but to give up its rights to Port Arthur because	they united to defeat Chinese nationalists during the Boxer Rebellion.
The Treaty of Berlin (1885) attempted to justify European imperialism in Africa by	cause instability in China and adversely affect the interests of European nations in the Far East.
The Fashoda Incident did not lead to war because	it needed a warm-water port from which to expand its own trading interests in the Far East.
That the imperial nations were prepared to work together to protect their joint interests in China is confirmed by the fact that	Britain and France were prepared to negotiate and compromise over their rival claims in Africa.

Reflection: Compare your answers with those of another student. How did you decide on the links between the two lists? Would you change your answers after talking with another student?

1.3 Why did Japan emerge as a world power and what was the impact on international relations?

Reasons for rapid modernisation and military development

Japan's rise as an imperial power in its own right was both sudden and dramatic. In the first half of the 19th century, Japan was still an unmodernised country with an almost medieval social structure. It had a rigid class system dating back centuries. The samurai had begun as a military elite but by this stage had largely become government officials, with their leader, the shogun, now an autocratic head of government. Farming, transport and industry had changed little for centuries, and the economy was still largely based on **bartering** rather than money; for example taxes were paid in rice.

 KEY TERM

Bartering: the trading of goods without the use of money; exchanging one thing in payment for another.

Fearing the potentially disruptive impact that Christian missionaries might have, Japan had effectively closed its borders to all foreigners in the 17th century, and at the same time prevented Japanese citizens from leaving. The Japanese did not welcome foreigners, and they successfully resisted pressure to establish trading rights with other nations. Russia (1804), Britain (1842) and the USA (1853) all tried to open up trade with Japan – and all had largely failed. The USA in particular was desperate to gain trading rights in Japan. There were three reasons for this:

- American commercial interests were pressurising the US government to open Japanese markets for their rapidly expanding industrial output.

- The American whaling fleet needed access to Japanese ports in order to take on vital supplies, especially coal.
- In 1849, the USA sent a warship, USS *Preble*, to Japan to rescue American sailors who had been shipwrecked off the Japanese coast. The Japanese were reluctant to let the *Preble* into port, but after the threat of force it successfully retrieved the sailors. The USA was angered by the fact that it was clear the sailors had been harshly treated by the Japanese.

Fillmore and Perry

Confronted with Japan's obstinate resistance to trade, in 1853–54 the USA sent a fleet of ships under the command of Commodore Perry. When the Japanese demanded that the ships leave, Perry turned his guns towards the town of Uraga. He demanded permission to deliver a letter from US President Fillmore, which made it clear that the USA expected trading access to Japan.

When the Japanese refused to agree to Fillmore's wishes, Commodore Perry threatened large-scale violence from the USA. Samurai swords were no match for modern guns, and the Japanese had no alternative but to open up their borders to trade with the USA. In 1854, Japan signed a treaty that allowed the USA trading access to two ports. In 1858, the Japanese signed another treaty that allowed foreigners access to more ports and designated cities within Japan.

Modernisation and industrialisation

This situation posed an enormous risk to Japan. With military backing, foreign merchants had already seized control of large areas of China, imposing their own laws and destroying local culture. There was an obvious risk that Japan would face the same fate and be divided up between competing foreign powers. To avoid this possibility, in 1867 the Japanese people demanded the restoration of an emperor as head of government, instead of the military shogun. Following the Meiji Restoration the following year, Emperor Meiji and his government set about modernising Japan in order to resist the imperial powers. By 1869, they had established a centralised administration, uniting all the previously independent regions of Japan under one government in one capital city. A new constitution was created, based on the German model. Whereas China had steadfastly refused to change in response to foreign interference, Japan realised that it would need to adopt Western ways in order to retain its independence.

In particular, the Japanese appreciated that they needed to develop their own military capabilities. This could not be achieved without rapid modernisation and industrialisation.

The Japanese modelled their education system, form of government, army, navy and industry on those of the foreign nations whose presence they most feared. Mines, iron foundries, factories and shipyards were quickly developed. Some of these were established by the government and then handed over to **private enterprise**. Others were built by samurai, such as Iwasaki Yataro, who founded the Mitsubishi shipyards. Railways and telegraph lines were laid, both to support industrial development and also to assist the government with its plans to unify the country. To cover the costs of this rapid modernisation, Japan concentrated on promoting its export trade, especially in textiles.

 KEY TERM

Private enterprise: businesses owned and managed by individuals, free of government restrictions.

Increasing prosperity facilitated the development of Japan's military strength. One-third of the national budget was spent on the army and navy. Military service became compulsory for all adult males, and by 1894, Japan possessed 28 modern warships. In schools, children were taught to be patriotic and to show total obedience to the emperor. The old Shinto religion, which viewed the emperor as descended from a god, was revived for the same reason.

The First Sino-Japanese War (1894)

Modernisation helped Japan maintain its independence and prevented it from suffering the same fate as China. In a remarkably short period of time, Japan developed from being a country threatened by the imperialistic ambitions of other nations to one capable of becoming an imperial power in its own right. The main reason for Japan's imperial ambitions in the late 19th century was economic. As a relatively small island nation, Japan possessed limited natural resources. Its industrial development, for example, was reliant on imported coal and steel. Much like the European imperial powers, the Japanese began to seek overseas possessions in order to gain the resources that they lacked.

The ongoing disintegration of China provided the opportunity for Japan to test its new military strength. Disputes over which country should control Korea led to the First Sino-Japanese War in 1894. The new, modern Japanese army quickly overran Korea, Manchuria and parts of China itself. When the Chinese capital, Peking (modern-day Beijing) came under threat, China surrendered. Under the terms of the Treaty of Shimonoseki (1895), China was forced to make territorial concessions to Japan, including the strategically important Port Arthur.

Japan's speedy and crushing victory over China came as a shock to the major European powers. It posed a serious threat to their own imperial interests in China and the Far East. Russia, in particular, greatly resented Japanese control of Port Arthur, whose warm-water port was vital to its own trading activities. With the support of France and Germany, Russia imposed diplomatic pressure on Japan to relinquish its control over Port Arthur. Faced with this 'Triple Intervention' of three major European powers, Japan had little choice but to back down. Port Arthur was returned to China, but Russia quickly established its own control over the region.

That Japan was unable to resist the combined pressure of Russia, France and Germany was not surprising. Few countries could have done. However, the situation made clear that Japan was not yet able to pursue its foreign and domestic policies without interference by the great powers. Humiliated, and mindful of Port Arthur, the Japanese decided to build more warships and wait for the opportunity to gain revenge against the Russians.

ACTIVITY 1.12

> I have no other object in sending Commodore Perry to Japan but to propose that the United States and Japan should live in friendship and have commercial intercourse with each other. I am desirous that our two countries should trade with each other, for the benefit both of Japan and the United States.
>
> Many of our ships pass every year from California to China, and a great number of our people pursue whale fishery near the shores of Japan. It sometimes happens, in stormy weather, that one of our ships is wrecked on Japan's shores. In all such cases, we ask and expect that our unfortunate people should be treated with kindness until we can send a vessel and bring them away.
>
> Our steamships, in crossing the great ocean, burn a great deal of coal, and it is not convenient to bring it all the way from America. We wish that out steamships and other vessels should be allowed to stop in Japan and supply themselves with coal, provisions and water. They will pay for them in money, or anything else you may prefer.
>
> These are the only reasons I have sent Commodore Perry, with a powerful squadron of ships, to Japan.
>
> **Letter from the President of the United States of America to the Emperor of Japan, 13 November 1852**

ACTIVITY 1.12 (CONTINUED)

a Look carefully at the extracts from President Fillmore's letter to the Japanese.

  i How would you describe the tone of the letter? Note down the phrases you would use as examples in your answer

  ii What requests did it make?

  iii Why do you think it mentions that Commodore Perry had 'a powerful squadron of ships'

b Make a list of the main factors which made the rapid modernisation of Japan possible? Which do you feel was the most important and why? Put the reasons next to your notes.

c Why, in the late 19th century, did Japan begin to look for overseas possessions?

d Why did Japan's victory in the First Sino-Japanese War both surprise and concern the major European nations?

KEY CONCEPT

Similarity and Difference

Historians study the ways in which people react to the situations that confront them, noting any similarities and differences they identify.

Prior to the 19th century, for example, China and Japan were **similar** in many ways – both maintained traditional methods which had lasted for centuries, and both resisted involvement with foreigners.

Yet, faced by the threat posed by foreign interference in the second half of the 19th century, China and Japan responded in very **different** ways. While China continued to follow its traditional beliefs and methods, Japan changed massively.

In small groups, compare and contrast the ways in which China and Japan responded to the threat posed by foreign interference in the second half of the 19th century.

International recognition of Japan as a world power

Russian expansion in the Far East

Having gained control of Port Arthur and the Liaodong peninsula in 1894, by 1900 Russia occupied the whole of Manchuria. This continued Russian expansion in the Far East caused alarm in Japan. Russia clearly had ambitions to seize Korea, which had been under Japanese control since the Treaty of Shimonoseki in 1895. The loss of Korea would greatly damage the Japanese economy and make Japan itself more vulnerable to a Russian attack.

Japan was not alone in being concerned by Russian expansion in the Far East. Britain saw it as a serious threat to its own commercial interests in China. As an island nation protected by its undisputed naval supremacy, Britain had followed a policy of 'splendid isolation', by which it had stayed out of European politics, avoided alliances with other countries and concentrated on the expansion of its own empire. By the beginning of the 20th century, it became clear that Britain needed to abandon this policy. There were a number of reasons for this. For example:

- it was becoming increasingly difficult for Britain to protect and maintain control over its vast empire
- the Boer Wars had exposed fundamental weaknesses in Britain's military capabilities
- the negative reaction of the other European powers to its involvement in the Boer Wars left Britain feeling isolated and vulnerable
- Germany had adopted a more aggressive foreign policy under Kaiser Wilhelm II – German acquisitions in Africa posed a threat to British possessions on the continent; more significantly, Germany's naval development programme threatened to undermine the supremacy of the British navy
- Russian expansion in the Far East was now posing a significant threat to Britain's commercial interests in China.

Anglo-Japanese Alliance (1902)

The British and Japanese governments decided to adopt a common approach to the problems posed by Russian expansion in the Far East. During 1901, negotiations took place between the British Foreign Secretary (Henry Petty-Fitzmaurice, 5th Marquess of Lansdowne) and the Japanese Ambassador to London (Hayashi Tadasu). These negotiations led to the signing of the Anglo-Japanese Alliance of 1902. Britain and Japan agreed to remain neutral if either country was involved in war. However, if either Britain or Japan faced war against two or more opponents, the other country would come to its aid. Britain recognised Japanese rights in Korea, while Japan agreed to use its fleet to protect British interests in the Far East.

The signing of the Anglo-Japanese Alliance was greeted favourably in both Britain and Japan. The British felt that their strategic and economic interests in the Far East were now adequately protected against Russian expansion. To the Japanese, the Alliance was a major triumph. Japan could now count on British support in a war against Russia if any other country, such as France or Germany, sided with the Russians. Moreover, the signing of the Alliance

marked the first time that Japan had been recognised as an equal by one of the major European powers. Some historians have argued that the Alliance established Japan's emergence as a world power in its own right.

ACTIVITY 1.13

Working in pairs:

a   make a list of reasons to explain why Britain formed the 1902 alliance with Japan

b   make a list of reasons why Japan formed the 1902 alliance with Britain

c   look carefully at Figure 1.13 – what can historians learn from this cartoon?

ALLIES.

"*Oh, East is East , and West is West . . . . .*
But there is neither East nor West, Border, nor Breed, nor Birth,
When two strong men stand face to face, tho' they come from the ends of the Earth!" – RUDYARD KIPLING.

Figure 1.13: A British cartoon, published in 1905. The text reads: "*Oh, East is East, and West is West... But there is neither East nor West, Border, nor Breed, nor Birth, When two strong men stand face to face, tho' they come from the ends of the earth!*" Rudyard Kipling (October 4, 1905)

The Russo-Japanese War (1904–05)

Japan now felt strong enough to seek a settlement with Russia. The Japanese were prepared to recognise Russian rights in Manchuria in exchange for Japanese rights in Korea. Convinced of their military superiority, the Russians refused to negotiate with the Japanese, and

28

instead invaded Korea. The Japanese response was rapid, dramatic and devastating, and brought Japan into a war with one of the world's great powers.

On 9 February 1904, Japanese warships entered Port Arthur, where a number of Russian ships were in dock, totally unprepared for battle. Two Russian battleships and a cruiser were destroyed by Japanese torpedoes. This began the Russo-Japanese War of 1904-05. With the Russian fleet widely dispersed across the world and Russian soldiers forced to endure a lengthy overland trip across Asia to reach the battlefield, the advantage clearly lay with Japan. It quickly established control over the local seas, which enabled it to move troops around without resistance. Once Port Arthur was taken (Figure 1.15), the Japanese moved into Manchuria, forcing the Russian troops to retreat to Mukden. After a three-month siege, involving over a million soldiers on both sides – and at the height of a bitterly cold winter – Mukden fell to the Japanese.

Russia's last hope lay with its fleet in the Baltic Sea, but the ships' journey to the Far East was long, tortuous and eventful. While steaming through the North Sea, the Russian ships mistook some British fishing boats for warships, and fired on them. The British were understandably outraged, and for a time the Russian fleet was pursued by a vastly superior fleet of British ships. As Britain was allied to Japan, it seemed likely that the rival fleets would engage in battle. While diplomatic negotiations succeeded in preventing this, Britain denied the Russian fleet access to the Suez Canal, forcing it to take the far longer route around Africa. Laden down with coal to fuel the steam engines, the Russian ships made slow progress and did not arrive in the Straits of Tsushima between Korea and Japan until May 1905.

The battle began on 27 May 1905, when Russian and Japanese ships finally faced each other in the straits. The slow-moving and outdated Russian vessels were no match for Japan's modern warships, which were under the command of Admiral Togo Heihachiro. By the following day, Japan had defeated the Russian navy. Facing humiliation abroad and revolution at home, the Russian tsar, Nicholas II, had no alternative but to seek a settlement with Japan. In August 1905, negotiations took place in Portsmouth, New Hampshire, USA, chaired by the American president Theodore Roosevelt. The following month, Japan and Russia signed the Treaty of Portsmouth, which clearly recognised Japan's overwhelming victory in the Russo-Japanese War. Russian influence in Manchuria was effectively ended, and Japan's rights over Korea were formally recognised.

Look carefully at Figure 1.14. It shows other countries looking on while the champion of Europe (Russia) takes on the champion of Asia (Japan).

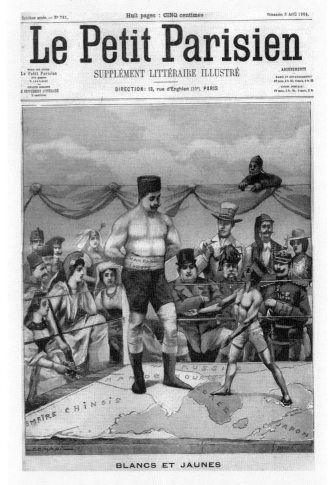

Figure 1.14: Cartoon published in the French magazine *Le Petit Parisien*, 1904

Consider the following questions in pairs or small groups.

a Put the illustration into context by commenting on the significance of its publication date.

b How are Russia and Japan depicted in the illustration?

c What is the meaning of the map on the floor of the ring?

d Why would other countries be so interested in the outcome of a conflict between Russia and Japan?

e Which of the two countries did the artist believe was most likely to achieve victory in the conflict between Russia and Japan?

f Do you think the artist considered Japan a major world power in 1904? Explain your answer.

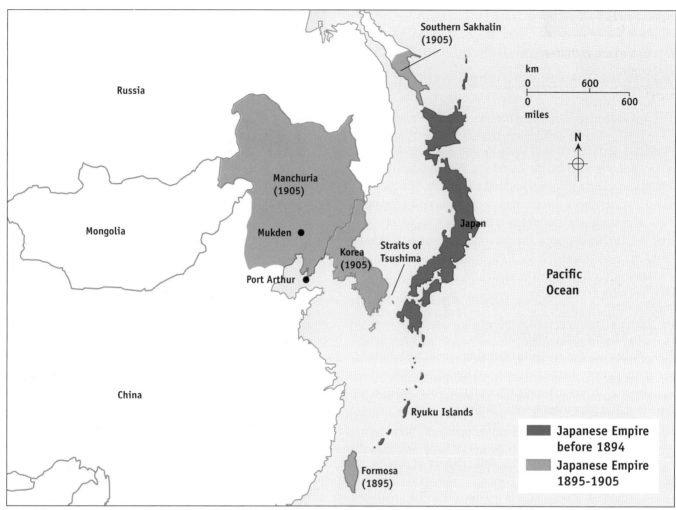

Figure 1.15: Japanese expansion 1894–1905

Figure 1.16: Japanese soldiers laying siege to Port Arthur, 1904

31

List the factors that enabled Japan to defeat a major European country in the Russo-Japanese War of 1904–05. Look at your list: would you agree that Japan's victory in the war of 1904–05 was the result of Russian weakness rather than Japanese strength?

Debate in pairs, one agreeing with the statement and the other disagreeing with it. After your debate, make notes on your conclusion.

Japan's role in the First World War and global position by 1918

In a period of less than 50 years, Japan had developed into a modern, industrial country with the military capacity to defeat a major European power. Japan entered the 20th century as an imperial nation, perceived as the champion of Asia against the **western powers**. Those Western powers, keen to protect and extend their own trading activities in the Far East, grew increasingly concerned by Japanese expansion within the region. This concern was heightened as a result of Japan's actions during the First World War.

Honouring its alliance with Britain, Japan entered the First World War by declaring war on Germany in 1914. Its primary role was to secure the sea lanes of the South Pacific and the Indian Ocean against the German navy. While the Western powers were fully occupied fighting the war in Europe, Japan took advantage of their absence from the Far East in a number of ways.

- Japan began to supply the Far East region with goods that the European countries could no longer provide. During the war years, 1914–18, Japan's exports of cotton cloth increased threefold, while its heavy industry was greatly expanded to fill the gap left by the absence of European imports of iron, steel and chemicals.
- To assist with this surge in exports, the Japanese merchant fleet almost doubled in size during the war years.
- The Japanese shipbuilding industry was also boosted by the fact that Japan supplied Britain and the Allies with shipping and other goods throughout the war.

- Japan attacked the German-controlled regions of China's Shantung (Shandong) Province. This enabled Japan to extend its own interests and influence in China, without facing opposition from the Western powers.

In January 1915, Japan presented the Chinese with what became known as the Twenty-One Demands. These were designed to dramatically increase Japanese political and economic power and influence over much of China. In effect, China would cease to be an independent country. When the Chinese initially refused to accept these demands, Japan issued an **ultimatum** on 7 May 1915:

> Despite the attitude of the Chinese Government, the Imperial Government of Japan, still warmly attached to the preservation of peace in the Far East, is still hoping for a satisfactory settlement in order to avoid the disturbance of relations. The Imperial Government hereby again offer their advice and hope that the Chinese government, upon this advice, will give a satisfactory reply by 6 p.m. on 9th day of May. It is hereby declared that if no satisfactory reply is received before or at the specified time, the Imperial Government will take steps they may deem necessary.
>
> **Ultimatum delivered to the Chinese Minister of Foreign Affairs by the Japanese Minister, 7 May 1915**

 KEY TERMS

Western powers: a term used to refer to the European countries with the most powerful economies, armies and navies, and the USA.

Ultimatum: a final demand that, if rejected, will lead to serious consequences such as war.

Following this ultimatum, the Chinese finally agreed to the Japanese demands on 8 May 1915. Under pressure from the USA, Britain and other countries with a vested interest in China, Japan was eventually forced to reduce its Twenty-One Demands. However, even the revised demands granted Japan similar rights in China to those enjoyed by the other great powers. Japan's use of threats and bullying tactics angered the Chinese and added to the other powers' growing suspicions of Japan.

- Between 1916 and 1918, Japan provided the Chinese with a series of loans, thereby further increasing its financial, commercial and economic influence over China.

The Western powers, particularly the USA and Britain, were greatly concerned by Japan's continued economic growth and attempts to extend its political and economic interests in the Far East. The USA saw Japan's attempts to exploit the weakness of China as a serious threat to the 'open door policy' and, therefore, to its own commercial interests in China. Britain, Japan's closest ally, feared that the Japanese intention was to take control over the whole of China. In 1902, Britain had signed the Anglo-Japanese Alliance to gain Japan's assistance in protecting its trading interests in China. Japan itself now seemed a threat to those interests. While the First World War continued, there was little that the USA or Britain could do about these concerns. Japan was a vital ally in the war against Germany.

ACTIVITY 1.16

a How did Japan benefit from the First World War?

b Why would Japan's increasing power and influence over China be of great concern to the Western powers?

c Initially, China refused to agree to Japan's Twenty-One Demands. Why do you think the Chinese government finally accepted the demands on 8 May 1915?

Ensure that your notes contain details of the ways in which Japan benefitted from the First World War

Reflection: Compare your analysis with that of another student. How did you decide which examples of Japan benefitting from the First World War to include? Did you include the same or different examples?

1.4 Why did the USA emerge as a world power and what was the impact on international relations?

Impact of the closing of the frontier on US foreign policy

If Japan's rise to world power status had been both rapid and dramatic, so too was that of the USA. At the beginning of the 19th century, the USA was a small nation, whose independence had only recently been formally recognised. It was confined by the Appalachian Mountains in the west, the Atlantic Ocean in the east, Canada in the north and Spanish territorial possessions in the south. Yet, by 1890, the USA had expanded across much of the North American continent.

For most of the 19th century, the USA focused on internal rather than international issues. It was preoccupied with westward expansion on the North American continent, and from 1861 to 1865, fighting a civil war that threatened to tear the country apart. Events in Africa, Asia and the associated rivalries between European nations had been of little concern to the USA. Americans had no real interest in wider international affairs, and followed a policy of **isolationism**. They looked inwards, seeking to develop in their own way without outside interference or involvement in foreign issues.

 KEY TERM

Isolationism: the policy of keeping one's country separate from the affairs of other nations, by avoiding alliances and international commitments.

Continental expansion

Louisiana was purchased from France in 1803, doubling the size of the USA at the time. Florida was taken from the Spanish in 1819. Settlers moved further and further west, towards and then across the Mississippi. Thousands moved into what is now Texas, but what was then a largely uninhabited part of Mexico. Mexico was weak and unstable, and the American settlers revolted against the Mexican government, establishing the Republic of Texas as an independent state in 1836 and becoming part of the USA in 1845. A boundary dispute between the USA and Britain was settled by the Treaty of Oregon in 1846, as a result of which the USA gained control over an area of forests and good agricultural land, with access to the Pacific Ocean. Victory in war against Spain led to the Treaty of Guadelupe Hidalgo (1848), by which the USA gained the present states of California, New Mexico, Nevada and Arizona, providing a longer Pacific coastline. In 1853, the USA purchased further land from Mexico in a deal known as the Gadsden Purchase. The purchase of Alaska from Russia in 1867 brought to an end the continental expansion of the USA in the 19th century.

The USA's rapid expansion across the North American continent led to international criticism. In particular, European nations interpreted the USA's **annexation** of Texas and involvement in the war against Mexico as the actions of an aggressive bully attacking a poorer and weaker country.

 KEY TERM

Annexation: taking possession of territory, usually by force or without permission

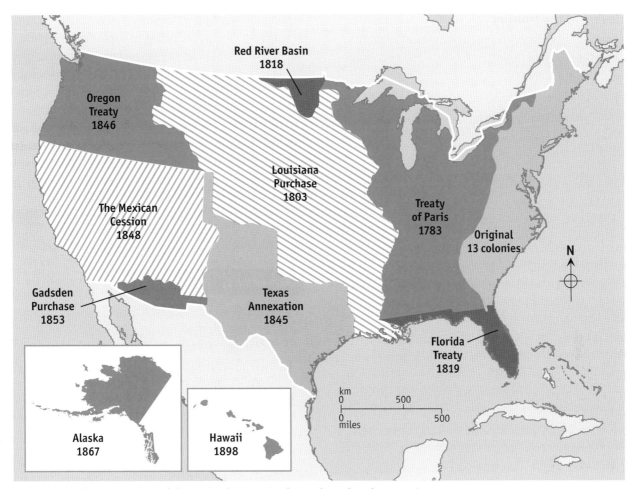

Figure 1.17: The expansion of the United States in the 18th and 19th centuries

Americans justified their territorial expansion by their belief in the concept of 'Manifest Destiny', which claimed that the USA was destined to expand into, settle and rule over the whole North American continent. The main ideas underpinning Manifest Destiny were:

- US expansion to the Pacific Ocean was logical and inevitable
- aggressive US nationalism was desirable
- the USA had the 'divine right' to continue expanding westwards until it had spread from the Atlantic to the Pacific
- the USA had a duty to spread its Christian values and culture
- incorporation into the USA would bring liberty and freedom to other North American territories.

The USA was also afraid that, if it did not acquire territories such as California, then some hostile imperial power might. By the early 19th century, virtually all the Latin American possessions of the once-great Spanish and Portuguese empires had gained independence. Only

Cuba and Puerto Rico remained under Spanish rule. Concerns that Spain would try to win back control of its former possessions in South America, and that this would encourage other European powers to extend their empires into the Americas, led the USA to approve the Monroe Doctrine in 1823. This stated that the USA would not interfere in European affairs, but that any attempt by European powers to intervene in the Americas would be viewed by the USA as an act of aggression and would be dealt with accordingly.

ACTIVITY 1.17

Discuss the following questions in small groups.

a Make a list of the various methods used by the USA to enable it to expand across the entire North American continent.

b How did the USA justify this expansion?

c Why did the USA establish the Monroe Doctrine in 1823?

The closing of the frontier

Having gained possession of much of the North American continent, the US government now needed to encourage people to settle in areas that it termed the 'Frontier' – areas which were wild, remote, dangerous and largely unexplored. The army was deployed to deal with the presence of Native Americans, who resented the attempts of white settlers to occupy their land. The US government regarded Native Americans as uncivilised savages, and brutal methods were used to deal with the 'Indian problem'. Gradually, the Native Americans were worn down, killed or confined to reservations. By 1900, fewer than 350 000 Native Americans were left.

Many of the early settlers in the Far West were miners, drawn by the prospect of finding gold. The government encouraged more permanent settlement of the frontier by enabling people to acquire cheap land on which to live and earn a living. The Donation Land Claim Act of 1850 allowed settlers to take ownership of up to 640 acres of land in Oregon without charge. This was followed by a series of Homestead Acts, the first of which was passed in 1862, which made land available to those willing to improve and farm it. As a result, more and more settlers were encouraged to move westwards, settle on farms and push back the frontier.

The 1890 census, a detailed government survey of the American population, revealed that settlements had been established across the entire USA. With no untamed areas left in which to settle, the government announced that the frontier was closed. The frontier had represented adventure, freedom and the opportunity to establish a new life. Many of the early settlers, for example, had sold their land for a profit to later arrivals and moved on in search of new and better land to cultivate. For the first time in its history, the USA had no frontier and these opportunities no longer existed.

In an essay entitled 'The Significance of the Frontier in American History', published in 1893, the historian Frederick Jackson Turner argued that the success of the USA was directly influenced by the country's westward expansion. He suggested that taming the wild and savage wilderness had shaped American culture and character, encouraging strength, ambition, initiative, self-reliance, violence and individualism. The closing of the frontier in 1890 effectively ended a period of expansion that Turner believed had been so important in shaping the character of the USA and its people.

The closing of the frontier was to have a profound effect on the USA's foreign policy. Americans began to look

abroad for new opportunities – a new frontier to tame, new economic opportunities to exploit and develop. Many senior American politicians and clergymen began to argue that it was the USA's duty to spread democracy and Christianity to less fortunate and 'backward peoples' in the world. For example, in his book *Our Country*, published in 1885, the clergyman Josiah Strong claimed that Americans belonged to the 'superior' Anglo-Saxon race, which should civilise the 'savage races'.

If the closing of the frontier provided an incentive for the USA to expand its influence overseas, a number of economic and political factors were simultaneously having the same effect.

ACTIVITY 1.18

a What dangers might face Americans who risked becoming settlers in the newly acquired and untamed western territories of the USA?

b Why do you think so many Americans were prepared to take such risks?

c Why did the US government announce the closure of the frontier in 1890?

d According to the historian Frederick Jackson Turner, why did the closing of the frontier have such a major impact on the USA?

e In what ways might the closing of the frontier encourage the USA to seek overseas territorial possessions?

Economic growth and the need for trade in the late 19th century

Throughout the last 30 years of the 19th century, the USA underwent a remarkable economic transformation, based on enormous industrial growth. A number of interrelated factors made this possible:

- the USA had large quantities of vital raw materials, such as coal, iron ore and oil
- population growth (31.5 million in 1880, 76 million in 1900), aided by increasing immigration from Europe and Asia, provided both labour and consumers
- the introduction of new methods for the mass-production of manufactured products
- a lack of government regulation enabled employers to manage their workforce in any way they chose
- the development of large-scale, highly profitable companies, known as corporations and trusts

- the mechanisation of farming enabled the mass-production of wheat and other crops
- the development of one of the most comprehensive railway systems in the world, facilitating the transportation of raw materials and finished products
- the availability of investment capital through banks and the **stock market** in New York – by 1880, the New York Stock Exchange on Wall Street had become the second largest money market in the world
- the government encouraged the growth of American industry by protecting it from foreign competition; tariffs (taxes) were imposed on imported foreign-manufactured goods to ensure that they were more expensive than home-produced ones; these tariffs could be as high as 50% of the cost of the imported goods.

As a result of these factors, the USA's output in key industries grew rapidly. For example:

- **coal** – less than 50 million tons were produced in 1870 – by 1890, this had risen to 262 million tons (the USA's closest rival, Britain, produced 219 million tons)
- **steel** – steel output rose from 380 000 tons in 1875 to 13 million tons by 1890 (the USA's closest rival, Germany, produced 6 million tons) – by 1900, Andrew Carnegie's US company was producing more steel than the whole of Britain
- **cotton** – in 1870, the USA produced 4.25 million bales of cotton – by 1890 this had risen to 10.6 million (the USA's closet rival, India, produced 3 million bales).

By 1900, the USA was outstripping its main European rivals in the output of key products. Nevertheless, the US economy suffered from an unstable banking system and overdependence on the domestic market. Anyone could set up a bank and small-scale banks would often invest unwisely. Railway speculator Jay Cooke's company borrowed $100 million; its bankruptcy in 1873 destroyed hundreds of banks. In 1893, bankruptcies in industries ranging from banks to railways sparked a crisis, which caused a shortage of cash. Industry laid off workers and unemployment rose from 3.7 million in 1892 to 12.3 million in 1894.

The sudden economic downturn in 1893 alerted businessmen to the dangers of over-reliance on the domestic market, and they suggested that the remedy was to sell more goods abroad. Large-scale farmers in the south and west, for example, argued that they needed access to overseas markets in order to maximise their profits. They campaigned against the government's policy

of protecting American industries from foreign imports by imposing high tariffs. They argued that this policy not only prevented them from selling their products abroad, but also increased their costs due to the high price of imported agricultural machinery. The Democratic Party also campaigned for the abolition, or at least the reduction, of import tariffs, arguing that free trade would be more beneficial to the American economy. The Republican Party, largely dominated by business and manufacturing interests, remained steadfastly in favour of protecting American industry from foreign competition. As Republican Senator William McKinley, later to become president of the USA, had explained in a speech in 1892, 'under free trade, the trader is the master and the producer the slave. Protection is but the law of nature, the law of self-preservation.' Republican dominance of American politics during the late 19th century meant that import tariffs not only remained, but remained at a high level.

Opportunities for the USA to expand its overseas trade were restricted. European nations practised **protectionism** throughout their empires, making it difficult for the USA to break into potentially lucrative markets. At the same time, the USA was facing growing competition for trade with South America, where European countries were increasing their commercial involvement. By 1900, for example, Britain had overtaken the USA as the main trading partner of Argentina, the largest South American market. As a result, access to markets in China and the Far East were increasingly viewed as vital for the USA's future prosperity.

 KEY TERMS

Stock market: a place where shares are bought and sold. Companies sell shares in order to raise the money (capital) required to establish their factories and businesses. People buy shares in a company as an investment in order to gain from its subsequent profits.

Protectionism: the placing of high tariffs (taxes) on imports in order to protect domestic industries from foreign competition. Protectionism is the opposite of free trade.

It was clear that the effective exploitation of the Far Eastern market would require investment in a strong navy to protect merchant ships, and the acquisition of overseas bases to protect US interests. That the USA should take these steps gained considerable support from the publication in 1890 of a book, *The Influence of Sea Power upon History*. Written by Captain A. T. Mahan, a former naval officer then lecturing at the USA's Naval War College, the book was both widely popular and extremely influential. Mahan argued that the evidence of history confirmed that a nation's greatness and prosperity depended on naval power. The idea that the USA should increase the size and strength of its navy as a means of enhancing and protecting overseas trade proved popular with many powerful Americans – not least the future president, Theodore Roosevelt, who had befriended Mahan at the Naval War College.

While many US politicians supported the idea that the USA should expand its overseas interests, others argued that maintaining the traditional policy of isolationism, and avoiding foreign entanglements and responsibilities, was the best way to protect US interests. In many ways, this debate was settled by events in Cuba.

ACTIVITY 1.19

Why were some American entrepreneurs able to become enormously wealthy during the late 19th century?

a Make a list of possible reasons.

b In pairs, compare lists and then re-arrange them into an order of significance – what you consider to be the most important reason at the top, and the least important at the bottom.

Reasons for, and impact of, the Spanish-American War (1898)

Cuba, located in the Caribbean in close proximity to the USA, was the last Spanish territorial possession in the region. In 1868, the Cubans revolted against their Spanish rulers, demanding independence. This was the first of three independence wars fought against Spain in Cuba, the last war starting in 1895. With their own anti-imperial background, Americans viewed the Spanish as brutal, anti-democratic rulers. Moreover, Cuba had become important to the US economy – a great deal of American money was invested in the production of sugar, tobacco and minerals, mainly nickel, on the island. American interests were therefore threatened by the situation in Cuba, not least because of the guerrilla tactics used by the Cuban rebels. In 1897, President William McKinley made an attempt to persuade the Spanish to reform their methods of governing Cuba, but this was publicly rejected by Spain in a manner American public opinion found insulting.

Reasons for the Spanish-American War

Although the USA officially remained neutral in the war between Spain and the Cuban rebels, it sent a battleship, the *Maine*, to Cuba to protect US citizens who had been caught up in the fighting. At 9.40 p.m. on 15 February 1898, the *Maine* exploded in Havana Harbour, killing 268 American sailors. This event sparked outrage in the USA. Although the US government believed that the explosion was the result of an accident, the American press argued that Spain was responsible, and it was heavily critical of the government's weak response to the incident.

ACTIVITY 1.20

a Which of the following statements about the article in the *New York Journal* (below) do you feel are true, and which are false? Make notes which explain your reasoning.

i The article believed that the US government had been right to keep out of the war between Cuba and Spain before the *Maine* incident.

ii The article argued that the US government should have intervened in the war between Cuba and Spain even before the *Maine* incident.

iii The article wanted its readers to believe that Spain had deliberately destroyed the *Maine*.

iv The article wanted the US government to declare war on Spain.

To five hundred thousand Cubans starved or otherwise murdered have been added an American battleship and three hundred American sailors lost as the direct result of the weak policy of our government toward Spain. If we had stopped the war in Cuba when duty and policy alike urged us to do, the Maine would have been afloat today, and three hundred homes, now desolate, would have been unscathed.

It was an accident, they say. Perhaps it was, but accident or not, it would never have happened if there had been peace in Cuba, as there would have been if we had done our duty. And it was an accident of a remarkably convenient kind for Spain. Two days ago we had five battleships in the Atlantic. Today we have four. A few more such accidents will leave us at the mercy of a Spanish fleet.

b The two headlines below appeared on the front pages of two other US newspapers on the same day. List the features they have in common.

SPANISH TREACHERY!

DESTRUCTION OF THE WARSHIP MAINE WAS THE WORK OF AN ENEMY

THINK LIKE A HISTORIAN

Newspapers, television, radio and the internet are very powerful in shaping people's views about particular issues in the modern world. They report facts and provide opinions. In small groups, discuss the differences between facts and opinions. What problems do the combination of the two in one publication or broadcast cause today?

The closing of the frontier and the publication of Mahan's book in 1890 encouraged many influential Americans to argue that the USA should extend its influence outwards – to the Caribbean and the Pacific Ocean. Arguably the most important of these was **Theodore Roosevelt**. Appointed Assistant Secretary of the Navy in 1897, he continued the process of developing the size and strength of the US navy that had started in 1882. A year before the sinking of the *Maine*, he had argued that it was in the USA's best interests to eject the Spanish from Cuba. He argued that war against Spain was advisable 'on the grounds both of humanity and self-interest, taking one more step toward the complete freeing of America from European dominion.' He added that such a war would benefit 'our military forces by trying both the navy and the army in actual practice'.

While President McKinley sought a diplomatic solution to the rising tensions following the sinking of the *Maine*, Roosevelt was already preparing for war. He ordered US naval vessels to occupy key ports, such as Manilla Bay in the Philippines with the aim of denying Spanish ships access to safe harbours and supplies.

In April 1898, President McKinley formally declared war on Spain. Historians have debated the reasons for this decision, and a variety of different arguments have been suggested:

- it was inspired by an aggressive and patriotic press campaign that inflamed public opinion following the *Maine* incident
- it was intended to protect American business interests in Cuba
- it was inevitable, given the misrule of the Spanish and the geographical closeness of Cuba to the USA
- the USA feared an independent Cuba that it could not control
- the USA desired more territory in order to extend its commercial interests
- the US government wanted to distract the American people from the effects of the economic depression.

Roosevelt became president of the USA in 1901, and was re-elected by a landslide in 1904. He believed that the USA should play a major role in world affairs, and he supported the move towards US imperialism. He negotiated the Treaty of Portsmouth that ended the Russo-Japanese War in 1905, for which he was awarded the Nobel Peace Prize.

The war was short-lived. The US navy, with its modern, well-equipped ships, destroyed a Spanish fleet at Manila Bay. A second Spanish fleet was defeated at Santiago de Cuba. In order to protect the security of Spain itself, the Spanish government recalled its remaining ships. Without naval support, the Spanish were unable to resist the combined efforts of the Cuban freedom fighters and the small number of US soldiers who had landed in Cuba. Spain had no alternative but to surrender. The USA ignored the Cubans' contribution and maintained that it was a purely American victory. The USA did not include, or even seriously consider, Cubans in the final peace settlement with Spain, the 1898 Treaty of Paris.

The Treaty of Paris and the impact of the Spanish-American War

The Treaty of Paris left the USA in effective control of a nominally independent Cuba. In addition, Spain was forced to hand control of its other former possessions, including the Philippines, Puerto Rico and Guam to the USA. The USA had become an imperial power.

Almost immediately, the Filipinos rebelled and, in order to retain control, the USA was forced to fight a far longer and more costly war (1899–1902) than the one against Spain. Anti-imperialists, such as the Democratic presidential candidate William Jennings Bryan, protested against the acquisition of foreign territories, arguing that it was a betrayal of the USA's isolationist traditions. However, Bryan's defeat by the sitting president, William McKinley, in the 1900 presidential election suggests that the majority of the American public supported the USA's move towards imperialism.

37

Acquiring the Philippines provided the USA with control of a region that could act as a strategic base to supply and defend American trading interests in China and the Far East. The USA had become an imperial power and began following policies designed to extend its global influence. Events in Hawaii provide a clear example of this. Following a series of trade treaties commencing in the 1840s, Hawaii had become important to the USA as a base for supplying American whaling vessels and a source of sugar cane. By 1870, American interests dominated much of the local economy, and in 1887 the USA established a naval base at Pearl Harbor. Realising the strategic importance of Hawaii to American trade with the Far East, and in line with its new imperial policy, the USA formally annexed Hawaii in 1898.

Less than a year into his second term, McKinley was assassinated, and Vice-president Theodore Roosevelt was sworn in. Roosevelt fully supported the new imperialistic direction of US foreign policy, believing that it was 'incumbent on all civilized and orderly powers to insist on the proper policing of the world'. He was to play a decisive role in the USA's adoption of a more imperialistic foreign policy.

In 1901, arguing that the Cubans were not yet ready to rule themselves, the US Congress passed the Platt Amendment to the Cuban Constitution. This gave the USA control of Cuban foreign, financial and commercial affairs. The USA was also granted rights over key land in Cuba, including a number of naval bases, such as Guantanamo Bay. With US soldiers still on the island, the Cubans had little option but to accept the Platt Amendment by treaty in 1903. A far-reaching takeover of Cuban land by Americans followed, and American businesses began to move into Cuba on a large scale.

There had long been a desire in the USA to connect the Atlantic and Pacific Oceans by canal, thus avoiding the long and dangerous sea journey around the tip of South America. In the 1860s, the US Secretary of State William Seward had attempted to start negotiations for the building of a canal to achieve this. These negotiations were, however, stopped by the US Senate. By 1902, the situation had changed. The USA had become an imperial nation, with a desire to extend its overseas trade, which renewed its interests in building a canal. The Spooner Act of 1902, enthusiastically supported by President Roosevelt, authorised the USA to purchase the assets of a French company that had unsuccessfully tried to construct a canal through what is now Panama, which was then under the control of Colombia.

When the Colombians showed no interest in the treaty, the USA provided support to a Panama independence movement. Panamanian independence followed in 1903, with rapid recognition by the USA. The presence of the US

navy off both the Atlantic and Pacific coasts of Panama made any retaliation by the Colombians impossible. The USA then acquired a strip of Panamanian land, some 16 km (10 miles) wide, through which the canal could be built. The Panama Canal was finished by 1914, built largely with American money and engineering skills. The canal was to play a major part in the development of the USA as a Pacific power.

In 1904, President Roosevelt announced a Corollary (addition) to the Monroe Doctrine. The Monroe Doctrine of 1823 was intended to protect the independent countries of the Americas by warning Europe to stay out of the region. The Corollary now sanctioned US armed intervention if any country in the region was threatened by internal or external factors. In effect, the USA was establishing a sphere of influence within the Caribbean region, within which it had the right to intervene whenever it considered its interests (particularly economic) were at risk. In 1905, for example, Roosevelt sent the US marines to the Dominican Republic, allegedly to prevent European powers taking action to collect debts owed to them. However, protection of massive US investment was a more likely reason for American intervention.

Roosevelt explained the purpose of the Corollary in a speech in December 1904:

> All that this country desires is to see the neighbouring countries stable, orderly, and prosperous. Any country whose people conduct themselves well can count upon our hearty friendship. If a nation shows that it knows how to act with reasonable efficiency and decency in social and political matters, if it keeps order and pays its obligations, it need fear no interference from the United States. Chronic wrongdoing, or an impotence which results in a general loosening of the ties of civilized society, may in America, as elsewhere, ultimately require intervention by some civilized nation, and in the Western Hemisphere the adherence of the United States to the Monroe Doctrine may force the United States, however reluctantly, in flagrant cases of such wrongdoing or impotence, to the exercise of an international police power.
>
> **Speech by President Roosevelt to Congress, December 1904**

President Roosevelt also started a major expansion of the US navy. He argued that a strong navy was essential to protect American economic interests, given that European nations and Japan were all increasing their own naval capabilities. Roosevelt ordered the building of 16 new battleships.

ACTIVITY 1.21

Look carefully at the cartoon in Figure 1.18, which was published in an American magazine in 1906.

a Who is depicted as captain of the American ship?

b Why is the ship's gun drawn so large?

c Who or what does the character on the left represent?

d Why is the character in the middle crying?

e Why are the words 'Monroe Doctrine' attached to the gun?

f What point do you think the cartoonist was trying to make?

Figure 1.18: Cartoon published in the American magazine *Puck* in 1906

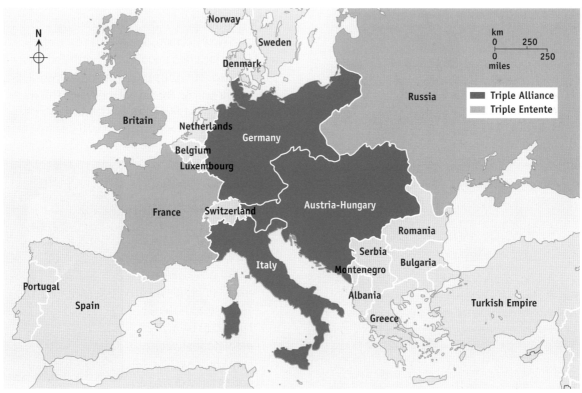

Figure 1.19: Europe in 1914, showing the division between the members of the Triple Alliance and the Triple Entente.

Between 1907 and 1909, Roosevelt sent the ships on an international tour to make sure that the world was fully aware that the USA was now a major naval power.

Roosevelt's policies were, of course, in marked contrast to the USA's isolationist tradition. Roosevelt justified them in two ways. First, such policies were necessary to protect America's trading and commercial interests. Second, they were to prevent European (especially German) intervention in the Americas, something that was seen as a real threat to the USA's security.

By 1914, therefore, the USA had emerged as a prosperous and strong regional power, with an ever-increasing influence over world financial markets and a new-found commitment to its own form of imperialistic expansion.

KEY CONCEPT

Cause and Consequence

Historians seek to explain why certain events or circumstances occurred, and to evaluate their possible consequences. For example, consider these issues relating to the emergence of the USA as a major world power with expansionist aims.

Cause – Look at this list of possible reasons why the USA became involved in overseas expansion in the 19th and early 20th centuries. In small groups, discuss the relative importance of each reason and then rearrange the list into an order of significance.

The USA became involved in overseas expansion because of:

- the need to increase and protect the USA's commercial interests
- the closing of the frontier
- victory in the war against Spain
- the need to prevent European nations threatening the security of the USA
- the opening of the Panama Canal

Consequence – With the advantage of hindsight, historians can see how the USA developed into the position of great international power which it occupies today. However, historians also need to consider how the USA's adoption of imperialistic ambitions by the early 20th century was interpreted at the time. In the same small groups, discuss the possible consequences of the USA's emergence as an imperial power for other countries, such as the major European nations, Japan, China and independent states within the Americas.

Reasons for, and impact of, the USA's entry into the First World War

The First World War began in Europe, and was the result of growing tensions between the major European countries during the late 19th and early 20th centuries.

In June 1914, Archduke Franz Ferdinand, heir to the throne of Austria-Hungary, was assassinated by a Serbian nationalist in Sarajevo. Austria-Hungary declared war on Serbia. Always suspicious of Austria-Hungary in the Balkans, Russia mobilised and declared war on Austria-Hungary. In support of Austria-Hungary, Germany declared war on Russia and – due to the requirements of its military planning – on France. German troops entered Belgium on their way to attack France, leading Britain to honour its 1839 commitment to defend Belgian neutrality and declare war on Germany.

The war surprised the countries' leaders by quickly becoming bogged down; modern weapons made quick victories more difficult and the armies found themselves trapped in defensive trenches, unable to advance with no-one knowing how to make a successful attack. Into this war of heavy losses and little movement came people from across the world as soldiers were brought in from several empires. The British army included soldiers from Canada, Australia, New Zealand, Africa and the Indian subcontinent, the French included people from north and west Africa and Vietnam. Honouring its 1902 alliance with Britain, Japan entered the war on the side of the Allies. This was war on a scale never seen before – truly a world war.

WOODROW WILSON (1856–1924)

The Democrat Wilson was elected as president in 1912 and narrowly won a second term in 1916. He made the decision to bring the USA into the First World War in 1917. He considered himself to be a mediator between rival European nations and played a leading role in the peace negotiations at the end of the war. Wilson suffered a stroke in 1919, but continued to serve as president until 1921.

However, it was a world war not involving a country that, by 1914, had unquestionably emerged as a major world power. The USA, under President **Woodrow Wilson**, could see no reason to become involved in a war raging thousands of miles away and which had resulted from conflicts between rival European nations. The USA's isolationist tradition meant that it was unwilling to interfere in European affairs.

Moreover, American interests were not initially threatened by the war. Indeed, the USA benefitted from it, taking over both German and British markets in South America and making money by setting up loans to countries involved in the conflict. As a result, Wilson remained firmly neutral in policy. He had avoided any formal links with either of the two armed camps that had developed in Europe, and did all he could to mediate between the warring nations. Wilson's neutrality policy was enormously popular in the USA, and he was re-elected in the 1916 presidential election based on his commitment that the USA would remain neutral and not become involved in the war.

Germany had a rather different view of American neutrality. While trade with the USA was theoretically open to all nations fighting in the war, Britain and France had a distinct advantage over Germany. With its navy largely controlling the Atlantic shipping routes, Britain and its allies could purchase and transport food and industrial products from the USA, while Germany could not. Moreover, American bankers tended to be heavily pro-British and, as a result, Germany was denied access to US loans readily available to its enemies. Senior members of the German government began to see the USA as far from neutral, believing that it was actively assisting Germany's enemies.

Reasons for the USA entering the war: German submarine warfare

Increasingly, American interests were being adversely affected by German actions. Convinced that the USA was supplying Britain and its allies with weapons and other military equipment, in 1915 German U-boats (submarines) began regularly attacking ships crossing the Atlantic. This threatened to seriously undermine the USA's attempts to maintain its trading links with Europe. At first, the Germans would issue warnings to the ships so that passengers could be evacuated before the attack began. In 1915, however, the *Lusitania* was sunk without warning, killing

more than 120 Americans. There was outrage across the USA, and President Wilson issued a stark warning to Germany.

KEY TERM

Pacifist: a person who opposes war or violence as a means of settling disputes.

Wilson's response caused a split in the US government. The Secretary of State, William Jennings Bryan resigned on 9 June 1915. A **pacifist** who firmly supported American isolationism, Bryan believed that the president's warning was too strongly worded, and likely to be interpreted as the prelude to a declaration of war against Germany. Bryan's argument was supported by those who remained totally opposed to entering the war. Moreover, there was some evidence that the *Lusitania* had been carrying munitions, which, as the Germans argued, made it a legitimate target. Bryan was replaced by Robert Lansing, who was convinced that the USA could not remain neutral forever and would eventually have to enter the war against Germany.

In 1916, another passenger ship, the *Sussex*, suffered the same fate as the *Lusitania*. Three Americans died, and Wilson threatened Germany with breaking diplomatic relations if the same were to happen again.

The German government's response, in which Germany promised to not attack passenger ships, diffused the situation for a time.

Germany's use of unconditional attacks against all passenger and merchant ships entering an exclusion zone that it had imposed around Britain and France clearly had an adverse effect on what the USA considered its legitimate trading interests. However, the immediate trigger for the USA's entry in the war came in 1917.

Reasons for the US entering the war: the Zimmerman Telegram

In early 1917, the British intercepted and decoded a telegram from the German foreign secretary, Arthur Zimmerman, to the German ambassador in Mexico. The telegram appeared to instruct the ambassador to discuss with the Mexicans the possibility of Mexico invading the USA from the south if it entered the war on the side of Britain and France. Germany appeared to be offering to help Mexico attempt to reclaim territories lost to the USA following the Mexican-American War of 1848.

Britain was initially concerned that informing the USA of the contents of the Zimmerman telegram, and proving its authenticity, would require revealing details of British codebreaking activities. However, with American anger growing as there was no sign of the German U-boat campaign ending, and desperate for a new and powerful ally, Britain made the US ambassador in London aware of the telegram. President Wilson was convinced that American interests were now very much under threat.

On 6 April 1917, the USA declared war on Germany. President Wilson described this as 'an act of high principle and idealism . . . a crusade to make the world safe for democracy'. Despite the USA's long-standing anti-war sentiment, American politicians voted overwhelmingly in support of the decision to declare war.

American public opinion was largely supportive of the decision to go to war. Anti-Mexican sentiment was strong in the USA, and anti-German feelings had grown following press reports of U-boat attacks on American ships. Nevertheless, there remained some opposition to the USA's involvement in a war that many considered to be an exclusively European affair. Even after its authenticity was proved beyond doubt, some elements of the press continued to insist that the telegram was an elaborate forgery. Pacifists opposed the war on philosophical grounds. The large German and Irish-American communities, both of which held anti-British views, openly resented the fact that their country was fighting on the British side.

In January 1918, President Wilson delivered a speech to the US Congress in which he outlined the USA's war aims and his vision for the future.

> The USA entered this war because violations of right had occurred which made the life of our own people impossible unless they were corrected and the world secure once and for all against their recurrence. What we demand in this war, therefore, is that the world be made fit and safe to live in; and particularly that it be made safe for every peace-loving nation which, like our own, wishes to live its own life, determine its own institutions, be assured of justice and fair-dealing by the other peoples of the world as against force and selfish aggression.
>
> **Speech by President Wilson to Congress, 8 January 1918**

Wilson then listed what became known as his 'Fourteen Points', which, he argued, should form the basis of peace negotiations once the First World War ended. These reflected Wilson's thinking about why the war had broken out and how it had been conducted. They were also part of the way in which Wilson justified the war to the American people, clearly important given his previous stance.

He wanted to see:

1 no more secret treaties between countries

2 nations able to sail and trade freely on the sea

3 protectionist barriers to trade removed and countries practising free trade

4 nations reducing their armed forces

5 rival imperial claims settled by negotiation rather than conflict, taking into account the wishes of the native people

6 Russia reintegrated into world diplomacy and land lost to Germany restored

7 land taken from Belgium during the war returned to it

8 France freed from German occupation and land taken from France by Germany in 1871 returned to France

9 Italian frontiers redrawn to match the nationality of the local people

10 peoples in the former Habsburg empire given independence

11 all foreign forces withdrawn from the Balkan nations

12 peoples in the former Turkish (Ottoman) empire given independence, and the Dardanelles made free to shipping

13 an independent, self-governing Poland with access to the sea

14 an international organisation in which member nations could discuss their disagreements and deal with them by negotiation rather than war: a League of Nations.

Once the decision had been taken to enter the war, Wilson and the USA threw themselves into the conflict with enormous effort and total commitment. There was a huge outpouring of patriotic sentiment, symbolised by various parades and characterised by a deplorable growth in anti-German violence. Large numbers of young men rushed to enlist. Concerned about opposition to the war from pacifist groups, President Wilson created the Committee on Public Information (CPI) with the aim of promoting the USA's war effort. Under the leadership of George Creel, the CPI mounted a massive pro-war publicity campaign. Wilson organised a massive anti-German propaganda campaign, while huge sums of money were raised by taxation and borrowing to fund the war effort.

Impact of the USA's entry on the course of the war

The US navy played an important role in ensuring that the German U-boats were finally defeated in the Atlantic, so that vital supplies (such as food, iron, steel and munitions) for Britain and France, as well as US soldiers, could cross the ocean. Over 2 million American soldiers crossed to France, and they played a key role in the fighting during 1918. War-weary Allied soldiers greeted them enthusiastically on the Western Front, where they arrived at a rate of 10 000 a day. Some historians have argued that the arrival of American troops made little difference to the eventual outcome of the war, suggesting that the Allies had already established a strategic advantage. However, at a time when Germany was unable to increase the size of its fighting forces, these American soldiers provided large numbers of fresh recruits for Germany's enemies. However, these new recruits unquestionably helped the Allies both to resist the German Spring Offensive and, subsequently, to mount their own counter-offensive.

For the USA, the First World War was both short and successful. No fighting had taken place on American soil, and many of its industries had expanded to meet increased wartime demand. In addition to supplying its Allies with vital resources, the USA had been able to extend its markets in areas such as South America and the Far East, formerly dominated by European nations. Prior to 1917, Britain had funded its war effort by taking out loans from private American banks. Following its declaration of war against Germany, the US government itself provided loans to Britain and the Allies. These loans would have to be repaid with interest once the war was over.

The war had proved to be highly beneficial for the American economy and American business. By 1918, the USA was unquestionably the greatest financial power in the world. Moreover, its president clearly believed that the USA had both the right and the responsibility to play a leading role in negotiations leading to the post-war peace settlement. Not only had the USA emerged as a major world power, by 1919 it had arguably become the most powerful and important.

ACTIVITY 1.22

a Why didn't the USA enter the First World War in 1914?

b What evidence suggests that American public opinion remained opposed to US entry into the war in 1916?

c Why did the USA declare war on Germany in April 1917?

d How did President Wilson justify the USA's entry into the First World War to the American people?

e In what ways did the USA benefit from the First World War?

f Which of the following statements most accurately reflects President Wilson's aims in listing his Fourteen Points? Discuss your answers in small groups.

  i Wilson wanted to prove that the USA was now a world power.

  ii Wilson wanted to avoid future wars.

  iii Wilson wanted the USA to control Europe after the war.

  iv Wilson wanted to punish Germany for causing the war.

Reflection: How did you decide which statement was the most accurate? Would you change how you completed this section of the activity following the discussion?

Exam-style questions

Source analysis questions

Read all four sources and then answer both parts of question 1.

The American debate about imperialism, 1899–1900

SOURCE A

When I realised that the Philippines had dropped into our laps, I confess I did not know what to do with them. And, one night it came to me:

1 That we could not give them back to Spain – that would be cowardly and dishonourable.

2 That we could not turn them over to France or Germany, our commercial rivals in the Far East – that would be bad business.

3 That we could not leave them to themselves – they were unfit for self-government.

4 That there was nothing left for us to do but to take them and to educate, uplift, civilise and Christianise the Filipinos.

The next morning, I sent for our map maker and told him to put the Philippines on the map of the USA; there they are, and there they will stay while I am president.

Republican President William McKinley, speaking in an interview, 1899

SOURCE B

We believe that the policy known as imperialism is hostile to liberty and tends towards militarism. We reaffirm that all men, of whatever race or colour, are entitled to life, liberty and the pursuit of happiness. We insist that the subjugation of any people is criminal aggression. We condemn the policy of the US government in the Philippines in pursuit of un-American gains. We denounce the slaughter of Filipinos as a needless horror and protest against the extension of American territory by Spanish methods. We demand the immediate ending of the war against liberty, started by Spain and continued by us.

We urge the US government to announce to the Filipinos our purpose to concede to them their independence for which they have so long fought and which is theirs by right. The USA has always protested against the doctrine of international law which permits the domination of the weak by the strong. The USA cannot act upon the belief that might makes right.

From a statement by the American Anti-Imperialist League, 1899

SOURCE C

The Philippines are ours forever. And just beyond the Philippines are China's unlimited markets. We will not abandon this opportunity or renounce our part in the mission of our race to civilise the world. God has marked us as His chosen people to lead the regeneration of the world. Our largest trade in the future must be with Asia. The Pacific is our ocean and is the ocean of the commerce of the future. China is our natural customer. Most future wars will be conflicts for commerce. The power that rules the Pacific, therefore, is the power that rules the world. And, with the Philippines, that power is and will forever be the USA. Two years ago we had no commercial, naval or military base in the Pacific. Today, we have the Philippines, located at the most commanding commercial, naval and military point in the ocean, rich in natural resources and peopled by a race which civilisation demands shall be improved.

From a speech by Republican Senator Albert Beveridge, 1900

SOURCE D

This nation has always been quick to express its sympathy with those who were fighting for civil liberty. We believe in the principles of self-government and, if we now reject this belief, the USA will lose prestige and influence among other nations. The argument that this earth belongs to those who have the power to acquire it does not justify the taking of the Philippines. The spirit which justifies the forcible annexation of the Philippines will justify the seizure of other islands and the domination of other people, and with wars of conquest we can expect a growth of our army and navy. This will impose a large financial burden on our people. Those who support imperialism argue that it will benefit our commercial interests. This is an argument based upon the theory that war can be rightly waged for financial advantage, and that it is profitable to purchase trade by force. I favour the expansion of trade by every legitimate and peaceful means, but I am not willing to gain trade by human blood. It is not necessary to own people in order to trade with them.

From a speech by Democratic Senator William Jennings Bryan, 1900

1 a Compare and contrast the views expressed in Sources A and B regarding the USA's actions in the Philippines.

b How far do Sources A to D support the view that Americans were in favour of the USA becoming an imperial nation?

Essay based questions

Answer both parts of the questions below.

2 a Explain why Britain experienced difficulty in defeating the Boers in the period from 1880 to 1902.

b To what extent did imperial rivalry pose a threat to peace in Europe during the late 19th century?

3 a Explain why the USA entered the First World War in 1917.

b 'Victory in the war against Spain (1898) was the main reason for the USA's emergence as an imperial power.' How far do you agree?

Sample answers

Here is a sample answer to Question 1(a).

In the late 19th century, public opinion in the USA was divided over the issue of imperialism, and these two sources reflect that division. Source B is clearly opposed to imperialism, which it claims threatens 'liberty', involves the 'domination of the weak by the strong' and goes against American beliefs and traditions. As a result, it condemns the actions

45

of McKinley's government in the Philippines, describing it as 'criminal aggression' and 'needless slaughter'. President McKinley clearly recognised that there was likely to be opposition to US involvement in the Philippines, which is why he uses Source A to stress that the USA did not deliberately seek control over them – they simply 'dropped into our laps' following victory in the war against Spain. McKinley then proceeds to justify US control over the Philippines by suggesting that his government had no choice – the Philippines could not be given back to Spain or to commercial rivals such as France or Germany.

The main difference between the two sources is that, whereas Source B argues that the Filipinos deserved liberty and freedom, Source A claims that they were unfit to govern themselves and therefore needed the USA to 'educate, uplift, civilise and Christianise them'. Therefore, while Source A highlights the positive aspects of imperialism (in much the same way as European nations had justified their imperialistic actions in Africa and Asia), Source B stresses its negative aspects.

> This answer demonstrates good understanding of the views expressed in the two sources, and is fully focused on the requirements of the question. The opening sentence provides contextualisation, showing how the two sources fit into the contemporary wider debate within the USA regarding the issue of imperialism and American involvement in it. Contextual knowledge is also used effectively in the final sentence, showing how McKinley's attempt to justify US imperialism in the Philippines was based on the same arguments as those used by imperialistic European nations.

There are two main areas in which the answer could be improved:

- There needs to be some attempt to explain why the two sources express such contrasting views. This could be achieved by stressing that President McKinley was a Republican, a party which supported US expansion through imperialism. Conversely, Source B comes from the American Anti-Imperialist League, which, as the name clearly implies, was totally opposed to imperialism.

- The reasons why some Americans opposed imperialism are clearly expressed in Source B. Further contextualisation could be provided by explaining why other Americans, such as McKinley and his Republican Party, supported it by looking at the economic, political and strategic advantages they hoped to achieve by taking control of the Philippines.

Here are two sample answers to the following exam question:

Explain why Japan was victorious in the Russo-Japanese War of 1904–05.

ANSWER 1

There are a number of reasons why Japan was victorious in the Russo-Japanese War.

1. *Japan had the element of surprise. The Russians were not expecting an attack on Port Arthur.*

2. *Japan gained control of the local seas and could move troops around without resistance.*

3. *Russian soldiers had to endure a lengthy trip across Asia to get to the scene of battle.*

4. *The Russian Baltic Fleet took a long time to get to the battle scene, giving the Japanese navy time to prepare for battle.*

5. *The Japanese had better ships and military equipment than the Russians.*

The writer shows a clear understanding of the question, and the ability to identify relevant material to address it. It is fully focused on the requirements of the question. However, the answer lacks depth. A number of valid points are made, but these are not fully explained or developed. For example, why did it take so long for the Russian Baltic Fleet to *get to the scene of battle*, and why were the Japanese better equipped than the Russians? It is never a good idea to include lists in your answers because this tends to prevent in-depth analysis – for example, by showing how the various causal factors are interconnected and reaching conclusions about their relative significance.

ANSWER 2

Arguably, the most important factor in Japan's victory was Russian arrogance and complacency. Russia considered itself to be a major European power and was convinced that Japan posed no real threat to its interests in the Far East. As a result, Russia refused to negotiate with Japan over their conflicting interests in Manchuria and Korea. Moreover, the Russian base at Port Arthur was totally unprepared for any Japanese attack.

Once the Japanese had taken Port Arthur, they had gained control over the local seas, enabling them to move troops around without resistance. Russian soldiers, on the other hand, had to undergo a lengthy journey across Asia. This gave the Japanese the time and opportunity to move into Manchuria. The Japanese troops were well-led, totally organised and better-equipped than their Russian counterparts. Tired after their long journey, and lacking effective leadership, the Russians finally lost Mukden after a three month siege.

The main Russian fleet was in the Baltic Sea, and had a long way to travel in order to engage with the Japanese. It encountered problems with the British fleet in the North Sea and, because of Britain's 1902 alliance with Japan, was refused access to the Suez Canal. Its slow moving ships, laden down with coal, were forced to go round the southern tip of Africa. The fleet did not reach the Straits of Tsushima until May 1905, by which time the Japanese navy was fully prepared. The slow moving, outdated Russian ships were no match for Japan's modern warships.

Japan's rapid modernisation and industrialisation in the second half of the 19th century had enabled it to develop the military capability to defeat a major European power in war. While Russia relied on outdated ships, armaments and military tactics, Japan could deploy a thoroughly modern army and navy. However, there is little doubt that Russia (in common with most of the other major European powers) had grossly under-estimated the Japanese.

This is a high-quality answer based on detailed knowledge and understanding.
All of the points made in Answer 1 are included, but are more fully developed. For example, the reasons why it took so long for the Russian Baltic fleet to reach the Straits of Tsushima are fully explained, while the fact that the Japanese had up-to-date military equipment is set in the context of Japan's rapid modernisation and industrialisation in the second half of the 19th century. The answer is fully-focused on the requirements of the question, and is analytical rather than simply descriptive. It demonstrates the inter-connection between various causal factors and makes a reasoned and supported judgement regarding what might be considered the most significant factor.

ACTIVITY 1.23

Do you think that Japan's victory in the war of 1904-05 was the result of Russia's military weaknesses? You will need to draw on much the same factual knowledge as the answer above, but used it in a rather different way. Using your own knowledge and the sample answers above:

a   identify points that agree with the statement in the question

b   identify points that disagree with the statement in the question

c   decide whether, on balance, you agree or disagree with the statement

d   prepare and deliver a presentation to explain and justify your decision.

Summary

After working through this chapter, make sure you understand the following key points:

- what imperialism is and the reasons why it became a major element in the policies of certain late-19th century European nations

- the reasons for, and impact of, European imperialism, particularly in Africa and China

- the potential for conflict which late-19th century imperialism created, and how conflict was usually avoided

- how two non-European nations, Japan and the USA, became world powers, and the impact which this had on international relations.

Further reading

Aldred, J. (2004). *British Imperial and Foreign Policy 1846–1980.* **Heinemann.** Chapter 4 analyses the reasons why Britain took part in the scramble for Africa. Chapter 5 explains why there was so much domestic support for British imperialism in the late 19th century.

Chamberlain, M. (2010). *Scramble for Africa.* **Routledge.** Parts 1, 2 and 3 provide background knowledge and analysis of the reasons for, and the impact of, the 'scramble for Africa'. Part 4 contains a great deal of original source material.

Charles Rivers Editors, (2017). *The Scramble for Africa: The History and Legacy of the Colonisation of Africa by European Nations during the New Imperialism Era.* **CreateSpace.** A short and interesting little book, which provides a great deal of useful information about the people and countries involved in the scramble for Africa.

De Pennington, J. (2005) *Modern America: 1865 to the Present.* **Hodder.** Chapter 4 provides a useful analysis of the ways in which the USA's foreign policy changed during the late 19th and early 20th centuries.

Farmer, A. and Stiles, A. (2015) *The Unification of Germany and the Challenge of Nationalism 1789–1919.* **Hodder.** Chapters 5 and 6 contrast the policies pursued by Bismarck with those of Kaiser Wilhelm II after 1890. Particularly useful are the sections on foreign policy, which reflect on Germany's relations with other countries.

Goodlad, G. (1999). *British Foreign and Imperial Policy 1865–1919.* **Routledge.** Chapter 3 deals with Britain's involvement in New Imperialism, while Chapter 4 outlines the problems Britain faced during the Boer Wars. Chapter 5 analyses how, why and with what implications, Britain moved away from its policy of 'splendid isolation'.

Holland, A. and Holland, A. (2010). *Different Interpretations of British Imperialism 1850–1950.* **Heinemann.** This is a useful book for investigating how different historians have interpreted historical evidence in different ways, as outlined in Chapter 1. Chapter 2 deals with interpretations of Britain's involvement in New Imperialism.

Huffman, J. (2010). *Japan in World History.* **Oxford University Press.** Chapter 5 provides a detailed analysis of how Japan was modernised during the late 19th century and how it was transformed into a major world power. The first part of Chapter 6 deals with Japan's emergence as an imperial power.

Kearey, K. and Waller, S. (2015). *International Relations and Global Conflict c1890–1941.* **Oxford University Press.** Chapter 3 shows how imperial rivalry increased international tension in the late 19th century. Chapter 4 is useful background reading on relations between European countries by 1900, while Section 2 outlines the build-up to the First World War.

Lowe, J. and Pearce, R. (2001). *Rivalry and Accord: International Relations 1870–1914.* **Hodder.** Chapter 3 deals with imperial rivalry in the period from 1870 to 1914. Chapter 4 provides an analysis of the tensions in Europe resulting from Kaiser Wilhelm II's adoption of a more aggressive foreign policy.

Lynch, M. (2016). *China 1839–1997.* **Hodder.** Chapters 1 and 2 provide good background knowledge of the problems facing China in the 19th century and the ways in which it was exploited by imperial nations.

Walker, B. (2015). *Concise History of Japan.* **Cambridge University Press.** Chapters 9, 10 and 11 analyse the ways in which Japan modernised during the late 19th century, leading it to become a major world power with an imperial foreign policy.

Waugh, S. and Clements, P. (2015). *The Making of a Superpower: USA 1865–1975.* **Hodder.** Chapter 3 provides useful information on the USA's adoption of an imperial foreign policy. Chapter 4 deals with the background to the USA's eventual entry into the First World War.

Webster, A., Carr, R. and Waller, S. (2016). *The British Empire c1857–1967.* **Oxford University Press.** Sections 1 and 2 provide detailed analysis of British imperialism in the period from 1857 to 1914, and how this affected Britain's relations with other countries. These sections are also useful for investigating how public opinion in Britain reacted to imperialism.

Chapter 2
The League of Nations and international relations in the 1920s

Learning Objectives:

In this chapter, you will:

- understand the difficulties associated with reaching agreement on, and implementing, the terms of the peace settlement at the end of the First World War
- learn why and how attempts were made to ease international tensions during the 1920s
- find out about the successes and failures of attempts to improve international relations during the 1920s
- analyse the creation, early development and effectiveness of the League of Nations during the 1920s.

Timeline

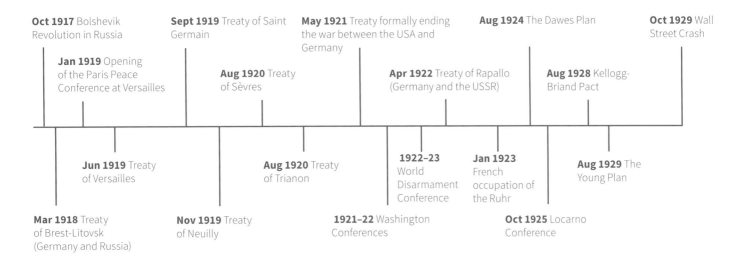

Oct 1917 Bolshevik Revolution in Russia

Jan 1919 Opening of the Paris Peace Conference at Versailles

Mar 1918 Treaty of Brest-Litovsk (Germany and Russia)

Jun 1919 Treaty of Versailles

Sept 1919 Treaty of Saint Germain

Aug 1920 Treaty of Sèvres

Aug 1920 Treaty of Trianon

Nov 1919 Treaty of Neuilly

May 1921 Treaty formally ending the war between the USA and Germany

Apr 1922 Treaty of Rapallo (Germany and the USSR)

1922–23 World Disarmament Conference

Jan 1923 French occupation of the Ruhr

1921–22 Washington Conferences

Aug 1924 The Dawes Plan

Aug 1928 Kellogg-Briand Pact

Aug 1929 The Young Plan

Oct 1925 Locarno Conference

Oct 1929 Wall Street Crash

Before You Start

Figure 2.1: 'European Baby Show', cartoon from *The Detroit News* 1919

Look carefully at Figure 2.1. Using the information in Chapter 1.4, discuss the following questions in pairs or small groups.

1 Who is the main character depicted in the cartoon?

2 What is the context of the cartoon?

3 Why is the main character labelled as 'judge'?

4 Why are European nations depicted as babies?

5 Did the cartoonist believe that arranging a peace settlement at the end of the First World War would be easy? Explain your answer.

Introduction

The political effects of the First World War were devastating. The empires that had long dominated the map of Central and Eastern Europe disintegrated, leaving chaos and confusion. The **tsarist regime** in Russia was overthrown by revolution in 1917 and, as defeat became inevitable during 1918, the German emperor was forced to abdicate.

Under these circumstances, those responsible for drawing up the treaties that would end the First World War faced a very difficult task. Although the American president, Woodrow Wilson, was determined to bring about a fair and lasting peace, he met resistance from European politicians who were equally determined to gain revenge and ensure future security for their own countries. As a result, the peace settlement that emerged between 1919 and 1920 consisted of harsh terms imposed by the victorious nations on those that had been defeated. Old tensions and rivalries remained, while many potential new ones were created.

A lasting peace seemed even more unlikely when, despite encouragement by Wilson, the **US Senate** refused to **ratify** the settlement agreed at the Paris Peace Conference. Instead, the USA reverted to its traditional policy of isolationism, keeping out of foreign affairs as much as possible. Equally significant for future international stability was the fact that Russia, whose new revolutionary government seemed determined to spread **communism** as far as possible, was not invited to the peace talks and took no part in the negotiations for the treaties that would define the post-war world.

> ## KEY TERMS
>
> **Tsarist regime:** the political system which existed in Russia at the beginning of the 20th century. All power lay in the hands of the tsar, the official title of the Russian emperor. Although Tsar Nicholas II's power had been curtailed following a revolution in 1905, he retained almost total control over Russia until his abdication following a revolution in March 1917.
>
> **The US Senate:** the more powerful of the two 'houses' of the US Congress – the other being the House of Representatives. The USA can only enter into treaties with other countries with the approval of the Senate.

> ## KEY TERMS
>
> **Ratify:** to give formal acceptance to something. For example, the diplomats negotiating at a conference can agree the terms of a treaty, but they do not come into effect until they have been formally accepted (ratified) by their government.
>
> **Communism:** a system of government based on the idea of a classless society in which there is common ownership of the means of production, such as farms and factories. It is very different from capitalism, under which individuals can become wealthy through the ownership of land, factories etc.

All countries were keen to avoid the horrors of another war, and many attempts were made to improve international relations during the 1920s, including the establishment of the League of Nations. For a time, these seemed to be successful and were greeted with both enthusiasm and relief. However, tensions continued to simmer beneath the surface.

2.1 Why was there dissatisfaction with the peace settlements of 1919–20?

Key terms and implications of the peace treaties (Versailles, Trianon, Neuilly, Saint Germain, Sèvres

As leader of the Russian Bolshevik Party, Lenin played a leading role in the October Revolution of 1917. He led the Party to power, establishing a communist government in Russia and was head of the Russian state (later the USSR) from 1917 until his death in 1924.

VLADIMIR ILYICH ULYANOV (LENIN) (1870–1924)

In January 1918, when US President Woodrow Wilson outlined his vision for future world peace in his Fourteen Points speech (see Chapter 1.4), the First World War was still raging and its outcome remained far from clear. The new Russian leader, **Lenin**, desperately trying to establish his Bolshevik government, believed that it was essential for Russia to end its involvement in the First World War, a war that was having a devastating effect on the Russian economy and its lower classes. Wilson had hoped his speech would encourage Russia to remain in the war and, at the same time, urge Germany to seek a peace settlement. Both hopes were dashed in March 1918 when Lenin's new Bolshevik government signed the Treaty of Brest-Litovsk with Germany. The terms of the treaty were extremely harsh on Russia, and certainly not in line with Wilson's Fourteen Points. Russia was to lose Poland, Estonia, Latvia, Lithuania, Ukraine, Georgia and Finland – areas containing much of Russia's best farmland, raw materials and heavy industry. In the event, Russia lost 25% of its population, 25% of its industry and 90% of its coal mines.

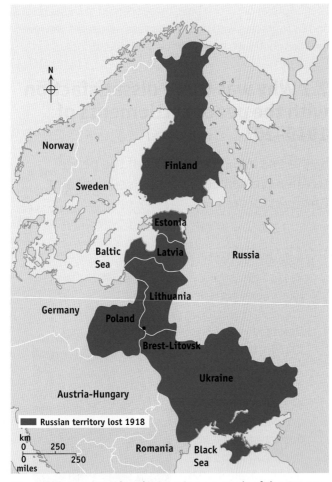

Figure 2.2: Territory lost by Russia as a result of the Treaty of Brest-Litovsk with Germany in 1918

With Russia now out of the war, Germany no longer had to fight on two fronts. In addition, Germany had gained a vast amount of new land and resources as a result of the Treaty of Brest-Litovsk. This allowed Germany to launch a major offensive on the Western Front, and for a time it seemed as though the Central Powers might secure victory after all.

However, the Allies launched a major counter-offensive that ran through the summer and autumn of 1918. German supply lines had been over-extended during their earlier offensive, and German troops were starved of food and vital equipment. Gradually, they were driven back. Realising that the situation was becoming hopeless, German military commanders decided to launch one last major naval battle against the British in the English Channel. They hoped this would prevent reinforcements and supplies reaching Allied troops in Europe. Convinced that this was a suicide mission for an already hopeless cause, the German sailors mutinied, and this sparked a wider revolution within Germany. Wilhelm II was forced into exile and formally abdicated on 28 November 1918. Germany became a republic (referred to by historians as the Weimar Republic), and the new government sought peace terms based on Wilson's Fourteen Points.

In January 1919, representatives of nearly 30 victorious nations met at Versailles, near Paris. The aim of this Paris Peace Conference was to develop a settlement that would finally end the First World War and, in the words of the French President Raymond Poincaré, 'prevent a recurrence of it'. This was no easy task.

ACTIVITY 2.1

Discuss and make notes on the following questions in pairs:

a Explain two reasons why the Treaty of Brest-Litovsk helped Germany's war effort.

b German troops had caused extensive damage in France during the war. Even as they retreated in 1918, they looted and destroyed much of Northern France. How might this affect French public opinion about how Germany should be dealt with at the Paris Peace Conference?

c Do you think that Paris was an appropriate place to hold the peace conference? Explain your answer.

d Only the victorious nations were invited to attend the Paris Peace Conference. What problems do you think this might cause?

First, events were taking place across Europe over which the peacemakers had no control. Revolutions occurred throughout the former Austro-Hungarian, Russian and Turkish empires. In Russia, the Bolsheviks were engaged in a civil war against other revolutionary parties and those who were keen to restore the monarchy. The Western powers, such as Britain and France, fearful of revolution in their own countries, provided some support to these anti-Bolshevik groups.

Under these circumstances, it was essential for decisions to be reached quickly. Inevitably, therefore, decision making came to rest with the Council of Four, consisting of President Woodrow Wilson (USA), Prime Minister David Lloyd George (Britain), Prime Minister **Georges Clemenceau** (France) and Prime Minister Vittorio Orlando (Italy). In reality, Italy had little influence. Orlando's inability to speak English greatly restricted his participation in negotiations. Moreover, once it became clear that Italy would not receive all of its territorial claims, Orlando temporarily withdrew the Italian delegation from the conference in anger. As a result, the main decisions were taken by the 'Big Three'.

Perhaps the most significant factor shaping the decision-making process was the disagreements between Britain, France and the USA over how the defeated Germany should be treated.

Figure 2.3: The Council of Four at the Paris Peace Conference; from left to right – Lloyd George (Britain), Orlando (Italy), Clemenceau (France) and Wilson (USA). This photograph was taken by Edward N. Jackson, Wilson's official photographer during the Paris Peace Conference. Does this information about the photographer change your interpretation of the photograph?

Clemenceau was a French politician who served as prime minister of France 1906–09 and 1917–20. In line with French public and political opinion, he insisted on a harsh settlement being imposed on Germany at the Paris Peace Conference.

GEORGES CLEMENCEAU (1841–1929)

France, Clemenceau

Clemenceau wanted to destroy Germany economically and militarily. He wanted to avenge France's humiliating defeat in the Franco-Prussian War (1870–71), and gain revenge for the devastation that France had suffered as a result of German aggression in the First World War. Moreover, he wanted to ensure that Germany could never again threaten French borders. In particular, Clemenceau wanted to secure a guarantee of British and American support in the event of any future German attack against France. In his determination to inflict a harsh settlement on the Germans, Clemenceau lived up to his nickname – 'The Tiger'.

UK, Lloyd George

Lloyd George wanted a less severe settlement. It was in British interests that Germany, a potentially important consumer of British exports, be allowed to recover quickly. However, British public opinion was strongly anti-German, and Lloyd George had just won an election on the promise that he would 'make Germany pay'. Britain therefore sought a settlement that would punish Germany while, at the same time, making its future economic recovery possible. The world's leading exporter in 1913, Britain had been overtaken by both the USA and Japan by 1919. Moreover, it has been estimated that the First World War cost Britain over £3.25 billion. Britain desperately needed to enhance its overseas trade, and Germany provided a potentially lucrative market for British exports.

53

USA, Wilson

Wilson, whose country had suffered far less severely than its European allies during the war, wanted a lenient peace based on the Fourteen Points and his slogan 'peace without victory'. He believed that imposing a harsh treaty on Germany would cause resentment and make future conflict more likely. Wilson thought that the greed and selfishness of the rival European nations had been a major contributing factor to the outbreak of the First World War, and saw himself as a mediator between these nations. In truth, however, Wilson had very little understanding of the complex problems facing Europe in 1919. Moreover, he could no longer claim to fully represent the government of the USA, as the Democrats had lost control of the Senate in the midterm elections. The war had become increasingly unpopular in the USA. The Republican Party, the political opponents of Wilson's Democratic Party, was strongly against American involvement in the Paris peace talks, believing that these were essentially a European matter. By the time Wilson arrived in Paris, the Republican Party held a majority in the Senate. As the US politician Theodore Roosevelt pointed out: 'Our allies and our enemies and Mr Wilson himself should all understand that Mr Wilson has no authority to speak for the American people at this time.'

Under these circumstances, it is perhaps unsurprising that what emerged from the Paris peace talks bore only limited resemblance to Wilson's vision of a fair and just settlement. Five separate treaties were agreed, each dealing with one of the First World War's defeated nations (none of which was invited to the Paris peace talks): the Treaty of Versailles with Germany, the Treaty of Saint-Germain with Austria, the Treaty of Neuilly with Bulgaria, the Treaty of Sèvres with Turkey and the Treaty of Trianon with Hungary.

ACTIVITY 2.2

Look carefully at the answer below to the following question:

Why, in 1919, did Wilson, Clemenceau and Lloyd George disagree about how best to treat the defeated Germany?

US President Wilson wanted a fair and just settlement which was not too harsh on Germany. On the other hand, French Prime Minister Clemenceau, The Tiger, showed determination to inflict a harsh settlement on Germany.

ACTIVITY 2.2 (CONTINUED)

Like Clemenceau, Lloyd George, Britain's Prime Minister, wanted to punish Germany for causing the war, but agreed with Wilson that the punishment should not be too severe.

This answer is based on sound knowledge, but it does not actually address the question. It describes how the three men's opinions differed rather than explaining why.

How would you adapt this answer in order to make it more relevant to the demands of the question?

KEY CONCEPT

Historians seek to identify and analyse the ways in which people, either individually or in groups, respond to the circumstances confronting them.

Similarity and difference

Look carefully at this question:

Compare and contrast the views of Britain and France regarding how to deal with Germany at the Paris Peace Conference.

'Compare and contrast' questions require the identification and explanation of similarities and differences.

- Make a list of the similarities in the views of Britain and France.
- Make a list of the differences in the views of Britain and France.

In pairs, discuss your lists, making amendments where necessary.

Write an answer to the question. (Basic answers would simply describe the similarities and differences. More effective answers would contain analysis – explaining why Britain and France held their respective views.)

In pairs, discuss your answers, making any appropriate amendments.

The Treaty of Versailles

The Germans fully expected a reasonable settlement based on Wilson's Fourteen Points, a peace proposal that had been widely publicised since January 1918 and that was popular with the anti-war movement in Germany. German representatives were not allowed to take part in the peace negotiations, and when they were presented with the Treaty of Versailles, they were horrified at the terms. Despite its objections, Germany had no alternative but to accept the treaty – failure to do so would have meant the continuation of war and an attack on Germany itself. In committing to a peace process, they had already abolished the monarchy and pulled back the army – they were in no position to renew fighting. Germany signed the Treaty of Versailles on 28 June 1919, in doing so accepting the loss of some 70,000 square kilometres (27,000 square miles) of land, containing some 7 million people:

- Alsace and Lorraine returned to France
- Eupen and Malmédy went to Belgium
- North Schleswig returned to Denmark
- the Saar Valley, a heavily industrialised region, was to be administered by the League of Nations for 15 years, during which France could use its coal mines: at the end of this time, a **plebiscite** would determine whether it should belong to France or Germany
- the Rhineland, part of Germany along its border with France, was to be demilitarised, meaning that no troops could be stationed there; this gave France the security it so badly wanted, but meant that Germany would be unable to defend this part of its border

- much of West Prussia went to Poland, allowing it access to the sea through the 'Polish Corridor', dividing Germany from its province of East Prussia
- the port of Memel (modern Klaipėda) went to Lithuania
- Estonia, Latvia and Lithuania, which Germany had gained through the Treaty of Brest-Litovsk, were established as independent states
- Germany lost her African colonies, which became **mandates** under League of Nations supervision.

KEY TERMS

Plebiscite: a referendum (vote) giving local people the opportunity to express their opinion for or against a proposal relating to a constitutional issue.

Mandates: overseas territories taken from the defeated countries at the end of the First World War. Responsibility for these territories was passed to other countries, which would administer them on behalf of the League of Nations.

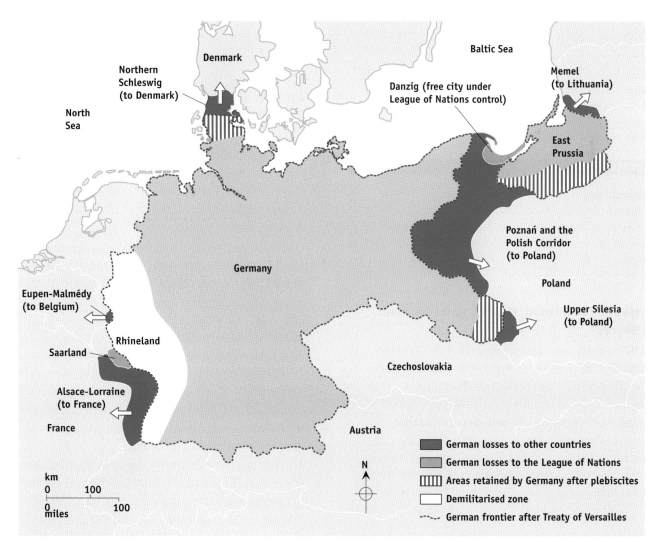

Figure 2.4: The European territory lost by Germany as a result of the Treaty of Versailles

For Germany, these territorial losses were both economically devastating and politically humiliating. The country was geographically split in two by the 'Polish Corridor', had lost control of the major industrial region in the Saar and been forced to return the economically lucrative Alsace and Lorraine to France. Many German-speaking people moved from areas that now came under the control of other countries. Those who remained were often persecuted for Germany's role in the war.

In addition to these land losses, the treaty imposed several other humiliating terms on Germany. German armaments were limited to a maximum of 100 000 troops, with no tanks, military aircraft or submarines, and a maximum of six battleships. This was intended to weaken Germany's armed forces so much that it could not pose a threat to other European countries in the future. For the same reason, *Anschluss* (union) between Germany and Austria was forbidden in an effort to prevent the two German-speaking countries uniting.

A further devastating term of the Treaty of Versailles was the 'War Guilt Clause'. This blamed Germany and its allies for the outbreak of the First World War, and allowed the victorious nations to impose **reparations** for the damage the war had caused. Imposing reparations on Germany was also intended to economically weaken the country so that it could not threaten other countries in the future.

KEY TERM

Reparations: money that one country has to pay another as compensation for war damage. The 'War Guilt Clause' was included in the Treaty of Versailles in order to provide legal justification for making Germany pay reparations to the victorious countries.

The treaties of Trianon, Neuilly, Saint Germain and Sèvres

Having finalised the Treaty of Versailles with Germany, the Paris Peace Conference now turned its attention to the other defeated nations (Austria-Hungary, Turkey and Bulgaria). In many ways, Wilson's notion of giving independence and **self-determination** to the peoples who formerly belonged to the Habsburg, Turkish and Russian empires was becoming a reality. The disintegration of those empires had already resulted in the emergence of new states. The Paris peacemakers had the difficult task of trying to formalise

the resulting chaos. Their decisions formally confirmed the existence of new national states – Yugoslavia, Poland, Czechoslovakia, Austria and Hungary – which became known as the '**successor states**'.

KEY TERMS

Self-determination: the principle that people of common nationality should have the right to form their own nations and govern themselves. Wilson's definition of a 'nationality' (based on common language) was both too simplistic and inappropriate for the situation in Eastern Europe at the end of the First World War.

Successor states: a newly formed state whose territory and population were previously under the sovereignty of another state.

Each of the defeated nations was dealt with separately through a series of four treaties.

- The Treaty of Saint-Germain was signed with Austria in September 1919. By the terms of this treaty, Austria lost:
  o Bohemia and Moravia to Czechoslovakia.
  o Dalmatia, Bosnia and Herzegovina to Yugoslavia
  o Bukovina to Romania
  o Galicia to Poland
  o Trentino, Istria, Trieste and parts of the South Tyrol to Italy.
- The Treaty of Neuilly was agreed with Bulgaria in November 1919. Bulgaria lost territory to Greece, Yugoslavia and Romania, had to reduce its army to no more than 20 000 and was instructed to pay reparations of over $400 million.
- Under the terms of the Treaty of Sèvres, signed in August 1920, Turkey lost territory to Greece and Italy. Other parts of the former Turkish Empire were mandated to France (Syria) and Britain (Palestine, Iran and Transjordan). The treaty also stated that the Dardanelles were to be permanently open to all shipping. Under the leadership of Mustafa Kemal, the Turkish National Movement was established with the aim of overturning the terms of the Treaty of Sèvres and expelling foreign soldiers from the country. Both had been achieved by October 1923 when the newly formed Republic of Turkey was proclaimed, with Kemal as its first president.
- The Treaty of Trianon with Hungary (August 1920) stated that Slovakia and Ruthenia were to become part of Czechoslovakia. Hungary also lost Transylvania to Romania, and Croatia and Slovenia to Yugoslavia.

These treaties reflected the collapse of the former Austro-Hungarian and Turkish Empires, but were also part of Wilson's idea of self-determination. Wilson's view of nationality was, however, based entirely on language and ignored other ethnic and religious factors. As a result, for example, 1.6 million people who considered themselves to be Hungarian would now be living under a foreign government in Romania. Moreover, concerns were raised that many of the newly created boundaries would make it impossible for some countries, such as Austria and Hungary, to be economically viable.

ACTIVITY 2.3

President Wilson had called for a 'peace without victory'. In pairs, discuss the reasons why the First World War's defeated nations would have been disappointed and angry about the outcomes of the Paris Peace Conference. What do you think were the possible implications of this?

Make sure that your notes contain both (a) the reasons for and (b) the implications of the defeated nations' anger over the Paris peace settlement.

Reflection: Discuss your list of implications with a partner.

Figure 2.5: A 1920 map Europe, showing the new national borders agreed in the peace settlements. The Austro-Hungarian Empire was broken up and the Ottoman Empire changed its name to Turkey. Nine new countries were created: Austria, Czechoslovakia, Estonia, Finland, Hungary, KSCS, Latvia, Lithuania and Poland.

Reparations

This was the wording of Article 231 of the Treaty of Versailles, and it is not difficult to see why it has become known as the 'War Guilt Clause'.

> The Allied and Associated Governments affirm and Germany accepts the responsibility of Germany and her allies for causing all the loss and damage to which the Allied and Associated Governments and their nationals have been subjected as a consequence of the war imposed upon them by the aggression of Germany and her allies.

In signing the Treaty of Versailles, Germany was effectively accepting its own responsibility, and that of its allies, for causing the First World War.

Given the tensions that had gradually built up in Europe during the late 19th and early 20th centuries, and the complicated series of events that led to the outbreak of war in 1914, it may seem unreasonable to expect Germany and its allies to accept full responsibility for it. The Germans themselves certainly thought so. However, there was a reason for the inclusion of the War Guilt Clause in the Treaty of Versailles. It provided some form of legal justification for expecting Germany and its allies to pay reparations.

Germany's enemies had suffered greatly during the First World War, both economically and in human terms. France, in particular, demanded compensation. Most of the war's major battles had taken place on French soil – whole towns and villages were destroyed, and France's main industrial region in Nord-pas de Calais had been devastated. Reparations would facilitate reconstruction, both in France and in other countries, such as Belgium, which had been so badly affected by the war.

The issue of reparations caused further disharmony between the 'Big Three' at Versailles. Wilson was entirely opposed to inflicting reparations on the defeated nations, arguing that this would cause resentment and instil a desire for revenge in Germany. Lloyd George, while agreeing with the principle of reparations, wanted to keep them as low as possible so that the German economy could recover quickly and re-establish its trading links with Britain. Clemenceau, whose country had suffered most during the war, demanded that high reparations be imposed on Germany. In addition to providing compensation for war damage, Clemenceau viewed reparations as a way of keeping Germany weak so that it could never threaten France again.

After lengthy debates, it was finally agreed at the Paris Peace Conference that reparations would indeed be imposed on Germany and the other defeated nations. The task of setting the actual amount that each country would have to pay was designated to a Reparations Commission that would meet in 1921. It was already clear, however, that most of the reparations requirements would be imposed on Germany and Bulgaria. The Treaties of Saint-Germain, Trianon and Sèvres acknowledged that Austria, Hungary and Turkey had very limited resources and would find it difficult to pay reparations.

When the Reparations Commission met in 1921 it considered the resources available to each of the defeated nations and took the views of their representatives into account before determining how much each country would have to pay. Considering the major economic problems facing Austria and Hungary, no reparations were imposed on them. Limited reparations were imposed on Turkey, but these were eliminated under the terms of the Treaty of Lausanne in 1923. A figure of £100 million was set for Bulgarian reparations, only a fraction of which had been paid by 1932 when the requirement was abandoned.

JOHN MAYNARD KEYNES (1883–1946)

Keynes was the leading economist of the early 20th century, and was a member of the British delegation at the Paris Peace Conference. In his book, *The Economic Consequences of the Peace* (1919), he argued that reparations were vindictive and would lead to problems because of Germany's inability to keep up with the payments.

As a result, the heaviest burden in terms of reparation payments fell on Germany, which was instructed to pay a total of £6.6 billion. The German representatives at meetings of the Reparations Commission were horrified. They argued that, with the German economy devastated during the First World War, the country was in no position to meet such demands. They were not alone in their condemnation of such a high reparations demand.

The British economist **John Maynard Keynes**, who had attended the Paris Peace Conference, argued that reparations at such a high level would simply add to the economic problems facing post-war Europe. In particular, he argued that reparations would lead to high **inflation**.

In his book *The Economic Consequences of the Peace*, published in 1919, Keynes's was heavily critical of the Paris peace settlement:

> The settlement includes no provisions for the economic rehabilitation of Europe, nothing to make the defeated Central Powers into good neighbours and nothing to stabilise the new states of Europe. It is an extraordinary fact that the fundamental economic problems of a Europe, starving and disintegrating before their eyes, was the one question which it was impossible to arouse the interest of Clemenceau, Lloyd George and Wilson. Reparation was their main excursion into the economic field, and they settled it without considering the economic future of the states whose destiny they were handling. Clemenceau was preoccupied with crushing the economic life of his enemy.
>
> **J. M. Keynes, *The Economic Consequences of the Peace* (1919), pp. 211–1**

In terms of reparations, Clemenceau's demands had held sway. Keynes's prediction that German reparations would cause economic problems in Europe was to prove correct. So too were President Wilson's fears that imposing reparations on Germany would lead to resentment and the desire for revenge.

KEY TERM

Inflation: a process that leads to an increase in the price of goods and services. It drives down the value of income and savings, discouraging investment and causing demands for increased wages. This, in turn, leads to higher prices, an inflationary spiral that can then result in increased unemployment.

ACTIVITY 2.4

Prepare notes on the following:

a Why was the War Guilt Clause included in the Treaty of Versailles?

b Complete the table below, outlining the views of Wilson, Lloyd George and Clemenceau regarding reparations: include why they disagreed about the issue.

WILSON	LLOYD GEORGE	CLEMENCEAU

c On the issue of reparations, did Keynes agree with Wilson, Lloyd George or Clemenceau? Explain your answer.

Reactions of victors and defeated powers

Many historians are critical of the Paris peace settlement of 1919–20, which was to have major short- and long-term effects on international stability. They argue that the five treaties were based on a series of compromises that satisfied none of the countries involved. It was representatives of the First World War's victorious nations which met in Paris to draw up the peace terms. The defeated nations, not allowed to attend the peace conference, simply had to accept the terms imposed upon them. While this inevitably led to resentment, the defeated nations were not alone in expressing their frustration and anger at the peace settlement. France, Russia, Italy and the USA, countries that had played a significant role in the Allied Powers' eventual victory in the First World War, were also disappointed.

France had wanted and expected a much harsher settlement imposed on Germany. Indeed, Clemenceau had argued for the creation of an independent Rhineland state, and proposed that Germany be broken up to permanently weaken it. Fear that the settlement left Germany strong enough, both economically and politically, to once again threaten the security of France was to dominate French foreign policy throughout the 1920s.

Russia was not invited to send representatives to the peace conference and was not consulted at all about the terms of the settlement. France and Britain argued that, having withdrawn from the First World War by signing the Treaty of Brest-Litovsk, Russia had no right to attend the conference. Moreover, fearful of revolution spreading, the Western powers refused to have any diplomatic relations

59

with Russia's Bolshevik government. This left Russia feeling increasingly isolated, much of its former territory divided up amongst newly created nations, including the Baltic states of Lithuania and Estonia.

Despite its membership of the Triple Alliance alongside Germany and Austria-Hungary, Italy did not enter the First World War when it began in 1914. However, in April 1915, Italy signed the Treaty of London with Britain in return for promises of major territorial gains along the Adriatic coast once victory was achieved. Italy thus joined the war on the side of the Triple Entente – Britain, France and Russia. Italy's involvement in the war, while not particularly significant militarily, was to prove expensive, both in human and financial terms. Over 600 000 Italian soldiers

were killed and 950 000 seriously wounded. The Italian government spent more in the three years of war than it had in the previous 50. Once the war was won, the Italian people expected the promises made in the Treaty of London to be honoured. To the majority of Italians, the Paris peace settlement was a bitter disappointment. The major decisions were taken by the 'Big Three', Wilson, Clemenceau and Lloyd George. The Italian delegation, led by Prime Minister Vittorio Orlando, had been largely ignored and humiliated. Although Italy had gained Trentino, South Tyrol, Istria and Trieste, its claims to parts of Dalmatia, Albania, Fiume, Adalia (Antalya on the south Turkish coast) and some of the Aegean islands had been denied. To the Italians, it appeared that other countries, particularly Yugoslavia, had gained at Italy's expense.

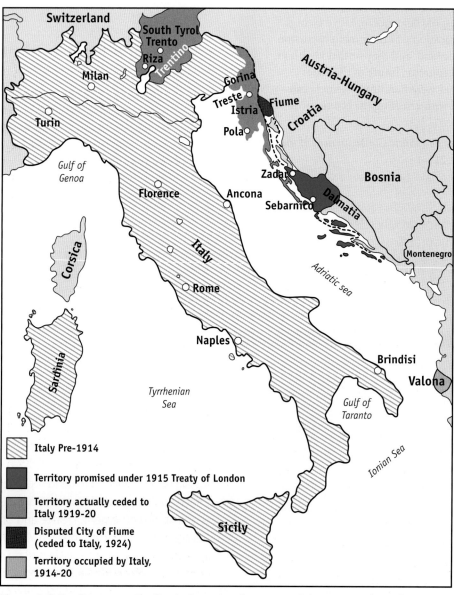

Figure 2.6: Territory promised to Italy under the terms of the Treaty of London 1915

US President Woodrow Wilson had played a leading role in determining the terms of the Paris peace settlement, and made strenuous efforts to convince the American people to support them. However, public opinion in the USA was largely opposed to the settlement. Many Americans believed that its terms were too harsh on Germany and that this would cause resentment and encourage the desire for revenge. Most argued that to support the settlement and, in particular, to join the League of Nations, would inevitably involve the USA in future wars. The US Senate, dominated by Wilson's Republican political opponents, refused to ratify the peace settlement, and the USA subsequently signed its own separate treaty with Germany.

For the First World War's defeated nations, the implications of the peace settlement were far worse. To the Bulgarians, their country much reduced in size and its economy severely damaged, the settlement was seen as a national catastrophe. Turkey no longer controlled its once great Ottoman Empire and remained under the authority of an Allied army of occupation.

Austrians and Hungarians alike were angered by the way in which the Paris peace settlement had divided up the territories of the former Habsburg Empire between newly formed nation states. They argued that the First World War's victorious nations had created new boundaries without regard to cultural, linguistic and ethnic factors. Austrian and Hungarian requests that plebiscites should be held to determine the wishes of local people had been ignored.

The terms of the Treaty of Versailles caused great resentment in Germany, resentment that was to have major implications for the future. German objections focused on two main issues. First, German representatives were not allowed to attend the peace talks – they simply had to accept whatever terms were imposed upon them. Second, the terms were not based entirely on Wilson's Fourteen Points as Germany had hoped.

There is some justification for German objections to the Treaty of Versailles:

- at a time of intense political instability, 100 000 troops might not be sufficient even to maintain law and order within Germany itself, let alone defend the country against external attack; moreover, while Germany was forced to disarm, it was clear that none of the other major European powers had any intention of doing so – this posed a threat to German security
- although they were set up as mandates under the supervision of the League of Nations, Germany's former colonies in Africa were effectively taken over by Britain, France and South Africa
- millions of people who were German in terms of their language and culture would now be living under foreign rule in countries such as Poland and Czechoslovakia
- although part of Germany, East Prussia was separated from the rest of the country by the Polish Corridor
- the War Guilt Clause caused particular resentment in Germany given the complicated series of events that had led to the outbreak of war in 1914
- the amount established for reparations was extremely high and, as the Germans would argue, virtually impossible for them to repay.

These harsh terms led to widespread anger in Germany. One German newspaper declared:

> In the place where, in the glorious year of 1871, the German Empire in all its glory had its origins, today German honour is being carried to its grave. Do not forget it! The German people will, with unceasing labour, press forward to reconquer the place among the nations to which it is entitled. Then will come vengeance for the shame of 1919.
>
> *Deutsche Zeitung*, 28 June 1919

These views were clearly shared by a leading German politician, who informed the Reichstag (German parliament) in 1919:

> In these conditions, there is no trace of a peace of understanding and justice. It is purely a peace of violence which, for our Fatherland, is thinly veiled slavery, and out of which will result not peace for the whole of Europe, but merely further bloodshed and tears.
>
> **Prime Minister of the Prussian Diet Paul Hirsch, quoted in *The Times*, 12 May 1919**

However, although the terms were harsh, they were not as severe as Clemenceau had hoped. The French were concerned that the treaty left Germany strong enough to rebuild for the future and, once again, pose a threat to their security. Germany's territorial losses in Europe were restricted to those areas it had gained as a result of previous wars. Indeed, Germany remained potentially the strongest economic power in Europe. Many have argued that, having ignored Wilson's Fourteen Points when inflicting the Treaty of Brest-Litovsk on Russia, Germany had little right to expect those points to form the basis of their own peace settlement.

ACTIVITY 2.5

How justified were German objections to the Treaty of Versailles? Complete the table below and remember these key points:

- remain fully focused on the precise needs of the question throughout – be careful to avoid unfocused narrative (i.e., providing factual information that does not make a relevant point)
- ensure that your answer is balanced – that you show understanding of both sides of the argument
- make a clear and supported judgement – on balance, were German objections justified or not?

JUSTIFIED	UNJUSTIFIED

KEY TERM

Dictator: an absolute ruler who controls a country without being accountable to an electorate or an elected national assembly, and with no limits to their power set by a constitution.

Bordering Italy, Austria, Hungary, Romania, Bulgaria, Greece and Albania, Yugoslavia became involved in territorial disputes. In an effort to protect itself, Yugoslavia made a series of friendly agreements with other countries. In the early 1920s, for example, it formed the 'Little Entente' with Czechoslovakia, Romania and France. In 1924, it joined an alliance with Greece, Romania and Turkey. Despite these agreements, Yugoslavia remained a weak and vulnerable country. With backward agricultural methods and limited industry, Yugoslavia became heavily dependent on Western loans.

Problems in 'successor states' created by the post-war settlements

Maintaining a commitment to self-determination was not as straightforward as Wilson had envisaged. His belief that nationality could be determined by language was too simplistic for the complicated situation in Eastern Europe, where there were so many ethnic groupings, all with conflicting ambitions. In redrawing the map of Eastern Europe, the peacemakers had left around 30 million people living in minority groups under foreign rule, making border disputes inevitable. The 'successor states' that emerged as a result of the break-up of the great European empires all suffered similar difficulties in the immediate post-war years. These problems were caused by the multinational composition of their populations, border disputes, economic difficulties and political instability.

Yugoslavia

Yugoslavia, formally established in December 1918, was made up of the previously independent kingdoms of Serbia and Montenegro, together with territory that had been part of the Habsburg Empire. It became home to people of varying ethnic and religious backgrounds — Serbs, Croats, Bosnians, Slovenes, Magyars, Germans, Albanians, Romanians and Macedonians, Orthodox and Roman Catholic Christians, Jews and Muslims. In this situation, religious and ethnic disputes were inevitable and developing effective democratic institutions was virtually impossible. In 1929, the king, Alexander I, banned all political parties and proclaimed himself **dictator**.

Poland

After more than a century of being partitioned by foreign powers, such as Germany and the Habsburg and Russian Empires, Poland re-emerged as an independent nation in November 1918. The Paris Peace Conference confirmed Poland's independence in June 1919. Of Poland's population of 27 million, fewer than 18 million were Poles and more than 1 million were German. These statistics, together with the fact that there were 14 political parties in the country, meant that attempts to maintain true democracy led to weak and unstable governments. In 1926, Jósef Pilsudski led a military coup and established himself as dictator.

Border disputes were to bring Poland into conflict with Germany, Czechoslovakia, Lithuania and Russia. Polish leaders wanted to extend Poland's territory beyond that which had been agreed at the Paris Peace Conference, in particular by gaining control over Ukraine and Lithuania, areas that had been part of Poland prior to its partition in the 18th century, when they came under the control of Russia. In 1919, Polish troops entered Ukraine. Their initial success was halted by a Russian counter-offensive in 1920, and, for a time, it seemed as though Poland would be utterly defeated. However, Polish forces were able to defeat the Russians at the Battle of Warsaw and resumed their own offensive. The war between Poland and Russia was ended by the Treaty of Riga (1921), which added a strip of land some 160 km (100 miles) wide to Poland's eastern border.

Czechoslovakia

The Czechoslovak First Republic emerged from the collapse of the Habsburg Empire in October 1918, and its existence as an independent state was confirmed by the Paris peace settlement. In addition to Czechs and Slovaks, Czechoslovakia contained Russians, Magyars, Poles, Jews and more than 3 million German speakers. The German-speaking populations of Bohemia, Moravia and the Sudetenland made up a sizeable **minority group** that persistently claimed it was being discriminated against. Despite these potential problems, Czechoslovakia was able to maintain a democratic system of government. Blessed with raw materials, rich agricultural land and productive industries, it remained relatively prosperous throughout the 1920s. Czechoslovakia had taken care to develop protective alliances with Yugoslavia, Romania, Italy and France.

KEY TERM

Minority group: a group of people bound together by, for example, common nationality, language or religion, living in a country dominated by other groups. As a result, they often lack political rights and are often discriminated against.

Austria

Landlocked and with most of its industrially productive areas given to Poland and Czechoslovakia by the Treaty of Saint Germain, Austria experienced enormous economic problems. The country was increasingly reliant on foreign loans and inflation ran high throughout the 1920s, leading to political instability. The majority of Austrians believed that the solution to their problems was union with Germany, but this was expressly forbidden by the post-war peace settlement. Indeed, foreign loans were only given in response to Austria's commitment not to seek union with Germany.

Hungary

The immediate aftermath of the First World War led to political chaos in Hungary. The Hungarian Communist Party seized control and the Hungarian Soviet Republic under the leadership of Béla Kun was announced on 21 March 1919. In an attempt to remove all potential opposition, Kun's government mounted a violent campaign, referred to as the 'Red Terror'. At the same time, Hungarian troops invaded Czechoslovakia with the aim of extending Hungary's borders. When, due to French intervention, Hungarian forces were forced to retreat, Kun ordered his army to invade Romania. The invasion was quickly defeated and facing the threat of Romanian forces on Hungarian soil Kun's government collapsed. Hungarian military leaders formed a new, heavily anti-communist government, which took violent reprisals, referred to as the 'White Terror', against those who had supported Kun. Hungary was now under the control of an authoritarian regime, which, like Kun, was determined to regain lost lands. Under the terms of the post-war settlements, Hungary had lost around two-thirds of its population and much of its industrial land to Czechoslovakia, Romania and Yugoslavia. Like Austria, Hungary suffered from major economic problems during the 1920s, and became increasingly reliant on foreign loans.

Given the disappointment of the First World War's victorious nations, the resentment of those that had been defeated and the problems faced by the 'successor states', it is easy to see why many historians are critical of the Paris peace settlement. However, such criticisms take little account of the difficult circumstances that faced those responsible for drawing up the peace settlement. Satisfying the competing demands of the victorious nations was a virtually impossible task. In Eastern Europe, the peacemakers had little option but to recognise situations that had already emerged following the disintegration of the Habsburg, Turkish and Russian empires towards the end of the war. In fact, far fewer people were living under foreign rule in 1920 than had been the case in 1914. As an American delegate at the peace talks claimed: 'it is not surprising that they made a bad peace: what is surprising is that they managed to make peace at all.'

63

ACTIVITY 2.6

In small groups, discuss the following:

a What problems were common to all of the 'successor states'?

b What factors caused these problems?

c How fair is it to blame these problems on the decisions taken at the Paris Peace Conference?

Make sure that your notes cover the problems faced by the 'successor states'.

ACTIVITY 2.7

Look carefully at Figure 2.7.

a Answering the following questions in pairs will help you to interpret what point the cartoonist was trying to make.

   i Identify the four men depicted to the right of the pillar.

   ii What task had these men just completed?

   iii Which of the four men appears to be the leader?

   iv Which of the four men appears to have been the least important?

   v What has the child hidden to the left of the pillar just been reading?

   vi Why do you think this child is labelled as '1940 CLASS'?

   vii Why is the child weeping?

   viii What is meant by the heading 'PEACE AND FUTURE CANNON FODDER'?

   ix 'The Tiger' says, 'Curious, I seem to hear a child weeping'. Who was 'The Tiger'? Why would he find it 'curious' that the child was weeping?

b Using your answers to these questions, decide which of the following statements are true and which are false, explaining your reasons in each case.

   i The cartoonist thought that the Paris peace settlement would lead to lasting peace.

   ii The cartoonist thought that France had got too much of its own way at the Paris Peace Conference.

   iii The cartoonist thought that Britain should have played a more significant role at the Paris Peace Conference.

   iv The cartoonist thought that the Paris peace settlement was a bad peace that would inevitably lead to another war in the future.

   v The cartoonist thought that the Paris peace settlement was entirely based on Wilson's Fourteen Points.

64

Figure 2.7: Cartoon published by the *Daily Herald*, a British newspaper, in 1919. The title reads 'PEACE AND FUTURE CANNON FODDER' The caption reads: 'The Tiger: "Curious! I seem to hear a child weeping!"'

Reflection: Discuss with another student how you decided which statement was true or false. Would you change your answers to the activity following this discussion?

●●● THINK LIKE A HISTORIAN

Look at the kind of political cartoons that you find in newspapers and magazines today.

What methods do the cartoonists use to:
- make us laugh
- shape our opinions?

🔑 KEY TERM

Fascism: a political philosophy which advocates state control over all aspects of society and the economy and is heavily nationalistic. In a fascist state, power is held by a small elite, usually under the direction of a dictator, and all political opposition is banned. A fascist government maintains power through control of the country's armed forces.

2.2 How and why did international tensions remain high in the period between 1920 and 1923?

Crises and tensions

If drawing up the terms of the peace settlement had been difficult, implementing them proved even more so. International tensions remained high in the post-war years for a number of reasons. The tensions between the USA, Britain and France, which had characterised negotiations at the Paris Peace Conference, increased when the US Senate rejected the peace settlement. Russia, whose Bolshevik government had not been invited to the Paris peace talks, remained isolated as fears of communist-style revolution spread across Europe. These fears led to the appointment of an anti-communist government in Italy under the leadership of **Benito Mussolini**, whose territorial campaigns in defiance of the Paris peace settlement added to the tensions caused by various border disputes.

BENITO MUSSOLINI (1883–1945)

Mussolini led the **fascist** movement in Italy, forming the Fascist Party in 1919 and ruling Italy from 1922 to 1943. He swiftly established a dictatorship and launched a campaign to control all aspects of Italian life. His decision to support Hitler during the Second World War proved disastrous, and he was dismissed by the king in 1943. Mussolini was executed by communists in 1945.

US isolationism

Despite the leading role President Wilson had played in negotiating the various peace treaties, public opinion in the USA was divided on the issue of whether the USA should ratify the Paris peace settlement and join the League of Nations. Most Democratic Party senators supported President Wilson's argument in favour of internationalism – that the USA should play a full and active part in international affairs. Most Republican Party senators opposed internationalism and argued in favour of isolationism – that the USA should keep out of international affairs unless its own interests were at stake.

ACTIVITY 2.8

a List and explain the reasons that Borah gives to justify his view that the USA should reject the Paris peace settlement.

b Did Borah believe that the Paris peace settlement would lead to lasting peace?

c Was Borah an internationalist or an isolationist?

We have entangled ourselves with European concerns. We are dabbling and meddling in their affairs. We have surrendered the great policy of 'no entangling alliances' upon which the strength of this Republic has been founded. How shall we keep from meddling in the affairs of Europe or keep Europe from meddling in the affairs of America? It is in conflict with the right of our people to govern themselves, free from all restraint, legal or moral, of foreign powers. America must, both for the happiness of her own people and for the moral guidance and greater contentment of the world, be permitted to live her own life. We are told that the treaty means peace. Even so, I would not pay the price. Would you purchase peace at the cost of our independence? But the treaty does not mean peace. If we are to judge the future by the past, it means war.

Speech by William E. Borah to the US Senate, 19 November 1919

Since the Republican Party held a majority in the Senate, the USA decided in favour of isolationism. In November 1919, the US Senate rejected the Paris peace settlement and refused to allow the USA to join the League of Nations. Determined not to become involved in another war, and believing that the terms of the peace settlement made future conflict inevitable, most Americans were convinced that the USA should return to its traditional isolationist policy.

The USA's decision not to ratify the Paris peace settlement and, instead, to make a separate peace with Germany in 1921, had a profound effect on relations between European countries. In particular, it contributed to France's already significant feelings of insecurity. The French now had no guarantee of American support in the event of an attack by a resurgent Germany. Furthermore, Britain was clearly seeking to withdraw from European affairs, focusing primarily on its relations with Australia, Canada and New Zealand. While Britain argued that disarmament was the key to future peace within Europe, France, fearful of a revival of German power, was totally opposed to it. To the British, it appeared that France posed a greater threat to future peace than Germany. As a result, there seemed little likelihood that Britain would guarantee French security. This left France isolated and consequently even more determined to prevent Germany's post-war recovery.

Attitudes towards Russia

Russia, now under communist rule, was viewed with suspicion and fear by its former allies and enemies alike. In a European-wide climate of social and economic hardship, many governments feared revolution in their countries in the post-war years. Concern over the potential spread of communism was so great that many Western European nations, together with Japan, became involved in the Russian Civil War in an attempt to prevent Lenin's Bolsheviks winning control of the country. For France, this situation meant the loss of another potential ally against a revitalised Germany. For Russia, it meant isolation and vulnerability.

There were, therefore, a number of underlying factors leading to international tension in the immediate post-war period. This tension was greatly increased by several issues which arose between 1919 and 1923.

German hyperinflation

Despite the USA's decision to isolate itself politically from Europe, it continued to have a major effect on European economies. During the First World War, the USA had provided large loans to assist its European allies. Now it insisted on the full repayment of these war debts.

For most European countries, ravaged by the effects of war and struggling to rebuild their economies, the only way to meet these debt repayments was by ensuring that Germany paid its reparations.

In the wake of its defeat, Germany claimed that it was in no position – politically, socially or economically – to meet these demands. Fighting on the Western Front during the First World War had been largely confined to France and Belgium, and Germany emerged from the war with most of its industrial infrastructure intact. However, Germany had borrowed heavily to finance its war effort, and the combined effects of repaying these debts and meeting reparations requirements were catastrophic for the German economy. Much as Keynes had predicted, German inflation spiralled out of control. The value of Germany's currency (the mark) fell dramatically, as shown in the table below:

Early 1921	$1 = 90 marks
Early 1922	$1 = 320 marks
December 1922	$1 = 7400 marks
November 1923	$1 = 4.2 trillion marks

Figure 2.8: German children using banknotes as building blocks during the hyperinflation crisis, 1923. How reliable do you think this photograph is?

In effect, Germany's currency had become worthless. In January 1922, a loaf of bread cost 250 marks; by November 1923, the price had soared to 200 000 million marks. Germany was suffering from an extreme form of inflation, which economists call hyperinflation, causing enormous hardships to its population. Germany's Weimar government, faced with numerous uprisings, struggled to maintain control over the country. Not strong enough to fix wages and prices, the government simply issued paper money, which rapidly became worthless, making the problem worse.

Ruhr crisis

Germany's economic problems were heightened by the actions of France and Belgium. In 1923, angered by Germany's failure to make reparations payments, French and Belgian troops occupied the Ruhr – one of Germany's most important industrial regions – with the aim of seizing coal and timber by way of payment. The German government ordered a policy of passive resistance, which effectively paralysed industry in the Ruhr as miners and factory employees refused to work. Although the French and Belgians largely failed in their aim to seize goods from German factories and mines, the economic effect of the loss of output from such a vital industrial region was catastrophic for Germany, further fuelling its rising inflation. Naturally, this made it even less likely that Germany would be able to meet its reparations requirements in the future.

Attitudes towards Germany

Relations between Britain and France were strained as a result of their different attitudes towards German recovery, which were highlighted by the Ruhr crisis. Britain, keen to re-establish the lucrative trading partnership between the two countries, encouraged Germany's economic revival. France, on the other hand, was determined to keep Germany as weak as possible for as long as possible. Britain opposed French actions in the Ruhr, considering them effectively an act of war.

Corfu Incident

The threat of communism had a particularly significant impact in Italy. Having borrowed heavily to finance its involvement in the First World War, Italy's attempts to repay these debts led to damaging inflation. The value of the Italian lira fell from five to the dollar in 1914 to 28 to the dollar by 1921. In addition to this massive increase in the cost of living, Italians also faced high unemployment as industry reduced production to pre-war levels and the number of people seeking jobs was increased by the return of more than 2 million soldiers. These circumstances inevitably led to disorder. Strikes organised by trade unions in 1919 and 1920 quickly descended into rioting and looting. In many industrial cities, workers took control of their factories and established councils to manage them. With the formation of the Italian Communist Party in January 1921, it seemed only a matter of time before a revolution began.

Formed in 1919, under the leadership of Benito Mussolini, the Italian National Fascist Party had gained a reputation for violence, its black-shirted members regularly attacking communist headquarters and newspaper offices. Nevertheless, the party had achieved increasing support from those sections of Italian society that had most reason to fear communism – industrialists, landowners, middle-class property owners, the Roman Catholic Church and King Victor Emmanuel III. In 1922, faced with the threat of revolution following the Communist Party's call for a general strike, the king asked Mussolini to form a government. Italy became the world's first fascist state.

In line with the aggressive nationalism which characterised fascism, Mussolini made it clear that his aim was to make Italy 'great, respected and feared'. 'The Twentieth Century', he declared, 'will be a century of Italian power.' His early actions certainly seemed to reflect these grand statements. In March 1923, Italian troops took possession of the Adriatic port of Fiume. This action was in defiance of the Paris peace settlement, which had declared Fiume a 'Free City', to be used jointly by Italy and Yugoslavia. In August 1923, four Italians were killed while engaged in a League of Nations attempt to resolve a border dispute between Greece and Albania. Believing that Greece was responsible for the deaths, Mussolini ordered Italian troops to bombard, and subsequently occupy, the Greek island of Corfu. Greece appealed to the League of Nations, which instructed Italian troops to withdraw from Corfu. Mussolini refused to accept the League's authority, and the Italian occupation continued until Greece paid a substantial amount of compensation. While Britain and France saw Mussolini as a useful ally against the threat of communism, his refusal to abide by the decisions made at the Paris Peace Conference was a cause of concern throughout Europe.

Other disputes and tensions

Elsewhere in Europe, other border disputes arising out of the decisions made at the Paris Peace Conference soon occurred. Turkey defied the peace settlement completely when its troops retook some of the land in 1922, including Smyrna and parts of Anatolia, awarded to Greece by the Treaty of Sèvres (see Chapter 2.1). In doing so, Turkey became the first country to successfully challenge the post-war settlement, and in 1923 a revised treaty – the Treaty of Lausanne – replaced the original agreement. As a result, Turkey regained some land it had lost, including Smyrna, Thrace and the Aegean islands of Imbros and Tenedos. This went some way to restoring Turkish national pride, which had been badly damaged by the Treaty of Sèvres. Turkey's success set a precedent for challenging the Paris peace settlement.

Beyond Europe, tensions increased between the USA and Japan. Japanese power in East Asia had grown enormously during the First World War. Japanese expansion in East Asia was of grave concern to the Western powers, which were keen to protect and extend their own trading activities in the region. The USA in particular increasingly viewed Japan as a threat to its open door policy in China (see Chapter 1.4).

(see Chapter 2.1)
(see Chapter 1.4)

The period from 1919 to 1923 was, therefore, characterised by international tension. Germany was weakened and resentful. France and Russia, albeit for different reasons, felt isolated and vulnerable. The USA had returned to a policy of isolationism, while Britain was focusing more on its imperial connections than on its relations with Europe. Italy, now under Mussolini's leadership, was seeking to overcome its humiliation at the Paris Peace Conference by territorial expansion. Border disputes were commonplace, and Turkey had become the first country to successfully challenge the Paris peace settlement. At the same time, countries were trying to come to terms with the economic consequences of the First World War.

Aims and impact of international treaties and conferences

Despite these simmering tensions, no country wanted another war. With this in mind, several attempts were made to improve international relations during the immediate post-war period.

The Washington Conference (1921–22)

There was a clear need to reduce growing tensions in East Asia arising from Japanese expansion in the region, tensions that threatened to cause a naval arms race and, possibly, lead to war. In 1921, therefore, the USA invited nine nations to Washington DC to discuss naval reductions and the situation in East Asia. Britain, Japan, France and Italy were invited to join the USA in talks on reducing naval capacity. Belgium, China, Portugal and the Netherlands were invited to join in discussions on the situation in East Asia.

The Washington Naval Conference led to a series of treaties, which at the time seemed to guarantee peace in East Asia.

- **The Five Power Treaty** (signed by the USA, Britain, France, Japan and Italy) – Japan agreed to withdraw from some of its recently acquired Chinese territory and to limit its navy to three-fifths the size of the British and US navies. In return, the Western powers agreed not to develop any new naval bases near Japan. All five countries agreed to limit their warship tonnage – Britain and the USA to 500 000 tons each, Japan to 300 000 tons, France and Italy to 175 000 tons each.

- **The Four Power Treaty** (signed by USA, Britain, France and Japan) – the four countries agreed to respect each other's rights in the Pacific and Far East, and to deal with any future disagreements by negotiation rather than military action. This treaty formally ended the 1902 alliance between Britain and Japan. Britain had

ACTIVITY 2.9

In pairs:

a identify the factors which caused international tension in the period from 1919 to 1923

b Rank these factors in order of significance

c discuss your ranked lists in a whole-class seminar

d how far do you feel the Paris peace settlement was responsible for international tension in 1919–23?

Use the table below to help you reach a conclusion.

TENSION CAUSED BY THE PEACE SETTLEMENT	TENSION CAUSED BY OTHER FACTORS

become increasingly embarrassed by this alliance for two main reasons – first, because the reason for it (Britain's naval rivalry with Germany) no longer existed; second, because, in the event of any conflict between the USA and Japan, Britain would be obligated to side with Japan.

- **The Nine Power Treaty** (signed by all nine countries attending the conference) – this treaty guaranteed protection for China against invasion and agreed to uphold the 'open door' policy, allowing equal opportunity for all countries seeking to trade with China.

The treaties arising out of the Washington Conference undoubtedly reduced tensions in East Asia. All of the countries involved had been willing to compromise in the interests of maintaining peace. However, the treaties were far from perfect. For example, although the Five Power Treaty limited the tonnage of each nation's warships, it did not include all types of shipping. As a result, there was a race to build cruiser ships that could be deployed in the event of war. Moreover, the treaties lacked a means of enforcement – they did not specify what action would be taken if a country violated the agreements it had made.

Contemporary opinions of the treaties arising out of the Washington Naval Conference varied enormously. The *American Army and Navy Journal* argued in 1922 that:

> The agreements made at the Washington Conference have placed the USA in danger. The USA has sacrificed itself to bring about peace. It should be pointed out that such treaties cannot be regarded as a guarantee against war, since similar agreements have failed many times in the past.

Conversely, a Japanese businessman, also writing in 1922, argued:

> If the Washington Conference fails it will not be due to the Japanese. It would have been fair to give equality to Japan. The USA should have granted this. The delegates should have been reminded of the opening address in which the President urged the delegates to be unselfish and think responsibly about the future of the world.

In the same year, William H. Gardiner, President of the US Navy League, suggested that:

> The Washington treaties are not a means of reducing the American fleet, but a way of increasing the efficiency of the American navy. The same holds true for Britain and Japan. Of the 1.65 million tons to be destroyed, over half are ships so old that they can no longer be considered fit to fight.
>
> **William H. Gardiner, 'A Naval View of the Conference',** *Atlantic Monthly*, **April 1922**

ACTIVITY 2.10

a   Compare and contrast the views of the *American Army and Navy Journal*, the Japanese businessman and William H. Gardiner regarding the treaties arising from the Washington Conference.

Remember to consider:
- similarities and differences between the sources
- the reliability of each source.

Remember that:
- you need to consider both sides of the argument in order to develop a balanced assessment
- you need to make a supported judgement.

b   How far do you agree with the view that the 'Washington Conference achieved nothing significant'?

Use the table below to help you reach a conclusion –

AGREE	DISAGREE

The Genoa Conference (1922)

At the suggestion of David Lloyd George, the British prime minister, representatives of 30 European countries met in Genoa, Italy, to discuss ways of easing their post-war economic problems. France was represented by its prime minister, Raymond Poincaré. Despite their political and diplomatic isolation, both Germany and Soviet Russia were invited to the conference, Lloyd George believing that their inclusion was vital to achieving the aim of 'the economic reconstruction of Europe, devastated and broken into fragments by the agency of war'.

That Britain and France had very different attitudes towards Germany is clearly shown by this extract, from a British political magazine:

> A major issue is at stake regarding the forthcoming conference in Genoa. M. Poincaré wants the physical security and prosperity of France by means of holding Germany down and taking large reparations from her and meanwhile maintaining an expensive army and navy. On the other hand, Mr Lloyd George stands for toleration, conciliation and cooperation with Germany. M. Poincaré has tried to prevent the Conference altogether. Mr Lloyd George told him that Britain would carry on in any case, and that if France refused to attend she would be the greatest loser. M. Poincaré probably felt that he could not afford to forfeit the good opinion of the world by not attending.
>
> 'France and the Genoa Conference', the *Spectator*, 4 March 1922

70

The conference, which ran from 10 April to 19 May 1922, focused largely on the issue of German reparations. Facing its own massive economic problems, Germany was struggling to keep up with the schedule of payments. Britain, with a vested interest in restoring its German trading links, argued that the massive reparations imposed on Germany would undermine European economic recovery and should therefore be reduced. France, fearing a revival of German power and opposing anything that seemed to weaken the terms of the Treaty of Versailles, insisted that reparation payments should be made in full.

The Genoa Conference achieved nothing. The USA, still pursuing its isolationist policy and determined to avoid involvement in European affairs, declined to attend. In the face of France's unwillingness to compromise, Germany quickly withdrew from the conference. Feeling increasingly isolated and sensing an opportunity to develop their relationship with Germany, the Russians also backed out.

ACTIVITY 2.11

Do you think that there was ever the slightest possibility that the Genoa Conference would achieve anything meaningful?

Make notes on each of the following points to help you:

- the aims of the conference
- factors that would make it difficult to achieve these aims
- the differing attitudes of Britain, France, Germany and Russia
- that the *Spectator* was a British magazine – how might a French magazine have described the same issue?

Make sure that your notes contain reasons why the Genoa Conference failed.

The Rapallo Pact (1922)

The First World War and the Paris peace settlement had left both Germany and Bolshevik Russia isolated and vulnerable. Representatives of both countries had attended the Genoa Conference, and they continued to hold joint discussions once the conference broke up in disarray. These discussions led to a treaty in 1921 by which Germany recognised the Bolsheviks as the legitimate government of Russia – the first foreign government to do so. Further negotiations, conducted by Georgi Chicherin and Walther Rathenau, foreign ministers of Russia and Germany respectively, led to the signing of the Treaty of Rapallo on 16 April 1922. Under the terms of the treaty, referred to as the Rapallo **Pact**, Russia and Germany agreed to renounce all territorial claims against each other, and to 'cooperate in a spirit of mutual goodwill in meeting the economic needs of both countries'.

 KEY TERM

Pact: a formal agreement. It could mean a treat between two or more countries as in the case of the Rapallo Pact, or an a agreement to recommend a course of action, as in the case of the Hoare-Laval pact (see p. 73).

In facilitating increased trade between Germany and Russia, the treaty was of great economic benefit to both. The treaty also led to industrial and military collaboration that enabled Germany to evade many of the terms of the Treaty of Versailles. Major German companies, such as Krupp, built factories in Russia producing the very tanks, artillery, aeroplanes, poison gas and other military equipment the treaty specifically banned them from manufacturing. Germany also organised military training in Russia for German officers who had been dismissed from the army in compliance with the Treaty of Versailles. Russia's major weakness during the First World War had been the lack of modern military equipment and training. The Russian armed forces were now able to learn from German military expertise and technological skills.

The signing of the Treaty of Rapallo caused great concern elsewhere in Europe, particularly in France and Poland. The French, fearful of communism spreading from Bolshevik Russia and determined to keep Germany weak and isolated, felt threatened by the increasingly friendly relations between these two countries. The Poles were well aware that both Germany and Russia claimed parts of the territory that comprised post-First World War Poland. Flanked by Germany to the west and Russia to the east, Poland's security was clearly under threat. Moreover, Poland's own hopes of territorial expansion at the expense of both Germany and Russia were curtailed.

The Treaty of Lausanne (1923)

The Treaty of Sèvres had never been formally ratified. While the Ottoman (Turkish) government had signed the Treaty, Greece refused to do so because of its claims to more former Ottoman Empire territory. This issue was further complicated when the Turkish National Movement, under the leadership of Mustafa Kemal, gained control over Turkey. Kemal's government rejected the Treaty of Sèvres, claiming some of the territory that the treaty had taken from the former Ottoman Empire.

With the aim of preventing this situation leading to further border disputes, representatives of all the countries involved met in Lausanne, Switzerland. Discussions were tense, and there were constant protests from the Turkish representatives. Nevertheless, agreement was finally reached, and the Treaty of Lausanne was signed on 24 July 1923.

The opening words of the treaty read:

> France, Britain, Italy, Japan, Greece and Romania of the one part and Turkey of the other part, being united in the desire to bring to a final close the state of war which has existed in the East since 1914, being anxious to re-establish the relations of friendship and commerce which are essential to the mutual well-being of their respective peoples, and considering that these relations must be based on respect for the independence and sovereignty of states, have decided to conclude a Treaty for this purpose.

In addition to settling the borders of Turkey, Greece and Bulgaria, the treaty formally recognised the independence of the Republic of Turkey, with Kemal as head of state. Turkey's requirement to pay reparations was ended. In effect, Turkey had become the first country to mount a successful formal challenge to the Paris peace settlement.

ACTIVITY 2.12

In pairs, discuss and make notes on following questions.

a   Russia and Germany were very different politically. They had been enemies during the First World War, and Germany had inflicted damaging terms on Russia in the Treaty of Brest-Litovsk. Given these factors, why did Russia and Germany sign the Treaty of Rapallo in 1922?

b   Why were other European countries deeply concerned by the signing of the Treaty of Rapallo?

Make sure that your notes contain both (a) the reasons for and (b) the implications of the signing of the Treaty of Rapallo.

Compare and discuss your answers in small groups. How would you change your notes based on your discussion?

If the treaties arising from the Washington Naval Conference had gone some way to relieving Western concerns caused by Japan's rise to power in the Far East, little had been achieved in terms of relieving tensions in Europe. The French refusal to compromise at the Genoa Conference had undermined Britain's attempt to improve relations between France and Germany. Failure to reach agreement on the issue of German reparations led to the subsequent French invasion of the Ruhr industrial area. Moreover, the failure of the Genoa

71

Conference led to closer relations between Germany and Russia, culminating in the Treaty of Rapallo, which was widely perceived as a threat to stability within Europe. This stability was further threatened by the Treaty of Lausanne, the first international agreement to clearly demonstrate that, under certain circumstances, the Paris peace settlement could be successfully challenged and amended.

Changing relations between the major powers

The ending of the First World War led to global economic chaos. Countries, such as France and Belgium, needed to rebuild their industrial infrastructure following the devastation of war damage. Britain had lost over 40% of its merchant fleet during the war, significantly reducing its ability to trade. At the same time, these countries had to repay their war debts to the USA. Japan, which had gained major economic advantages from the war, now found that it faced renewed commercial competition from other countries. The German economy, confronted with war debts and reparations requirements, declined into a period of hyperinflation. Even the USA, which had gained financial benefits during the war, found that its trading opportunities were reduced because of economic weaknesses elsewhere in the world. Unemployment rose as wartime production ceased and soldiers returned from the war. Economic hardships led to social problems, which in turn posed the threat of civil disturbance and revolution. In these circumstances, it is not surprising that international tensions remained high in the immediate post-war period.

A number of key issues shaped relations between the major powers in the period from 1919 to 1923.

Fear of communism/USSR

The threat of revolution was heightened by events in Russia (USSR). The Bolsheviks' rise to power in October 1917 caused alarm across Europe. France and Britain were especially concerned, as they lost a vital ally when the new Russian government withdrew from the First World War by signing the Treaty of Brest-Litovsk with Germany. It soon became clear that Lenin intended to spread revolution as far as possible. Russian agents and propaganda appeared in all the major European cities.

In March 1919, communists from all over the world were invited to a conference in Moscow, which marked the inauguration of the Third International or **Comintern**. Its chairman, Grigori Zinoviev, proclaimed that 'in a year the whole of Europe will be Communist'. Given the political and economic turmoil Europe faced at this time, widespread revolution did indeed seem a genuine possibility. Even in

the USA, fear that revolution might spread from communist Russia led to a nationwide panic, known as the Red Scare, in 1919 and 1920. Some countries (including Britain, France, the USA and Japan) actively supported the Bolsheviks' opponents in the Russian Civil War.

> **KEY TERM**
>
> **The Comintern:** also known as the Third International or the Communist International, was a communist organisation founded in Moscow in 1919. Its aim was to encourage worldwide communist revolution.

By 1921, the Bolsheviks were clearly established in Russia. However, their hopes of a worldwide communist revolution under Russian leadership had not materialised. Lenin now accepted that Russia's future depended on peaceful coexistence and economic cooperation with other countries. In March 1921, Britain was prepared to sign a trade treaty with Russia, in effect recognising the Bolsheviks as the legitimate Russian government. France, however, remained deeply resentful of Bolshevik success in Russia. Not only had it robbed France of a potential ally in the event of any future attack by Germany, but it also increased the threat of revolution in France itself. Moreover, the Bolshevik government's refusal to repay Russian debts to France resulted in great anger. It was largely at French insistence that Russia was not represented at the Paris Peace Conference.

French concerns regarding Bolshevik Russia were heightened when the Treaty of Rapallo was signed in 1922, restoring full diplomatic relations between Russia and Germany, and ending the political and economic isolation of both. The treaty caused great concern across Europe, but particularly in France and Poland.

The impact of decisions taken by the USA

The USA's decision not to ratify the Paris peace settlement had major implications for international relations. It undermined the legitimacy of the various treaties that emerged from the Paris Peace Conference, and seriously damaged the credibility of the proposed League of Nations. In particular, it was a cause of great concern in France. Under the terms of the Treaty of Versailles, both Britain and the USA guaranteed to help France in the event of any future German invasion. When the USA refused to ratify the treaty, Britain used this as an excuse to cancel its own commitment. With no guarantee of American or British help, France was left feeling betrayed and vulnerable.

During the war, the USA had provided its European allies, such as Britain and France, with sizeable loans, to be repaid with interest once the war was over. In 1919, Britain and France urged the USA to cancel these debts. They justified this request by pointing out that the USA had benefitted from significant economic advantages during the war, and that its post-war economy was in a much healthier state than their own. Rejecting these requests, the USA insisted that the loans be repaid in full. For European nations, already suffering from major economic problems in the immediate aftermath of the First World War, this posed a further financial problem.

In order to repay their debts to the USA, Britain and France were reliant on the reparation payments they were due to receive from Germany. Yet Germany, with its currency collapsing and confronting the problem of hyperinflation, was in no position to meet its reparation requirements. While Britain was prepared to compromise with the German government, France continued to insist that Germany meet its reparation requirements in full.

French attitudes towards Germany

France had been invaded by Germany twice in the space of less than 50 years. After the humiliating defeat in the Franco-Prussian War (1870–71) and the devastating effects of German aggression between 1914 and 1918, it is hardly surprising that France's main priority was to ensure that Germany could never again become a threat. At the Paris Peace Conference, Clemenceau had demanded that a harsh settlement be imposed on Germany, and, to some extent, his demands had been met in the Treaty of Versailles. However, the USA's decision not to ratify the treaty meant that France no longer had the guarantee of American and British assistance in the event of any future aggression by Germany.

Under these circumstances, France adopted a tough and uncompromising policy towards Germany throughout the period from 1919 to 1923. The aim was to ensure that Germany remained too weak, both militarily and economically, to pose a threat to French security. For this reason, France insisted that Germany should pay the full amount of reparations, as clearly demonstrated by French refusal to compromise at the Genoa Conference. Since this was to be paid over a period of 66 years, the French could feel assured that Germany would remain economically weak for a long time to come – too weak to contemplate further aggression against France.

When Germany fell behind in its reparations payments, France was prepared to adopt drastic measures to force the Germans to pay. This resulted in the French occupation of the Ruhr region in 1923. This extreme measure, effectively an act of war, proved counter-productive for two main reasons:

1 it greatly increased the problem of inflation, which was already undermining the German economy; this made it even more difficult for Germany to meet its reparations requirements

2 it severely damaged France's relations with Britain, which had its own reasons for wanting to encourage the recovery of the German economy; this had the effect of making France feel further isolated and even more insecure.

ACTIVITY 2.13

Working in pairs or small groups:

a identify and analyse the reasons why French soldiers occupied the Ruhr in 1923

b discuss how far you agree with the view that 'the French government's decision to occupy the Ruhr was a diplomatic mistake'.

Complete the following table to help you during the discussions.

MISTAKE	NOT A MISTAKE

Reflection: Join a different group or pair and compare how you completed your tables. Do you see any differences between your tables? Would you change your table after your discussion?

2.3 How successful were attempts to improve international relations from 1924–29?

Economic recovery and improved relations

At the beginning of 1924, international relations remained extremely tense, particularly in Europe. Still struggling to cope with the economic problems that confronted them in the aftermath of the First World War, there seemed little to unite European nations, and much to divide them. Border disputes continued to break out as various countries challenged the decisions made at the Paris Peace Conference. Moreover, French and Belgian soldiers were occupying German territory in the Ruhr.

A number of main factors combined to gradually reduce these tensions over the next five years.

League of Nations and diplomacy

Despite the fact that its membership did not include the USA, Russia or any of the First World War's defeated nations, the newly created League of Nations was able to negotiate peaceful resolutions to a number of border disputes.

> In a speech delivered in 1946, Joseph Paul-Boncour, French representative at the League of Nations, stressed the importance of this:
>
> > During a number of years, in the period following the peace treaties, the League of Nations settled various grave disputes, all of them involving areas which might have become battlefields if the League had not settled the disputes in their initial stages.
> >
> > Speech by Joseph Paul-Boncour at the closing session of the League of Nations, April 1946

Economic recovery and reconstruction

The economies of the major European nations had been devastated by the First World War. In addition to physical damage, former markets had been lost, primarily to the USA and Japan. The high costs involved in sustaining military action had resulted in high taxation, extensive foreign borrowing and rising inflation. In order to finance the war effort, countries had left the **gold standard**. This enabled them to print more paper money, but had the serious effect of weakening the value of their currencies, leading to inflation.

KEY TERM

The gold standard: a monetary system by which the value of a currency is directly linked to the value of gold. Being on the gold standard is intended to give a nation's currency international credibility.

Albeit slowly, the economies of European nations began to recover. Realising that private enterprise would find it impossible to finance the reconstruction of infrastructure and industry, governments took the lead. Both France and Britain, for example, appointed Ministers of Reconstruction – Louis Loucheur and Christopher Addison

respectively. Their work was severely hampered by financial constraints, but gradually economic confidence was restored. Entrepreneurs and businessmen were increasingly willing to invest their capital again. Members of the public provided governments with loans by purchasing bonds offering guaranteed interest rates. By 1925, Britain had returned to the gold standard. France followed suit in 1926, Italy in 1927 and, by 1928, virtually all of the world's nations had done so.

The role of the USA

Just as in Europe, the ending of the First World War led to a period of high inflation and rising unemployment in the USA. Nevertheless, the USA emerged from the war as the world's leading economy. No fighting had taken place on American soil, and its industries and infrastructure remained intact. It had gained new markets, and the necessities of war had encouraged it to increase manufacturing production and efficiency. It would also benefit from the repayment of war debts by its former European allies. The USA was about to experience an economic boom – a period referred to as 'the Roaring Twenties', characterised by a massive rise in consumerism.

Despite its outward commitment to a policy of isolationism, the USA was to play a significant role in easing international tensions during the 1920s. Its vast financial resources would help to overcome the problem of German reparations and, in so doing, lead to an improvement in relations between France and Germany.

Aims and impact of international treaties and conferences

By 1924, it had become more important than ever to find a solution to the problem of German reparations. There were three main issues:

1 French and Belgian troops were occupying German territory, effectively an act of war which posed a clear threat to peace in Europe

2 Germany claimed that it was unable to make the reparation payments as required under the terms of the Treaty of Versailles

3 the USA continued to insist on full repayment of the loans it had made to its allies during the First World War; Britain and France argued that they could only afford to repay these debts if they received reparation payments from Germany.

In order to address these problems, a conference was held in London during 1924. Chaired by the American banker, Charles Dawes, the conference was attended by representatives from the USA, Britain, France, Italy and Belgium. What emerged from this conference is known as the Dawes Plan, which had four main elements:

1 it was agreed that French and Belgian troops should withdraw from the Ruhr as quickly as possible and that the region should be returned to full German control

2 Germany's reparation payments were restructured; although no reduction was made to the total amount Germany would have to pay in reparations, it was agreed that its annual payments would be restricted to what 'she could reasonably afford'

3 it was agreed that Germany's national bank, the Reichsbank, should be restructured and supervised by representatives of the other countries attending the conference

4 Germany received a sizeable foreign loan, mainly from the USA; this was intended to stabilise the German economy so that Germany would be in a better position to meet its reparations requirements in the future.

Assured that they would continue to receive reparations, France and Belgium withdrew from the Ruhr and tensions were reduced.

The Dawes Plan seemed to mark a significant change in French policy towards Germany. Previously, France had adopted a hard-line attitude, insisting that Germany paid reparations on time and in full. This had been one of the main reasons for the failure of the Genoa Conference and had led to the French occupation of the Ruhr. This new French willingness to compromise opened the way for further negotiations designed to reduce tensions between France and Germany, thereby enhancing stability within Europe.

ACTIVITY 2.14

Why do you think France was willing to compromise in 1924 when it had steadfastly refused to do so in 1922?

The USA was following an isolationist policy during the 1920s. Why, then, did US representatives play such a major role in devising the Dawes Plan?

KEY CONCEPT

Historians study patterns of development over time, identifying and analysing areas of continuity and areas of change.

Change and continuity

A number of problems had arisen over the issue of Germany's requirement to pay reparations.

In pairs, identify what these problems were.

In attempting to address these problems, the Dawes Plan reflects the idea of continuity and change:

- **continuity** – no changes were made to the Treaty of Versailles; the War Guilt Clause still applied and no changes were made to the full amount which Germany was expected to pay in reparations

- **change** – Germany's annual reparations payments were reduced, thereby extending the period in which the full amount had to be paid; foreign loans were provided to help Germany deal with its economic problems and foreign supervision of the Reichsbank meant that other countries would be able to monitor Germany's economic situation and know how much it could afford to pay in reparations each year.

The Locarno Conference (1925)

The resort of Locarno in Switzerland was the setting for a series of agreements designed to create greater stability and security in Europe. The most significant outcome of the Locarno Conference was that Germany, France and Belgium promised to respect their joint frontiers. This meant that the borders agreed at the Paris Peace Conference were jointly confirmed and accepted. No military action could be taken unless it was considered defensive.

In addition, a Treaty of Mutual Guarantee was agreed. This stated that Britain and Italy would come to the assistance of any country that fell victim to an act of aggression in violation of the Locarno Treaties. Britain thus pledged to come to France's aid in the event of a future German attack – an agreement that finally gave the French the security they had desired for so long.

Mussolini's aggressive actions in Fiume and Corfu during 1923 had caused concern across Europe. At Locarno, Mussolini adopted a more cautious and diplomatic approach, forging effective working relationships with representatives from Britain, France, Germany and Belgium. Despite his ambitious foreign policy aims, Mussolini was well aware that the Italy of the 1920s was in no position, economically or militarily, to challenge the major European powers of Britain and France.

He also realised that, as the only fascist nation and with a reputation for aggressive foreign policies, Italy was in danger of becoming isolated. Being an isolated nation in the 1920s meant being vulnerable. Mussolini played an important role in securing the agreements reached at Locarno, gaining a reputation as a statesman with whom other European nations could safely negotiate. This was a sign that Mussolini's Italy was being accepted by the other leading European nations as a major power in its own right. If not yet either 'great' or 'feared', at least Italy was 'respected'.

The original idea of holding the Locarno Conference came from Gustav Stresemann, the German foreign minister, who wanted to restore German prestige and privileges as a leading European nation. To achieve this, he was willing to accept Germany's losses in the Treaty of Versailles.

The Locarno Conference seemed to mark a major turning point in international affairs, symbolised by the effective working relationship which had developed between Aristide Briand, the French foreign minister, and Gustav Stresemann. To emphasise Germany's good intentions towards France, Stresemann also accepted the permanent loss of Alsace, Lorraine, Eupen and Malmédy. In doing so, he hoped to win assurances from Germany's former enemies that there would be no future incursions such as the invasion of the Ruhr. Moreover, it enabled Germany to be accepted as a member of the League of Nations in 1926.

The treaties were greeted with relief and enthusiasm across Europe, Lord Balfour, the former British prime minister, even claiming 'The Great War ended in 1918. The Great Peace did not begin until 1925'.

However, some historians have been more critical, pointing out that the Locarno Treaties gave no guarantees regarding Germany's borders with Poland and Czechoslovakia. Moreover, it was clear that Britain was not fully committed to taking military action to enforce the agreements made at Locarno – Britain's responsibilities were limited by clauses requiring aggrieved nations to make an initial appeal to the League of Nations.

That the French were, perhaps, less sincere than they seemed to be in forging better relations with Germany is clearly implied by a cartoon published in a British newspaper in 1925 following the conference (Figure 2.9).

76

ACTIVITY 2.15

The Locarno Treaties seemed to reduce tensions in Europe, in particular because they appeared to provide evidence of improved relations between France and Germany. Look carefully at the cartoon (Figure 2.9), and then discuss the following questions in pairs.

a   Why has the cartoonist depicted the three characters standing on pieces of paper?

b   How does the cartoonist suggest that France, despite the Locarno Treaties, still did not really trust Germany?

c   What does the cartoonist suggest about the role played by Britain at the Locarno Conference?

d   The historian Sally Marks has described the Locarno Treaties as 'a fragile foundation on which to build a lasting peace'. How far does the cartoon agree with this view?

THE CLASP OF FRIENDSHIP (FRENCH VERSION).

Figure 2.9: Depicted, from left to right – Briand, Austen Chamberlain (British Foreign Secretary) and Stresemann

The Kellogg-Briand Pact (1928–29)

That the French still felt insecure despite the agreements reached at Locarno is clear from the fact that, in 1927, Briand proposed a pact between France and the USA to outlaw war between them. US President Calvin Coolidge and Secretary of State Frank Kellogg were initially opposed to the idea, concerned that such an agreement might force the USA to intervene in the event of France being threatened in the future. They suggested that the pact should be extended to all countries wishing to become involved.

Figure 2.10 French Foreign Minister Aristide Briand (seated left) and American Secretary of State Frank Kellogg (seated right), the architects of the Kellogg-Briand Pact. Who do you think was the intended audience for this photograph?

The result was the Kellogg-Briand Pact of 1928, which was subsequently signed by over 60 nations, including the USA, France, Britain, the USSR, Germany, Italy and Japan. The Kellogg-Briand Pact officially came into effect on 24 July 1929 and technically still exists (Barbados being the most recent signatory in 1971). By signing the pact, nations renounced war and agreed to settle disputes by peaceful means. For France, the pact appeared to provide protection from any future German aggression. For Germany, the USSR and Japan it offered international recognition as equal and trustworthy partners. Britain interpreted the pact as another means, outside the League of Nations, to preserve international peace and stability. However, the pact contained no indication of what steps might be taken against any country that subsequently broke the agreement, and this lack of clarity ultimately made it worthless. The USA only signed on the understanding that it retained the right to self-defence and would not be required to take action against any nation breaking the agreement. Retaining its isolationist policy, the USA was not making any formal commitment by signing the pact.

The Young Plan (1929)

The USA knew that, despite the Dawes Plan, once Germany had to meet its full annual reparations payments it would no longer be able to afford its interest payments on American loans. As a result, a committee chaired by the American banker Owen Young met to discuss the possibility of reducing the total figure that had been agreed for reparations in the aftermath of the peace talks.

Negotiations were not easy, especially as the Germans added new demands, including the return of the Polish Corridor and Upper Silesia. However, the outcome of these negotiations throughout 1928 and 1929 was the Young Plan, which reduced the final sum of German reparations from £6.6 billion to £2 billion. In essence, this was an admission that the figure set in 1921 was too high and unrealistic. In addition, the international controls over the German economy that had been established by the Dawes Plan were dismantled. These were significant steps for Germany.

The Young Plan was probably the best example of France's apparent new willingness to compromise. Previously (at the Genoa Conference, for example), France had steadfastly refused to agree to any reduction in German reparations requirements. By 1929, the French appreciated that continuing to insist on full reparations would leave France isolated and less secure. Moreover, both Britain and France realised that Germany's ability to pay any reparations at all was entirely dependent on American loans; as a result, they had little alternative but to agree with the US-inspired Young Plan.

In terms of reducing international tension, great progress appeared to have been made in the period from 1923–29. The League of Nations had proved successful in settling a number of border disputes. France had adopted a less hard-line approach towards Germany, even to the point of accepting reduced reparations payments under the Young Plan. Germany had formally accepted the terms of the Treaty of Versailles, and the Locarno Conference seemed to symbolise a new era of friendly relations within Europe. All of the major powers, even the USA, which had steadfastly refused to join the League of Nations, had renounced war by signing the Kellogg-Briand Pact.

Tensions remained, however. The French still held a deep distrust of Germany, their acceptance of the Young Plan largely being the result of international pressure. Neither the Locarno Treaties nor the Kellogg-Briand Pact contained any formal guarantees that countries would take action to enforce their terms.

ACTIVITY 2.16

In 1929, the USA was still following an isolationist policy. This meant avoiding involvement in international affairs, such as the dispute in Europe over German reparations. Despite this, the USA felt that it was important to find a peaceful solution to this dispute. Here are four possible reasons to explain this apparent contradiction, only three of which are accurate. Which is the odd one out and why?

1   The USA realised that its First World War allies, such as Britain and France, could only afford to repay their war debts to the USA if they received reparations from Germany. Therefore, it was in the USA's best interests to solve the problem of German reparations.

2   The USA wanted to ensure that Germany paid interest on its American loans. Germany was finding it difficult to do this at the same time as paying reparations. Therefore, it was in the USA's best interests to reduce the amount of reparations which Germany had to pay.

3   The USA had a vested interest in ensuring that the German economy recovered as quickly as possible. American businessmen saw Germany as a potentially valuable trading partner.

4   The USA wanted to join the League of Nations. Helping to solve the problem of German reparations would demonstrate the USA's commitment to ensuring international peace. This would make it more likely that the USA would be accepted as a member of the League.

Changing relations between the major powers

As a result of the agreements reached in the period from 1924 to 1929, relations between the major powers were significantly improved. However, it is clear that underlying tensions remained.

France

After the summer of 1924, by which time it was clear that the Ruhr occupation had failed in its purpose and damaged its relations with Britain, France began to adopt a more conciliatory approach towards Germany. Accepting that it was unrealistic to expect Germany to keep up with its reparations payments, France agreed

to the Dawes Plan as a suitable compromise. Relations between France and Germany significantly improved, aided by the good working relationship that existed between the French foreign minister, Briand, and his German counterpart, Stresemann. France's new spirit of cooperation with Germany was clearly reflected in the Locarno Treaties, the Kellogg-Briand Pact and the Young Plan.

Despite this, France remained sceptical of German intentions and deeply concerned about its national security. That Britain would assist France in the event of any future German attack, in line with the assurances it made at Locarno, was far from guaranteed. In signing the Kellogg-Briand Pact, the USA was not prepared to commit itself to taking action against any country in breach of its terms. As a result, the French continued to feel vulnerable.

In an attempt to gain greater security, France began developing a series of alliances with states in Eastern Europe, including Poland (1921), Czechoslovakia (1924), Romania (1926) and Yugoslavia (1927). This network of alliances became known as the 'Little Entente'. France also strongly encouraged the development of an effective League of Nations. In truth, neither of these strategies proved particularly effective. France's 'Little Entente' partners were relatively weak and it soon became apparent that the League of Nations lacked the power to enforce its decisions on anything other than minor issues.

French relations with Russia also remained tense. Although France restored formal diplomatic relations with Russia in 1924, it made little attempt to enhance this relationship. France had been deeply concerned when Russia and Germany signed the Treaty of Rapallo in 1922. From the French perspective, the treaty would enhance the risk of revolution spreading from Bolshevik Russia and assist Germany in its economic and political recovery. French concerns were heightened in 1926 when Russia and Germany signed the Treaty of Berlin, extending the Rapallo agreement for a further five years.

Britain

Britain likewise remained deeply suspicious of Russia's communist government and its close relationship with Germany. Although, in 1921, Britain was one of the first countries to establish diplomatic relations with the Bolshevik government, its relationship with the USSR fluctuated throughout the 1920s. Fears that the USSR was encouraging independence movements in British-ruled

India led Britain to break off diplomatic relations with Russia in 1927. These were not restored until another trading agreement was reached in 1929.

USA

Although the USA appeared to be following a policy of isolationism, as demonstrated by its lack of interest in joining the League of Nations and lack of participation in European relations, it was impossible for it to keep out of world affairs completely and, indeed, not in its national interests to do so. As a result, American policies and actions had a profound effect on other countries and the relationships between them. American overseas trade and foreign investment continued to grow throughout the 1920s. Inevitably, the USA wanted to protect its international interests. On occasions, this took precedence over strict adherence to isolationism.

In particular, the USA had a vested interest in encouraging the recovery of European economies. Such a recovery would ensure that the USA received repayment of war debts from its wartime European allies, and provide enhanced markets for American exports. It was for this reason that the USA provided Germany with substantial loans following the implementation of the Dawes Plan. However, this led to the nonsensical situation whereby Germany used American loans to pay reparations to Britain, France and Italy, who then used the same money to repay their debts to the USA.

The issue of German reparations had arguably been the most significant factor in causing tension in Europe prior to 1924. The Dawes Plan, backed by the USA's financial resources, had greatly eased these tensions. French acceptance of the plan led to improved relations between France and Germany, subsequently endorsed by the agreements reached at Locarno. The USA was not represented at the Locarno Conference, but it most certainly influenced its outcome by finding a solution to the reparations problem.

Germany

Under Stresemann, Germany was prepared to compromise in order to ease its economic problems, achieve national security and regain international

recognition as a major, and trustworthy, power. At Locarno, Stresemann formally accepted the terms of the Treaty of Versailles, in particular by recognising Germany's requirement to pay reparations and guaranteeing its borders with France and Belgium. As a result, Germany was permitted to join the League of Nations, as a permanent member of the Council, in 1926.

USSR

The USSR remained largely isolated throughout the 1920s. Although Britain, France and Italy had restored diplomatic relations with the USSR by 1924, thereby recognising the Bolsheviks as its legitimate government, they still feared the spread of communism. In particular, the USSR's close relations with Germany following the Treaty of Rapallo were a cause of concern across Europe. Moreover, distrust of the USSR was not confined to Europe – the USA did not establish diplomatic relations with the USSR until 1933. The Russians themselves still resented the fact that they had not been allowed to attend the Paris Peace Conference or join the League of Nations, an organisation they increasingly perceived as simply a means of preserving the international power and influence of Britain and France.

ACTIVITY 2.17

Taking into account what you've learned so far, do you think that relations between European nations were better in 1929 than they had been in 1920? To help you consider this: (a) identify and list evidence which supports the view (b) identify and list evidence which challenges the view (c) decide which evidence seems stronger (d) write a paragraph which states your opinion - make sure it is both clear and explained. (e) discuss your opinion in pairs. Remember you are being asked for your opinion – there is no 'right' answer.

Reflection: How did discussing your opinion with your partner change how you would answer the question? Would you include these changes if you were answering a similar question by yourself?

2.4 How successful was the League of Nations during the 1920s?

Aims, membership and structure of the League

By including this statement in his 'Fourteen Points' speech (see Chapter 1.4), US president Woodrow Wilson made it clear that he fully supported the concept of an international organisation designed to prevent future wars. It is often assumed that the idea of creating a League of Nations was Wilson's brainchild, but this was not the case.

> A general association of nations must be formed under specific **covenants** for the purpose of affording mutual guarantees of political independence and territorial integrity to great and small states alike.
>
> **Speech by President Wilson to Congress, 8 January 1918**

80

KEY TERMS

Covenants: binding agreements made between nations.

'The war to end all wars': a phrase derived from the title of a book, *The War that will End War*, by the British author H. G. Wells in 1914. It was subsequently used by President Wilson in his attempts to ensure that there would never be another major war.

The First World War was the first large-scale conflict to take place between industrialised nations. This was warfare on an unprecedented scale where, for the first time, the number of civilian deaths matched those of military personnel. This was 'the Great War', **'the war to end all wars'**. Anti-war sentiment spread across the globe, together with a determination that such a catastrophe must never be allowed to happen again. Even while the war was still raging, statesmen in many different countries had reached the conclusion that there needed to be major changes in the way that international relations were conducted in order to avoid a future disaster on the same scale.

As early as 1915 (before the USA entered the First World War), the League to Enforce Peace (LEP) was established in New York by a group of notable citizens, including former president William Howard Taft. At a conference in Philadelphia in 1915, the League proposed an international agreement in which participating nations would agree to 'jointly use their economic and military force against any one of their number that goes to war or commits acts of hostility against another'. In the same year, a British League of Nations Society had been founded in London.

In 1916, the senior British politician Lord Robert Cecil submitted a memorandum to the British government advocating an international organisation to settle future disputes between nations and help preserve world peace. Leon Bourgeois and Paul Hymans, who represented France and Belgium respectively at the Paris Peace Conference, had made similar proposals to their governments. In 1918, Jan Smuts of South Africa, who unsuccessfully argued in favour of more lenient terms for Germany in the Treaty of Versailles, published a treatise entitled 'The League of Nations: A Practical Suggestion'. The **Nobel Peace Prize** was awarded to Wilson in 1919 and Bourgeois in 1920 for their work in establishing the League of Nations.

KEY TERM

Nobel Peace Prize: one of five Nobel Prizes created by Alfred Nobel, a Swedish industrialist. It is awarded annually to those who have done the most to encourage international peace and harmony.

If Wilson cannot claim to have come up with the idea of a League of Nations, he certainly became one of its strongest advocates. At the Paris Peace Conference in 1919, Wilson acted as chairman of a multinational commission set up to agree on the precise wording of the League of Nations' Covenant, a list of rules by which the League would operate. The commission consisted of two representatives each from the USA, Britain, France, Italy and Japan, together with one representative each from Belgium, China, Portugal and Serbia. Representatives from Czechoslovakia, Greece, Poland and Romania were later added.

While there was considerable support for the idea of establishing a League of Nations designed to ensure future international peace, there was less agreement between delegates about how such a League should be organised. After much negotiation and compromise, delegates at the Paris Peace Conference finally agreed on the precise wording of the Covenant of the League of Nations, a document that outlined the League's aims, structures and methods of working. On 28 June 1919, the League of Nations was formally established by Part I of the Treaty of Versailles. By signing the Covenant, the following states became founder members of the League of Nations: Argentina, Australia, Belgium, Bolivia, Brazil, Canada, Chile, China, Colombia, Cuba, Czechoslovakia, Denmark, El Salvador, France, Greece, Guatemala, Haiti, Honduras, India, Italy, Japan, Liberia, the Netherlands, New Zealand, Nicaragua, Norway, Panama, Paraguay, Persia, Peru, Poland, Portugal, Romania, Siam, Spain, Sweden, Switzerland, South Africa, United Kingdom, Uruguay, Venezuela, Yugoslavia.

ACTIVITY 2.18

Look carefully at the list of countries that were founding members of the League.

a Which important countries were not members?

b Explain why each of these countries did not become founding members.

c What problems might the League of Nations face as a result of the non-membership of these countries?

It was at Wilson's insistence that the Covenant of the League of Nations was included in each of the separate peace treaties that emerged from the Paris Peace Conference. In addition, and despite his own failing health, Wilson endured a gruelling tour of the USA in an attempt to convince the sceptical American public of the importance of the League of Nations, both for the world in general and for the USA in particular.

The opening section of the covenant makes it clear that member states were committing themselves to 'promote international co-operation and to achieve international peace and security' and accepting the 'obligation not to resort to war'. In essence, the League had three main aims – preventing future wars, administering the post-war peace settlements and promoting international cooperation.

Preventing future war

It was the firm belief of many statesmen, Wilson among them, that the horrors of the First World War could have been avoided if only there had been an international organisation designed to settle disputes between nations before they descended into armed conflict. The League of Nations was designed to play this role in the future in an attempt to ensure that the Great War really was 'the war to end all wars'. It would achieve this in a number of ways.

- Promote disarmament – Article 8 of the covenant begins 'Members of the League recognise that the maintenance of peace requires the reduction of national armaments to the lowest point consistent with national safety'.

- Abolish secret diplomacy – Wilson strongly believed that the main cause of the First World War was the secret diplomacy that had led to the Triple Alliance and the Triple Entente. In reality, both of these rival alliances had been created by a series of treaties that were essentially defensive rather than aggressive. If the full details of these treaties had been known and understood by everyone, they would have caused less fear and panic. Under Article 18 of the covenant, any future treaty entered into by a member state would have to be registered with and published by the League of Nations.

- **Arbitration** – member states agreed to arbitration by the League of Nations of any dispute between them (Article 13). The League of Nations would investigate the dispute, considering the rights and wrongs of each party. It would then pass judgement on how the dispute should be settled. The League's decision would be binding on both parties.

- Develop **collective security** – member states would work together against any country whose actions were seen as a threat to peace by acting aggressively or ignoring decisions made by the League. This could take the form of **economic sanctions** or, if these failed, joint military action (Article 16).

KEY TERMS

Arbitration: the settling of a dispute between two parties by an impartial third party.

Collective security: the idea that if any member state of the League was threatened, all the other member states would work together to defend it.

Economic sanctions: refusing to trade with a nation that was acting in defiance of the League's judgements. It was hoped that such economic pressure would force the aggressor nation to back down.

ACTIVITY 2.19

In pairs or small groups:

a list the methods that the League of Nations was intending to use in order to prevent future wars

b discuss what problems the League might face when putting these methods into practice.

Make sure that your notes contain details of the League of Nations' aims and the methods it was intending to use to achieve them.

81

Administering the post-war peace settlements

There were two main ways in which the League of Nations would work to ensure that the terms of the peace settlements were carried out.

1   Arranging plebiscites – for example, the Treaty of Versailles determined that the Saar Valley should be administered by the League of Nations for a period of 15 years, after which a plebiscite would be held so that local people could decide for themselves whether the area should belong to France or Germany. In 1935, the League of Nations duly arranged this plebiscite and the Saar region voted to return to Germany.

2   Organising mandates – as a result of the peace treaties ending the First World War, many colonies were taken away from the defeated nations. In cases where it was felt that these territories were not yet ready for full independence, they would be run as mandates. This meant that their administration was entrusted to another country (known as the Mandatory) appointed by the League of Nations. The Mandatory had to submit an annual report to the League of Nations, which established a Mandate Commission to review the progress of each mandated territory. This system was outlined in Article 22 of the covenant.

Promoting international cooperation

The League of Nations aimed to actively work towards improving relations between member states and the lives of their citizens. This would be achieved by:

- seeking to improve working conditions and wage levels throughout the world through an International Labour Organization (ILO)
- repatriating prisoners of war and resettling refugees
- providing loans to new countries, such as Austria and Hungary
- encouraging the development of education
- promoting improvements in public health, such as the prevention and control of disease

Structure

In line with the agreements reached at the Paris Peace Conference, the main organs of the League of Nations were the General Assembly and the Council. These were supported by other institutions, including the Secretariat, the Permanent Court of International Justice, and various commissions and committees established to investigate and deal with specific issues that arose.

The General Assembly

The General Assembly met annually in Geneva, a location selected because Switzerland seemed to symbolise the desire for peace. A neutral country that had taken no part in the First World War, Switzerland was also the base for the **International Red Cross**. Each member state could send up to three representatives to meetings of the Assembly, and each state was able to cast one vote. The Assembly's main role was to decide general policy, to deal with the admission of new members of the League and to handle the organisation's finances. Any decision taken by the Assembly had to be **unanimous**.

KEY TERM

International Red Cross: organisation founded in Geneva, Switzerland, in 1863 with the aim of easing the suffering of those adversely affected by war and armed conflict across the world. The International Committee of the Red Cross has been awarded the Nobel Prize on three occasions, in 1917, 1944 and 1963.

Unanimous decision: a decision that is agreed by everyone. In the League of Nations General Assembly, for example, a single country could prevent a decision being taken by voting against it.

The Council

This was a smaller body, whose main function was to settle political disputes between nations. It held four ordinary sessions each year, with extra meetings (known as extraordinary sessions) being called in times of emergency. The Council met a total of 107 times between 1920 and 1939. As with the General Assembly, decisions taken by the Council had to be unanimous. The Council was made up of permanent and non-permanent members:

- **Permanent members** – there were four original permanent members: Britain, France, Italy and Japan. The USA was to have been a permanent member but decided not to join the League of Nations. Germany became a fifth permanent member when it joined in 1926. When Germany and Japan both left the League in 1933, the USSR was added as a permanent member.

- **Non-permanent members** – initially, there were to be four of these, elected every three years by the General Assembly. The first non-permanent members were Belgium, Brazil, Greece and Spain. The number of non-permanent members was increased to six in 1922, nine in 1926 and 11 in 1933.

ACTIVITY 2.20

In pairs, discuss your impressions of the photograph taken at the first meeting of the League of Nations General Assembly. Your discussion should include issues such as:

- Why were there so many people present?
- How appropriate was the layout of the room?
- How easy would it be for this meeting to reach unanimous decisions?

Make sure that your notes cover the organisational structure of the League of Nations.

Figure 2.11: Delegates at the first meeting of the League of Nations General Assembly, 15 November 1920

The Secretariat

The Secretariat carried out the day-to-day work of the League: preparing agenda, publishing reports and dealing with vital routine matters. It was based in Geneva and directed by a Secretary-General, the first of whom was the British diplomat Sir Eric Drummond, who held the post from 1919 to 1933.

The Permanent Court of International Justice

Based at The Hague in the Netherlands, the **Permanent Court** was designed to deal with legal disputes between states.

 KEY TERM

The Permanent Court of International Justice: often referred to as the World Court, the Permanent Court of International Justice achieved some success in the 1920s, but increasingly became less used during the 1930s. Although the World Court ceased to exist in 1946, the United Nations established the International Court of Justice to replace it.

Its role was outlined in Article 14 of the Covenant of the League of Nations:

> The Court shall be competent to hear and determine any dispute of an international character which the parties thereto submit to it. The Court may also give an advisory opinion upon any dispute or question referred to it by the Council or by the Assembly.

The Permanent Court consisted of 15 judges of different nationalities who were elected for a period of nine years by the General Assembly. The Court ran from 1922 to 1946.

ACTIVITY 2.21

Class discussion:

a   What is significant about the countries that were permanent members of the Council?

b   Why did the Council have both permanent and non-permanent members?

c   Why was the Council smaller than the Assembly?

d   Which was the more powerful body – the Council or the Assembly?

Commissions and committees

A number of commissions and committees were established by the League of Nations to deal with specific problems. The main commissions dealt with issues such as the mandates, disarmament, refugees and slavery. There were committees for matters relating to international labour, health, child welfare, drug problems and women's rights. These commissions and committees achieved some notable successes during the 1920s. They facilitated the **repatriation** of some 400 000 prisoners of war, set up refugee camps, began the process of finding preventions for diseases such as malaria and leprosy, closed down a number of Swiss companies that were selling illegal drugs, and arranged for the freedom of some 200 000 slaves in countries such as Burma. However, little progress was made during the 1920s in terms of disarmament, restricting working hours or extending the rights of women.

KEY TERM

Repatriation: returning people, such as prisoners of war, refugees or migrants, to their country of origin.

Collective security and the League's involvement in the resolution of disputes: successes

In order to achieve its main aim of preventing war, the League of Nations developed a system known as collective security. Members of the League would jointly take economic and, if necessary, military action against any country that was posing a threat to peace.

The system was established by Article 16 of the covenant:

> Should any Member of the League resort to war in disregard of the Covenant, it shall be deemed to have committed an act of war against all other Members of the League, which hereby undertake immediately to subject it to the severance of all trade or financial relations.
>
> It shall be the duty of the Council in such case to recommend what effective military, naval or air force the Members of the League shall severally contribute to the armed forces to be used to protect the Covenant of the League.

The intention was that any future dispute between nations should be referred to the League, which would carefully review all of the issues involved. The League would then decide how best to resolve the dispute, and insist that all of the countries involved accepted its decision. If a country refused to do so and began preparing for war, League members would be asked to impose economic sanctions against it. If these failed to have the desired effect, League members would collectively threaten military action. It was assumed that, confronted by the combined strength of the League's member states, aggressive countries would be forced to back down.

This system enabled the League to play a key role in the successful resolution of a number of political disputes during the 1920s.

Teschen 1920

With its rich deposits of coal, the Teschen (Cieszyn) area had been one of the wealthiest and most industrialised regions of the former Austro-Hungarian Empire. In 1919, violence erupted between Czechoslovakia and Poland, which both claimed the region. The League arbitrated the dispute, splitting the region between the two countries in 1920. Although neither Poland nor Czechoslovakia was entirely satisfied with the League's decision, both accepted it and the fighting ceased.

The Åland Islands 1921

The League was equally successful in resolving a dispute over the Åland Islands (a group of some 6 500 islands situated midway between Sweden and Finland). Although the population of the islands was exclusively Swedish-speaking, the Åland Islands had belonged to Finland since the early 1900s. Most inhabitants wanted the islands to become part of Sweden, but Finland was reluctant to lose sovereignty over them. The Swedish government raised the issue with the League of Nations.

After detailed consideration, the League of Nations decided that the islands should remain with Finland. Both Finland and Sweden accepted the League's decision, and the threat of war was averted.

The Swedish government was not pleased with the decision. This is clear from its response to the League:

> It is with profound disappointment that Sweden learns of the League's decision. In supporting the cause of the people of the Aaland [sic] Islands, Sweden was not influenced by the desire to increase its territory. It only wished to support the just aspirations of the island population to reunite itself to its mother-country. This population has declared its unanimous wish not to be bound to a country to which it had been joined by force. Sweden had hoped that the League, which was established to assure justice in international relationships, would have favoured a solution in line with the principle of self-determination. It had hoped that the League of Nations would have filled, at least on this occasion, the role of the champion and defender of right. The League's decision will shake the confidence that countries which support international law have in the League of Nations. Sweden loyally accepts the decision, but hopes that the day will come when the aspirations of the people of the Aaland Islands will be triumphantly vindicated.
>
> **Swedish government's response to the Council of the League of Nations, 24 June 1921**

This was a very cleverly worded response. For example:

- it claims that Sweden had not been 'influenced by the desire to increase its territory' and that it was simply supporting the wishes of the local population to be governed by Sweden rather than Finland, which had gained the Islands 'by force' – this implies that Finland, rather than Sweden, had been the aggressor state

- it implies that, in making its decision, the League was not acting in the 'role of champion and defender of right' or supporting 'justice in international relationships'

- it also claims that the League's decision was not 'in line with the principle of self-determination', which had been one of President Wilson's key objectives at the Paris Peace Conference

- it claims that the League's decision was not in line with international law and that it 'will shake the confidence that countries which support international law have in the League of Nations'

- it implies that the League's decision would not bring an end to the dispute, because the Åland Islanders would continue to seek justice

- despite all these points, the response makes it clear that 'Sweden loyally accepts the decision' reached by the League of Nations.

Looking at the Swedish government's response in isolation, it could easily be concluded that the League of Nations had made a major mistake in deciding to leave the Åland Islands in the possession of Finland. The Swedish government's response is biased – it looks at the problem of the Åland Islands only from its own viewpoint.

In fact, there were perfectly logical reasons for the League's decision: it was based on detailed consideration of all the issues involved by a specially appointed commission, and provided the outcome that was most likely to ensure future peace in the islands. Moreover, it contained specific guarantees to protect the rights of Swedish people in the islands to maintain their own language and culture.

ACTIVITY 2.22

Discuss the following questions in pairs or small groups.

a Why do you think the Swedish government 'loyally' accepted the League's decision despite disagreeing with it?

b The Swedish government states – 'It had hoped that the League of Nations would have filled, at least on this occasion, the role of the champion and defender of right'. What does the underlined section suggest about Sweden's opinion of the League of Nations?

Upper Silesia 1921

The people of Upper Silesia, an important industrial region, were divided over whether they wished to be part of Germany or Poland, both of which laid claim to the area. This led to a series of local riots between 1919 and 1921, at which point the League of Nations became involved. After careful consideration of the case, the League of Nations decided that the area should be divided between Germany and Poland. The League's decision was accepted by both Germany and Poland and, importantly, by the vast majority of the Upper Silesians themselves.

The Yugoslavia–Albania border dispute 1921

Also in 1921, the League was confronted with open warfare between Yugoslavia and Albania. Following ongoing disputes between the two countries over territory on their joint border, Yugoslav troops entered Albanian land in November 1921. The League of Nations sent a commission, made up of representatives from Britain, France, Italy and Japan, to investigate the cause of the disagreement. On the basis of the commission's recommendations, the League of Nations found in favour of Albania. Yugoslavia complained bitterly, but had no alternative but to withdraw its troops.

Memel 1923

The port of Memel (modern Klaipėda) and the surrounding area were placed under the control of the League of Nations by the terms of the Treaty of Versailles. However, Lithuania claimed the region and invaded in 1923. The League decided that the area around the port should belong to Lithuania, but that Memel itself should remain an 'international zone'. Lithuania accepted the decision. The action taken by the League of Nations was a success in the sense that it prevented bloodshed. However, there was some criticism of the League's decision because it seemed to condone the fact that Lithuania had been able to gain land by the use of force.

Mosul 1924

The city and region of Mosul had been part of the Turkish Empire until 1918. As a result of the Paris peace settlement, Mosul – an area in which oil had recently been discovered – became part of the British mandate of Iraq. Turkey demanded that it should be allowed to regain control of the region. In 1924, the League of Nations found

in favour of Iraq and, after reaching an agreement with Britain, the Turks accepted the decision.

The Greece–Bulgaria border dispute 1925

Following a border dispute, Greece invaded Bulgaria in 1925. Bulgaria ordered its troops to offer only token resistance in an effort to avoid open conflict.

> This matter was referred to the League of Nations:
>
> > Make only slight resistance, protect the fugitive and panic-stricken population . . . do not expose the troops to unnecessary losses, in view of the fact that the incident has been laid before the Council of the League of Nations, which is expected to stop the invasion.
> >
> > **General order issued by the Bulgarian Ministry of War, 22 October 1925**

This was a clear indication that Bulgaria had faith in the League to find a peaceful settlement to the dispute. The League condemned the invasion and called for Greece to withdraw and pay compensation to Bulgaria. Greece complied with the League's decision.

In each of these disputes, the League of Nations was successful in finding a solution that was accepted by both parties and that prevented possible wars. The key to the League's success in dealing with these disputes was the fact that its arbitration and decisions were accepted by all the parties involved. However, it should be noted that these were relatively minor disputes, none of which directly involved any of the world's major powers.

Collective security and the League's involvement in the resolution of disputes: challenges

Despite its success in resolving these relatively minor disputes, it quickly became clear that the League's powers were limited and its authority was increasingly challenged.

Vilna 1920

The first successful challenge to the League of Nations' authority came as early as 1920. A dispute arose between Poland and Lithuania, two countries whose borders had been defined by the post-First World War settlement agreed at the Paris Peace Conference. Vilna (Vilnius) was the capital of Lithuania, but its population was predominantly Polish. In 1920, Polish troops occupied the city. Following a request by Lithuania, the League of Nations ordered Poland to remove its forces and tried to arrange a plebiscite to decide the region's future. Although the Polish government initially agreed, it subsequently reinforced its troops in Vilna, and in 1922 annexed the city and its surrounding area. Poland had effectively defied the League of Nations and the territory remained in Polish hands until 1939. The key to understanding the League's failure in this case is the role played by Britain and France, both of which supported Poland's claim to Vilna. France in particular was keen to keep Poland as an ally in the event of any future conflict with Germany. Without the support of these two major powers, the League of Nations was powerless to enforce its decision. As early as 1920, therefore, the underlying weaknesses of the League of Nations were fatally exposed. Britain and France were putting their own national interests ahead of their commitment to the League.

ACTIVITY 2.23

Discuss the following questions in pairs or small groups.

a What action could the League of Nations have taken to force Poland to remove its forces from Vilna?

b Why would lack of support from Britain and France prevent the League from taking such action?

c What effect would the Vilna incident have on members' confidence that the League of Nations could deal with international disputes effectively?

The Treaty of Riga 1921

In 1920, Poland invaded Russian territory. By 1921, the Russians had no choice but to sign the Treaty of Riga by which Poland gained some 80 000 square kilometres (31 000 square miles) of territory. The League of Nations took no action against Poland's open aggression. There were two main reasons for this. First, Russia was not a member of the League at that time. Second, Russia's communist government was unpopular in Britain and France, neither of which had any interest in defending it.

The invasion of the Ruhr 1923

German failure to pay war reparations led to France and Belgium invading the Ruhr, Germany's most important industrial region, in 1923. By taking this action, two members of the League of Nations were effectively breaking the rules to which they had committed

themselves by signing the Covenant of the League. Both France and Belgium were represented on the League of Nations Council – France as a permanent member, Belgium as a non-permanent member. Since decisions of the Council had to be unanimous, the League was effectively prevented from taking action to deal with this incident. It was the Dawes Plan of 1924 that finally led to the withdrawal of French and Belgian troops from the Ruhr region, the League of Nations having been powerless to either prevent or end it.

The Corfu Incident 1923

In 1923, Italy blamed Greece for the death of three Italian officials monitoring the border between Greece and Albania. Mussolini demanded compensation and occupied the Greek island of Corfu. Greece appealed to the League of Nations, which ordered the Italian troops to withdraw. Mussolini refused to accept that the League had the authority to deal with this issue. He threatened to withdraw Italy from the League and referred the matter instead to the **Council of Ambassadors**. The Council decided that Greece should pay considerable compensation to Italy. This incident exposed two fundamental weaknesses of the League of Nations. First, as a member of the League of Nations Council, Italy was in a position to prevent the League from taking any action. Second, the League's decision was effectively overruled by another body – the Council of Ambassadors.

 KEY TERM

The Council of Ambassadors: an intergovernmental agency founded in 1920 with the task of implementing the terms of the Paris peace settlement and mediating territorial disputes between European states. Chaired by the French foreign minister, the other nations represented were Britain, Italy and Japan. In view of its decision not to ratify the Paris peace settlement, the USA had observer status only (it could oversee the rulings of the Council of Ambassadors but had no power to change them).

During the 1920s, therefore, it became clear that the League of Nation's effectiveness was heavily dependent on the attitudes of its most powerful members. With their support, the League was able to arrange and enforce peaceful settlements to a number of international disputes. Although disagreeing with the League's decision over the Åland Islands, for example, Sweden had no alternative but to accept it because of the threat of collective action backed by the economic and military strength of Britain, France and Italy. However, the League was ineffective when these powerful nations put their own interests above their commitment to the League of Nations as, for example, over the issues of the Ruhr invasion and the Corfu Incident. Even during the 1920s, therefore, many member states were already expressing concern that the League provided no real guarantee of international peace and security.

Weaknesses of the League

Even during the 1920s, therefore, when the League enjoyed some success in resolving international disputes, it was clear that its powers and authority were limited. There were a number of reasons for the League's weakness.

Created by an unpopular peace settlement

The League emerged from the treaties agreed at the Paris peace settlement. From the outset, therefore, the League was closely associated with treaties that were unpopular in many countries and which inevitably led to numerous territorial disputes. To many observers, the League of Nations was an organisation created by, and for the benefit of, the First World War's victorious nations – a perception reinforced by the fact that none of the defeated nations was initially allowed to join.

Member states

The League of Nations was conceived as a global organisation. However, of the world's major powers, only Britain, France, Italy and Japan were members of the League throughout the 1920s. Germany was not allowed to join until 1926, the USSR did not become a member until 1934 and the USA was never a member.

The USA's refusal to join the League of Nations

It is, perhaps, the supreme irony that the USA rejected the post-war peace settlement and the League of Nations, despite the fact that its president had been so instrumental in the creation of both. By the time Wilson returned to the USA from the Paris Peace Conference, the Republican Party had gained control of the Senate.

Most Republican senators shared the views of Henry Cabot Lodge:

> The independence of the USA is not only precious to ourselves but to the world . . . I have always loved one flag and I cannot share that devotion with a mongrel banner created for a League. Internationalism . . . is to me repulsive . . . The USA is the world's best hope, but if you fetter her in the interests and quarrels of other nations and the intrigues of Europe, you will destroy her power and endanger her very existence . . . We would not have our country's vigour exhausted or her moral force abated by everlasting meddling and muddling in every quarrel which afflicts the world.
>
> **Speech by Senator Henry Cabot Lodge to the Senate Foreign Relations Committee, on 12 August 1919**

For all Wilson's attempts to convince the American people of the League's importance, both to the world in general and to the USA in particular, the Senate voted against him on 19 November 1919. To most Americans, the best way of ensuring that the USA did not become involved in another war was a return to the policy of isolationism. The USA's refusal to join the League was a significant blow to its prospects of success, reducing both its credibility and its financial security.

The significance of the USA's refusal to join the League of Nations is evident in a cartoon published in a British magazine in 1919 (Figure 2.12).

Other organisations

The authority of the League of Nations was frequently undermined. For example, the Council of Ambassadors had been established to administer the post-war treaties until such time as the League of Nations was fully operational. In reality, it continued to function until 1931, and on several occasions disagreed with, and took precedence over, the League's decisions (as in the Corfu Incident). Similarly, countries often chose to ignore the League entirely, preferring to make separate agreements, such as the Locarno Treaties of 1925.

The need for unanimity

The Covenant of the League of Nations required that decisions, both within the General Assembly and the Council, must be unanimous. It was, perhaps,

ACTIVITY 2.24

1 Why did Senator Henry Cabot Lodge oppose US membership of the League of Nations?

2 Analyse the meaning of the cartoon. In particular, consider the following:

- How is the USA represented and what does this imply?
- In what ways is the wording on the sign to the left of the bridge sarcastic?
- What do you notice about the names on the bridge?
- What is significant about the keystone?

Did the cartoonist believe that the League of Nations could succeed without the involvement of the USA?

THE GAP IN THE BRIDGE.

Figure 2.12: 'The Gap in the Bridge', *Punch*, 10 December 1919

inevitable that it should do so. Countries would clearly not be willing to accept the possibility that their actions might be determined by the decisions of other nations. Thus, the requirement for unanimity provided them with the right of veto – the ability to prevent a decision being reached and acted upon. Moreover, this need for everyone to be in agreement slowed down the League's decision-making process, especially since many decisions required ratification by the General Assembly, which met only once a year. As a result, the League appeared both slow and indecisive.

Collective security

The League's ability to confront aggression and threats to world peace was entirely dependent upon the notion of collective security – League members working together to impose economic sanctions or, in the worst case situation, taking military action. This is reflected in Article 11 of the Covenant, which states 'Any war or threat of war, whether immediately affecting any of the Members of the League or not, is hereby declared a matter of concern to the whole League, and the League shall take any action that may be deemed wise and effectual to safeguard the peace of nations.'

In the absence of its own army, the League expected member states to provide troops if military action became necessary (Article 16). However, a resolution passed in 1923 established that each member state could decide for itself whether or not to provide armed forces in a crisis. This clearly undermined the entire principle on which collective security was based. In both Britain and France, where public opinion was strongly anti-war, there was an understandable reluctance to commit to military action. Governments in both countries believed that they were militarily weak and that war must be avoided at all costs.

National interests

At times, countries discovered that their commitments to the League of Nations were at odds with their own national interests. In 1921, for example, the League took no action in response to Poland's conflict with the USSR because neither Britain nor France had any desire to help a country that was not a member of the League and whose communist government they saw as a threat. Similarly, France would clearly not endorse any League action against its own occupation of the Ruhr in 1923.

In the final analysis, the League of Nations was only as strong as the willingness of its member states to support it. That willingness was often found wanting.

> **●●● THINK LIKE A HISTORIAN**
>
> Although the League of Nations ceased to exist in 1946, it was replaced by the United Nations (UN), which continues to work in the interests of international peace and cooperation. All independent sovereign countries are members of the UN.
>
> Think of some current or recent situations in which a country has put its own national interests ahead of its commitment to the UN. Consider each situation from (a) the country's point of view and (b) the needs of international peace.

Role and impact of the agencies

In many ways, the League's most successful achievements during the 1920s resulted from the work of its agencies.

The International Labour Organization (ILO)

The International Labour Organization was created by and financed through the League of Nations. Under the leadership of Frenchman Albert Thomas, the ILO enjoyed some success in improving working conditions around the world. Governments were persuaded to fix maximum working hours (per day and per week), to establish minimum wage levels, to provide sickness and unemployment benefits and to introduce old-age pensions. In 1928, for example, the ILO's decision to establish a minimum wage was ratified by 77 countries. By the end of the 1920s, social security schemes were common in Europe. Such measures made an enormous difference to the lives of underprivileged people. However, not all of the ILO's decisions were successfully implemented, For example, its attempts to ban night work and ensure that workers received paid holidays were rejected, one delegate arguing that such schemes would require his country 'to commit industrial suicide'.

The International Commission for Refugees

Under its director, the Norwegian Fridtjof Nansen, the International Commission for Refugees helped to resettle over half a million former prisoners of war who had been stranded in Russia at the end of the First World War. In 1922, the Commission was responsible for introducing the Nansen passport, the first internationally recognised identity card for stateless refugees. When violence erupted in Turkey during 1923, the Commission helped to find homes, food and jobs for almost one-and-a-half million refugees, working closely with other agencies to prevent the spread of diseases such as typhoid and cholera. In 1928, the International Commission was awarded the Nobel Peace Prize for its efforts to introduce the Nansen passport.

The Health Organization

In addition to dealing with specific problems, such as the health risks posed by large numbers of refugees in Turkey, the Health Organization achieved a great deal in investigating the causes and possible preventions of epidemics. It was successful in combating a typhus epidemic in Russia, and carried out research on diseases such as leprosy. Following its research, vaccines were introduced worldwide for diseases such as tuberculosis, diphtheria and tetanus.

The Mandates Commission

The Mandates Commission supervised the territories that had been taken from Germany and Turkey at the end of the First World War. Supervision was intended to ensure that these territories were well-governed and adequately prepared for their own independence. For example, the Commission facilitated the League's efficient administration of the Saar region until 1935, and then arranged a plebiscite in which the local people voted to return to Germany. The Commission demanded regular reports from the mandatory powers (Britain, France and Belgium) in order to ensure that they were following the strict rules laid down by the League. While the Commission did not have the power to carry out inspections to ensure the accuracy of these reports, there is clear evidence that the mandatory powers treated these territories differently from their other overseas possessions. For example, Britain allowed its mandate of Tanganyika to purchase American goods that were cheaper than their British equivalent. In truth, however, little was done to prepare these territories for future independence.

Financial assistance

The League of Nations was able to provide vital financial assistance to many countries facing economic difficulties. For example, Austria and Hungary were facing bankruptcy; the League arranged loans for the two nations, and sent commissioners to offer advice on how best to spend the money (1922–23). This set Austria and Hungary on the path to economic recovery.

Other achievements

The League of Nations played a significant role in responding to issues such as the exploitation of women and children, drug trafficking and slavery. It helped to free 200 000 slaves in places such as Sierra Leone and Burma. In 1930, the League investigated rumours of forced labour in the independent African state of Liberia, concluding that the president, Charles D. B. King, and senior government officials were guilty of exploiting the situation. The president was forced to resign and the League of Nations insisted that the new government carry out reforms.

These agencies continued to carry out impressive and important work during the 1930s. It is a fitting tribute to their achievements that, when the United Nations was established at the end of the Second World War, it retained many of the agencies. The ILO still exists, the United Nation's High Commissioner for Refugees (UNHCR) continues to address the problem of refugees, and the World Health Organization (WHO) carries on the vital work of seeking solutions to international health issues.

ACTIVITY 2.25

In pairs or small groups, make lists to demonstrate how the League of Nations was attempting to achieve each of its three stated aims:
- preventing future wars
- administering the post-First World War settlements
- promoting international cooperation.

How successful do you think the League of Nations was during the 1920s? Complete the following table to help you reach a conclusion

What criteria are you going to use in order to evaluate how successful the League was?	
Evidence of success based on your chosen criteria	
Evidence of failure based on your chosen criteria	

In a whole-class seminar:
- compare lists
- discuss how far the League of Nations was successfully achieving its aims.

Reflection: Review your answer to this activity. What evidence would you expect to see if the League of Nations was successfully achieving its aims?

Exam-style questions

Source analysis questions

Read all four sources and then answer both parts of question 1.

The American debate on whether to join the League of Nations, 1919–20

SOURCE A

I have always been a sincere advocate of an agreement between the leading nations to set up the necessary international machinery that would bring about a practical abolition of war. But it is inadvisable to join a League of Nations that would make it necessary for the USA to maintain a standing army. This would be needed to support new and independent governments that it is intended to establish among semi-civilized people. This could involve the USA in wars in Europe, Asia and elsewhere. Rather, we should disarm the defeated nations and then follow the example by disarming ourselves. If the world is disarmed there will be no more world wars. Nations should be left entirely independent to decide their own affairs.

A letter from Senator George Norris (Republican) to an American newspaper, the Nebraska State Journal, *18 March 1918*

SOURCE B

The Republicans are trying to defeat the plan for a League of Nations, which, if organised, will reduce military armament among all the great powers, and make war almost, if not, completely impossible. If the Senate destroys the League of Nations, then the USA must begin at once to arm on a greater scale than any other nation in the world, because we must be strong enough to beat all comers. This means a navy in the Atlantic big enough to overcome the combined navies of at least three European powers. It means a navy in the Pacific bigger than Japan. It means the greatest standing army we have ever had. If we want to promote human slaughter and increase taxation, we should defeat the League of Nations. If we must abandon the glorious ideas of peace for which this nation has always stood, we must do so with full knowledge that the alternative is wholesale preparation for war.

Public speech by Senator William G. McAdoo (Democrat), 1919

SOURCE C

The argument that the formation of a League of Nations would prevent war sounds fine, but would it hold good? In my opinion, the ultimate result of such a League would involve us in disputes which should (except for us being a member of the League) not concern us. Why should we make ourselves party to an agreement which would compel us to help protect the interests of a nation, such as Britain, whose dominions are world-wide and, therefore, the more likely to foster trouble? Let us follow the advice of our great leaders and 'keep out of entangling alliances'.

Letter to an American newspaper, the Evening Public Ledger *(Philadelphia), 28 March 1919*

SOURCE D

I am in favour of the League of Nations Covenant, of which our gallant and noble President is the proposer. I believe Mr Wilson will be able to accomplish the fulfilment of the Covenant despite all opposition. The League of Nations idea is a very delicate matter to handle, and no-one but our President, who possesses the necessary qualities, could really be at the head of it. The abuse and discredit given to our President by the Republicans would make one imagine that these men lack intelligence. They know the Covenant is good for humanity; they should boost the League instead of criticising it. Their criticism of every move President Wilson makes implies that they are foolish or influenced by political motives. The League of Nations will alleviate all unrest, discontent and anxiety, and will make the world safe for democracy. The League would promote commerce, civilisation and brotherly love. I sincerely hope our President sees his way clear, and happy will I be the day the Covenant is accomplished and put into operation.

Letter to an American newspaper, the Evening Public Ledger *(Philadelphia), 28 March 1919*

1 **a** Compare and contrast the views of Senators Norris (Source A) and McAdoo (Source B) on whether the USA should become a member of the League of Nations.

b How far do Sources A to D support the view that the League of Nations would be more likely to cause wars than prevent them?

Essay based questions
Answer both parts of the questions below.

2 **a** Explain why the Dawes Plan was developed in 1924.

b 'The Locarno Treaties of 1925 greatly reduced tension between European nations.' How far do you agree?

3 **a** Explain why France occupied the Ruhr region of Germany in 1923.

b How successful was the USSR in its attempts to establish improved relations with the rest of Europe during the 1920s?

Sample answers
Look carefully at these extracts from speeches made by the two candidates in the 1920 US presidential election.

SOURCE A

Can any American be willing to merge our nationality into internationality? We do not mean to live within and for ourselves alone, but we do mean to hold our ideals safe from foreign interference. Americans will not fail civilisation in the advancement of peace. We are willing to give, but we resent demand. We desire a world relationship which will maintain peace through justice rather than force, yet still hold us free from menacing involvement. It is better to be the free agents of international justice than to be shackled by a written agreement which surrenders our freedom of action and gives the League the right to proclaim America's duty to the world. No surrender of rights to a world council should ever summon Americans to war. There is sanctity in that right which we will not surrender.

Public speech by Senator Warren G. Harding (Republican), 1919

93

SOURCE B

The finest impulses of humanity, rising above national lines, seek to make another war impossible. Under the old order of international anarchy, war came overnight and the world was on fire before we knew it. It sickens our senses to think of another war. The League of Nations plans to make this impossible. Shall we act together with the free nations of the world in setting up a tribunal which would avoid war in the future? Shall we participate in the advancement of peace, or shall we follow the old paths trod by the nations of Europe, paths which always led to fields of blood? Shall we unite with our former allies to make the League effective, or shall we play a lone hand in the world, guarding our isolation with a huge army and an ever-increasing navy with all the consequent burdens of taxation? I am in favour of going into the League of Nations.

Public speech by Senator James M. Cox (Democrat), 1920

Now look at this sample answer to the question:

Compare and contrast the views expressed by Senators Harding and Cox regarding the role that the USA should play in helping to maintain future world peace.

The two senators agree that the USA should play a role in helping to maintain future world peace. Harding says that 'America will not fail civilisation in the advancement of peace'. Cox says that the USA should work together with other nations to 'avoid war in the future'.

However, they disagree on the issue of whether the USA should join the League of Nations. Harding is clearly opposed to the USA joining the League. He argues that joining the League would lead to 'foreign interference' in American affairs and the USA being forced into 'menacing involvement'. He says that the USA should remain 'free agents', rather than being 'shackled' to an agreement which would force the USA to take action against its will. In particular, he is concerned that the USA might be forced to take part in war on the instructions of the League.

Cox takes the opposite view. He argues that the League of Nations would make 'another war impossible'. Joining the League would enable the USA to 'participate in the advancement of peace'. The sentence 'shall we unite with our former allies to make the League effective' implies that the League would be likely to fail without American involvement. Cox claims that, if the USA did not join the League, it would need to enhance its army and navy in order to guarantee its own protection – this would not only mean increased taxation, but could also lead to the kind of arms race with other countries which led to the First World War.

Therefore, the two senators agree that it is important for the USA to help preserve world peace, but disagree about the best way to achieve this.

This answer is based on sound understanding of the arguments put forward by the two senators. It accurately identifies areas of agreement and disagreement, backed up by well-selected supporting evidence.

However, there is very little evaluation. This aspect could have been improved in two ways.

1 **Putting the two speeches into context** – Involvement in the First World War had become very unpopular in the USA. President Wilson (Democrat) argued that the best way of avoiding involvement in another war was for the USA to ratify the Paris Peace Settlement and join the League of Nations. Most Democrats, such as Senator Cox, supported this view. However, by the time Wilson returned from Paris, the Republican Party had gained control of the Senate. Most Republicans, such as Harding, opposed both the Paris Peace Settlement and US membership of the League of Nations. The two speeches reflect this debate. Harding was supporting the cause of isolationism, whereas Cox was in favour of internationalism. Both were seeking support from the American public in the forthcoming presidential election.

2 **Analysing the methods used by the two senators in attempting to gain support for their views** – Harding focuses on American nationalism and independence, both of which he claims were threatened by membership of the League of Nations. He uses language very skilfully to emphasise this threat – e.g. foreign interference, menacing involvement, shackled, surrender, resent demand, freedom of action. Cox focuses on the USA's responsibility to humanity and, like Harding, uses emotive language to support his argument – for example, 'fields of blood', 'finest impulses of humanity', 'participate in the advancement of peace'. Both speeches contain questions, each of which is clearly designed to have only one possible answer and, therefore, help to shape public opinion.

Taking on board all of these comments, write your own answer to the question.

ACTIVITY 2.26

Now look carefully at a cartoon published in a US newspaper *c.*1920 (Figure 2.13).

a Regarding the League of Nations, do you think the cartoonist agreed with Harding or Cox? Explain your answer.

b What did the cartoonist believe were the implications for the League of Nations of the USA's refusal to become a member? Explain your answer.

THE ACCUSER

Figure 2.13: Cartoon, *World Journal Tribune*, 22 March 1920

Summary

After working through this chapter, make sure you understand the following key points:

- the problems involved in creating a peace settlement at the end of the First World War
- details of the five treaties which comprised the Paris peace settlement
- the effects of the Paris peace settlement on international relations
- the impact of the Bolshevik revolution in Russia
- the impact of the USA's decision to return to an isolationist foreign policy
- attempts to ease international tension in the period from 1920 to 1933
- the establishment and early development of the League of Nations.

Further reading

Collier, M. (2009). *From Kaiser to Führer: Germany 1900–45*. **Edexcel.** Chapters 4 and 5 are useful for understanding the problems faced by Germany during the 1920s.

Goldstein, E. (2002). *The First World War Peace Settlements, 1919–25*. **Routledge.** A relatively short book containing some useful detail and analysis. Particularly relevant are: Chapter 1 on the background to the Paris Peace Conference, Chapter 2 on the Conference itself, Chapter 3 on the impact of the Paris Peace Settlement on Europe and Chapter 8 on the Locarno Treaties.

Henig, R. (1995). *Versailles and After*. **Routledge.** A relatively short book that is well worth reading in its entirety.

Henig, R. (2010). *The League of Nations*. **Haus.** Chapters 1–4 provide detailed information and analysis about the founding of the League of Nations and its development during the 1920s.

Housden, M. (2011). *The League of Nations and The Organisation of Peace*. **Longman.** Especially useful are Chapter 1 on the background to the establishment of the League and Chapter 3 on the League's early successes.

Kearey, K. and Waller, S. (2015). *International Relations and Global Conflict c1890–1941*. **Oxford University Press.** Chapter 14 provides useful information about the Paris Peace Conference. Chapters 15 and 16 deal with international tensions in the period 1919–23. Chapter 17 explains why tensions were reduced after 1923.

Robson, M. (2015). *Italy: The Rise of Fascism 1896–1946*. **Hodder.** The first two sections of Chapter 8 outline the aims and international implications of Mussolini's foreign policy during the 1920s.

Sharp, A. (2008). *The Versailles Settlement: Peacemaking in Paris 1919*. **MacMillan.** Chapter 2 is useful on the Paris Peace Conference, while Chapters 4 and 5 deal with various aspects of the Treaty of Versailles.

Williamson, D. (2015). *War and Peace: International Relations 1890–1945*. **Hodder.** Chapter 5 deals with the Paris peace settlement and international tension 1919–23. Chapter 6 is useful for understanding why relations improved in the later 1920s.

50Minutes.com. The Treaty of Versailles: The Treaty that Marked the End of World War I (50 Minutes.Com 2017) A very short account of the Treaty of Versailles, which provides useful detail on the main people involved and their impact on negotiations.

Chapter 3
The League of Nations and international relations in the 1930s

Learning Objectives:

In this chapter, you will:

- learn about the political impact of the Great Depression, and the rise of dictatorships that pursued aggressive foreign policies
- learn about the failure of collective security, and the League of Nations' inability to take effective action in response to international aggression
- understand the foreign policies adopted by Britain and France during the 1930s, and their impact on international relations
- analyse the reasons why the Second World War broke out in 1939, just 20 years after the conclusion of the 'war to end all wars'.

Timeline

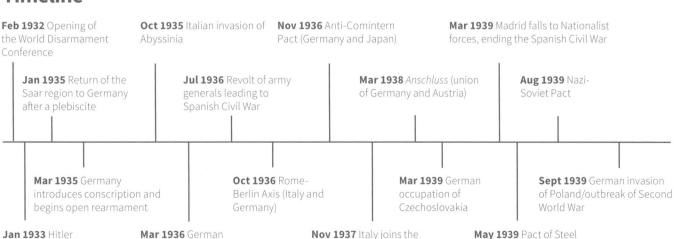

Feb 1932 Opening of the World Disarmament Conference

Oct 1935 Italian invasion of Abyssinia

Nov 1936 Anti-Comintern Pact (Germany and Japan)

Mar 1939 Madrid falls to Nationalist forces, ending the Spanish Civil War

Jan 1935 Return of the Saar region to Germany after a plebiscite

Jul 1936 Revolt of army generals leading to Spanish Civil War

Mar 1938 *Anschluss* (union of Germany and Austria)

Aug 1939 Nazi-Soviet Pact

Mar 1935 Germany introduces conscription and begins open rearmament

Oct 1936 Rome-Berlin Axis (Italy and Germany)

Mar 1939 German occupation of Czechoslovakia

Sept 1939 German invasion of Poland/outbreak of Second World War

Jan 1933 Hitler becomes Chancellor of Germany

Mar 1936 German occupation of the Rhineland

Nov 1937 Italy joins the Anti-Comintern Pact with Germany and Japan

May 1939 Pact of Steel (Italy and Germany)

Before You Start

During the 1920s there had been many attempts to improve international relations. By 1930, however, many problems still remained. For example:

- France still distrusted and feared Germany
- Germany still resented the harsh terms imposed by the Treaty of Versailles
- the USA's return to isolationism undermined the authority of the League of Nations.

1 Complete this list by identifying other issues that posed a threat to good international relations by 1930.

2 Write a sentence about each of the issues you have identified, explaining how you assess its relative importance.

3 Compare and discuss your lists in pairs or small groups.

Introduction

The gradual improvement in international relations that characterised the period from 1924 to 1929 owed much to the USA's economic strength. For example, France accepted the Dawes Plan and withdrew from the Ruhr because American loans provided the guarantee that Germany would meet its reparations requirements. This greatly reduced tensions between the major European nations, leading to agreements at the Locarno Conference in 1925 that seemed to guarantee future peace in Europe.

In October 1929, the USA's post-First World War economic boom ended in sudden and dramatic fashion. This led to the Great Depression, which was to have catastrophic repercussions worldwide. Large-scale unemployment led to social unrest and political extremism. Even in Britain, with its long tradition of **constitutional government**, extremist groups seemed to pose a real threat to democracy. The Communist Party of Great Britain, founded in 1920, grew in popularity, while the British Union of Fascists was established in 1932. Although **democracy** was able to survive in Britain, other countries with less stable constitutions were unable to resist the pressures of extremism.

KEY TERMS

Constitutional government: a system in which the powers of government are limited by a written constitution, as in the USA, or by an established political method and series of conventions, as in Britain. In both forms, the legality of what government does can be challenged and even overturned in independent law courts.

Democracy: a system of government in which the citizens exercise power by electing representatives to form a legislative body, such as a parliament.

As early as 1922, Benito Mussolini had led his Fascist Party to power in Italy. By 1933, Adolf Hitler had gained supremacy for his Nazi Party in Germany. Between 1936 and 1939 the rival forces of fascism, communism and democracy fought out a long and bloody war for control of Spain, culminating in victory for General Francisco Franco's nationalist and fascist forces. Mussolini, Hitler and Franco rapidly removed political opposition, establishing dictatorships in which they had ultimate control over the fate of their countries. By 1932, civilian and democratic forces had lost control of the political system in Japan, and the army was in charge. Following Lenin's death in 1924, Joseph Stalin set about removing his political rivals in Soviet Russia. By 1930, he had established himself as a dictator in the USSR.

The emergence of these dictatorships had a major impact on international relations. Fear of communism across the rest of Europe meant, effectively, that Soviet Russia was isolated, and therefore vulnerable. The alliance between Britain, France and Russia, which had proved so vital to success in the First World War, was no longer possible. The ultra-nationalist and aggressive foreign policies pursued by Hitler and Mussolini posed a significant threat, not only to the USSR, but also to other European countries. Japanese expansionism in Asia posed a threat to the interests of the USA and the other Western powers. The Spanish Civil War was a sign of things to come.

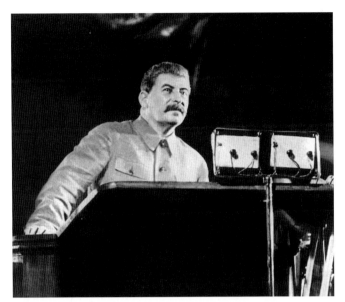

Figure 3.1: Soviet leader, Joseph Stalin (1878–1953). What impression does this photograph give of Stalin as a leader?

3.1 How did the rise of extremism affect international relations?

Impact of the Great Depression on political ideologies

The US economy, seemingly so strong and influential, collapsed in 1929. American industries were heavily dependent on the export market, their output vastly exceeding what could be sold within the USA itself. The USA practised protectionism, imposing high taxes on foreign imports in order to protect its own industries from competition. This effectively prevented other countries from making profits by selling their goods within the USA. Without such profits, these countries were increasingly unable to afford American products. In retaliation, some countries began to impose high taxes on American imports. As a result, foreign demand for American goods fell. As investors realised the potential implications of this, they rushed to sell their **shares**, creating a panic on the New York stock exchange on Wall Street. By 29 October 1929 – 'Black Friday' – shares in hundreds of businesses had become worthless. Thousands of American citizens were financially ruined. Many banks were forced to close down as people rushed to withdraw their savings. This was the Wall Street Crash. The Great Depression that followed affected not just the USA, but the whole world.

As demand for American products fell, manufacturers began to produce less. This meant that many workers lost their jobs at a time when there was no **unemployment benefit**. As more and more families were forced to reduce their spending, the demand for goods fell still further, leading to even more unemployment. This vicious circle continued, spiralling the USA deeper and deeper into an economic depression that lasted until the outbreak of the Second World War in 1939.

Other countries were soon affected, largely because their prosperity was dependent on American loans. As soon as the crash came, the loans stopped. The German economy immediately collapsed and Germany was no longer able to make reparation repayments. This, in turn, affected Britain, France and Italy, which relied on reparations to repay their own debts to the USA and to maintain their economic stability.

As international trade declined, all industrialised countries suffered from the same economic problems. Spiralling **deflation** affected Europe and Japan alike. High unemployment quickly followed, leading to social unrest. Everywhere, the threat of revolution seemed greater than ever before. It is in such circumstances that political extremism thrives. As poverty and hardship increased, the poor became disenchanted with elected governments, which they believed to be incapable of solving their problems, or were even responsible for them. Instead they adopted extremist political ideas, such as those of the communists and the fascists. At the same time, many middle-class people grew increasingly concerned about the adverse effects of social disorder and the threat of revolution on their livelihoods. They sought governments capable of restoring order and protecting their interests.

> ### KEY TERMS
>
> **Shares:** a means of investing money in businesses. Shares in a successful business rise in value. Investors aim to buy shares at low prices and then sell them when the value rises.
>
> **Unemployment benefit:** payments made by a state to people who are unable to find a job.
>
> **Deflation:** a general decline in prices, caused by a reduction in the supply of money and credit. During the Great Depression, deflation spiralled out of control. As prices of their products fell, employers reduced the wages of their workers, leading to a further downward turn in prices. As unemployment increased, fewer people were able to buy products, leading to a further reduction in prices. Many businesses collapsed.

Even in countries with well-established forms of constitutional government, such as Britain, France and the USA, support for fascist and communist organisations grew during the 1930s. In these countries, democracy was able to survive. However, in countries that lacked a strong democratic tradition, such as Germany, Japan and Spain, democratic forms of government collapsed.

ADOLF HITLER (1889–1945)

Austrian-born Hitler moved to Munich in 1913 and won medals for bravery in the First World War. He later adopted an extreme right-wing nationalist outlook and joined the German Workers' Party (later the Nazi Party). After years of commanding only a tiny amount of support, Hitler's party grew in popularity and he was appointed Chancellor of Germany in 1933, quickly establishing a dictatorship. His policies contributed to the outbreak of the Second World War in 1939.

The impact of the Great Depression on political extremism is most clearly evident in **Adolf Hitler**'s rise to power in Germany. As just one more unemployed soldier with a limited education and little hope of finding employment, Hitler seemed an unlikely political leader. However, his skill in delivering frenzied, almost hypnotic, speeches gained him a small following, and by 1921 he had become the leader of the National Socialist German Workers' Party (Nazis). To begin with, its members were mainly unemployed youths and soldiers returning from the First World War. Disenchanted and with little hope for the future, these men might have turned to communism, but instead they were drawn to Hitler's magnetic speeches. In spite of the falsity of his arguments, many people found the simplicity of them appealing.

Hitler was heavily critical of Germany's democratic post-war Weimar constitution. With so many political parties, he argued, none of them could gain an overall

majority in elections, leading to weak governments and the growing threat of communist revolution. He claimed that politicians had betrayed the country by seeking peace when Germany could still have won the First World War. These same politicians had agreed to the humiliating Treaty of Versailles, which, he stressed, was the cause of all Germany's post-war problems.

Well organised and violent gangs of Nazi supporters, known as **Stormtroopers**, attacked the meetings of rival political parties, and in 1923 the Nazi Party attempted a 'national revolution,' which is referred to as the Munich Putsch. This was easily put down, and Hitler was arrested and sentenced to prison.

KEY TERM

Stormtroopers: Nazi gangs that specifically used violence against Hitler's opponents. Far from hiding these violent methods, Hitler boasted about them. Worried about the possibility of a communist revolution, the authorities did little to stop them. When the head of the Munich police force was told that such gangs were causing bloodshed throughout the city, he replied that it was a pity there were not more of them.

Upon his release, Hitler found Germany somewhat revitalised. American loans under the Dawes Plan (1924) had helped to stabilise the economy, and Germany was forging better relations with other European nations through the Locarno Treaties. While this was good for the country, it did not bode well for Hitler's future success. With the situation improving in Germany, there would be less support for a political party built on extremist views. In the May 1928 elections, the Nazi Party gained only 810 000 votes out of the 31 million cast.

It was the Wall Street Crash and the ensuing worldwide depression that breathed new life into Hitler's political career. American loans, on which Germany's new prosperity was entirely dependent, suddenly stopped. The country was plunged back into a period of economic chaos and massive unemployment. Support for the Nazis began to grow, and in the elections of 1932 the Party gained 37% of the total votes cast. Although they still did not have an overall majority in the Reichstag (the German parliament), the Nazis had become the largest single party. On 30 January 1933, Hitler was appointed Chancellor of Germany.

Hitler had become Chancellor of Germany through legal and constitutional means, by exploiting the very weaknesses within the German constitution that he had criticised so vehemently. Once in the position of chancellor, it did not take Hitler long to remove all political opposition, end the constitution through which he had been elected and establish the **Third Reich**. Germany became a one-party, **totalitarian** state founded on extreme nationalism and the use of violence to maintain order and obedience. If Mussolini had established the world's first fascist state in Italy, Hitler had created the second.

KEY TERMS

Third Reich: the term used by Hitler that linked the present with Germany's past glories. The First Reich (empire) was the Holy Roman Empire (962–1806). The Second Reich followed the unification of Germany in 1871 and lasted until 1918.

Totalitarian: a system of government that is centralised, dictatorial and requires complete subservience to the state.

ACTIVITY 3.1

Working in pairs, make a list of reasons to explain why the Wall Street Crash led to worldwide social, economic and political chaos. Create a mind map out of this list, demonstrating how the different reasons were interconnected.

Impact of the rise of dictatorships on relations between powers

By 1933, four of the world's leading nations – Italy, the USSR, Germany and Japan – were governed by dictatorships through which the state controlled all aspects of life. These dictatorships maintained popular support by the extensive use of censorship and **propaganda**, crushing opposition through control over the armed forces. This clearly had an enormous impact on the lives of people living in those countries, but it also had an adverse effect on international relations. Tensions between the major powers, which had been gradually reduced during the 1920s, were renewed in the wake of the Great Depression and the establishment of dictatorships.

KEY TERM

Propaganda: the communication of a political or other message by appealing to people's emotions rather than their reason, encouraging them to be excited rather than to think.

Nazism in Germany

Hitler's rise to power was a major cause of concern across Europe. Although the issue of reparations had caused friction with other countries, particularly France, Germany had gradually developed better foreign relations during the late 1920s. This was particularly evident at the Locarno Conference in 1925, and culminated in Germany being admitted to the League of Nations the following year. It was evident that Hitler had no intention of continuing the policies that had made this possible. He had been making his views very clear since the early 1920s – he wanted Germany to be restored to its rightful position as a major European power and, in particular, to destroy the Treaty of Versailles. Such views were enormously popular in Germany.

While Hitler's statements were popular in Germany, they caused great alarm elsewhere in Europe. The French were particularly concerned. They had consistently aimed to keep Germany weak as a safeguard against any future German attack against France. A rearmed and powerful Germany would pose a threat to French security. In the late 1920s, France had been willing to compromise and develop friendly relations with Germany. With Hitler's rise to power, France reverted to the hard-line approach towards Germany that it had adopted in the period from 1919 to 1924.

Italy also had reason to fear Hitler's intentions, particularly his desire to form a union between Germany and Austria. One of Mussolini's major concerns was the post-First World War weakness of Austria. As a neighbouring nation, Austria's lack of political, economic and military strength meant that it would provide Italy with little protection should Germany regain its power and show signs of aggression. Indeed, a revival of German military strength and ambition seemed increasingly likely when Hitler's Nazi Party gained power. Consequently, Mussolini provided support to the anti-Nazi Austrian government of Chancellor Engelbert Dollfuss. When Dollfuss was murdered by Austrian Nazis in July 1934, Mussolini sent Italian troops to the border to prevent a suspected German invasion of Austria. Italy's actions were heavily praised in France and Britain, which increasingly viewed Mussolini as a vital ally against Hitler's Germany.

Stalin's Russia also had reason to be concerned by Hitler's rise to power. As the only communist country, Russia felt both isolated and vulnerable. Its only formal alliance was that with Germany, which began with the Treaty of Rapallo in 1922. In view of the German Nazi Party's strongly anti-communist views, this relationship was now under threat.

So too was Russian security. While in prison following the failed 'national revolution' in 1923, Hitler had written *Mein Kampf* (My Struggle), a book in which he outlined his political philosophy. In this book, Hitler argued that the German population was too large for the boundaries in which it was constrained. His stated solution was *Lebensraum* (living space), whereby Germany would take land in the east to provide more space for the expanding German population. The implication was clear – Hitler's long-term intention was to take land from both Poland and the USSR.

In an attempt to ensure the security of the USSR against Hitler's Germany, Stalin consistently tried to secure agreements with Britain and France. His attempts failed. Amid the social and economic chaos of the Great Depression, political stability was under threat in both Britain and France. Extremist political parties were growing in popularity, and revolution seemed a distinct possibility. Under these circumstances, the British and French governments viewed Stalin's communist Russia with distrust and fear. Indeed, most British politicians saw Stalin's Russia as a bigger threat than Hitler's Germany.

ACTIVITY 3.2

Look carefully at Hitler's foreign policy aims.

  a Why would they be popular in Germany?
  b Why would they cause concern elsewhere in Europe?
  c List the actions that Hitler would have to take in order to achieve these aims.

Military dictatorship in Japan

Increased international tension resulting from the rise of dictatorships was not confined to Europe. In countries that lacked a strong democratic tradition, existing forms of government found it impossible to cope. In Japan, a democratic form of government had only existed since 1889. Accustomed to a system in which the emperor held supreme power, the Japanese people had little respect for parliamentary democracy. They believed that politicians were weak, corrupt and open to bribery. As unemployment and poverty grew alarmingly following the Wall Street Crash, the Japanese blamed the elected government for their misfortunes. With social unrest increasing, the armed forces took control and the country became a military dictatorship.

In September 1931, against the wishes of Japan's elected government, elements of the Japanese army

had mobilised and taken control over the whole of Manchuria, part of China. This event led to the collapse of the Japanese democracy. With the democratically elected government unable to control Japan's armed forces, Emperor Hirohito replaced it with a government of National Unity under Admiral Makoto Saitō. Japan had become a military dictatorship, with the clear intention of further expansion in Asia. This caused great concern in a weak, unstable and vulnerable China, but it also threatened the regional interests of European nations and the USA.

In March 1933, Japan withdrew from the League of Nations and cancelled the arms limitations agreements made at the Washington Naval Conference of 1921–22 (see Chapter 2.2). In November 1936, Japan formed an alliance with Germany, known as the Anti-Comintern Pact. The Comintern, which had been established by the USSR's Bolshevik government to encourage worldwide communist revolution, was perceived as a threat by the governments of both Germany and Japan. In theory, the Anti-Comintern Pact was a defensive alliance, the governments of Germany and Japan agreeing to provide mutual support in the event of any future attack on either of them by the USSR. However, the union of two dictatorships, both following aggressive foreign policies, inevitably caused suspicion and concern internationally. The fact that Germany formally recognised Japan's control over Manchuria, thereby legitimising Japanese aggression, added to these concerns. The situation became even more intimidating in 1937, when a third dictatorship, that of Mussolini's Italy, joined the Anti-Comintern Pact. The alliance of three dictatorships, all ideologically opposed to communism and all following aggressive foreign policies, posed an obvious threat to the USSR. It also caused alarm in Britain, France and the USA, which perceived the Pact as a direct threat both to international peace and their own democratic institutions. Indeed, by the end of 1937, US President Roosevelt had concluded that the Pact's true intention was aimed at world domination.

Fascism in Italy

By 1934, Mussolini was widely respected abroad. He had fostered good relationships with Britain and France, played an important role at the Locarno Conference, and helped to prevent Hitler's designs on uniting Germany and Austria in 1934. However, in Italy little progress had been made towards achieving the ambitious aims of which he had boasted when he came to power. Italy was neither 'great' nor 'feared'. As a result of the Great Depression, Italy was facing severe economic and social problems, and Mussolini's popularity with the Italian people was declining. Mussolini was in need of a propaganda boost, some spectacular overseas success that would reunite the people behind him. He had seen, and been increasingly impressed by, the way Hitler had set about challenging the Treaty of Versailles, and how this had increased his popularity in Germany. He also saw the weak response to Hitler's aggressive foreign policy by the League of Nations, in particular from Britain and France. Mussolini became increasingly convinced that there was more to be gained by a close relationship with Germany than with Britain and France.

Figure 3.2: Hitler greeting Mussolini during negotiations in the Munich Conference in 1938, published in a German newspaper. What does this image suggest about the relationship between Hitler and Mussolini? Why do you think this photograph was published?

As a result, Mussolini completely reversed the thrust of his foreign policy. Rather than fearing and resisting the resurgence of German power, he began to support and, in many ways, imitate it. The diplomatic approach he had adopted between 1923 and 1934 was replaced by aggression and an even greater desire for glory. In 1935, therefore, Mussolini ordered Italian troops to invade Abyssinia (modern Ethiopia), one of the few parts of Africa not yet under European control. Hitler's Germany was the only major power that was not critical of this action. In 1936, Italy and Germany formed an alliance known as the Rome-Berlin Axis. In 1939, the terms of this alliance were extended in the Pact of Steel, a formal military alliance between Italy and Germany pledging mutual support in the event of war.

Elsewhere in Europe, the Pact of Steel was interpreted as evidence that Germany and Italy were preparing for war. Feeling particularly threatened, the USSR sought closer relations with Britain and France. However, the British and French governments, still fearing the spread of communism and believing the USSR to be an untrustworthy ally, were not prepared to commit to any formal alliance with the Soviets. While deeply concerned about the possible implications of the Pact of Steel, neither Britain nor France felt in a position to take any action against it.

The combined effects of the Great Depression and the development of aggressive dictatorships completely destabilised international relations during the 1930s. Events in Spain were soon to highlight the potentially serious implications of this.

ACTIVITY 3.3

Make notes on the key points of the following

a   Why were European nations and the USA concerned when Japan became a military dictatorship?

b   How would the League of Nations be affected by the fact that both Germany and Japan had withdrawn from it by 1933?

c   Why did Mussolini completely change his foreign policy after 1934?

Remember that including explanations of several relevant factors makes for a better answer than listing just a single point.

Foreign responses to the civil war in Spain

As in Japan and Germany, democracy was a victim of the Great Depression in Spain. Since 1885, Spain had been governed under the **constitutional monarchy** of King Alfonso XIII. This had never been a particularly efficient system, and it came under increasing threat as a result of major political divisions within the country. Many different political groups emerged, each wanting different things.

- Monarchists wanted to preserve the power of the king and the authority of the Roman Catholic Church. Their position was weakened by the fact that there were two different monarchist parties, the Bourbonists and the Carlists, supporting two different branches of the royal family.
- Liberals wanted reform in order to create a modern democracy such as that found in Britain. They argued that the powers enjoyed by the king and, especially, the Church should be reduced.
- Socialists wanted more extensive and more rapid social and economic reform than the Liberals. They argued that the state should take control of industrial and agricultural businesses so that everyone, and not just a few wealthy people, could benefit.
- Communists wanted a Russian-style revolution, involving the seizure of property, the abolition of all other political parties and the development of a classless society.
- Anarchists rejected all forms of authority, supporting a political philosophy that argued that there should be no government at all. Anarchists opposed unequal power relationships and exploitation, including those involving governments, employers and landowners. They advocated local associations that could form free associations with one another.
- Separatists wanted independence for their regions. Many Basques, Catalans, Andalusians, Aragonese and Castilians felt that preserving their regional identity was more important than showing allegiance to Spain as a country.

KEY TERM

Constitutional monarchy: a monarchy in which the king or queen is the head of state, with powers limited by a written constitution or by an established political method or series of conventions, as in Britain. They do not instruct the government. They may appoint or dismiss governments, but only as a result of those governments winning or losing elections, or votes in a national parliament.

ACTIVITY 3.4

It has become a convention to classify political groups as either left wing or right wing.

Left wing	Right wing
Groups that seek some degree of change to existing social, economic and/or political systems.	Groups that value tradition and largely oppose change to existing social, economic and/or political systems.
They generally believe in:	They generally believe in:
• equality • supporting those who cannot support themselves • high taxation to pay for the provision of services by government agencies and to enable some redistribution of wealth from the rich to the poor	• freedom • individuals taking responsibility for themselves • low taxation and minimum government interference

Which of Spain's political groups in the 1930s would you classify as left wing?

Which of Spain's political groups in the 1930s would you classify as right wing?

●●● THINK LIKE A HISTORIAN

Which political groups in your own or other countries would you class as left or right wing, and why?

With so many political groups, each with contrasting aims, it became impossible for any elected government to provide Spain with effective leadership. Convinced of the need for strong and stable government, army officers, under the leadership of Don Miguel Primo de Rivera, carried out a bloodless coup in 1923. With the support of the king, parliamentary government was removed, and Rivera established himself as dictator with absolute power over the country, governing in the absence of elections and a formal constitution.

As the catastrophic social and economic effects of the Great Depression hit Spain, Rivera lost the support of the army and was forced to resign. With him went the period of stability that his dictatorship had provided. Spain was plunged into turmoil again. Fearing bloodshed, King Alfonso abdicated in April 1931, and the new Republic of Spain was proclaimed.

This led to a period of political chaos, during which no single party was able to gain overall control within the Cortes (Spanish parliament). Right-wing groups (the Church, the army, wealthy landowners, industrialists and businessmen) formed a new party, the Spanish Confederation of the Autonomous Right (CEDA). At the same time, left-wing groups (socialists, communists and anarchists) unified in what became known as the Popular Front. It proved impossible for either the CEDA or the Popular Front to form an effective government capable of addressing Spain's social and economic problems. Social order collapsed, and Spain experienced a period of strikes, riots and acts of violence.

In July 1936, a leading right-wing politician, Calvo Sotelo, was killed by police. This convinced right-wing groups that a military dictatorship was the only way to overcome the escalating violence within Spain. On 17 July 1936, a group of army generals began a revolt in Morocco. General **Francisco Franco** was flown in from the Canary Islands to assume leadership of the conflict. Within a day, the revolt had spread to mainland Spain. The Spanish **Civil War** had begun. For three years, Spain was torn apart as Franco's right-wing Nationalists fought with the left-wing Republicans for control of the country. By 1939, the Nationalist victory was assured. Franco established a military dictatorship that incorporated elements of fascism.

FRANCISCO FRANCO (1892–1975)

Franco came from a military family, and by the time of the Spanish Civil War he had risen to the rank of general. He led the nationalist rebels to victory against the republican government in the war. Franco remained in power until his death in 1975.

KEY TERM

Civil war: a war between citizens of the same country.

ACTIVITY 3.5

a Which groups in Spain would be likely to support the revolt led by Franco and why?

b Which groups in Spain would be likely to oppose the revolt led by Franco and why?

If the army had expected a rapid and straightforward seizure of power, it was bitterly disappointed. Many Spaniards were prepared to resist a military takeover. Anarchist trade unionists in Barcelona fought against and defeated the army insurgents, executing their leaders. The government in Madrid, in which the Popular Front held a majority, issued workers with guns, which allowed them to overcome local army regiments fighting for the Nationalists.

By the end of July 1936, Franco's Nationalists controlled much of northern Spain and the southern areas around Cadiz and Seville. The republicans controlled the centre and north-east of Spain, most significantly the major cities of Madrid and Barcelona. Realising that taking full control of Spain was going to prove difficult, Franco appealed to Hitler and Mussolini for assistance, claiming that he was fighting to prevent a communist revolution in Spain.

Neither Hitler nor Mussolini had any real interest in Spain, but both could see the value of having a third fascist state in Europe, especially one that was situated on France's southern border. Consequently, from the outset of the Civil War, both Germany and Italy covertly supplied Franco with military equipment and troops. Their involvement in what was basically a private Spanish affair was to have a major impact on international relations.

Public opinion in the democratic states of Britain, France and the USA was divided. While some people saw Franco as yet another brutal fascist dictator determined to seize power, others perceived him as a vital bulwark against the spread of communism. However, when the republican government of Spain asked for British and French assistance against Franco, politicians in those countries adopted a more pragmatic approach. Desperate to avoid any action that might provoke Germany, Britain and France encouraged the League of Nations to establish a Non-Intervention Committee. This was intended to ensure

105

that no foreign aid entered Spain. Germany and Italy joined the Committee, but both ignored it. Denied British and French assistance, the republicans turned to the only country that seemed prepared to help – the USSR.

By the end of 1936, therefore, the Civil War was no longer an internal Spanish affair. It had become an international battleground for the rival ideologies of fascism and communism.

ACTIVITY 3.6

A Danish journalist, writing in 1937, commented on the League's response to events in Spain:

Look carefully at the journalist's comments.

In pairs or small groups, consider the following statements. Decide whether each statement is true or false, and give reasons for your decision.

The Danish journalist:

a   suggested that, when the Spanish Civil War initially broke out, the League of Nations had no right to intervene

b   believed that the League of Nations had a responsibility to intervene in the Spanish Civil War once foreign countries, such as Italy, became involved

c   claimed that the League of Nations could not intervene in the Spanish Civil War because there was no evidence that other countries, such as Italy, were becoming involved

d   argued that Italy was effectively waging war against Spain

e   opposed fascism

f   was a communist.

> Spain is another victim of Fascist weapons ... Events in Spain presented the Great Powers with a new problem. It was not a war between two countries, but a revolt against a constitutionally elected government, and the question was what attitude the other countries ought to adopt in these circumstances. The Great Powers chose neutrality ... an idea which originated in Britain ... At the beginning the war in Spain was regarded as a civil war. As there is no article in the Covenant to determine the League's attitude in a civil war, the non-intervention agreement was not in conflict with the Covenant. But when in August Italy sent army planes to Spain ... Spain's Foreign Secretary appealed to the Assembly in September. He pointed out the great danger to peace if it should become the custom for a country to support a rebellion in another country with military forces ... without any declaration of war. The Assembly demanded proofs. They were already available in the Non-Intervention committee in London ... Now it was evident that non-intervention was in conflict with the Covenant. In the face of a military attack on one of its members, the League of Nations has no right to declare itself passive. But the Assembly did not move.
>
> **Ellen Hørup, 'The League of Nations and Non-intervention',** *Politiken* **(1937)**

Italy, Germany and the USSR each had their own reasons for interfering in the Spanish Civil War.

• **Italy** – Mussolini was seeking glory, confirmation of his ability to lead Italy back to its former greatness as a major power with a leading role to play in European affairs. While Italy maintained the pretence of supporting the Non-Intervention Committee, it was impossible to hide the presence of some 50 000 Italian troops and over 750 Italian fighter planes around the battlefields of Spain. Within Italy itself, Mussolini boasted of the country's involvement in the Spanish Civil War. It provided propaganda material designed to maintain his popularity with the Italian people. He portrayed himself as leading the fight against communism, which posed a major threat to the stability of Italy.

• **Germany** – The Spanish Civil War provided an opportunity to test the efficiency and capability of Germany's rearmament programme. Moreover, Hitler encouraged Italian involvement in Spain in an effort to distract Mussolini from Germany's own plans to force a union with Austria. To prolong the Spanish Civil War, Germany not only supplied Franco's Nationalists with men and equipment, but Hitler also allowed German firms to sell arms to the Republicans.

- **The USSR** – Soviet leader Stalin also had a vested interest in prolonging the Spanish Civil War. Sensing that Germany posed the biggest threat to the security of the Soviet Union, Stalin had worked hard to maintain good relations with both Britain and France. While he certainly did not want Franco to take control of Spain, which would pose yet another fascist threat to the Soviet Union, he was also aware that neither Britain nor France would tolerate a communist government in Spain. As a result, Stalin authorised just enough aid to ensure that the Republicans could maintain their resistance, but not enough to enable them to gain outright victory.

Oblivious to these diplomatic intrigues, Spain continued to tear itself apart. Franco's well-armed professional soldiers met determined, if disorganised, resistance. The people of Madrid, encouraged by communist leaders such as Dolores Ibárruri, prepared to repel the Nationalist assault. Both men and women enlisted and were given basic training in methods of warfare. They were supported by International Brigades, communist-organised armies of foreign volunteers. British, French, Italian, German, Polish, Russian and American civilians poured into Spain by sea from Marseilles or along pathways across the Pyrenees. Some were driven by a desire to prevent the spread of fascism, but many were simply in search of adventure.

At a time of high unemployment, there were many people who saw involvement in the Spanish Civil War as a way of escaping from poverty and boredom.

Increasingly concerned about its own security and diplomatic isolation, the USSR stopped sending supplies and ammunition to the Spanish Republicans by late 1938. This naturally helped the Nationalist cause. In addition, Franco gained further support from Germany in exchange for a 40% share in the Spanish iron mines. These factors gave Franco the upper hand. In January 1939, Barcelona finally fell to the Nationalists. With the fall of Madrid two months later, Franco's victory was secured.

Adopting the title *Caudillo* (leader), Franco set about establishing a form of government that was, in many ways, similar to those of Mussolini and Hitler. Repression, military courts and large-scale executions became as common in Spain as they were in Italy and Germany. However, Spain did not completely follow the typical pattern of a fascist state. This was most evident in the fact that Franco was an ardent supporter of the Church, restoring its control over education, and he avoided the persecution of Jews. As events unfolded towards the end of 1939, Hitler expected Spanish support, but Franco kept Spain out of the Second World War. While Hitler and Mussolini were ultimately defeated, Franco survived and continued to rule Spain until his death in 1975.

107

ACTIVITY 3.7

Figure 3.3 is a poster issued during the Spanish Civil War. Look carefully at the markings on the bombs.

a Which side issued the poster and what was its purpose?

b Use the table below to note the reasons why Germany, Italy and the USSR became involved in the Spanish Civil War, and the impact of their involvement.

	REASONS	IMPACT
GERMANY		
ITALY		
THE USSR		

Figure 3.3: The text reads:
'*Comrades of the Rearguard, more shelters to avoid more victims*'

Aims and impact of Hitler's expansionist policies

Hitler's main foreign policy aims can be summarised as:

- ending Germany's commitment to the Treaty of Versailles
- recovering all lost territory, including the Polish Corridor
- developing the German army, navy and air force
- uniting all German-speaking people under the government of Germany, beginning by forming a union with Austria (*Anschluss*)
- supporting the concept of *Lebensraum*, providing more 'living space' for the German people by the acquisition of more territory – initially popularised within Germany at the beginning of the 20th century, *Lebensraum* became a fundamental principle of Nazism in the 1930s.

In the period from 1934 to 1938, Hitler achieved almost unqualified success in pursuit of these aims. Moreover, he did so without dragging Germany into another war. His methods were devious, dependent on a mixture of threats and conciliatory statements. His actions were frequently in open defiance of the Treaty of Versailles and, by his own admission, they were gambles with potentially serious consequences – he had no way of accurately predicting what the reaction of other countries might be.

Little by little, Hitler wore away the restraints the Treaty of Versailles had imposed upon Germany. He achieved this by convincing the major European nations, particularly Britain, that his motives were entirely honourable, justifiable and peaceful, while at the same time isolating countries that were the targets of his desire for the expansion of German power. Whether Hitler was following a meticulously devised plan of action towards war, or simply improvising as opportunities presented themselves, has become an issue of debate amongst historians.

In January 1935, the Saar region, with its valuable coal fields, was returned to Germany following a plebiscite of the local people (see Chapter 2.1). Although the plebiscite had taken place in line with the terms of the Treaty of Versailles, Hitler fully exploited the propaganda opportunity this provided in order to enhance his reputation within Germany. To assure the French of his peaceful intentions, Hitler also claimed that this put an end to all remaining grievances between Germany and France.

Rearmament

Developing Germany's armed forces was one of Hitler's objectives. In March 1935, in direct contravention of the Treaty of Versailles, he reintroduced **conscription**, claiming that this was in response to increases in the British air force and the announcement that France was to extend conscription from 12 to 18 months. Hitler also declared that it was his intention to increase the German army to a strength of 600 000 men – six times higher than the number permitted by the Treaty of Versailles. The treaty had also banned Germany from having an air force; in February 1935, Hitler publicly announced the establishment of the *Luftwaffe*, a new German air force that had been formed secretly in May 1933.

 KEY TERM

Conscription: compulsory military service for certain groups of society, such as men between certain ages.

It was clear from Hitler's comments at, and subsequent withdrawal from, the World Disarmament Conference, that he intended to rearm Germany in defiance of the Treaty of Versailles.

Initially, there appeared to be a strong reaction to German rearmament. British, French and Italian representatives met in Stresa in Italy to discuss their common concerns about Germany. On 14 April 1935, the prime ministers of Britain, France and Italy – Ramsay MacDonald, Pierre Laval and Benito Mussolini respectively – signed an agreement that established the Stresa Front. Its aim was to reaffirm the Locarno Treaties, maintain the independence of Austria and resist any future attempts to change the Treaty of Versailles.

From the outset, there were fundamental weaknesses in the Stresa Front that meant that it provided no real deterrent to Hitler's plans to rearm Germany. The terms of the agreement were vague, and did not specify what action Britain, France and Italy would take in support of its aims. In fact, although its implications were clear, the agreement was so vague that it did not specifically mention Germany at all. Realistically, preventing Hitler from carrying out his rearmament plans would have meant launching a full-scale invasion of Germany. None of the three countries was prepared to take such drastic action.

The Stresa Front's weaknesses were quickly exposed. In June 1935, Britain, without consulting its Stresa Front partners, entered negotiations with Germany which led to the signing of the Anglo-German Naval Agreement. Under its terms, Germany agreed to limit its navy to 35% the strength of the British navy. While this guaranteed British naval supremacy, Britain was effectively condoning a transgression of the Treaty of Versailles, which limited the size of the German naval fleet. The fact that Britain had signed this treaty without consulting either France or Italy clearly demonstrated the fragility of the Stresa Front alliance against Germany. With Britain's opposition to German rearmament effectively removed, Hitler continued to increase the size of his army, ordered the building of new battleships and began the process of developing a large and efficient air force. In effect, Hitler was tearing up the Treaty of Versailles – and no one was stopping him.

In October 1935, Mussolini launched the Italian invasion of Abyssinia, assuming that his Stresa Front partners would offer no opposition. He was both surprised and angry when Britain and France supported the League of Nations' sanctions against Italy. In response, Mussolini withdrew Italy from both the League of Nations and the Stresa Front.

ACTIVITY 3.8

Prepare notes on the key points of the following, and then discuss them in small groups

a   What were the aims of the Stresa Front and why did it fail to achieve its aims?

Make sure that your notes contain explanations of the following issues regarding the Stresa Front -

* The countries that were members of it
* Its aims
* The reasons for its failure

b   On each occasion that Hitler defied the Treaty of Versailles, both Britain and France issued strong statements condemning his actions. Make a list of reasons why Britain and France did nothing more than this.

Germany's rearmament, and Britain's apparent acceptance of it, caused considerable alarm in France, which, following the collapse of the Stresa Front, felt increasingly isolated and vulnerable. The USSR had similar concerns. Despite reservations about making an agreement with a communist country it considered untrustworthy, the French government signed a Treaty of Mutual Assistance with the USSR in 1935. The two countries agreed to support each other in the event that either of them were attacked by another European country.

Remilitarisation of the Rhineland (1936)

Hitler's foreign policy thus far had been based on the assumption that none of the other major European countries would take serious action against him. This was clearly evident in March 1936, when Hitler ordered German soldiers to enter the Rhineland, part of Germany along its border with France. The Treaty of Versailles had ordered the demilitarisation of the Rhineland, providing France with security against any possible German aggression in the future. Hitler argued that this was unreasonable, since it prevented Germany from defending this part of its border. Hitler's decision to defy the Treaty of Versailles by placing German soldiers in the Rhineland was a gamble. He was completely aware that his armed forces were not yet ready for a full-scale war – he issued strict orders that his troops should retreat if they met French resistance.

Hitler's gamble proved successful. No resistance was met. Although they protested vigorously, neither Britain nor France took any direct action to remove German soldiers from the Rhineland. Hitler had successfully regained full control over the Rhineland, and had done so without bloodshed. He was now fully convinced that Britain and France were not willing to go to war in defence of the Treaty of Versailles, and would not stand in the way of his determination to continue building up Germany's armed forces.

Hitler justified the remilitarisation of the Rhineland and the redevelopment of Germany's armed forces by arguing that he was merely righting the wrongs inflicted on Germany by the unfair Treaty of Versailles. Germany was simply exerting its right to defend itself. His arguments were largely accepted in Britain, which had long argued that the Treaty of Versailles had been too harsh. Moreover, many British politicians saw a strong Germany as providing a good defence against the spread of communism. Concerns regarding the long-term implications of Hitler's actions were greater in France and the USSR. German remilitarisation posed a clear threat to the security of France, especially now that German troops were strategically positioned on the French border in the Rhineland. In the USSR, there were concerns that the re-development of Germany's armed forces would lead to a German attack against Poland. This would not only adversely affect the USSR's own claims to parts of Poland, but would also threaten the security of the USSR itself. However, neither France nor the USSR felt strong enough to confront Hitler, and neither were prepared to go to war against Germany without the guarantee of British support.

ACTIVITY 3.9

Look carefully at the following two sources.

SOURCE A

The forty-eight hours after the march into the Rhineland were the most nerve-racking of my life. If the French had marched into the Rhineland, we would have had to withdraw with our tails between our legs, for the military resources at our disposal would have been wholly inadequate for even moderate resistance.

Adolf Hitler, commenting on the remilitarisation of the Rhineland

SOURCE B

Goering was visibly terrified by Hitler's decision to remilitarise the Rhineland. He gave me to understand that Hitler had taken this extremely risky step by his own decision, against the advice of his own generals.

Jósef Lipski (Polish Ambassador to Germany), commenting on his meeting with Hermann Goering (a senior member of Hitler's Nazi government), in 1936

a What do these two sources suggest about Hitler's leadership style?

b Why would Goering have been worried about Hitler's decision to remilitarise the Rhineland?

c Which European country would Hitler have thought most likely to resist Germany's remilitarisation of the Rhineland, and why?

d In fact, no country took any action in response to Germany's remilitarisation of the Rhineland. Why do you think this was?

Anschluss (1938)

Although expressly forbidden in the terms of both the Treaty of Versailles and the Treaty of Saint-Germain, *Anschluss* was one of Hitler's main foreign policy aims. It would unite German-speaking people, provide Germany with Austrian resources and undermine the treaties that Hitler so detested.

That Hitler fully intended to force a union between Germany and Austria became clear in 1934. With Hitler's encouragement, Austrian Nazis staged a revolt and murdered the Austrian Chancellor, Engelbert Dollfuss. Hitler's troops were ready to enter Austria on the pretext of restoring order, but in the event they were forced to back down when Mussolini sent Italian regiments to the Austrian border. This unexpected setback highlighted the fact that Germany did not yet possess the military strength to risk a war against Italy. Hitler had no alternative but to deny any involvement in the actions taken by the Austrian Nazis. On this occasion, Hitler's gamble had failed.

Later in 1936, Hitler both removed Mussolini as a potential hindrance to his plans by forming the Rome–Berlin Axis with Italy and gained a further ally by signing the Anti-Comintern Pact with Japan. Like Mussolini, Hitler provided military assistance to Franco during the Spanish Civil War. This enabled the German army and air force to gain vital military experience.

Figure 3.4: German soldiers enthusiastically welcomed in Innsbruck (Austria), 1938. Would you describe the photograph as an example of propaganda? Why or why not?

In March 1938, Hitler finally achieved *Anschluss* with Austria in clear defiance of the Treaty of Versailles. Following riots and demonstrations organised by Austrian Nazis, which the government of Chancellor Schuschnigg was powerless to control, German troops moved in and declared Austria part of Germany. As before, Britain and France protested but took no direct action. Unlike in 1934, Mussolini's Italy, now a German ally, also did nothing.

Hitler had achieved his long-standing aim of *Anschluss*, union between Germany and Austria. In so doing, he had gained access to valuable resources such as iron ore, added 7 million people to Germany's population and increased the size of its army by 100 000 men. Germany's strategic position within Europe had been greatly enhanced, posing an obvious threat to other countries, most notably Czechoslovakia, which was now surrounded on three sides by Nazi territory. Moreover, Hitler achieved this without bloodshed since no action was taken to oppose him. Yet again, Hitler's instinct that he could get away with international bullying proved correct.

Sudetenland (1938)

Having effectively isolated potential opposition from Europe's other major powers, and convinced that they would take no action against him, Hitler now set about bringing more German-speaking people into the Third Reich. There were around 3.5 million such people living in the Sudeten area of Czechoslovakia, many of whom joined the Sudeten German Party. Under their leader, Konrad Henlein, they claimed, with some justification, that they were being discriminated against by the Czech government. Riots and demonstrations broke out, many of them orchestrated by the Nazis.

In a speech on 12 September 1938, Hitler justified his claims to the Sudetenland:

> I am not asking that Germany be allowed to oppress three and a half million Frenchmen, nor am I asking that three and a half million Englishmen be placed at our mercy. Rather I am simply demanding that the oppression of three and a half million Germans in Czechoslovakia cease and that the inalienable right to self-determination take its place.

This is a very clever speech:

- it shows Hitler's full support for the German-speaking people of the Sudeten region, thereby encouraging them to continue their campaign for the Sudetenland to become part of Germany
- it argues that Germany's claim to the Sudetenland is both fair and reasonable since it is what the local people actually want; self-determination had, after all, been one of Woodrow Wilson's guiding principles at the Paris Peace Conference
- it aims to convince Britain and France that Germany's claim to the Sudetenland is just, and poses no threat to them.

NEVILLE CHAMBERLAIN (1869–1940)

Chamberlain became British prime minister in May 1937. He was a firm believer in the policy of **appeasement**, arguing that the best way of dealing with Hitler was by negotiation rather than confrontation. He finally accepted that appeasement had failed, and in 1939, declared war on Germany. He resigned in May 1940, and died of cancer later that year.

Edvard Beneš, the Czech president, believed that Hitler was deliberately stirring up these disturbances in order to justify a German invasion of Czechoslovakia in the guise of restoring order. Hitler's instinct that Britain and France would do nothing to hinder his designs on Czechoslovakia proved correct. The British prime minister, **Neville Chamberlain**, and his French counterpart, Édouard Daladier, put pressure on the Czech government to make concessions to Hitler. Chamberlain believed that Germany's claim to the Sudetenland was reasonable – an error of the Treaty of Versailles in need of correction. The Czechs were naturally reluctant to allow Germany to take over the Sudetenland, a part of the country that was so vital to its industrial infrastructure. Moreover, the Sudetenland, with its mountains and strategically located defences, was key to the security of Czechoslovakia. The loss of the Sudetenland would leave Czechoslovakia totally vulnerable to any subsequent German attack. If Chamberlain genuinely believed that Hitler's designs on Czechoslovakia would end with the acquisition of the Sudetenland, he was wrong. Hitler had already informed his generals that 'it is my unalterable decision to smash Czechoslovakia by military action in the near future.'

 KEY TERM

Appeasement: a policy of giving in to, rather than confronting, demands made by aggressive nations.

ACTIVITY 3.10

Group discussion:

a Why do you think Hitler was convinced that Britain and France would do nothing to help Czechoslovakia?

b In what ways does Hitler's speech on 12 September 1938 contradict what he told his generals?

Reflection: How did discussing the questions as a group help you to answer the questions in the activity? Did you find this approach helpful in answering the activity?

Czechoslovakia (1939)

As the prospect of war increased, a four-power conference was held in Munich on 29 September 1938. Hitler, Mussolini, Chamberlain and Daladier discussed the best way of resolving the problem of Czechoslovakia. It was agreed that Germany should take immediate possession of the Sudetenland. The Czech government was not invited to the meeting – it was simply informed that if it refused to abide by the decisions reached at Munich it could expect no assistance from either Britain or France. With resistance hopeless, the Czech government agreed. Beneš resigned.

At a private meeting on 30 September, Chamberlain and Hitler signed a document renouncing warlike intentions and agreeing to deal with any future issues by negotiation. Hitler promised that he had no more territorial demands in Europe.

Chamberlain used the huge press coverage of his return to Britain as an opportunity to demonstrate how successful he had been in gaining an understanding with Hitler. Holding up the signed piece of paper, he explained 'I believe it is peace for our time'. The British public was relieved that the threat of war had been averted, but many were not convinced that Hitler could be trusted to keep his promises.

It quickly became apparent that Hitler had no intention of honouring the agreements made at Munich. Having encouraged riots by urging Slovakia to seek independence from the Czech government in Prague, Hitler warned that Germany might have to take action to preserve law and order. The new Czech president, Emil Hácha, was summoned to Berlin and informed that Prague would be bombed to destruction if he did not agree to allow the German occupation of what remained of Czechoslovakia. Hácha had little choice but to submit and 'invite' the Germans to restore order in Czechoslovakia. On 15 March 1939, German troops crossed the Czech border. Once again, Britain and France took no action. Chamberlain argued that

the guarantee of Czech frontiers given at Munich did not apply because technically the German action was not an invasion; the Germans had been invited into the country.

Czechoslovakia ceased to exist. A country that had been created as part of the Paris peace settlement had survived for just 20 years. Hitler was now totally convinced that Britain and France would never declare war against Germany. This time, however, his instincts were wrong. Whereas his earlier actions could be justified by the claim that he was merely redressing the unfair terms of the Treaty of Versailles, his acquisition of Czechoslovakia was different. He had seized territory over which Germany could have no justifiable claim and he had broken the promises he had made at Munich. No longer could Hitler claim that he had only peaceful intentions.

Poland (1939)

Hitler now turned his attention towards Poland. In April 1939, he demanded the return of Danzig (modern Gdańsk) and German access across the Polish Corridor. In some ways these were understandable demands. Danzig's population was largely German-speaking, while the Polish Corridor had split East Prussia from the rest of Germany. However, Hitler's demands were in defiance of both the Paris peace settlement and the non-aggression treaty Germany had signed with Poland in 1934. Considering recent events in Czechoslovakia, the Poles were naturally concerned that Hitler's demands were a first step towards a full invasion of Poland. That their concerns were justified is evident from the fact that, on 1 September 1939, German troops crossed the border into Poland.

3.2 Why did the League of Nations fail to keep the peace in the 1930s?

The failure of disarmament

The outbreak of the Second World War in 1939 clearly highlighted the failure of the League of Nations, an organisation that had been established to maintain international peace. In truth, however, the League's failure had been almost universally recognised long before 1939. One of the main reasons for this was the League's inability to secure disarmament.

In his 'Fourteen Points' speech of January 1918 (Chapter 1.4), US President Wilson had argued that there should be a 'reduction of armaments by all nations'. With the intention of preventing the kind of arms race that had characterised the build-up to the First World War, this became one of the League's most important aims. All of

Europe's leading powers had committed themselves to arms reduction in both the Treaty of Versailles and the Covenant of the League of Nations. With the exception of Germany, none of the countries had kept to their commitment by 1930. To address this issue, the League organised the World Disarmament Conference, which formally opened in February 1932.

There was considerable optimism when the conference began under the chairmanship of the former British Foreign Secretary Arthur Henderson. Over 60 nations were represented, including both the USA and the USSR. The League of Nations had established a Preparatory Commission in 1925 and, by 1931, it reported that League members were genuinely willing to discuss the issue of disarmament.

This early optimism was to prove unfounded. Despite lengthy discussions, the conference failed to achieve any significant decisions regarding disarmament. One of the main reasons for this is the fact that the timing of the conference could not have been worse. Three separate issues arose during the conference, all of which undermined discussions about disarmament.

1   The depression that followed the Wall Street Crash of 1929 was beginning to have adverse social and economic effects across the world. Many countries felt threatened by possible revolutions, and wanted to maintain their armaments to counter this threat.

2   There was considerable concern about the implications of the Japanese takeover of Manchuria, which began in September 1931. Japan simply ignored the League's instruction to withdraw its forces from Manchuria, announcing its decision to withdraw from the League in February 1933. If the League of Nations was powerless to prevent such aggression, countries felt that they needed to maintain their own armaments to protect themselves. In addition to defying the League of Nations, by increasing the size and strength of its navy Japan was also breaking the commitments it had made at the Washington Conference. This posed a serious threat to US interests in East Asia, so the USA was determined to maintain its armaments in order to protect those interests.

3   Adolf Hitler gained power in Germany at the beginning of 1933, causing alarm across the rest of Europe. Hitler had always made it clear that his intention was to destroy the Treaty of Versailles and restore Germany's power and prestige. This posed a threat to other European countries, which wanted to maintain their armaments as security against possible German aggression.

With the World Disarmament Conference already disrupted by events in Manchuria, Hitler made demands that added a further problem. He pointed out that Germany had reduced its armaments to the very low levels prescribed by the Treaty of Versailles. Since none of the other major European nations had reduced their military capabilities in line with the commitments they had made at the Paris Peace Conference, he argued that Germany was in no position to defend itself against foreign invasion. Hitler therefore insisted that, if other countries were not prepared to disarm, Germany should be permitted to increase its own armaments in the interests of self-defence.

While Hitler's argument seemed perfectly reasonable to some of the delegates at the Disarmament Conference, it was totally unacceptable to the French. Still concerned that any revival of German military power posed a serious threat to France, the French government steadfastly refused to consider any measure of disarmament. Confronted with this French refusal to negotiate, Hitler withdrew Germany from both the Disarmament Conference and the League of Nations in October 1933.

Hitler subsequently justified his decision to withdraw from the League of Nations in a speech broadcast by radio to the German nation in March 1935:

In 1918, the German people, trusting in the guarantees of Wilson's Fourteen Points, laid down their arms after four years of valiant resistance in a war they had never wanted. Germany supported the concept of the League of Nations more enthusiastically than any other nation. This is why the German people accepted the absurd conditions of the Treaty of Versailles. Having suffered most from the consequences of war, our people faithfully supported the idea of restructuring relations between nations in the interest of ridding the world once and for all of similar horrors. The German people were convinced that the League would lead to a general international reduction in arms. While Germany fulfilled its obligations to disarm, other nations failed to perform theirs. Surrounded by highly armed nations of war, Germany was completely at the mercy of any threat which any of them might pose. Given other nations' refusal to disarm, the German government could not remain in the League.

Adolf Hitler, 'Proclamation to the German People', Berlin, 16 March 1935

On first reading, this speech makes Germany's argument at the World Disarmament Conference seem totally reasonable. Analysing the speech in depth, however, reveals that it is based on a heavily **biased** interpretation of events.

KEY TERM

Bias: the support or opposition of a particular opinion in an unfair way, such as by manipulating or distorting evidence.

- Hitler claims that 'Germany supported the concept of the League of Nations more enthusiastically than any other nation.' This is clearly untrue – because of its close association with the Treaty of Versailles, most German people in 1920 felt that the League was simply a way for the First World War's victorious countries to maintain their power over the defeated nations. As a defeated nation, Germany was not even allowed to join the League until 1926.
- He implies that Germany only accepted 'the absurd conditions of the Treaty of Versailles' because of its enthusiastic support for the League of Nations. In reality, Germany had no alternative but to sign the treaty because of its inability to continue fighting the war.
- He suggests that, because of its own forced reduction in arms, Germany was vulnerable to attack. In fact, Germany's western borders were guaranteed under the terms of the Locarno Treaties and, since 1926, Germany had the added protection of being a member of the League of Nations.
- He claims that the First World War had been a war which the German people 'never wanted'. In this statement, Hitler is clearly disputing the validity of the War Guilt Clause.

●●● THINK LIKE A HISTORIAN

With the aim of gaining public support, politicians often use bias in their speeches. Think of some current or recent examples.

In each case, consider how bias is used and for what purpose.

People have different opinions about, and interpretations of, the same issue. Is there a difference between opinion/interpretation and bias? If so, what is it?

ACTIVITY 3.11

a Based on the demands that Hitler made of the World Disarmament Conference, what conclusions can we reach about his future intentions? Look carefully at this list of statements – for each one, decide whether you agree or disagree with it and explain why. Then discuss your decisions in pairs or small groups.
  - Hitler intended to honour Germany's commitments under the terms of the Treaty of Versailles.
  - Hitler intended to increase Germany's armaments in defiance of the Treaty of Versailles.
  - Hitler was determined to continue negotiations with other countries with the aim of achieving international disarmament.
  - Hitler's views were very different from those expressed by Stresemann at the Locarno Conference (see Chapter 2.3)
  - Hitler's main aim was to rid 'the world once and for all' of the horrors of war.
  - Hitler simply wanted to ensure that Germany was safe from attack by any of 'the highly-armed nations of war' that surrounded it.
  - Hitler's demands would have caused alarm in other European countries, especially France.

b Make a list of the reasons why the World Disarmament Conference failed. Then, rearrange the list into an order of significance.

Germany and Japan, two of the world's major nations, were no longer members of the League, and both seemed committed to increasing their armaments. Interpreting this situation as a serious threat to their own national interests and security, the other major European countries and the USA felt the need to increase, rather than decrease, their armaments. As a result, the World Disarmament Conference broke up in disarray, having achieved none of its ambitious aims.

Reasons for and actions taken in response to the crises in Manchuria and Abyssinia

During the 1920s, the League of Nations had successfully resolved a number of international disputes, as outlined in Chapter 2. However, these had been relatively minor issues that did not involve any of the most powerful countries. The League's inability to deal effectively with events that did involve one or more major powers quickly became apparent.

The crisis in Manchuria

Japanese expansion in East Asia was a cause of concern to the USA and European nations, which saw Japan's increasing interests in China as a threat to their own trading rights. These concerns were heightened in 1931, when Japanese forces invaded Manchuria, an area of China in which Japan had extensive trading rights. China appealed to the League of Nations, which ordered Japan to withdraw. When Japan refused to comply, the League appointed a commission to investigate the rival claims of China and Japan. The commission was led by the British politician Lord Lytton, and consisted of four other members, representing Germany, Italy, France and the USA. While the commission was carrying out its fact-finding mission and preparing its recommendations to the League, Japanese forces continued their takeover of Manchuria. In 1932, Japan claimed full control over Manchuria and renamed it Manchukuo.

The commission spent six weeks in Manchuria in early 1932, investigating the rival claims of China and Japan. The commission's report (the Lytton Report) was published on 2 October 1932. It recommended that, while there was fault on both sides, Manchuria should be returned to Chinese sovereignty under the oversight of the League of Nations. At a meeting on 24 February 1934, the League of Nations voted in favour of accepting the Lytton Report's recommendations by a majority of 42 to 1. The only negative vote was cast by Yosuke Matsuoka, representing Japan.

Refusing to accept the League's decision, Japan continued with its military occupation of Manchuria. Under the terms of its Covenant, the League should have taken action against Japan. However, at the height of the worldwide depression, Britain and France were in no position to impose economic sanctions on Japan, and neither was prepared to go to war over this issue. Without the support of two of its most powerful members, the League was powerless to do anything in response to Japan's blatantly aggressive actions.

ACTIVITY 3.12

a   The USA was not a member of the League of Nations, yet its representative was included in the League's commission appointed to investigate the Manchurian issue. How many of the following statements might be used to explain this?

- By 1931, the USA had realised its earlier mistake and now wanted to join the League of Nations.

ACTIVITY 3.12 (CONTINUED)

- The USA had its own trading interests in China and the Far East which were threatened by the Japanese invasion of Manchuria.
- It was in the USA's best interests to work with the League of Nations to find a peaceful solution to the Manchurian issue.
- By 1931, the USA was determined to end its policy of isolationism.
- The League of Nations believed that it stood a better chance of securing a peaceful solution to the Manchurian issue by working closely with the USA.

b   Why do you think the League did not force Japan to remove its forces from Manchuria while the Lytton Commission was undertaking its fact-finding mission?

The crisis in Abyssinia

The League's failure to take effective action in response to the Japanese takeover of Manchuria was repeated when Mussolini's Italy invaded Abyssinia in 1935. Emperor Haile Selassie of Abyssinia appealed to the League of Nations for assistance (Abyssinia had become a member of the League in 1923). The situation confronting the League of Nations could not have been clearer. A powerful member of the League was displaying blatant and unjustified aggression towards one of its weaker and more vulnerable members. The League of Nations unanimously condemned this act of aggression, and discussed what methods it should use to force Italy to withdraw from Abyssinia.

Once again, however, the League's ability to take effective action was hampered by the national interests of its two most powerful members. Britain and France were reluctant to give their full support to Abyssinia for three main reasons:

1   they saw Italy as a vital ally against the growing power of Germany – the three countries had only recently formed the Stresa Front with the aim of resisting any further attempts by Germany to change the Treaty of Versailles

2   Mussolini had suggested that Italy was prepared to go to war with any country which imposed sanctions against it

3   neither Britain nor France was prepared to go to war, especially against a country whose alliance they felt was so important to the future stability of Europe; still

less were they prepared to go to war in defence of a far-away African country, whose independence and security were of no direct interest to them; moreover, as Mussolini was keen to point out, there was little difference between Italian actions in Abyssinia and the earlier imperialistic involvement of Britain and France in Africa.

Britain and France faced a dilemma. On the one hand they wanted to be seen to honour their commitment to the League of Nations. On the other, they wanted to avoid taking any action that might damage their vital relationship with Italy. They attempted to solve this dilemma by engaging in secret diplomacy.

Outwardly, Britain and France seemed to be supporting, even encouraging, the League's decision to impose economic sanctions against Italy. However, these sanctions were limited and did not apply to vital resources such as oil, coal and steel. In truth, the sanctions had little effect on Italy's ability to maintain its fight for Abyssinia. At the same time, however, British and French diplomats were secretly meeting with their Italian counterparts to discuss ways of settling the Abyssinian problem without going to war. The outcome of these secret meetings was a proposal put forward jointly by Samuel Hoare, the British foreign secretary, and Pierre Laval, the French prime minister. This proposal, known as the Hoare-Laval Pact, recommended the partition of Abyssinia in such a way that Italy would have been granted effective control of the country.

When details of the Hoare-Laval Pact became common knowledge, the British and French governments faced a hostile reaction. Public opinion in both countries was still largely supportive of the League of Nations and believed that something should be done to end Italy's unjustified aggression towards Abyssinia. At the League itself, member states expressed their anger and disappointment that the pact was, in effect, recommending that Italy be rewarded for its aggression. Confronted by this wave of opposition, the British and French governments were forced to repudiate the pact. Both Hoare and Laval resigned from their posts. The historian A. J. P. Taylor described the Hoare-Laval Pact as a 'betrayal of the League' and, indeed, the event that 'killed the League'

The League's limited economic sanctions against Italy remained in place, but were ineffective in preventing Mussolini's acquisition of a vulnerable African state and were quickly abandoned. Annoyed that the League had imposed any sanctions at all, Mussolini withdrew Italy's

membership and moved towards a closer alliance with Hitler's Germany.

While the British and French attitude towards both the Manchurian and Abyssinian crises can be seen as selfish and damaging to the League's credibility, it was also logical. The heaviest burden of any League action, either economic or military, would inevitably fall on Britain and France. Most of the other members of the League were small nations, lacking the financial and military resources to take effective action. From the British and French perspective, it seemed foolish to go to war against Italy in defence of an African country of no real interest to either of them.

This situation was aggravated by the fact that there was a certain lack of trust between Britain and France. Politically divided and increasingly concerned by the resurgence of Germany under Hitler, France was reluctant to take any action without the guarantee of British support. The Anglo-German naval agreement of 1935, in which Britain effectively condoned German rearmament, convinced the French that Britain was an unreliable ally. At the same time, British politicians viewed France as weak and offering no guarantee of genuine support in a crisis.

ACTIVITY 3.13

a Identify evidence to support A. J. P. Taylor's view that the Hoare-Laval Pact was responsible for the death of the League

b Identify evidence that suggests that the League was already 'dead' even before the Italian invasion of Abyssinia.

c To what extent was the British and French response to Italian aggression against Abyssinia based on their fear of war?

Complete the table below to help you make a judgement.

FEAR OF WAR	OTHER FACTORS

The crisis in Spain

If the League failed to take effective action against the aggressive acts of Japan and Italy, it was equally weak in its response to foreign involvement in the Spanish Civil War. In September 1936, the Spanish Republican government appealed to the League of

Nations for assistance against the Nationalist rising that began the Spanish Civil War. However, members of the League were not prepared to intervene in what they perceived as an internal Spanish matter. At the suggestion of Britain and France, the League established a Non-Intervention Committee that aimed to prevent any foreign involvement in the Spanish Civil War. Representatives of 27 countries, including Germany and Italy, were involved in this committee.

This initial approach was fully in line with the Covenant of the League, which established the principle that the League could not interfere with the internal affairs of a member state. However, it soon became clear that Italy and Germany were breaking the non-intervention agreement by providing military assistance to General Franco's Nationalist forces in their rebellion against Spain's elected republican government. Under the terms of the Covenant, the League now had a duty to stop this foreign involvement in the Spanish Civil War.

Under the direction of Britain and France, however, the League continued to take no action, claiming that there was insufficient evidence of German or Italian interference in Spain. In reality, the evidence was overwhelming, but neither the British nor the French government was prepared to go to war against Italy and Germany.

In desperation, Julio Álvarez del Vayo, Spain's Minister of Foreign Affairs, addressed the League of Nations Assembly on 11 December 1936:

> The youth of Spain fall in their thousands, the victims of fascist aeroplanes and the foreign war materials delivered month after month despite the Non-Intervention Agreement. Women and children in Madrid have been butchered in hundreds by bombing planes under the orders of rebel generals and foreign states which have, in fact, begun a war. An international war is raging on Spanish soil. Every foreign mission which has visited Spain has brought back fresh evidence of this monstrosity. The worst thing that could happen to the League of Nations would be to contribute by its own silence and inaction to the spread of this war.

Faced with the League's continued refusal to become involved, Spain's Republican government gained military aid from Soviet Russia. While this both spread and extended the war, it could not prevent Franco's Nationalist forces gaining victory by 1939.

ACTIVITY 3.14

Julio Álvarez del Vayo's speech to the League of Nations Assembly contains emotive language – his words and phrases were carefully chosen to achieve an emotional response from his audience. For example, his use of the word 'butchered' was designed to have a more powerful effect than simply saying 'killed'.

In pairs or small groups:

a identify other examples of emotive language in his speech

b discuss his reasons for using emotive language in his speech.

Japanese invasion of China

In 1937, Japan began a full-scale invasion of China. China's appeals to the League of Nations were greeted with sympathy, but no practical assistance. There were two main reasons for this. First, with their own economies suffering enormously as a result of the Great Depression, neither Britain nor France was in a position to impose economic sanctions against Japan. Second, this was the period of appeasement in which key nations were desperate to avoid taking any action that might lead to war. Japan was no longer a member of the League of Nations and had formed an alliance with Germany in 1936. The only way to force Japan to end its invasion of China was to take military action – something Britain and France were not prepared to do.

During the 1930s, therefore, the League of Nations failed to respond effectively to the aggressive acts of three of the dictatorships – Germany, Italy and Japan. Moreover, all three nations had withdrawn from the League, leaving Britain and France as its most influential members. With Britain and France committed to pursuing a policy of appeasement, there was little possibility that the League would be able to confront aggression.

Changing attitudes of the major powers towards the League of Nations

For the League of Nations to be genuinely effective, it required the full commitment of the major powers. They alone had the economic and military power necessary to enforce the League's decisions. During the 1930s, the major powers became less committed, and it was largely for this reason that the League was unable to respond effectively to acts of international aggression.

In truth, Mussolini's Italy had never been a fully committed member of the League. As early as 1923, Mussolini had completely ignored the League's instruction that Italian troops be withdrawn from the Greek island of Corfu (Chapter 2.4). Italy remained in the League only so long as it appeared to provide some guarantee of national security and it was in Mussolini's interests to maintain good relations with Britain and France. In response to the League's imposition of sanctions following Mussolini's invasion of Abyssinia, Italy withdrew its membership.

Hitler, too, was heavily critical of the League, not least because it had been created by the Paris peace settlement. Hitler viewed the League as a method whereby Britain and France could maintain their power over Europe in general, and Germany in particular. He deeply resented the fact that Germany had not been permitted to become a member of the League when it was created, and was only allowed to join in 1926 having formally accepted what he considered the unfair terms of the Treaty of Versailles. He was quick to withdraw Germany from the League following the failure of the World Disarmament Conference in 1933.

At the end of the First World War, Japan's democratically elected government seemed genuinely committed to the League and its principles, as demonstrated by its willingness to compromise at the Washington Naval Conference (see Chapter 2.2). Moreover, Japan's rise to world power status was formally recognised when it became a permanent member of the League Council.

As democracy collapsed, the military dictatorship in Japan viewed membership of the League as a hindrance to its ambitions for territorial expansion. The League's decision to support China's claim to Manchuria was deeply resented in Japan, which immediately withdrew its membership and ignored the League's instruction for Japanese troops to withdraw.

The League of Nations was viewed with deep suspicion in the USSR. The League had been established by the Paris Peace Conference, to which Russian delegates were not invited, and Russia was initially prohibited from becoming a member. To the Soviet government, it appeared that the League's purpose was to maintain the isolation of the USSR and the power of Europe's leading nations, Britain and France. By 1934, however, circumstances had changed. The revival of Germany, and its rearmament under Hitler, posed a serious threat to the national security of the USSR. With its potential enemies, Germany and Japan, no longer members of the League, it seemed

an opportune moment to seek membership. In September 1934, the USSR joined the League as a permanent member of the Council. However, even as a member, it remained heavily critical of the League, particularly regarding its failure to apply the principle of collective security in defence of its members.

In 1934, for example, Maxim Litvinov, the Soviet representative, told the League of Nations Assembly:

> The aggressor states such as Japan and Italy are now still weaker than a possible bloc of peace-loving nations, but the policy of non-resistance to evil and aggression, which the opponents of sanctions propose to us, can have no other result than further strengthening and increasing the forces of aggression. The moment might arrive when their power has grown to such an extent that the League of Nations, or what remains of it, will be in no condition to cope with them even if it wants to. With the slightest attempt of aggression, collective action as envisaged in Article 16 of the Covenant of the League of Nations must be brought into effect. The programme envisioned in the Covenant of the League must be carried out against the aggressor, decisively, resolutely and without any wavering.

From its establishment, and in the absence of the USA, leadership of the League had fallen largely on its two most powerful and influential members, Britain and France. Their initial commitment to the League and its principles had faded by the 1930s. They began to see membership of the League as a burden, often in conflict with their own national interests. This was most clearly evident in their response to Italy's invasion of Abyssinia. Outwardly supporting League sanctions against Italy, they were secretly determined to take no action that might destroy what they considered to be their vital alliance with Mussolini. Without the full commitment of Britain and France, the League was effectively powerless.

Determined to avoid involvement in another war, and suffering from the economic effects of the Great Depression, British and French politicians were reluctant to spend vital resources on the kind of collective military action envisaged by Article 16 of the League Covenant.

The League's failure to confront acts of aggression greatly concerned and angered many of its members. Countries that were relatively weak and vulnerable depended on the League for their national security. They had believed that the collective influence and power of the League's members would be deployed to protect them from attack. The League's failure to take effective action in defence of two of its members – China and Abyssinia – undermined this belief.

ACTIVITY 3.15

Discuss the following questions in pairs or small groups.

a Why would the League's failure to confront Japanese aggression in Manchuria concern and anger many of the League's member states?

b What action did Litvinov believe the League should have taken in response to Japanese aggression in Manchuria?

c Why didn't the League take such action?

d Why did the League impose only limited sanctions in response to Italy's invasion of Abyssinia?

e What did Litvinov fear would be the eventual outcome of the League's failure to confront aggression?

Reflection: In pairs, consider the ways in which the League of Nations responded to the crises in Abyssinia and Manchuria.

Identify similarities in the League's response to these two threats to international peace. Then identify differences in the way the League responded to them. Do you agree on the same similarities and differences? How can these differences be explained?

During the 1930s, therefore, the weaknesses of the League of Nations were fully exposed. It had failed to secure international disarmament, and done nothing to prevent German rearmament in total defiance of the Treaty of Versailles. It seemed increasingly incapable of preventing, or responding effectively to, international aggression. As a result, it lacked the ability to achieve its primary purpose, maintaining international peace and stability. Countries that were seeking territorial expansion simply ignored it, and by 1935, Germany, Japan and Italy had all withdrawn from it. In their absence, the League became increasingly reliant on the leadership of Britain and France. While both claimed that they remained fully supportive of the League and its aims, neither Britain nor France was prepared to go to war in order to enforce its decisions, especially if it was against their own national interests to do so.

3.3 Why, and with what effects, did Britain and France pursue a policy of appeasement?

Over the issues of Manchuria and Abyssinia, the League of Nations had failed to take effective action against the kind of aggression it had been established to prevent. This failure to take decisive action against countries displaying aggressive foreign policies is known as appeasement. During the 1930s, the British and French pursuit of a policy of appeasement played a crucial role in the failure of the League of Nations to confront international aggression. In hindsight, it is easy to criticise appeasement as a foolish policy that both destroyed the League and made another world war more likely. Indeed, as early as July 1940, a book entitled *Guilty Men* was published in Britain – it was heavily critical of appeasement and the politicians who had supported it. During the 1930s, however, there seemed compelling reasons to justify appeasement.

Impact of economic and military considerations for foreign policy
Economic considerations

Public opinion in both Britain and France was heavily against involvement in another war. There was no desire to repeat the horrors of the First World War, while technological developments made it clear that any future war would be far worse, with enormous civilian casualties caused by the aerial bombing of major cities. Evidence of this was already available in Spain, where the civilian populations of Madrid (1936) and Guernica (1937) suffered as a result of heavy aerial bombing.

Moreover, suffering from the devastating economic effects of the Great Depression, neither Britain nor France could realistically afford the high costs of preparation for war. If avoiding involvement in war was a priority for British and French politicians, so too was maintaining the international trade on which their economies depended. These two priorities help to explain the failure of the League of Nations to take effective action in response to the Japanese invasion of Manchuria in 1931. Under the terms of its Covenant, the League should have imposed economic sanctions against Japan as a means of forcing it to withdraw its troops. Britain and France had extensive trading links with Japan and were reluctant to lose them. British representatives at the League argued that imposing economic sanctions against Japan would be counterproductive – it would adversely affect the economies of those countries imposing sanctions, while Japan would simply extend its trading links with nations willing to defy the League's sanctions. Britain was also concerned about its overseas possessions, especially Hong Kong and Singapore. There was a risk that Japan would attack these areas if Britain imposed sanctions against it, leading to war.

Over the issue of Manchuria, Britain and France were putting their own national interests above their commitment to the League of Nations. Without the support of its two most powerful and influential members, the League was powerless to take effective action against Japan. Similarly, Britain and France were reluctant to take strong action following Italy's invasion of Abyssinia in 1935. Mussolini was seen as a vital ally against the rising power of Hitler's Germany, and, as a result, the League's response was limited to minor and largely ineffective economic sanctions.

Responding effectively to Hitler's aggressive actions would also have enormous economic repercussions for Britain and France. It was clear that military intervention was the only way to ensure the removal of German troops from the Rhineland and to monitor the area to prevent their subsequent return. Such expensive action seemed unjustified when, in effect, Germany was simply occupying its own territory. Similarly, taking action in response to the *Anschluss* would involve Britain and France in an expensive and highly risky war in Central Europe.

Military considerations

The military strategies followed by both the British and French governments during the 1930s were based primarily on self-defence. France developed what became known as the Maginot Line – a series of concrete fortifications and weapon installations – along its borders. This was intended to deter any future aggression by Germany. Britain's armed forces were already seriously overstretched defending its large and widespread empire. British military policy prior to 1932 was based on the 'Ten Year Rule' – the assumption that Britain would not be involved in a major war for at least ten years. By the time the 'Ten Year Rule' was abandoned, Britain was suffering from the adverse economic effects of the Great Depression, and in no position to devote large expenditure to enhancing its armed forces. The British government's priority, therefore, was ensuring the defence of Britain itself and its empire.

As a result, it was in British and French interests to avoid unnecessary confrontation. Providing military

assistance to China in its attempt to end Japan's occupation of Manchuria was simply not possible. Nor was defending Abyssinia against Italian aggression, or ensuring the removal of Italian and German troops from Spain. Neither Britain nor France was in a position to mount the type of military campaign in Central Europe, which would have been necessary in order to confront Hitler's aggression. Moreover, as a result of the Anti-Comintern Pact, any action against Germany would also involve Britain and France in war against Japan in the Far East.

ACTIVITY 3.16

From what you have learned so far, do you think that Britain and France followed a policy of appeasement in the 1930s for economic rather than political reasons?

a Make two lists, one explaining economic reasons for appeasement, the other explaining political reasons.

b Use your lists to help you develop your opinion.

Changing nature of relations with the USSR and impact on foreign policy

Amidst the social and economic problems caused by the Great Depression, communist revolution was widely perceived as the biggest threat facing European democracies, such as Britain and France. Many politicians felt that Hitler's Germany, with its well-known opposition to communism, provided a vital buffer against the westward expansion of the Soviet Union. As the British politician Lord Lothian said in 1935, 'I am convinced that Hitler does not want war. What the Germans are after is a strong army which will enable them to deal with Russia.'

Although Britain and France had restored diplomatic relations with the USSR by 1924, both remained deeply suspicious of it. The USSR's close links with Germany following the Treaty of Rapallo (1922), and its worldwide distribution of pro-communist propaganda, caused great concern. France, in particular, was convinced that the USSR was intent on conquering territory in Eastern Europe, including territory Poland had taken from the USSR in 1921, threatening the borders that had been established by the Paris peace settlement and subsequent treaties.

At the same time, the USSR showed little interest in forging closer political links with Britain and France. Stalin was heavily critical of British and French imperialism, and described the League of Nations as an institution designed to maintain their control over foreign territories and their domination of international affairs.

By 1934, circumstances dictated a fundamental change in the relationship between Britain and France on the one hand, and the USSR on the other. Germany and Japan had shifted from democracy to military dictatorship, and this caused great concern in the USSR. Stalin was well aware that Hitler's foreign policy aims centred on the seizure of Eastern European and Russian territory. Moreover, Japan's aggressive expansionism posed a major threat to Russian interests in the Far East. At the same time, Britain and – particularly – France felt threatened by Hitler's determination to overturn the Treaty of Versailles and Japan's refusal to comply with the League's decision that it should withdraw its troops from Manchuria.

With these concerns in common, relations between the USSR and the Western democracies began to ease. In 1935, for example, France and the USSR signed a Treaty of Mutual Assistance, agreeing to support each other in the event of either being attacked by another European country. The USSR's sense of isolation was further reduced when it signed a Treaty of Alliance with Czechoslovakia in 1935. Mutual fear of German expansion had brought these countries together. While Britain remained unwilling to sign any formal alliance with a country that it considered both dangerous and untrustworthy, it was at least prepared to entertain talks with Soviet diplomats after 1934. Even the USA, which had steadfastly refused to recognise Soviet control over Russia, finally did so in 1933, when its own Far Eastern interests were threatened by Japanese expansionism. Japan's occupation of Manchuria and its obvious desire to extend its influence in other parts of China, threatened to undermine the USA's trading interests. Moreover, Japan's decision to defy the treaties agreed at the Washington Naval Conference by enhancing the size and strength of its navy posed a clear threat to the USA's naval presence in the Pacific.

At the same time, France was encouraging the League of Nations to accept the USSR as a member. Despite its earlier forthright opposition to the League, circumstances now dictated that it was in the USSR's best interests to join it.

On 18 September 1935, the USSR joined the League of Nations, becoming a permanent member of the Council. However, Minister for Foreign Affairs, Maxim Litvinov, made it clear that the USSR could not accept all of the League's resolutions and considered that its charter was seriously flawed. Moreover, not all members of the

League had supported Soviet membership when the issue was debated in the Assembly – three (the Netherlands, Portugal and Switzerland) had voted against it, and seven had abstained.

In truth, the apparent improvement in relations between the USSR and the Western democracies was the result of mutual convenience rather than trust. Britain and France remained firmly opposed to the USSR's political ideology, and resented its continued widespread distribution of pro-communist propaganda. British and French politicians interpreted the USSR's provision of military aid to the Republicans in the Spanish Civil War as a further attempt to encourage the spread of communism. To a certain extent, this explains Anglo-French reluctance to encourage the League to take action when there was clear evidence that Italy and Germany were actively supporting Franco's Nationalists – this would have meant supporting a Republican cause increasingly perceived as communist in nature. At the same time, the USSR was heavily critical of the League's failure to respond effectively to Italy's invasion of Abyssinia. To the Soviets, this was a clear example of Britain and France endorsing Italian imperialism rather than fulfilling their commitment to the League's stated aim of preventing international aggression.

Despite these ongoing differences, Stalin felt that it was in the best interests of the USSR's security to develop closer military alliances with Britain and France. This became even more imperative when Germany and Japan formed the Anti-Comintern Pact, subsequently joined by Italy and some Eastern European countries such as Hungary. Outwardly, the pact was designed to suppress communist activity, but Stalin was fully aware that it was an alliance that posed a genuine threat to the USSR. Britain, however, was reluctant to commit itself to an alliance with a country it considered both unreliable and undemocratic. Feeling isolated, insecure and vulnerable, the USSR made a decision that caused shock and fear throughout Europe and in the USA – it formed an alliance with Germany.

ACTIVITY 3.17

a   Why did the USSR become a member of of the League of Nations in 1935, despite its earlier criticism of it?

b   Why did Stalin try to achieve closer relations with Britain and France in the late 1930s, and why did his efforts fail?

of the Rhineland, effectively destroying the agreements reached at the Locarno Conference in 1925, posed an obvious threat to the security of France. The French government referred the matter to the League of Nations, arguing that the League had an obligation to take collective action in order to enforce treaty agreements and ensure the removal of German troops from the Rhineland. The League's ability to respond effectively was thwarted by Britain's refusal to support any action that might involve it in a war against Germany. The British government was adamant that the best way of dealing with the crisis was by negotiation with Hitler.

From Hitler's perspective, the lack of effective action in response to Germany's remilitarisation of the Rhineland had exposed major weaknesses in the relationship between Britain and France, and the growing distrust between them. His instinct that they would do nothing to prevent his further attempts to undermine the Treaty of Versailles proved correct when Germany, unopposed, secured the *Anschluss* in March 1938.

Attitude towards the *Anschluss*

With its entire western half now surrounded by Germany, Czechoslovakia was the country most threatened by the *Anschluss*. On 11 March, Hitler had assured the country that it had nothing to fear from Germany's intention to take control of Austria. Besides, Hitler was well aware that Czechoslovakia was too weak to resist Germany without support from the other major European powers. He also knew that Italy would not oppose him; Mussolini, who had resisted Hitler's earlier attempt in 1934, was now Hitler's closest ally following the formation of the Rome–Berlin Axis and had made it clear that Austria was of no interest to him. Any meaningful opposition to the *Anschluss*, therefore, could only come from Britain and France and, as before, both lacked the political will to take action against Hitler.

France was in a state of political turmoil, its entire government having resigned on 10 March 1938 after failing to secure support for its plans for dealing with the country's economic problems. It was in no position to react decisively to Germany's takeover of Austria, and besides, could not have done so without British support. It was certainly not prepared to become involved in a war in Central Europe in defence of Austrians, most of whom seemed to support their country's union with Germany. Therefore, despite the fact that the *Anschluss* represented a clear breach of the Paris peace settlement, France took no action against it – a clear act of appeasement.

On Baldwin's retirement, Neville Chamberlain had become British prime minister in May 1937. Chamberlain was an ardent supporter of appeasement, and was determined to negotiate with, rather than antagonise, Hitler. Some politicians opposed Chamberlain's appeasement policy. For example, Anthony Eden resigned from his post as foreign secretary in 1938 because of Chamberlain's willingness to negotiate with Mussolini. Similarly, **Winston Churchill** argued that the *Anschluss* posed a major threat to European peace, and that Britain should take strong and decisive action in response to it.

WINSTON CHURCHILL (1874–1965)

Churchill became a politician in 1900, and by the First World War was serving as First Lord of the Admiralty, in command of the British navy. He openly opposed the policy of appeasement pursued by Britain during the 1930s. After the failure of appeasement and the outbreak of the Second World War, Churchill became British prime minister. He led Britain through the war years and was voted in again as prime minister in 1951.

However, Chamberlain had the support of British public opinion, which was still heavily opposed to any action that might lead to Britain's involvement in another major war. The *Anschluss* did not seem to pose any threat to Britain, and besides, most of Austria's population seemed to be in favour of it. To the majority of British people, it seemed foolish to risk going to war with Germany in support of Austrian independence against the wishes of the Austrians themselves. Moreover, as a result of the Anti-Comintern Pact, there was the very real risk that such a war might escalate to include Italy and Japan.

Under these circumstances, Britain and France issued strongly worded condemnations of Germany's takeover of Austria, but took no direct action in response to it. Neither the British nor the French governments were prepared to use force – just as Hitler had predicted.

ACTIVITY 3.18

In his speech on 14 March 1938, Chamberlain made it clear that the *Anschluss* caused great concern in both Britain and France. Why, then, did they take no action against it?

In pairs or small groups, compare your answers and discuss how they might be improved.

Czechoslovakia and the Munich Crisis

Chamberlain's determination to pursue a policy of appeasement, and his belief that it was the best way of dealing with the threat Hitler's actions posed to peace, was most clearly evident at the Munich Conference in September 1938.

Despite his earlier assurances that Czechoslovakia had nothing to fear from Germany, Hitler was clearly intent on taking control of the Sudetenland region of the country. His justification was that he was supporting the large number of German-speaking people living in the region, who were being unfairly treated by the Czech government. For Germany to take part of a country that had been established by the Paris peace settlement would unquestionably pose a major threat to peace in Europe.

Munich Crisis

Initial negotiations designed to reach an agreed resolution to the problem had proved fruitless. Initially asking only for areas where 50% or more of the population was ethnic German, Hitler had increased his demands to include the whole of the Sudetenland region. The loss of such a strategically important area, containing over 70% of Czechoslovakia's heavy industry, would effectively leave the country defenceless, something the Czech government could clearly not accept. As negotiations faltered, it seemed increasingly likely that the situation would lead to a major European war. Under the terms of the Paris peace settlement, and in line with their commitment to the League of Nations, Britain and France would be obligated to protect Czechoslovakia against German aggression.

As so often before, Hitler achieved German territorial expansion without the need for bloodshed. The Munich Conference, attended by the political leaders of Germany, Britain, France and Italy (Hitler, Chamberlain, Daladier and Mussolini respectively), effectively gave in to Hitler's demands. The government of Czechoslovakia was neither invited to the conference nor consulted about the decisions reached by it. Despite the USSR's alliances with both France and Czechoslovakia, Stalin was also not invited to the Conference.

The Munich Conference reached decisions that were designed to prevent a major European war. It was agreed that Germany should take control of the whole of the Sudetenland, in return for Hitler's guarantee that he had no more territorial ambitions. Other Czech territories were given to Poland and Hungary, in line with the concept of self-determination for ethnic minorities. Czechoslovakia was left defenceless and only nominally independent. The Czech government was informed that it must accept the Munich Agreement, or fight Germany alone.

Historians perceive the Munich Conference as the clearest example of appeasement. They argue that, in a desperate attempt to avoid a major war, Britain and France were effectively giving in to Hitler's demands. Both Britain and France were ignoring their commitment to uphold the Paris peace settlement. Moreover, France was ignoring its obligations under the terms of its defensive alliance with Czechoslovakia.

Chamberlain, convinced that Hitler's demands were both justified and reasonable, returned to Britain proudly boasting that the Munich agreements guaranteed peace in Europe.

Daladier was less convinced than Chamberlain. He was convinced that Germany's success in gaining the Sudetenland would lead to further territorial demands by Hitler, posing a threat to countries such as Poland. He agreed to go along with the decisions made at Munich only because he was well aware of the fact that France was neither militarily nor financially prepared for war. He returned to France anticipating a hostile reception from the French people. Instead he was applauded as the man who had helped to prevent a war.

The apparent ending of the threat of imminent war was greeted with great relief in both Britain and France. Elsewhere, too, Chamberlain and Daladier were seen as great statesmen for their efforts in preserving peace. Newspapers in both Sweden and Norway campaigned for Chamberlain to be awarded the Nobel Peace Prize. The prime minister of Egypt sent a telegram to Chamberlain thanking him for averting war and describing him as the 'statesman who saved civilisation from destruction'.

Not everyone was convinced, however. Some British politicians, most notably Winston Churchill, criticised Chamberlain for weakly giving in to Hitler's bullying tactics. They argued that Hitler could not be trusted to honour the commitments he had made in Munich. In October 1938, British politicians discussed the Munich Agreement in parliament. Here are extracts from two of the speeches:

ACTIVITY 3.19

Compare and contrast the views expressed about the Munich Agreement by Chamberlain and Churchill during the parliamentary discussion in October 1938.

You need to consider issues such as

- areas of agreement – for example, both Chamberlain and Churchill wanted to avoid Britain's involvement in a major war
- areas of disagreement – for example, Chamberlain argued that the Munich Conference was a success, while Churchill felt it was a failure
- the ways in which they each justify their views
- what they were trying to achieve by making their speeches

At the end of the parliamentary debate, British MPs voted on whether or not to support Britain's strategy at the Munich Conference – 369 voted in support, 150 voted against.

a What does this suggest about the British attitude towards appeasement in 1938?

b Use the table below to note the arguments used by those who supported the policy of appeasement and those who opposed it-

SUPPORTING ARGUMENTS	OPPOSING ARGUMENTS

In my view, the strongest force of all … was that unmistakable sense of unanimity among the peoples of the world that war must somehow be averted. The peoples of the British Empire were at one with those of Germany, of France and of Italy, and their anxiety, their intense desire for peace pervaded the whole atmosphere of the conference … Ever since I assumed my present office my main purpose has been to work for the pacification of Europe … The path which leads to peace is long and bristles with obstacles. The question of Czechoslovakia is the latest and perhaps the most dangerous. Now that we have got past it, I feel that it may be possible to make further progress along the road to sanity.

Neville Chamberlain to the House of Commons, 3 October 1938

We have sustained a total and unmitigated defeat … The utmost he [the Prime Minister] has been able to gain for Czechoslovakia … has been that the German dictator, instead of snatching his victuals [food] from the table, has been content to have them served to him course by course … The Czechs, left to themselves and told they were going to get no help from the Western Powers, would have been able to make better terms than they have got … I have always held the view that the maintenance of peace depends upon the accumulation of deterrents against the aggressor … I venture to think that in the future the Czechoslovak State cannot be maintained as an independent entity … Czechoslovakia will be engulfed in the Nazi regime.

Winston Churchill to the House of Commons, 5 October 1938

Reflection: What other evidence could you use to make a judgement about public opinion of appeasement in both Britain and France during the late 1930s?

Of all the successor states formally established by the Paris peace settlement, Czechoslovakia had arguably been the most successful. Possessing raw materials, good agricultural land and productive industries, Czechoslovakia had a sound economic base, and it had managed to maintain a democratic form of government despite the multi-ethnic nature of its population. Moreover, it had seemingly ensured its national security by making a series of protective alliances, most notably with France and the USSR. As a result of agreements reached at the Munich Conference, Czechoslovakia was severely weakened. Without any consultation with its government, Czechoslovakia was forced to give up territory that was vital to both its economic well-being and its ability to defend itself. Moreover, its most important ally, France, had been party to the decisions made at Munich. Czechoslovakia, formally renamed Czecho-Slovakia, was left totally exposed to invasion.

The outcome of the Munich Conference also caused disappointment, anger and concern in the USSR. Despite the fact that the USSR had, like France, signed a treaty of mutual assistance with Czechoslovakia, Stalin was not invited to the conference. In his absence, Britain and France had agreed to allow Germany to take control of Czech territory, greatly weakening a country that formed a defensive barrier between Germany and the USSR. From Stalin's perspective, Britain and France had colluded with Hitler, rewarding his aggressive actions in a manner that threatened the national security of the USSR. Stalin concluded that, just as they had done nothing to defend Czechoslovakia, Britain and France would take no action in response to any future aggression Hitler might launch against the USSR. The Munich Conference, therefore, led to a fundamental change in Stalin's foreign policy in the interests of the USSR's security. Rather than seeking better relations with Britain and France, which he now considered to be unreliable and untrustworthy allies, Stalin decided to seek negotiations with Hitler.

While the appeasement policies of Britain and France may have seemed logical, and indeed popular, at the time, they clearly had catastrophic effects. They undermined the effectiveness of the League of Nations to the extent that Japan and Italy were allowed to get away with blatant acts of aggression in Manchuria and Abyssinia respectively. Appeasement had allowed Hitler to progressively destroy the Treaty of Versailles – through rearmament, remilitarisation of the Rhineland, the *Anschluss* and, at Munich, acceptance of his claims over territory that was vital to the future viability of Czechoslovakia. By the late 1930s, appeasement had helped to create a situation in which three countries, all dictatorships committed to territorial expansion and in alliance with each other, posed a significant risk to international peace.

3.4 Why did war break out in 1939?

British rearmament in response to Germany's expansionism

It quickly became apparent that Churchill's prediction was accurate – Hitler had no intention of keeping the promises he had made at Munich. On 15 March 1939, German troops began the takeover of the remainder of Czechoslovakia. Even those who had appeased Hitler for so long realised that it was time for confrontation.

Speaking in Birmingham on 17 March 1939, Chamberlain accepted that the policy of appeasement had failed.

> I went there [Munich] first and foremost because in what appeared to be an almost desperate situation, that seemed to me to offer the only chance of avoiding a European war. And I might remind you that, when it was first announced that I was going, not a voice was raised in criticism. Everyone applauded that effort … The first and most immediate object of my visit was achieved. The peace of Europe was saved … I have no need to defend my visits to Germany last autumn, for what was the alternative? Nothing that we could have been done … could possibly have saved Czechoslovakia from invasion and destruction … I had another purpose, too, in going to Munich. That was to further the policy … which is sometimes called European Appeasement … I felt that … by the exercise of mutual goodwill and understanding … it should be possible to resolve all differences by discussion and without armed conflict … In view of those [Hitler's] repeated assurances, given voluntarily to me, I considered myself justified in founding a hope upon them that, once this Czechoslovakian question was settled … it would be possible to carry farther that policy of appeasement … I am convinced that after Munich the great majority of the British people shared my hope.

Chamberlain went on in the speech to consider the possibility that Hitler's actions against Czechoslovakia might be 'a step in the direction of an attempt to dominate the world by force'. As a direct warning to the German chancellor, he continued: 'No greater mistake could be made than to suppose that, because it believes war to be a senseless and cruel thing, this nation has so lost its fibre that it will not take part to the utmost of its power in resisting such a challenge if it were ever made … We value peace, but we value freedom even more'.

ACTIVITY 3.20

In pairs or small groups, discuss the following:
- How does Chamberlain define the policy of appeasement?
- What methods did Chamberlain use in his speech in an attempt to justify the policy of appeasement?
- Why would Chamberlain have been embarrassed by the events of 15 March 1939?

Chamberlain clearly hoped that his strong words would deter Hitler from any further aggressive actions. In truth, Britain was militarily ill-prepared to fight a major war. At the end of the First World War, Britain had significantly reduced its military capabilities. The British government adopted the 'Ten Year Rule', which was based on the assumption that Britain would not be involved in a major war for the next ten years. This led to a major cutback in defence spending, from £766 million between 1919–20 to £189 million in 1921–22, and £102 million in 1931–32.

KEY CONCEPT

Historians analyse the reasons why changes occur, particularly when these changes are sudden and very different from what had gone before.

Continuity and change

Chamberlain had always followed an appeasement policy, believing that this was the best way to avoid Britain's involvement in another major war. As late as 15 March 1939, when German troops entered Czechoslovakia, Chamberlain was still claiming that Hitler had not broken the promises he made at Munich.

By 17 March 1939, Chamberlain's attitude had changed. He was speaking critically of Hitler and making it clear that Britain would resist any future German aggression.

How can we explain this sudden change?

As international tensions increased following Japan's invasion of Manchuria, Britain abandoned the 'Ten Year Rule' in 1932. Senior military commanders were expressing concern that, in the event of war, Britain would be unable to defend its empire, its trade and even its own security. In response, the British government appointed a Defence Requirements Sub-Committee (DRC) to identify how best to address deficiencies in Britain's ability to defend its national interests. The DRC's first report, submitted in 1934, suggested that Britain would be likely to face involvement in a major war within five years. Hitler's Germany was not seen as the major immediate threat to peace. The report argued that the priorities were first to defend British interests in the Far East against Japanese expansionism, and second to protect British-owned India.

The DRC did, however, identify Germany as a significant threat to British security in the long-term. To address these concerns, the DRC recommended that Britain spend an additional £75 million on defence over the next five years. At a time when Britain was experiencing major economic problems as a result of the Great Depression, it could ill-afford such expenditure. There were other priorities, such as housing, health and education – all of which would be more politically acceptable to a British public heavily opposed to war. While accepting many of the DRC's report's recommendations, the British government reduced the additional defence spending to £50 million, spread over ten tears rather than five.

The DRC's priorities had changed by the time it submitted its second report in 1936. It now argued that war against Germany, Italy and Japan was extremely likely. It also gave the stark warning that this would be a war that Britain could not win. Accordingly, the DRC suggested that Britain should greatly increase its rearmament programme, but, at the same time, continue with its appeasement policy in the hope that Hitler could be deterred from further aggression.

The British government accepted the DRC's report and set about implementing its recommendations. Appeasement remained the main policy, with Chamberlain increasingly convinced that Germany's own economic problems would eventually force Hitler to end his aggressive foreign policy. At the same time, Britain began the process of developing its defence capabilities. Its Royal Air Force, which was still relying on First World War biplanes as late as 1935, was provided with new planes, mainly Spitfires and Hurricanes. As it became increasingly clear that Germany and Japan were greatly enhancing their naval resources, the Royal Navy was provided with new battleships and aircraft carriers, while some of its other ships were modernised. The aim was to ensure that the British navy was powerful enough to defend both Britain itself and its empire. Priority was afforded to the RAF and the navy, which were seen as vital to Britain's national defence. By 1939, Britain was committed to building 9 battleships, 25 cruisers, 43 destroyers and 19 submarines. In view of the enormous expenditure involved in developing the RAF and the navy, less was spent on the army. For the British government, the idea of sending armed forces to fight in Europe was very much a last resort. While the army was promised modern weapons and tanks, these took time to be manufactured and only limited progress had been made by the outbreak of war in 1939.

In response to the imminent threat of war posed by Hitler's claims over the Sudetenland region of Czechoslovakia, a British Expeditionary Force (BEF) was established in 1938. In the event of war breaking out, the BEF would be stationed in France to prevent Germany from threatening Britain by gaining access to the French ports. Government subsidies were provided to encourage many privately owned factories to produce military equipment. Between 1938 and 1939, the production of anti-aircraft guns increased four-fold, and 20 new radar stations were built around Britain's coastline.

In effect, Britain was preparing for a war that seemed increasingly likely – but a war it still hoped to avoid by continuing the appeasement strategy of negotiating with Hitler. Impressive though this rearmament programme sounds, it should be remembered that its primary purpose was the defence of Britain rather than preparation for fighting a war on European soil. In reality, Britain was ill-prepared to launch an attack on Hitler's Germany. On the day war broke out, the British army was composed of only 897 000 men. At the same time, the French army numbered 5 million, and, during the Second World War, over 13 million soldiers served in the German army. Whereas Britain had spent £350 million on armaments in 1937–1938, Germany had spent £1 600 million. By the end of 1938, Britain had fewer than 1 000 modern aircraft – Germany had 2 800.

ACTIVITY 3.21

In pairs, discuss whether you think Britain was unprepared for war in 1939. Following your discussion, make detailed notes using the table below to help you form a judgment.

AGREE	DISAGREE

The British guarantee to Poland and the failure of appeasement

With Czechoslovakia now under German control, there could be little doubt that Poland would be Hitler's next target. Just as in Czechoslovakia, there were a large number of German-speaking people living in Poland. Moreover, Hitler had long made it clear that he viewed the Polish Corridor, which effectively divided Germany into two parts, as yet another unfair outcome of the Treaty of Versailles. Confronted with this situation, Chamberlain's government completely reversed its policy – having done nothing to protect Czechoslovakia, it now provided Poland with a guarantee of British support in the event of a German attack.

At a time when Britain lacked the means to mount a full-scale war in Europe, Chamberlain was providing the Polish government with a guarantee of immediate British assistance in the event of a German attack on Poland. Under the terms of the Anglo-Polish agreement, Britain was making a commitment to fight a war in continental Europe. Having been criticised for following a policy of appeasement that had clearly failed, Chamberlain was now criticised for pledging British support to Poland. Many British politicians argued that providing Poland with a guarantee of British support would inevitably lead to Britain's involvement in a major war – and a war that Britain could not win. The British politician Duff Cooper, for example, wrote in his diary: 'Never before in our history have we left in the hands of one of the smaller powers the decision whether or not Britain goes to war.'

Chamberlain was clearly of the opinion that Britain's message of support for Poland would deter Hitler from taking action against it. There was some justification for this viewpoint. Many German generals (including Brauchitsch, Halder and Keitel) thought that Hitler should adopt a more diplomatic approach to foreign policy following the conquest of Czechoslovakia. They believed that any further aggressive action, particularly against Poland, would inevitably lead to an unwelcome war against Britain and France. However, Hitler remained convinced that he could continue his aggressive foreign policy without other major European powers intervening. He argued that it would be impossible to maintain the German economy 'without invading other countries or attacking other people's possessions'.

In April 1939, Hitler demanded the return of Danzig and for German access across the Polish Corridor. In some ways these were understandable demands. Danzig's population was largely German-speaking while the Polish Corridor had split East Prussia from the rest of Germany. Even Churchill, arguably the most vocal opponent of appeasement, argued that Britain should encourage Poland to make concessions to Germany over Danzig and the Polish Corridor. In view of recent events in Czechoslovakia, the Poles were naturally concerned that Hitler's demands were merely the first step towards a full-scale German invasion of Poland. Moreover, Hitler's demands were in defiance of a non-aggression treaty that Hitler had signed with Poland in 1934. With the guarantee of British support, the Polish government was in no mood to make concessions. As a result of Britain's guarantee to Poland, Hitler delayed the commencement of his invasion of Poland. Originally planned for 26 August, it did not begin until 1 September.

On 27 April 1939, as the threat of war loomed, the British government instituted the Military Training Act, which required all fit and able British men aged 20–21 to have six months of military training. At the same time, Britain entered negotiations with France and the USSR with the aim of forming an alliance to defend Poland against German aggression. With Britain and France too far away to send immediate assistance to the Poles, it was hoped that such an alliance would deter Hitler since it would involve Germany's armed forces having to fight on both western and eastern fronts. Despite his reservations about Britain and France following their appeasement of Hitler at the Munich Conference, Stalin made it clear that he was prepared to commit the USSR to a full military alliance against Germany. However,

these negotiations quickly broke down. This was partly because Poland refused to allow Russian troops to enter Polish territory – much of Poland had been part of the Russian Empire, and the Poles distrusted the USSR's motives. The failure of the negotiations was also partly due to Chamberlain being unable to hide his obvious dislike and distrust of communist Russia. Without an alliance with Britain and France, Stalin looked for another way to maintain the security of the USSR.

ACTIVITY 3.22

a Look carefully at this extract from a letter written by the British prime minister Neville Chamberlain in March 1939. Identify four reasons that Chamberlain gives to explain why he opposed an agreement between Britain and Russia.

> I must confess to the most profound distrust of Russia. I have no belief whatever in Russia's ability to maintain an effective offensive, even if it wanted to. And I distrust Russia's motives, which seem to me to have little connection with our ideas of liberty, and to be concerned only with getting everyone else by the ears. Moreover, Russia is both hated and suspected by many of the smaller states, notably by Poland.

b Look carefully at these views expressed by Winston Churchill in a speech to the British parliament on 19 May 1939. In what ways did he disagree with Chamberlain regarding a possible alliance with Russia?

> I have been quite unable to understand what the objection is to making an agreement with Russia. The proposals put forward by the Russian government contemplate a triple alliance between Britain, France and Russia. The alliance is solely for the purpose of resisting further aggression and protecting the victims of aggression. What is wrong with this simple proposal? We have already given guarantees to Poland. Consequently, if Poland is attacked we shall be at war, and so will Russia. If we are ready to be an ally of Russia in time of war, to join hands with Russia in defence of Poland, why should we shrink from becoming an ally of Russia now, when we may by that very fact prevent the breaking out of war?

c Looking back over this chapter, how would you describe and assess Stalin's foreign policy during the 1930s?

Reasons for the Nazi-Soviet Pact

Convinced that Britain and France would do nothing to defend Poland from a German attack, the main obstacle to Hitler's plans was the USSR. Since the USSR had its own historic claims to parts of Poland, Stalin might well resist any German attempt to take possession of it. Indeed, Stalin had long been convinced that Hitler's ultimate intention was to attack the USSR, and an invasion of Poland could be seen as preparation for this. Stalin's attempts to form an alliance with Britain and France had failed – neither was willing to commit themselves to a formal alliance with a country they considered untrustworthy and intent on spreading communism internationally. At the same time, Stalin had reason to distrust Britain and France following their appeasement of Hitler at the Munich Conference.

Just as Stalin feared Germany under its fascist dictator, so Hitler had spent his entire political career denouncing

communism. To the astonishment of the rest of Europe, Germany and the USSR signed a treaty of friendship and non-aggression on 24 August 1939, following negotiations conducted in secret by their respective foreign ministers, Joachim von Ribbentrop and Vyacheslav Molotov. That Stalin would be prepared to sign an agreement with Hitler, whose aggressive intentions clearly posed a significant threat to the security of the USSR, seemed inconceivable. So too did the fact that Hitler would willingly enter an agreement with a country whose political philosophy he detested, and which would be an obvious target in pursuit of his policy of *Lebensraum*.

Outwardly, this Nazi-Soviet Pact (sometimes referred to as the Molotov-Ribbentrop Pact) was simply an economic agreement extending trading links between Germany and the USSR, together with a mutual pledge not to attack each other. However, it contained a secret agreement that

ACTIVITY 3.23

Look carefully at Figures 3.5 and 3.6, two cartoons relating to the Nazi-Soviet Pact.

SOMEONE IS TAKING SOMEONE FOR A WALK

Figure 3.5: Cartoon from a British newspaper, 1939. Caption reads 'Someone is taking someone for a walk'.

Figure 3.6: Cartoon from a US newspaper, 1939. Title reads 'Little Goldilocks Riding Hood'. The wolf is labelled 'Nazi Germany' the bear is labelled 'Soviet Russia' and Goldilocks is labelled 'Poland'.

a Discuss the following questions in pairs or smal groups.
- What does Figure 3.5 suggest about the Nazi-Soviet Pact?
- What does Figure 3.6 suggest about the Nazi-Soviet Pact?
- What methods do the cartoonists use to put across their message?
- Which cartoon do you feel is more effective and why?

b Compare and contrast the usefulness of the two cartoons for historians studying the Nazi-Soviet Pact. Ensure that your answer considers when the cartoons were published; the motives of the cartoonists; the audiences the cartoons were addressing; what the cartoons suggest about the Nazi-Soviet Pact; the methods used by the cartoonists to put across their ideas; how the cartoons compare with our own knowledge of the Nazi-Soviet Pact.

Germany could attack Poland without the interference of the USSR. In exchange for Stalin's non-intervention in Germany's invasion of Poland, Hitler promised that the USSR would receive eastern parts of Poland, Finland, Estonia and Latvia.

It is unlikely that Hitler intended to honour this promise, but Stalin was fully aware of this and there were logical reasons for his decision to sign the pact. His attempts to form an alliance with Britain and France in the interests of the USSR's national security had failed. Moreover, British and French appeasement of Hitler, particularly at the Munich Conference, had convinced Stalin that they would do nothing to oppose any German attack on the USSR. At the same time, the USSR's interests in the Far East were coming under threat, Japanese forces having made incursions into Soviet Union territory near Manchuria in May 1939. There was a very real possibility that the USSR could face war on two fronts against the combined power of Germany, Japan and Italy, allies in the Anti-Comintern

Pact. Stalin reasoned that signing an agreement would at least delay any subsequent German attack on the USSR, giving him time to build up his armed forces in preparation for it.

Stalin informed one of his senior officials: 'Of course, it's all a game to see who can fool whom. I know what Hitler's up to. He thinks he's outsmarted me, but actually it's I who have tricked him.'

The signing of the Nazi-Soviet Pact was equally beneficial for Hitler. It provided a guarantee that the USSR would do nothing to interfere with his plans for an invasion of Poland. He was already convinced that Poland could expect no assistance from Britain and France, which, he believed, remained committed to the policy of appeasement that had prevented them from taking action in defence of Czechoslovakia. Once Poland had been taken, there would be nothing to prevent Hitler invading the USSR itself.

The rest of Europe understood that the Nazi-Soviet Pact was a treaty of convenience between two dictators who neither liked nor trusted each other. However, the implications of it were clear. There was no longer any possibility of an alliance between Britain, France and the USSR in an attempt to encourage Hitler to restrain his aggressive intentions. Appeasement had been based on the assumption that Hitler's demands were both reasonable and justified, and that the best way of dealing with him was by negotiation. However, Hitler had blatantly ignored the promises he made at the Munich Conference by taking control of the whole of Czechoslovakia. Now, the national security of Poland was clearly under the threat of German aggression. The prospect of a full-scale European war, something the Munich Conference had so desperately tried to avoid, seemed greater than ever.

The invasion of Poland

With Soviet neutrality now assured, there seemed to be nothing stopping Hitler from carrying out his planned invasion of Poland. His generals were still urging him to at least delay the invasion. They argued that the German army (the *Wehrmacht*) was not ready to fight in the east against the Poles and, at the same time, against Britain and France in the west. Hitler dismissed their concerns. He remained convinced that Britain's prime minister Chamberlain and France's Daladier were weak and would do anything to avoid war. Britain's guarantee of support for Poland was, in his opinion, a bluff. Moreover, he believed that a German **blitzkrieg** offensive would quickly achieve

a decisive victory in Poland before Britain and France could react.

KEY TERM

Blitzkrieg: literally meaning 'lightning war', *blitzkrieg* was a military tactic used by Germany in the Second World War. It was based on the concentrated use of aeroplanes, tanks and artillery to disrupt the enemy, allowing German troops to move in and achieve rapid victory.

On 31 August 1939, Nazi soldiers wearing Polish uniforms staged a phony 'invasion' of Germany, an 'unforgivable act of aggression' that Hitler used as justification for the German attack on Poland. On 1 September 1939, German soldiers marched into Poland, supported by 1 300 aircraft.

At 8 a.m. on the same day, the Polish government requested military support from Britain and France. Still hopeful that Hitler could be persuaded to back down, and militarily unprepared for the speed of Germany's offensive, Britain and France were in no position to take immediate action. At 9.30 p.m., the British government issued an ultimatum to the German foreign minister, Joachim von Ribbentrop.

The ultimatum was ignored. At 11 a.m. on 3 September 1939, Prime Minister Chamberlain spoke to the British people via a radio broadcast:

> This morning, the British Ambassador in Berlin handed the German Government a final note stating that unless we heard from them by 11 am that they were prepared at once to withdraw their troops from Poland, that a state of war would exist between us. I have to tell you now that no such undertaking has been received, and that consequently this country is at war with Germany.

Shortly after this announcement, France also declared war on Germany. Hitler's instincts had been wrong. The invasion of Poland was a gamble too far. On the day war was declared, Britain passed the National Service (Armed Forces) Act, which made all men between the ages of 18 and 41 liable for conscription. By the end of 1939, over 1.5 million men had been conscripted into the British armed forces. In support of Germany, Stalin sent Soviet military forces to the Soviet-Polish border. Having negotiated a ceasefire agreement with Japan, preventing further Japanese inroads into Soviet territory near Manchuria, Stalin ordered an invasion of Eastern Poland on 17 September 1939, advancing up to the line agreed in the Nazi-Soviet Pact.

Twenty years after the conclusion of the First World War, the 'war to end all wars', the world was at war again.

The Second World War may have started as a result of the German invasion of Poland, but its causes are more complex. The combined effect of a number of factors, both long- and short-term, led to war. For example:

- problems created by the Paris peace settlement, and in particular the German resentment caused by the harsh terms of the Treaty of Versailles
- the failure of the League of Nations to deal effectively with problems, particularly aggressive acts by countries such as Germany, Italy and Japan
- the world economic crisis that followed the Wall Street Crash and which played a major role in enabling fascist dictators to gain power
- the fear of communism, which assisted the rise of fascist dictatorships and effectively prevented an alliance between Britain, France and the USSR against Hitler's aggression
- appeasement, which gave Hitler the opportunity to develop large and well-equipped armed forces, and led him to believe that he could carry out increasingly provocative acts without opposition
- Stalin's willingness to sign the Nazi-Soviet Pact, which effectively made the German invasion of Poland inevitable
- while Germany could argue that it had a legitimate claim to the Sudetenland, Danzig and access to the Polish Corridor, Hitler's decisions to take the whole of Czechoslovakia and invade Poland could have no justification and made war unavoidable.

ACTIVITY 3.24

On 3 September, Chamberlain announced Britain's declaration of war in a speech broadcast on the radio.

Look carefully at Chamberlain's radio speech, and then discuss the following questions in small groups.

a Why do you think Britain declared war in defence of Poland when it had done nothing to protect Czechoslovakia?

b How did Chamberlain use the speech to justify the policies he had adopted in response to Hitler's aggression?

c What reasons did Chamberlain give to justify Britain's declaration of war against Germany?

ACTIVITY 3.24 (CONTINUED)

You can imagine what a bitter blow it is to me that my long struggle to win peace has failed. Yet I cannot believe that there is anything more or anything different that I could have done that would have been more successful. Up to the very last it would have been quite possible to have arranged a peaceful and honourable settlement between Germany and Poland, but Hitler would not have it. He had evidently made up his mind to attack Poland whatever happened. His action shows convincingly that there is no chance of expecting that this man will ever give up his practice of using force to gain his will. The situation in which no word given by Germany's ruler could be trusted has become intolerable. He can only be stopped by force.

Reflection: How did you identify reasons which Chamberlain gave to justify Britain's declaration of war? Would you change how you identified these reasons after your discussion?

133

Historians disagree about the long-term motives and ambitions of Hitler's foreign policy, and in particular whether it had always been his intention to involve Germany in a major war.

In the period immediately after the Second World War, historians such as Hugh Trevor-Roper argued that Hitler had always intended for Germany to become involved in a major war. They claimed that his long-term aim had consistently been the conquest of Russia and that the acquisition of Poland was merely the prelude to an attack on Stalin's USSR. Sooner or later, they claim, this policy was bound to lead to a war against the other major European powers. Evidence for this theory comes from Hitler's own words in *Mein Kampf*, the book he had written long before he rose to power in Germany and in which he stated that the German population was too large for the boundaries in which it was constrained. His solution was *Lebensraum*. It is also known that Hitler explained his expansionist ideas to key army personnel at a meeting in 1937; this is recorded in the Hossbach Memorandum, a summary of the meeting made by Colonel Friedrich Hossbach.

Martin Gilbert, writing in the 1980s, argued that Hitler intended to fight a major European war in order to remove the stigma attached to Germany's embarrassing defeat in the First World War. 'The only antidote to defeat in one war', Gilbert claims, 'is victory in the next.' Ian Kershaw (1999) agrees, stating that 'Hitler had never doubted, and had said so on innumerable occasions, that Germany's future could only be determined through war.'

In 1989, the German historian Eberhard Jäckel argued that Hitler consistently worked for 'the establishment of a greater Germany than had ever existed before. The way to this greater Germany was a war of conquest fought mainly at the expense of Soviet Russia.'

Other historians, most notably A. J. P. Taylor writing in 1961, challenge this theory, arguing that Hitler had never intended a major war. They suggest that Hitler was an opportunist, taking advantage of situations as they occurred, and that his foreign policy had not been based on a step-by-step plan of conquest. Such a long-term plan would have been impossible, they claim, because Hitler could not have predicted how Britain and France would react to developments such as rearmament and the occupation of the Rhineland. As evidence to support this view, they cite Hitler's own concerns that, in 1936, German soldiers might be forced to withdraw from the Rhineland if they met resistance from other European countries. They suggest that the idea of *Lebensraum* was merely a propaganda tool to gain further support for the Nazi Party and was never intended as a plan for aggressive action.

Alan Bullock suggests that Hitler never intended or wanted a world war and, least of all, a war against Britain and France. Such a war would make it much harder for Hitler to defeat the USSR since it would force Germany to fight on two fronts, against the USSR in the east and against Britain and France in the west. The weak British response to Hitler's aggression between 1933 and early 1939 had convinced him that Britain and France would not interfere with his designs on Poland, leaving the way open for a German attack on the USSR. He had every reason to believe that Britain and France would do nothing to support Stalin's communist regime.

KEY CONCEPT

Interpretation

Historians often interpret the same events in different ways, reaching different conclusions. The examination requires you to interpret events and reach your own conclusions.

In pairs, look carefully at the following statements. For each, decide whether you agree or disagree with it, and explain why.

- Hitler always expected, and indeed wanted, a war against Britain and France.
- Hitler's aim was to gain more territory for Germany without going to war.
- Hitler was simply an opportunist, taking advantage of situations as they arose.
- Hitler's foreign policy was based on a detailed long-term plan that would inevitably lead to war.
- The only war that Hitler wanted was one against the USSR.
- Hitler had every reason to believe that Britain and France would do nothing in response to the German invasion of Poland.

Exam-style questions

Source analysis questions

Read all four sources and then answer both parts of question 1.

British reaction to the outcome of the Munich Conference, 1938

SOURCE A

Be glad in your hearts. Give thanks to your God. People of Britain, your children are safe. Your husbands and your sons will not march to war. Peace is a victory for all mankind. If we must have a victor, let us choose Chamberlain. For the Prime Minister's conquests are mighty and enduring – millions of happy homes and hearts relieved of their burden. To him the laurels. And now let us go back to our own affairs. We have had enough of those menaces, conjured up from the Continent to confuse us.

Editorial in The Daily Express, *a British newspaper, 30 September 1938*

SOURCE B

On his return to London, large crowds cheered Mr Chamberlain. The cries were all for 'Neville', and he stood there waving his hand and smiling. 'My good friends', Mr Chamberlain said – it took some time to quiet the crowd so that he might be heard – 'This is peace with honour. I believe it is peace for our time.' No one in this country who examines carefully the terms under which Hitler's troops march into Czechoslovakia today can feel other than unhappy. Certainly the Czechs will hardly appreciate Mr Chamberlain's phrase that it is 'peace with honour'. If Germany's aim was the economic destruction of Czechoslovakia, the Munich agreement goes far to satisfy it. Czechoslovakia is rendered helpless, and Hitler will be able to advance again when he chooses, with greatly increased power.

Editorial in The Manchester Guardian, *a British newspaper, 1 October 1938*

SOURCE C

We all feel relief that war has not come this time. However, we cannot feel that peace has been established. The Munich agreement has not been a victory for reason and humanity. It has been a victory for brute force. The events of these last few days constitute one of the greatest diplomatic defeats that this country has ever sustained. There can be no doubt that it is a tremendous victory for Herr Hitler. Without firing a shot, by the mere display of military force, he has achieved a dominating position in Europe. He has destroyed Czechoslovakia, the last fortress of democracy in Eastern Europe, which stood in the way of his ambition. He has opened his way to the food, the oil and the resources which he requires in order to consolidate his military power. He has successfully defeated the forces that might have stood against the rule of violence.

Clement Attlee MP, addressing the British Parliament, 3 October 1938

SOURCE D

Chamberlain has pulled off a masterly coup. Nobody else could have done the trick and I have no doubt that prayer helped the result. He will be the darling of the Western world for a while. There will be some nasty moments as the Germans march into the Sudeten territory and the worthless Czechs flee before them. I am convinced that Hitler will not now go to war. My own impression is that Europe, including the Nazis, has now turned its back on world war, if only because a general war means letting Russia loose in Europe. I believe a final settlement, including disarmament, may be possible if Chamberlain's lead is followed up.

Lord Lothian, a member of the British House of Lords, in conversation with a colleague, October 1938

1 a Compare and contrast the views expressed in Sources A and B regarding the agreement which emerged from the Munich Conference.

b 'In October 1938, the British people believed that the risk of war with Germany was over.' How far do Sources A to D support this view?

Essay based questions

Answer both parts of the questions below.

2 a Why did Germany become involved in the Spanish Civil War?

b 'By the end of 1938, Hitler had completely destroyed the Treaty of Versailles.' How far do you agree?

3 a Why was Stalin prepared to sign the Nazi-Soviet Pact?

b 'A foolish and pointless gesture.' How far do you agree with this assessment of Britain's guarantee to support Poland in 1939?

Sample answers

Here is a sample answer to the source-based question:

'In October 1938, the British people believed that the risk of war with Germany was over.' How far do sources A to D support this view?

Since coming to power in Germany, Hitler had pursued an aggressive foreign policy in blatant defiance of the Treaty of Versailles. German rearmament, re-occupation of the Rhineland and achievement of Anschluss with Austria had all caused great concern in Britain and in other European countries such as France. Hitler`s claims to the Sudetenland area of Czechoslovakia posed a genuine threat to peace within Europe since Britain and France had a commitment to protect Czechoslovakia, a nation effectively created by the Paris Peace Settlement, from German aggression. To the British people, desperate to avoid involvement in another major conflict, war against Germany seemed inevitable. There was, therefore, understandable relief when the British Prime Minister Chamberlain, together with his French counterpart Daladier, reached agreement with Hitler at the Munich Conference in late September 1938.

Chamberlain returned to Britain proudly claiming that he had achieved 'peace with honour' and that the promises Hitler had made at Munich meant an end to the threat of war. That there was widespread support within Britain for Chamberlain`s achievement at Munich is reflected in sources A, B and D. The Daily Express newspaper (Source A) clearly believed that the Munich agreement ended the threat of war – 'Your husbands and your sons will not march to war.' It expresses great relief ('Give thanks to your God.') and argues that Chamberlain should be highly praised for his 'mighty and enduring' conquests. A similar view was held by the British politician Lord Lothian (Source D), who argues that Chamberlain had achieved a 'masterly coup' and that 'nobody else could have done the trick'. Lord Lothian clearly agreed with the Daily Express that the Munich agreement ended the threat of war – 'I am convinced that Hitler will not now go to war'. Reporting on the reaction to Chamberlain`s return to Britain from Munich, the Manchester Guardian (Source B) describes the 'large crowds' cheering the Prime Minister and chanting his name – a clear indication of the widespread support for the Munich agreement and belief that the threat of war was over. Even the British politician Clement Attlee (Source C), who was clearly opposed to the Munich agreement, admitted that 'we all feel relief that war has not come this time'.

However, not everyone supported the agreement which Chamberlain had made with Hitler at Munich or believed that it genuinely ended the threat of war. The Manchester Guardian (B) argues that the Munich agreement rendered Czechoslovakia defenceless and that Hitler would subsequently invade the whole country. It concludes by suggesting that 'Hitler will be able to advance again when he chooses, with greatly increased power'. The implication is that the Munich agreement may have delayed a war, but had not prevented one. This interpretation is shared by Clement Attlee in Source C. He argues that at Munich, Chamberlain had simply given in to Hitler`s aggressive demands and that, as a result, Hitler would demand even more. Describing the Munich agreement as a 'diplomatic defeat' for Britain, Attlee suggests that it would enable Hitler to 'consolidate his military power' and subsequently 'defeat the forces that might have stood against the rule of violence'.

The four sources reflect the British people`s contrasting views regarding Chamberlain`s policy of appeasement. Lord Lothian (D) was a firm believer in appeasement as the right way of dealing with Hitler`s demands, and this is clearly reflected in his praise of Chamberlain following the Munich agreement and his belief that the threat of war had been averted. The Daily Express (A) clearly shared this view, as did the large crowds which assembled to praise Chamberlain on his return from

Munich. Conversely, the Manchester Guardian (B) and Clement Attlee (C) were clearly opposed to appeasement, arguing that it simply gave in to Hitler's aggressive and unjustified demands, delaying rather than averting the risk of war.

> The answer demonstrates excellent understanding of the sources in their historical context. It successfully groups the sources according to their support for or challenge of the hypothesis, and makes effective use of cross-referencing (eg showing areas of agreement between Sources A and D, and Sources B and C). There is some attempt at provenance evaluation although this is largely restricted to the statement that 'Lord Lothian was a firm believer in appeasement', used as a way of explaining his support for Chamberlain's actions at Munich.
>
> The answer does have two major weaknesses:
> - The opening paragraph, while providing important contextual information, makes no reference at all to the sources. As a result, this introduction gives no indication of the argument which the answer will develop in direct response to the actual question. It would have been better to incorporate this contextual information into the analysis of the sources themselves.
> - The answer is clearly balanced – it shows good understanding of the arguments which might be used to both support and challenge the hypothesis. However, it never reaches an actual conclusion regarding how far the sources support the view that 'in October 1938, the British people believed that the risk of war with Germany was over'. In effect, the answer provides much of the analysis necessary to develop a fully-focused and explicit argument, but never actually does so.

Here are two sample answers to the following question:

How far had Hitler achieved his foreign policy aims by April 1938?

ANSWER 1

From the moment he gained power in Germany, Hitler adopted an aggressive foreign policy. First, he removed Germany from the League of Nations and then began rearming Germany, breaking the Treaty of Versailles.

In 1935, Hitler ordered the invasion of Abyssinia and in 1936 German troops reoccupied the Rhineland, an area which was supposed to have no military presence.

Hitler tested the efficiency of his redeveloped military by taking part in the Spanish Civil War. By 1937, Hitler had formed an alliance with both Italy and Japan. This was known as the Anti-Comintern Pact. The following year, Hitler

ensured the union of Austria and Germany, another act which broke the Treaty of Versailles.

Hitler then turned his attention to Czechoslovakia. Having negotiated Germany's control over part of the country, he then sent in German troops to take over the rest of it.

In order to remove possible opposition to his planned attack on Poland, he formed a treaty with the USSR. Hitler then invaded Poland and was shocked when Britain and France came to the aid of the Poles. The Second World War had begun.

> This is an entirely narrative answer – it simply describes Hitler's foreign actions without addressing the actual question.
>
> There is no attempt to explain what Hitler's foreign policy aims actually were – without this, it is impossible to evaluate how far he had achieved them by April 1938. While much of the answer is factually accurate, there are some errors. For example, it was Mussolini's Italy rather than Hitler's Germany which invaded Abyssinia.
>
> The final two paragraphs are irrelevant. Germany's takeover of Czechoslovakia and invasion of Poland took place in 1939 – outside the date range specified in the question.
>
> **[The aim of *positive marking* is to reward positive aspects of an answer, rather than punish weaknesses. Therefore marks would not be deducted for factual errors or content which is irrelevant, but no marks would be awarded for knowledge when it is misapplied either.]**
>
> This is a weak answer. The writer clearly has some knowledge, but displays limited depth of understanding.

ANSWER 2

Once he gained power in Germany, Hitler made his foreign policy aims very clear. In particular, he wanted to destroy the Treaty of Versailles and regain Germany's place as a major world power. To achieve this, he intended to rebuild Germany's army, navy and air force, form a union with Austria (Anschluss), recover all lost German territory and bring all German-speaking people under Germany's control. By April 1938, Hitler had achieved all these things.

In 1933, Hitler withdrew Germany from both the World Disarmament Conference and the League of Nations. He then began rearming, in defiance of the Treaty of Versailles. He cleverly signed a naval agreement *with Britain in 1935 – an agreement by which Britain accepted Germany's rearmament. The following year, he remilitarised the Rhineland, again in defiance of the Treaty of Versailles.*

By 1937, Hitler had formed the Anti-Comintern Pact with Italy and Japan. Closer relations with Italy's leader, Mussolini, removed possible opposition to Anschluss. Mussolini had helped prevent Hitler's plans for Anschluss in 1934, but was now an ally. In 1938, Anschluss was achieved, yet another destruction of the Treaty of Versailles.

By April 1938, therefore, Hitler had achieved his foreign policy aims. Germany was once again regarded as a major world power, and the Treaty of Versailles had been destroyed. Moreover, he had achieved all this without having to go to war.

This answer is based on a good understanding of the question. A relevant argument is developed, supported by appropriate factual evidence.

The opening paragraph outlines Hitler's foreign policy aims – this is essential, because it provides the criteria by which to evaluate how far he had achieved them by April 1938.

The final sentence of the first paragraph introduces the argument which the answer will develop. This argument remains consistent throughout and is reinforced in the conclusion.

[Inconsistency is a common weakness in answers to questions of this type. Answers often appear to contradict themselves – the argument seems to change as the answer progresses, so that the introduction and the conclusion do not match. This is caused by inadequate planning.]

However, this answer has one major weakness – it lacks balance. The argument is completely one-sided – it does not consider the possibility that Hitler may not have achieved all his foreign policy aims by April 1938. For example:

- all German-speaking people were not under Germany's control by April 1938 – e.g. there were many living in Czechoslovakia and Poland
- Hitler had not recovered all lost German territory – e.g. the Polish Corridor
- another of Hitler's stated aims was *Lebensraum* – no progress had been made on this by April 1938.

Now write your own answer to the question, remembering to develop a consistent and balanced argument.

Summary

After working through this chapter, make sure you understand the following key points:

- the impact on international relations of the growth of political extremism and the rise of dictatorships in the 1930s
- the reasons why the League of Nations failed to take effective action in response to the kind of international aggression it had been established to prevent
- the reasons for, and the impact of, the adoption of a policy of appeasement by Britain and France
- the long- and short-term causes of the Second World War.

Further reading

Hall, K., Brown, D. and Williams, B. (2015). *Nationalism, Dictatorship and Democracy in 20th Century Europe.* **Pearson.** The section on Germany contains a useful analysis of the extent to which Hitler was responsible for the Second World War. The section on Spain provides a good account of the Spanish Civil War.

Henig, R. (2005). *The Origins of the Second World War 1933–1941.* **Routledge.** A short book which analyses the short- and long-term causes of the Second World War.

Hinton, C. and Hite, J. (2000). *Weimar and Nazi Germany.* **Hodder.** Section 3 Chapter 20 analyses the reasons for Hitler's foreign policy success in the period to 1939.

Kearey, K. (2015). *International Relations and Global Conflict c1890–1941.* **Oxford University Press.** Sections 5 and 6 provide good background coverage of international relations in the 1930s.

Kershaw, I. (2001). *The Hitler Myth:* **Image and Reality in the Third Reich. Oxford University Press.** Chapter 5 provides a well-written analysis of Hitler's foreign policy in the period up to 1939.

Overy, R. J. (2009). *The Inter-War Crisis*, 1919–1939. **Routledge.** Chapter 5 is useful for understanding the impact of the Great Depression. Chapter 6 analyses the reasons for the rise of dictatorships. Chapter 7 deals with the reasons why war broke out in 1939.

Stedman, A. D. (2014). *Alternatives to Appeasement: Neville Chamberlain and Hitler's Germany.* **I. B. Tauris.** A book which analyses what alternatives Britain had to appeasement. Particularly useful is Chapter 3 on the League of Nations.

Traynor, J. (2007). *Mastering Modern German History 1864–1990.* **Palgrave Macmillan.** Chapter 11 provides detailed information on Hitler's foreign policy and its impact on international relations.

Waller, S. and Rowe, C. (2016). *Revolution and Dictatorship: Russia* **1917–53. Oxford University Press.** Chapter 20 outlines the USSR's international relations during the 1930s.

Williamson, D. (2015). *War and Peace:* **International Relations 1890–1945. Hodder.** Chapters 7 and 8 provide good coverage of the major events of the 1930s, and analysis of how these affected international relations. The first part of Chapter 9 outlines the impact of the Japanese invasion of Manchuria.

Chapter 4
China and Japan 1912–1945

Learning Objectives:

In this chapter, you will:

- understand the reasons for the growth of Chinese nationalism 1912–1945
- understand the reasons for, and implications of, the increasing popularity of both the Kuomintang and the Chinese Communist Party 1912–1927
- learn about the reasons for, and implications of, increasing rivalry between the Kuomintang and the Chinese Communist Party 1927–1945
- assess the failure of democracy in Japan and its implications for Japan itself, China and wider international relations.

Timeline

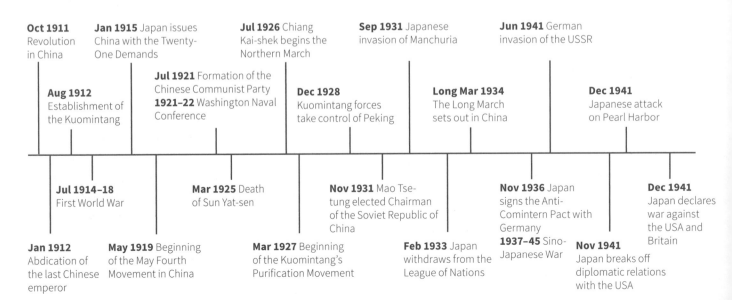

Oct 1911 Revolution in China

Jan 1915 Japan issues China with the Twenty-One Demands

Jul 1926 Chiang Kai-shek begins the Northern March

Sep 1931 Japanese invasion of Manchuria

Jun 1941 German invasion of the USSR

Aug 1912 Establishment of the Kuomintang

Jul 1921 Formation of the Chinese Communist Party
1921–22 Washington Naval Conference

Dec 1928 Kuomintang forces take control of Peking

Long Mar 1934 The Long March sets out in China

Dec 1941 Japanese attack on Pearl Harbor

Jul 1914–18 First World War

Mar 1925 Death of Sun Yat-sen

Nov 1931 Mao Tse-tung elected Chairman of the Soviet Republic of China

Nov 1936 Japan signs the Anti-Comintern Pact with Germany

Dec 1941 Japan declares war against the USA and Britain

Jan 1912 Abdication of the last Chinese emperor

May 1919 Beginning of the May Fourth Movement in China

Mar 1927 Beginning of the Kuomintang's Purification Movement

Feb 1933 Japan withdraws from the League of Nations

1937–45 Sino-Japanese War

Nov 1941 Japan breaks off diplomatic relations with the USA

Before You Start

1 Look again at Chapter 1.1 and 1.2 regarding the impact of imperialism on China in the late 19th century.

Identify appropriate evidence to support each of the following statements:

a 'In the 19th century, China lacked a government that was capable of maintaining control over the country.'

b 'It was not just European nations that sought to gain political and economic influence in China.'

c 'By the end of the 19th century, Chinese nationalism was beginning to develop.'

d 'Foreign nations were prepared to work together, rather than in opposition to each other, in their attempts to exploit China.'

e 'The Boxer Rebellion (1898–1901) completely undermined the authority of the Chinese government.'

2 Discuss your answers in pairs or small groups, making any necessary changes or additions.

3 Which country do you think posed the biggest threat to China by 1912, and why?

Introduction

Confronted with external challenges from the West and internal pressure from a series of large-scale rebellions, China's collapse began in the middle of the 19th century. By 1912, its last emperor was forced to abdicate, ending a system of government that had lasted for thousands of years. The newly proclaimed **republic** was unable to prevent the ongoing disintegration of China into separate provinces, where powerful **warlords** and their private armies established unchallenged control. Rival political groups emerged, their desire to restore order and unity in China dependent on the increasingly large armies they controlled. China was on course for civil war.

> **KEY TERMS**
>
> **Republic:** a state in which political power is held by representatives of the people rather than a monarch.
>
> **Warlords:** regional chieftains who led private armies and competed with each other for control over territory.

For Japan, China's plight created a power vacuum in East Asia that presented both a danger and an opportunity. There was a significant risk that the Western powers (the USA and European nations) would seek to exploit China's weakness in order to enhance their own economic and political influence in the region. This would undoubtedly pose a threat to Japan. Conversely, China's inability to defend itself offered the possibility that Japan could establish itself as the supreme power in East Asia. With the dual aim of protecting its own security whilst increasing its own regional power, Japan had become involved in wars against China (1894–95) and Russia (1904–05). It had sought conquest in Taiwan (1894), South Manchuria (1905) and Korea (1910). Its international prestige had been enhanced by a treaty with Britain in 1902. And, during the First World War when the Western powers were otherwise engaged, Japan emerged as a major power in East Asia.

Japan's seemingly aggressive rise to power caused alarm in Europe and the USA, concerned that their own economic interests in East Asia were under serious threat. These fears seemed to have been allayed by Japan's willingness to compromise at the Washington Naval Conference (1921–22). However, as Japan descended into military dictatorship in the 1930s, it once again embarked upon an aggressive foreign policy that was to lead it into conflict, first with China and subsequently with the Western powers.

> ### The names of Chinese people, places and organisations
>
> Chinese names do not easily transliterate into other languages. A number of different systems have been used to transliterate Chinese names into English.
>
>

The well-established system (known as the Wade-Giles romanisation) was widely used until the 1950s, when the Pinyin system was introduced. As a result, you may come across different versions of the same name during your reading. For example:

Traditional (Wade-Giles)	Pinyin
Kuomintang	Guomindang
Chiang Kai-shek	Jiang Jieshi
Mao Tse-tung	Mao Zedong
Yenan	Yan'an

Throughout this chapter, Wade-Giles spellings are used for Chinese names. The Pinyin version is given in brackets after the first mention of the name.

4.1 What were the implications of the 'warlord era' that affected China from 1916 to 1928?

Issues facing China

During the 19th century, the power and authority of China's ruling family, the Manchu **dynasty**, was gradually eroded. The Western powers, keen to exploit the trading opportunities which China offered, increasingly gained control over many of the Chinese provinces. Defeat against Japan in the First Sino-Japanese War (1894–95) confirmed China's weaknesses (see Chapter 1.3). During the Russo-Japanese War (1904–05), two foreign countries were fighting on Chinese territory for control of Manchuria. The Manchu government could do nothing to prevent it or influence its outcome.

The authority of the Manchu government was also challenged by internal rebellions demanding reform and modernisation. The Manchu empress, Tzu-Hsi (Cixi Taihou), was steadfastly opposed to reform, and enlisted the support of warlords and the foreign powers to put down rebellions. Whereas Japan's response to foreign intervention had been to modernise and adopt Western methods, Tzu-Hsi **purged** her government of all those who supported modernisation.

> **KEY TERMS**
>
> **Dynasty:** a line of hereditary rulers of a country. The Manchu (Ch'ing (Qing)) dynasty ruled China from 1644 to 1912.
>
> **Purge:** from the Latin word *purgare*, which means to purify. To purge in a political context means to remove people who are considered undesirable or harmful.

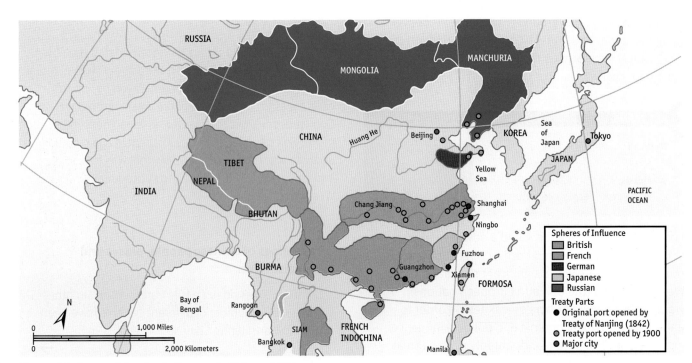

Figure 4.1: Areas of foreign influence in China c.1900

Angered by their government's failure to prevent foreigners gaining increasing power and influence within China, Chinese nationalists took up arms in the Boxer Rebellion (1898–1901). Initially opposed to the rebellion, the Manchu government eventually supported it, declaring war against the foreign powers. An eight-nation alliance of Britain, Russia, Japan, France, the USA, Germany, Italy and Austria-Hungary put down the rebellion and engaged in looting and atrocities. The Manchu government was ordered to pay compensation for the damage that had been done to foreign-owned property during the uprising.

At the same time, China's traditional culture and customs were being undermined. Schools began offering a Western-style education, thousands of young Chinese were sent abroad to be educated and hundreds of European books were translated into Chinese. The traditional examination system, based on Confucian ideas, was abolished in 1905. China also began the process of industrialisation. Coal mines, iron foundries and cotton factories were established, and transport infrastructure was developed with the construction of roads and railways. China was becoming Westernised – a process that was accompanied by increasing demands for reform. Many of the newly educated Chinese argued that, if China was to become a modern nation capable of defending itself against foreign interference, its political systems would need to be significantly changed.

One of the most influential figures in the growing campaign for reform in China was **Sun Yat-sen** (Sun Yixian). Dismayed by China's backwardness and fragmentation, Sun became increasingly convinced that his country needed to adopt Western styles of democracy, agriculture and industry. He founded the Revive China Society in 1894, and in 1905 merged with other anti-government groups to form the Tongmenhui (Revolutionary Alliance), which was committed to overthrowing the Manchu dynasty and forming a republican government in China. Fearing execution when his attempts to start a revolution against the Manchu dynasty failed, Sun Yat-sen left China in 1895. He toured Europe and the USA raising money for the Save China League, and continued to develop his vision for how China should be governed in the future.

Inefficient, corrupt and increasingly unpopular, the Manchu dynasty's hold on power in China suffered a severe blow in 1908 when the Empress Tzu-Hsi died, leaving three-year old

Sun Yat-sen was educated abroad and graduated as a doctor of medicine. He became a professional revolutionary, touring Europe and the USA to raise funds for the Save China League. Risking imprisonment and possible execution, he returned to China several times to campaign for a revolution against the Manchu dynasty, but he was in the USA when the revolution finally took place in 1911.

Pu Yi as heir to the throne. In October 1911, a revolution began amongst soldiers in Wuchang, who were incensed that the government was continuing to pay compensation to the hated foreigners for the Boxer Rebellion. The uprising, which has become known as the Xinhai Revolution, rapidly spread, and most provinces declared themselves independent of the central government in Peking (Beijing). In response, the Manchu government asked **Yuan Shih-kai**, who held great influence within the army, to return from retirement to take up the post of prime minister. Once in power, Yuan gained control of the powerful **Beiyang army**.

 KEY TERM

Beiyang army: the imperial Chinese army established by the Manchu Dynasty in the 19th century.

Yuan Shih-Kai was a warlord and a general in the Chinese army. He gained considerable influence within the Manchu dynasty, helping to defend it against rebellions. When the Manchu dynasty ended, he became president of the Republic of China, but was forced to resign when he lost the support of the army in 1915. He died shortly afterwards.

143

Following the Wuchang uprisings, Sun Yat-sen returned to China and the Revolutionary Alliance joined with other parties to form the **Kuomintang** (Guomindang). Sun was elected as 'Provisional President of the United Provinces of China' at a formal meeting of the independent provinces in December 1911. Sun formally announced the establishment of the Republic of China in January 1912, with its government based in Nanking. In reality, Sun's authority was severely restricted. There was no constitution, the treasury was empty and the Chinese provinces were far from united. Moreover, the country was now divided between the north and south, since the Manchu government, led by Yuan Shih-kai and backed by the Beiyang army, was still in power in Peking.

For a time, it seemed that China might descend into a full-scale civil war. In order to avoid this, negotiations took place between Sun Yat-sen and Yuan Shih-kai. It was agreed that Yuan would arrange for the emperor's abdication, and that China would be unified as a republic with Yuan as president. In March 1912, Following Pu Yi's abdication, Yuan was declared president of the Republic of China with a government, known as the Beiyang Government, based in Peking. A monarchy that had lasted for nearly 2500 years had been formally ended. China was now a republic. A republic, however, with no tradition or experience of constitutional forms of government.

Yuan Shih-kai and the disintegration of China

The new president of the Republic of China, Yuan Shih-kai (Yuan Shikai), was a man of considerable military experience who commanded the support of the army. Yuan's background and political beliefs were different from those of Sun. Opposed to reform, he had helped the Empress Tsu-Hsi retain power in the aftermath of the Boxer Rebellion and had become a highly influential figure within the Manchu government.

As commander of the army division responsible for the protection of Peking, Yuan held great power as this account from 1907 clearly demonstrates:

> In the hunting park, three miles to the south of Peking, is quartered the Sixth Division, which supplies the guards for the Imperial Palace. Commanded by Yuan Shih-Kai, this Division is the pride of the modern Chinese army. Yuan completely controls all the approaches to the capital, and holds a force which he may utilise to protect the Palace from threatened attack or to crush the Empress should he himself desire to assume imperial power.
>
> **Douglas Story,** *Tomorrow In the East* (1907), **pp. 224–26**

In elections following Yuan's appointment as president, the KMT won the popular vote, and planned to appoint its chairman, Sung Chiao-jen, as prime minister. Sung had campaigned to limit the role of the president in China's government. Yuan, however, quickly established himself as a **military dictator**. Political opponents were suppressed and, although it was never proven, it was widely believed that Yuan was responsible for Sung's assassination in 1913. Fearing for his own life, Sun Yat-sen fled to Japan, urging a rebellion against Yuan's government. With the army's full support, Yuan had no difficulty in putting down this rebellion in 1913, and consolidated his own power by banning the KMT as a political organisation and dismissing its members from the government. All hopes that China might develop a democratic form of government were dashed.

With the backing of the Beiyang army, Yuan gradually assumed almost complete control of the government. In 1914 he dismissed the Chinese parliament and issued a new constitution that gave the president complete power over China's military, economy, foreign policy and civil laws.

However, Yuan's authority over China was far from complete, as many of the provinces continued to oppose any form of centralised government. Moreover, Yuan's popularity was severely damaged when he was forced to accept Japan's Twenty-One Demands in 1915 (see Chapter 1.3). These demands gave Japan considerable influence over China's affairs, and to many Chinese it appeared that Yuan's government was just as weak as that of the Manchu dynasty in confronting foreign interference.

Convinced that his position as Chinese leader was secure, Yuan made a serious error of judgement in December 1915. He issued an order cancelling the republican form of government, and proclaimed himself Emperor of China. This caused widespread anger across the country. Revolutionary groups had no wish to see the restoration of a monarchy. More significantly, this move lost him the vital support of the army. Several of the provinces refused to recognise him as emperor, with Yunnan, Kweichow, Kwangsi, Kwangtung, Chekiang, Shensi, Szechuan and Honan all declaring independence. Realising the hopelessness of the situation, Yuan resigned and died shortly afterwards. He had been emperor for just 83 days.

Yuan Shih-Kai's fall from power in 1915, and his death the following year, removed the one person who had seemed capable of preserving order and unity in China. Although the former vice-president, Li Yuan-Hung (Li Yuanhong), became president, he lacked the full support of the army. Denied a strong central government, and increasingly vulnerable to foreign intervention, China disintegrated into hundreds of small states, each controlled by a warlord and the private army at his command. The territory a warlord controlled could range from a few small towns and villages to vast areas such as Manchuria. These warlords were more concerned with their own political powers than with China's national interests. They fought each other in bloody campaigns, each determined to gain wealth and prevent one warlord becoming more powerful than another. To further their individual interests, they were loosely organised into groups and temporary alliances. Their actions caused misery and hardship to China's mainly **peasant** population.

> ### KEY TERM
>
> **Peasants:** Agricultural labourers and (usually small-scale) farmers.

It has been estimated that the total size of the various warlord armies rose from around 500 000 in 1916 to over a million by 1918 and two million in 1928. There were two main reasons for this. First, the Chinese army broke apart following the resignation of Yuan Shih-Kai, its former members drifting into the armies of the various warlords. Second, warlords usually allowed their soldiers to retain a share of whatever they looted or stole from the local Chinese people. To young men in poor rural areas, joining a warlord army seemed a good way of avoiding poverty.

The main aim of the majority of warlords was to gain wealth. They increased taxes within the areas they dominated, and seized control of profitable businesses. This provided the funds necessary to pay their armies. Large numbers of peasants were driven from their land, which was taken over by the soldiers. Some peasants were forcibly conscripted into the warlord armies, while others joined the growing number of Chinese unemployed, which, by 1925, had reached 168 million.

Although the government in Peking had little practical authority in China, it did have the ability to access foreign loans and customs revenue, and therefore was a source of wealth. As a result, various warlords fought for control of the government, leading to instability and corruption, which further weakened the central government.

Not all warlords were motivated entirely by greed for wealth and power. Some made a genuine attempt to improve the lives of the people living in the areas they dominated. For example, Yan Xishan (Yen His-Shan), who controlled Shanxi Province, avoided conflict with other warlords and introduced reforms, such as improved education for girls. The overwhelming majority of warlords, however, were corrupt, violent and selfish rulers, caring little for the local people.

In 1917, following a short, failed revolution that aimed to restore Pu Yi as emperor, Sun Yat-sen returned to China from his exile in Japan. He formed a KMT government based on the 1912 constitution in Canton, in opposition to the government in Peking. However, he relied on assistance from southern warlords in order to maintain control, and was unable to extend KMT authority beyond the Canton area in southern China.

By 1918, therefore, the disintegration of China was complete. The Peking government was weak and had limited authority in the country. As a result, it was unable to carry out vital social and economic reforms. This, together with warlord activity, led to China's economic stagnation. Moreover, the country was politically divided – in the north, warlords were fighting for control of the Peking government, while, in the south, Sun Yat-sen had established a KMT government in Canton. Neither government had the ability to exert control over China's various provinces, where the warlords established their own laws and dictated the lives of ordinary Chinese people.

Ineffective central government, the absence of social and economic reforms and the violence associated with the warlords created circumstances that encouraged radical and revolutionary ideas to emerge and take hold. Hatred of the warlords gave the different revolutionary groups a common aim, providing the foundation for them to work together.

> **ACTIVITY 4.1**
>
> Working in pairs discuss the following questions:
>
> **a** Compare and contrast the political views of Sun Yat-sen and Yuan Shih-kai.
>
> **b** Of these two political views, which do you think was most appropriate for China's needs in the early 20th century? Explain your reasoning.
>
> **c** Why was Yuan Shih-kai unable to hold on to power, and what does this suggest about the problems facing China in the early 20th century?
>
> **d** In your notes, make a list of the problems which faced China in c1900.

Reasons for and impact of the May Fourth Movement

Dismayed by the various problems facing their country, and angered by the chaos inflicted by the warlords, many Chinese intellectuals and writers argued that reform was essential if China was to recover and survive. By 1915, they formed the New Culture Movement, which claimed that China's weakness was caused by its outdated social, political and religious traditions. The movement suggested that the way to restore China's unity and strength was to adopt Western values, such as democracy and individual liberty. This could only be achieved through mass education and changing a culture that relied on a rigid class system and unquestioning obedience to those in power.

The ideas put forward by the New Culture Movement were attractive to Chinese students. At Peking University, for example, student publications, such as *New Youth* and *New Tide*, were heavily critical of traditional Chinese culture which, they claimed, had prevented the country from modernising. They advocated the adoption of Western culture, which would enable China to industrialise, end foreign interference, destroy the unwelcome power of the warlords and reunify. It was students, supported by many of their teachers, who instigated the events of 4 May 1919.

Having fought with the victorious Allies in the First World War, the Chinese assumed that at the end of the conflict they would be able to reclaim the territories in Shantung Province that Germany had occupied since the late 19th century. However, China's representatives were largely ignored at the Paris Peace Conference, which initially decided that the German areas in Shantung should go to Japan. To many students, already committed to the ideas of the New Culture Movement and supporters of Chinese nationalism, this was an unacceptable humiliation.

Radical students at Peking University decided to take action, and drafted a manifesto outlining their aims:

> Japan's demand for rights in Shantung Province is going to be agreed to by the Paris Peace Conference. Japan's diplomacy has secured a great victory, while ours has led to a great failure. This is the last chance for China in its life and death struggle. Today we swear two solemn oaths with all our fellow countrymen. First, China's territory may be conquered, but it cannot be given away. Second, the Chinese people may be massacred, but they will never surrender. Our country is about to be annihilated. Up, brethren!

KEY TERM

Manifesto: a written statement of the beliefs, aims and policies of a person or group of people. Political parties, for example, publish manifestos prior to an election.

On 4 May 1919, some 5 000 students, from Peking University and several other educational establishments, gathered in the streets of Peking. Chanting nationalist slogans, they demonstrated against Japan's occupation of Shantung Province and the weakness of China's national government. They shouted 'do away with the Twenty-One Demands', demanded a boycott of Japanese products and insisted that the government should refuse to sign the Paris peace settlement. Further demands included that three government officials accused of collaborating with the Japanese should be forced to resign. In the chaos that followed, the home of one of these government officials was set on fire.

Fearing the breakdown of law and order, the government dispersed the protesters and arrested almost 40 of its leaders. However, what began as a student demonstration in Peking rapidly spread. In response to the actions taken by the government, students across China went on strike. Angered by the continued detention of student leaders, 100 000 workers in Shanghai declared a week-long general strike in early June. The growing tensions were only eased when the government released the student prisoners and refused to sign the peace treaty granting control of Shantung Province to Japan.

The May Fourth Movement (Wusi Yundong), as these protests have become known, initially appeared to have a positive impact. The Paris Peace Conference accepted the views of the Chinese government, and decided that control of Shantung Province should rest with China after all. In reality, however, this made little difference. China's national government lacked the power and authority required to enforce this decision. Chinese warlords secretly made deals that gave Japan extensive rights in Shantung in exchange for financial support for their own territorial ambitions.

Nevertheless, despite the fact that the student protests appeared to achieve little at the time, many Chinese historians believe that the May Fourth Movement constituted an intellectual revolution that had a major impact on the future of China. They argue that the movement marked the beginning of the struggle to restore the integrity and maintain the unity of China. It did so by promoting Chinese nationalism and encouraging the adoption of more modern social, political, economic and cultural ideas. The movement advocated the eradication of traditional Confucian values, and their replacement with Western concepts of democracy, individual freedom and the development of science and industry. It led to changes in the written form of the Chinese language, making it more accessible and helping to spread literacy. It marked the emergence of a working class, increasingly aware of the power it possessed through industrial action such as strikes. Perhaps most importantly, it helped to shape the early ideologies of China's main political parties, such as the Kuomintang. The Chinese Communist Party (CCP), founded by a group of intellectuals in 1921, traces its own origins back to the May Fourth Movement, as evidenced by a commemorative poster issued by the CCP (Figure 4.2).

147

Figure 4.2: A poster published by the Chinese government in 1959, commemorating the May Fourth Movement.

ACTIVITY 4.2

Describe the ways in which the May Fourth demonstrators hoped China would develop in the future. Your answer should include social, economic, political and cultural issues.

Outline your points using the table below:

SOCIAL	
ECONOMIC	
POLITICAL	
CULTURAL	

Reasons for the growth of the Kuomintang under Sun Yat-Sen

The Chinese Communist Party was established by people, such as Chen Duxiu, who had been actively involved in the May Fourth Movement. Its aim, as stated by Chen Duxiu himself, was 'to establish by revolutionary means a state of the working class in order to create a government and laws to put a stop to internal and external pillaging'. At first, the CCP was a small and relatively insignificant group of intellectuals. Fewer than 20 people attended its first meeting in 1921, and its membership remained below 1 000 by 1925. However, the CCP quickly established connections with, and gained support from, Soviet Russia.

A communist government had been established in Russia following the 1917 revolution. With the aim of encouraging communist groups elsewhere in the world, the new Russian government founded the Comintern (Communist International) in March 1919. The Comintern viewed the revolutionary statements of many Chinese intellectuals as an opportunity to spread communist ideology in Asia. Indeed, the official establishment of the CCP in 1921 resulted from a series of meetings between Chen Duxiu and a Comintern agent.

The Comintern was well aware that the CCP lacked the size and influence required to bring about significant political change in China. It seemed logical for the CCP to join forces with Sun Yat-sen's Kuomintang (KMT) party, which had a larger membership and which was also advocating political reform. Meetings between Sun Yat-sen and Adolf Joffe, a Russian diplomat, resulted in the formation in 1923 of the First United Front – a union between the CCP and the KMT. Chinese communists became members of the KMT.

The KMT was not a communist party, although Sun realised the advantages to be gained by working with the recently formed CCP. In particular, this brought valuable assistance, both financial and organisational, from Soviet Russia. Russian advisors helped to create a more efficient structure for the KMT across southern China, and were important in developing the KMT's army into a more effective fighting force. A military academy was established at Whampoa to train KMT officers. To head the Academy, Sun chose **Chiang Kai-shek** (Jiang Jieshi), who was sent to Moscow to receive military training. Chiang's brief was to ensure that the KMT could both defend itself against attack by warlord armies and also begin to expand its power base outside the Canton area.

In a speech to mark the formal opening of the Whampoa Military Academy, Sun explained its importance:

> Why do we need this Academy? You all know that the Chinese Revolution has gone on for thirteen years. After thirteen years of revolution, the Republic is just an empty name and, even today, the revolution is a complete failure. Our hope is that from today on we will be able to remake our revolutionary enterprise and use the students of this Academy as the foundation of the revolutionary army of the future. Without a good army, the Chinese revolution is doomed to failure. In opening this Academy here today, our only hope is to create a revolutionary army to save China from extinction.

Speech by Sun Yat-sen at the opening ceremony of the Whampoa Military Academy, 16 July 1924

ACTIVITY 4.3

Discuss why the USSR encouraged a union between the KMT and the CCP. You will need to focus on the Chinese context, not the Soviet (USSR) one. What advantages do you think the USSR saw from such a union? What risks do you think were involved?

General Chiang Kai-shek (Jiang Jieshi) had received military training in Japan prior to the First World War. As an ardent nationalist, he joined the KMT and quickly became influential. He was charged with developing the KMT's military capabilities. He emerged as leader of the KMT following Sun Yat-sen's death in 1925.

CHIANG KAI-SHEK 1887–1975

Although they enjoyed a close friendship, Sun Yat-sen and Chiang Kai-shek had different backgrounds, characters and political beliefs. Sun, the son of a peasant farmer, spent much of his life in the west, exposed to western methods of education and political ideologies. He developed a firm belief in the importance of democracy and political reform. Chiang, on the other hand, was the son of a wealthy landowner. Educated in China and Japan, he was steeped in Chinese traditions and culture, believing that their preservation was vital to the country's resurgence. Sun was the intellectual thinker, the revolutionary philosopher, sharing many of the beliefs that had led to the May Fourth Movement. Chiang was the soldier, the man of action opposed to fundamental changes in China's social and political traditions. They did, however, have one thing in common – total commitment to Chinese nationalism and the development of a unified country independent of foreign influence and interference.

The Three Principles

Sun Yat-sen's political philosophy and aims are most clearly expressed in what he referred to as the Three Principles, as outlined in his book *Fundamentals of National Reconstruction* published in 1923. These principles, he claimed, 'were in some cases copied from our traditional ideals, in other cases modelled on European theory and experience'. He defined the Three Principles as:

1 **nationalism** – for China to become a strong and unified country, respected abroad and without foreign interference; Sun argued that China 'should strive to maintain independence in the family of nations … in the hope that we may forge ahead with other nations towards the goal of ideal brotherhood'

2 **democracy** – for China to adopt a democratic system of government, in which the people could elect their own leaders rather than being controlled by dynasties or warlords; to prepare the Chinese people for democratic self-government, an effective education system would be required

3 **social and economic reform** – the ending of China's rigid class system and improved conditions for the peasants and working classes; he argued that China should adopt more efficient agricultural practices and while there should be some redistribution of land to the peasants, Sun was opposed to the confiscation of property from wealthy landowners as advocated by many communists.

> As Sun wrote in 1925:
>
> For 40 years I have devoted myself to the cause of the people's revolution with but one end in view – the elevation of China to a position of freedom and equality among the nations. My experience during these 40 years has convinced me that to attain this goal we must bring about an awakening of our own people and ally ourselves in common struggle with those people of the world who treat us as equals.
>
> **Letter from Sun Yat-sen to the Kuomintang, March 1925**

Convinced that it was imperialism by Western nations that had caused the disintegration of China, Sun became increasingly reliant on Russian support. It was the Russians who treated the Chinese 'as equals', and it was Russian advice that seemed to offer the best way of removing imperialist foreign influence in China.

Popular support for the KMT increased, particularly in Kwangtung (Guangdong) Province where it was based and where its aims became widely known. There were several reasons for this:

- the KMT reflected the growth in Chinese nationalism, its primary aim being to create a unified China free from foreign interference
- Sun's Three Principles were very much in line with the views of those students and intellectuals who supported the May Fourth Movement
- the KMT appeared to offer the prospect of ending the violent chaos caused by the warlords — in particular, shopkeepers, merchants and businessmen saw the KMT as the best chance of protecting their profits from warlord greed and competition caused by foreign interests in China
- collaboration with the communists broadened the appeal of the KMT – its popularity increased amongst those sections of Chinese society, such as peasants and factory workers, who were already attracted by the CCP's promise of social and economic reform.

However, although well established in Kwangtung Province in the south, the KMT had no authority in the rest of the country, which remained firmly in the control of regional warlords, whose constant feuds continued to bring disunity and disorder. Moreover, the growth in support for the KMT disguised fundamental differences in the aims of its members. It had become a party united only by its desire to create a reunited China, free of foreign interference and warlord power. There was little agreement regarding how that reunified and independent China would be governed. Communist members of the KMT wanted a revolution to bring about major political, social and economic reform. Shopkeepers, merchants and businessmen, fearing that such a revolution would destroy their social status and profits, wanted a China governed in the traditional manner.

ACTIVITY 4.4

a Why do you think little progress had been made towards the achievement of Sun Yat-sen's aims by the time of his death in 1925?

b Do you think Sun Yat-sen's decision to collaborate with the CCP and the USSR was sensible? Explain the reasons for your answer.

The Northern Expedition

Divisions within the KMT were highlighted when, in March 1925, Sun's death led to a power struggle for leadership of the party. As effective head of the KMT armed forces, the National Revolutionary Army (NRA), Chiang Kai-shek considered himself an obvious candidate. However, by January 1926, communists held most of the strategically important posts within the KMT and many key roles within the NRA, a clear threat to Chiang's desire for leadership of the party. On 20 March 1926, in what has become known as the Canton Purge, Chiang deployed the NRA to remove communists from key positions within the KMT and declared himself as its leader.

Despite growing support, due in small part to collaboration with the CCP, the KMT's authority remained confined to Kwangtung Province. The rest of China was still dominated by the warlords and their private armies. If the KMT was to achieve its aim of reunifying China under a single government, in line with Sun's first Principle, it would need to confront and defeat the warlords. Preparations for this had begun as early as 1922, and by July 1926 Chiang felt ready to put the plans into action. He began the Northern Expedition, a military advance northwards through China.

By the end of 1926, the KMT had defeated two warlord armies and gained control over all land in China south of the Yangtze River. This rapid success of the KMT forces can be explained by a number of factors.

- The Expedition was the result of four years of detailed planning. Careful consideration had been given to issues such as the route to be taken and where best to confront the warlord armies. Russian advisers had helped to develop the KMT's military strength and political organisation so that is was in a better position to retain control over areas taken from the warlords.

- Despite the fact that Chiang was clearly opposed to communism, the Northern Expedition retained the assistance of Soviet military advisers. Stalin believed that a united China would be of benefit to the USSR – a friendly country that would end the Soviet Union's isolation.

- The NRA was extremely well organised and had been well prepared for the situations it would encounter during its march northwards through China. Its officers had undergone detailed training, largely at the Whampoa Military Academy but, in some cases, in the USSR or Japan. Moreover, the NRA was well equipped with modern weapons from the USSR, Germany and Japan.

- Conversely, the warlord armies were largely disorganised and, compared to the NRA, poorly equipped. They were designed to control and exploit local people, such as peasants, who were in no position to defend themselves. Their soldiers were either young men keen to make a living by looting, or **mercenaries** paid by the warlords. Many of these armies simply dispersed when confronted by the highly efficient NRA, their warlord leaders seeking refuge elsewhere in China. Some of the warlords, hoping to retain their regional power by defeating rival warlords, allied their armies with the NRA.

- Ordinary Chinese people were weary of the violence and exploitation incited by the warlords. They welcomed and supported the KMT forces, believing that they would restore order and bring peace.

- Many Chinese people joined the KMT forces as they marched through southern China. The army at Chiang's disposal grew from 100 000 in July 1926 to over 250 000 by the end of that year.

 KEY TERM

Mercenary: a soldier who joins an army purely for money rather than to support a cause.

In 1927, divisions appeared within the leadership of the KMT, which for a time threatened to halt the NRA's relentless march northwards. KMT members were split between those who supported Chiang Kai-shek and those who felt that Wang Ching-wei (Wang Jingwei) was a more credible leader. Wang had been a close associate of Sun Yat-sen, and shared his dream of bringing democracy and social reform to China. Although not a communist himself, Wang was prepared to work closely with the CCP. The traditionalist Chiang, on the other hand, had little interest in social reform, and was clearly opposed to the political ideas of the communists. By April 1927, the KMT had established two separate Chinese governments – one in Wuhan, led by Wang Ching-wei, and one in Nanchang, led by Chiang Kai-shek.

Despite this, KMT forces continued their march northwards, taking control of Hankow, Shanghai and Nanking during 1927. Peking itself fell to KMT forces in 1928. There was some justification to Chiang's claim that China had now become a unified country. KMT flags replaced those of the Peking government on public buildings. Moreover, the KMT Nationalist Government was quickly recognised overseas as the legitimate government of China. Chiang moved the centre of government from Peking to Nanking, which remained a KMT stronghold.

In many ways, the Northern Expedition was a great success for the KMT. Chiang appeared to have removed the power of the warlords, checked the influence of the Chinese Communist Party, and, in effect, become the political and military leader of China. It seemed that Sun Yat-sen's first Principle, nationalism and a reunified China, had been achieved.

In reality, however, the KMT's control over China was undermined by a number of factors. Although nominally controlling the whole country, in reality KMT authority was restricted to central and southern areas of China, northern areas remaining under warlord control.

Although defeated, the warlord armies had not been destroyed; they had simply dispersed. Moreover, most of the warlords themselves were still alive. It did not take long before the warlords reformed their armies and decided to work together in opposition to the KMT. Moreover, some of the military commanders who had helped to secure the success of the Northern Expedition opposed Chiang's leadership of the Nationalist government. In collaboration with some of the most powerful warlords, they established a rival government in Peking. KMT forces loyal to Chiang took six months to defeat them in what became known as the Central Plains War of 1930.

The Northern Expedition had brought the KMT into conflict with another opponent, one that was considerably more powerful than the warlords. Japan was concerned that the KMT's success would have an adverse effect on Japanese interests in China. Following the Twenty-One Demands, Japan had greatly increased its influence within China. This was especially the case in Manchuria, where Japan had developed extensive industrial and transport facilities. In early May 1928, as KMT forces moved through Shantung Province, they were confronted by the Imperial Japanese Army. In what has become known as the Jinan (Tsinan) Incident, several thousand KMT soldiers and Chinese civilians were killed. While this did not prevent the KMT's relentless march towards Peking, it was clear that Chiang's leadership of China would continue to face a formidable opponent in Japan.

The success of the Northern Expedition owed much to popular support for the KMT, due to a large extent to its collaboration with the CCP. It had become clear, however, that Chiang was deeply opposed to the CCP and had no enthusiasm for the social and economic reforms it advocated. Moreover, the Northern Expedition had exposed major divisions within the KMT. These divisions were to have serious implications for the party's attempt to form a credible national government of China.

151

ACTIVITY 4.5

Look carefully at this question:

'The main reason for the success of the Northern Expedition was the support it received from the USSR.' How far do you agree?

From what you have learned so far, do you think that the main reason for the success of the Northern Expedition was the support it received from the USSR? Use the following procedure to help you, making detailed notes as you do so:

- identify the ways in which support from the USSR assisted the Northern Expedition
- identify other factors that assisted the Northern Expedition
- decide which factor you feel was the most important in ensuring the success of the Northern Expedition
- make a judgement based on your notes.

Reflection: Working in pairs, swap your draft answers. Read your partner's answer and make written comments on it. Discuss your findings; how would you change your draft answer following your discussion?

4.2 How effectively did Chiang Kai-shek deal with the communists in the period 1927 to 1936?

The Shanghai massacres and the extermination campaigns

The success of the Northern Expedition owed much to the fact that the KMT had gained increasing support from peasants and factory workers, attracted by the communist promise of land redistribution and industrial cooperatives. Chiang was deeply opposed to such measures, and began to see the communists as an embarrassing ally. Moreover, Chiang's leadership of the KMT was threatened by the existence of Wang Ching-wei's rival government in Wuhan, established in 1927. Wang's supporters argued that Chiang was a power-mad soldier, intent on turning China into a military dictatorship under his personal control. Conversely, Chiang claimed that Wang's government had been infiltrated by communists, and was determined to seize power through revolution that would destroy Chinese traditions. These divisions within the KMT came to a head in April 1927.

In early 1927, the CCP, under the leadership of Chou En-lai (Zhou Enlai), organised a series of **insurrections** by industrial workers in Shanghai. By late March, the local warlord had been defeated. While Wang congratulated the communists for gaining control of Shanghai, Chiang was incensed that the action had been taken without his knowledge or permission. Chiang began what has become known as the Purification Movement – a deliberate and calculated attempt to remove all communist influence within the KMT.

On 6 April 1927, Chiang ordered the closure of the CCP's headquarters in Shanghai. On 9 April, he declared **martial law**, claiming that this was to restore order by ending the violence and strikes that were adversely affecting Shanghai. On 11 April, Chiang ordered KMT leaders in Shanghai to begin a purge of communists. He enlisted the support of Shanghai's infamous 'Green Gang', a group of gangsters, opium smugglers and criminals. Issued with KMT uniforms and weapons, the 'Green Gang' contributed to the violent suppression of communist supporters in Shanghai. KMT soldiers attacked CCP buildings, murdering leading communists and trade union leaders, and arresting striking workers. When students and factory workers gathered to protest against the violence, they were fired on, resulting in at least 100 deaths.

KEY TERMS

Insurrection: an organised and violent attempt to overthrow those in a position of authority.

Martial law: the imposition of direct military control over civilian affairs in response to a temporary emergency.

On Chiang's orders, the purge of communists, subsequently referred to as the 'White Terror', rapidly spread beyond Shanghai into other areas of China controlled by his forces, such as Changsha (Hunan Province) and Canton (Kwangtung Province). The number of deaths resulting from it was hotly disputed – while the KMT government suggested 5 000, the CCP claimed 50 000. Independent sources indicate that about 12 000 communists were killed or disappeared in a three-week period, and that almost 4 000 were killed in Shanghai alone.

Despite going into hiding, many communist leaders and activists were hunted down and murdered as the extermination campaign continued. There was an attempt by the communists to fight back. In August 1927, for example, communist soldiers under the leadership of Chou En-lai gained control of Nanchang. However, they were quickly defeated by KMT troops loyal to Chiang. Wang's government in Wuhan collapsed after being attacked by a warlord sympathetic to Chiang's leadership of the KMT. Wang's political career from then until his death in 1944 was inconsistent – at times, he occupied senior positions within Chiang's government, while at other times he tried, with little success, to establish governments that challenged Chiang's leadership of both the KMT and China. However, by the late summer of 1927, Chiang had established himself as the undisputed leader of the KMT. With the fall of Peking to KMT forces in 1928, Chiang declared himself political and military leader of China.

However, Chiang's violent suppression of the CCP and its members resulted in the withdrawal of Russian support for the KMT. As a result, the KMT no longer had access to the Russian political and military advisers who had helped to develop it as a political party, and who had played such a prominent role in facilitating the success of the Northern Expedition. Denied Russian-supplied weapons and other military equipment, the KMT was forced to spend vital financial resources purchasing them from elsewhere. Moreover, the Purification Movement may have removed communists from membership of the KMT, but it had not destroyed the CCP. Although weak and confined to the isolated and mountainous region of Kiangsi Province, the CCP still existed. **Mao Zedong** was emerging as the leader of a communist army known as the Revolutionary Army of Workers and Peasants. Deeply opposed to the KMT, Mao and his followers were to become a persistent and increasingly formidable enemy of Chiang Kai-shek.

The Long March 1934-35

Mao Tse-tung had been present at the meeting that established the CCP in 1921. By 1927 he held senior posts both within the CCP and the KMT, gaining a reputation as a highly effective organiser of trade unions and peasant associations. Endangered by Chiang's Purification Movement, the CCP took to the mountainous regions of Kiangsi Province, where Mao developed and commanded a Revolutionary Army of Workers and Peasants. By 1931, Mao had joined his army with that of Chu Teh (Zhu De), creating the Workers and Peasants' Red Army of China, later simply known as the Red Army.

Also in 1931, Mao helped to establish – and was elected chairman of – the Soviet Republic of China. Impressive though this sounds, the reality is that Mao controlled only a small area, with an army consisting of ill-equipped and poorly trained peasants. Nevertheless, Chiang considered that the continued existence of the CCP posed a threat to the KMT's control of China. It restricted the KMT government's authority within Kiangsi Province, and the CCP's policies of social and political

reform were increasing its popularity with peasants and factory workers.

Chiang carried out five 'extermination campaigns' against the CCP between 1930 and 1934. Forced to fight a guerrilla war against the more organised armies of the KMT, costly in terms of both money and soldiers, Mao also faced opposition to his leadership of the Communist Party in Kiangsi. Mao's strategy of concentrating on gaining the support of the peasants rather than trying to gain influence in the industrial towns controlled by the KMT was not universally popular amongst fellow communist leaders. Mao's determination to retain control led to his systematic and violent suppression of all opposition. In December 1930, for example, Mao ordered the arrest of around 4 000 members of the Red Army, falsely claiming that they were KMT sympathisers. In response, a Red Army battalion in Futian mutinied. Under Mao's orders, the mutiny was crushed, and between 500 and 700 communist soldiers were arrested, interrogated and executed in what is referred to as the Futian Incident. Mao's attempts to consolidate his own power by removing potential opposition to his leadership continued into 1931. Mao's supporters carried out a series of purges that claimed thousands of lives – estimates vary between 10 000 and 70 000.

Born in 1893, the son of a wealthy peasant farmer, Mao became well educated. While working in the library of the university in Peking, he was exposed to Marxist political philosophy. He became a communist, convinced that China's future lay in the hands of the peasants and working classes. He was impressed by Lenin's achievements following the Russian Revolution of 1917, and became convinced that China could follow a similar path.

MAO TSE-TUNG 1893–1976

As the world learned of events unfolding in Kiangsi Province, foreign journalists began depicting Mao as a terrorist whose methods were no different from those of the warlords. For example, the British newspaper, The Times, reported in August 1929:

> The name of Mao has been infamous on the borders of Fukien and Kwantung for two years past. Twice he has been driven to refuge in the mountains, being too mobile to catch, but at the first sign of relaxed authority he comes down again to ravage the plains. Mao calls himself a communist, and wherever Mao goes he begins by calling on the farmers to rise and destroy the capitalists. But he is really the worst kind of brigand.

Mao had a rather more pragmatic attitude towards the use of violence. In his perception, the resurgence of China could only be achieved as a result of revolution, and revolution inevitably and unavoidably implied violence. As he wrote:

> Revolution is not a dinner party, nor an essay, nor a painting, nor a piece of embroidery. It cannot be so refined, so leisurely and gentle, so temperate, kind, courteous, restrained and magnanimous. A revolution is an insurrection, an act of violence by which one class overthrows another.
>
> Mau Tse-tung, 'Report on an Investigation of the Peasant Movement in Hunan', 1927
>
> Every communist must grasp the truth, 'political power grows out of the barrel of a gun'.
>
> **Mau Tse-tung, 'Problems of War and Strategy', 1938**

In early 1934, however, Mao was more concerned with survival than revolution. In the autumn of 1933, Chiang launched another major attempt to destroy the CCP base in Kiangsi Province. Rather than simply attacking the communists, Chiang planned to surround and starve them into submission. KMT forces moved forward slowly, building a series of defences as they did so. The strategy appeared to be succeeding – within 12 months, the KMT had seized over half of the territory controlled by the communists in 1933, killing some 60 000 members of the Red Army in the process.

The KMT tactics also led to a split within the CCP's leadership. On the advice of Russian agents, the CCP decided to launch a full-scale attack on the KMT forces surrounding Kiangsi Province. Believing that such an attack was bound to fail, Mao was deeply opposed to it. Accused of being unwilling to do anything to protect the Kiangsi peasants who were being killed by the KMT, Mao was removed from the CCP's leadership committee. Mao's instincts were, however, proved correct. The communist advance was quickly halted by KMT forces, and the CCP suffered serious losses of both men and equipment.

Starving and surrounded, the CCP's defeat seemed inevitable. Mao suggested an attempt to break out and mount a surprise attack on the rear of the KMT's forces. Instead, the CCP leadership decided on a full-scale retreat from Kiangsi Province, with the aim of reaching Yenan (Hunan) in Shensi Province, an area in northern China that had not yet fallen under KMT control. This retreat, now referred to as the Long March, began in October 1934. Around 90 000 communists embarked on a journey of up to 9 700 km (6 000 miles), a journey that was to take 368 days.

The early stages of the Long March gave little cause for optimism. It took well over a month to break through the lines of defences with which the KMT had surrounded Kiangsi. Having done so, the communists were instructed to march in a straight line, making their movements easily predictable. Moreover, in addition to weapons and ammunition, they were carrying items, such as furniture, which slowed down their progress and that were of no practical use under the circumstances. It did not take long before they were attacked by KMT forces at Xiang. In the ensuing battle, the Red Army lost 45 000 men, over half of its fighting force. The survivors were constantly pursued by the KMT, intent on destroying the CCP once and for all.

These early disasters were blamed on the CCP's leadership, and control of the Red Army was handed over to Mao in January 1935. He immediately made three tactical changes. First, unnecessary items were discarded, enabling the marchers to move more quickly. Second, rather than marching in a straight line, he ordered his followers to progress in a manner that was less predictable. Thirdly, he split the Red Army into smaller

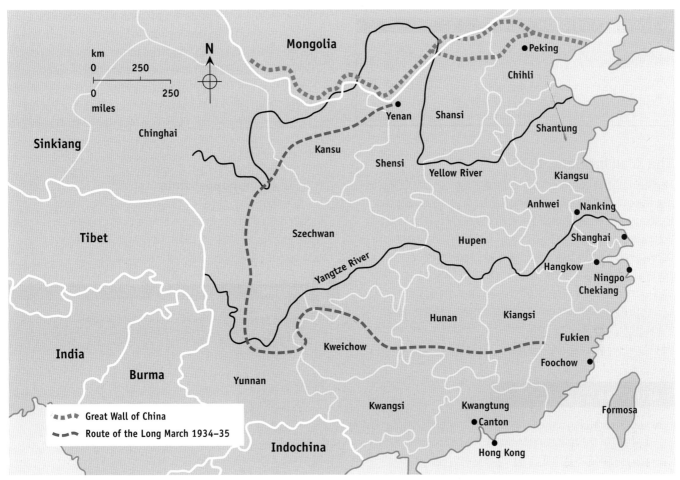

Figure 4.3: China, showing the major towns and regions and the route of the Long March

units, making them far less easy to detect. These revised tactics greatly reduced the risk of further devastating contact with the pursuing KMT forces.

However, the KMT was not the only problem confronting the communists on their epic journey northwards. The route took them across difficult terrain, including 18 mountain ranges, 24 rivers and an area of deep marshes known as the Chinese Grassland. In the mountainous regions near the border with Tibet, the marchers were attacked by Tibetans. In some of the more isolated regions of northern China, the marchers faced the armies of warlords that even the KMT had been unable to defeat.

Eventually, between 10 000 and 20 000 survivors of the Long March reached Yenan in Shensi Province, an area that had not yet fallen under the control of the KMT. This enabled Mao, by now the undisputed communist leader, to develop a safe base and gave him time to rebuild his depleted army. At great cost in terms of human life and suffering, the Long March had enabled communism to survive in China.

ACTIVITY 4.7

Prepare a written answer to this question:

Do you think the Long March should be seen as a defeat or a victory for the CCP?

Make sure that you take the following points into account:

- you are being asked to make a judgement – this must be clearly expressed and supported by appropriate evidence
- your assessment needs to be balanced – you need to show understanding of the ways in which the Long March could be viewed as **either** a defeat **or** a victory.

Using a table, such as the one below, will help you to achieve this and to reach a reasoned judgement.

DEFEAT	VICTORY

The Xi'an Incident, 1936

Maintaining the continuous campaigns against the CCP was not the only issue facing Chiang Kai-shek as he attempted to secure his leadership of China in the early 1930s. Following the Twenty-One Demands, Japan had established considerable economic and political interests in China, particularly in Manchuria. Japan's determination to protect and extend these interests posed another major threat to Chiang's KMT government. Japanese troops stationed in Manchuria, increasingly concerned by Chiang's attempts to reunify China, urged Japan's government to take full control of the area. When the government refused, the soldiers took matters into their own hands. In September 1931, they engineered a small explosion close to the Japanese-owned South Manchuria Railway line near the town of Mukden, claiming that it was a deliberate act by anti-Japanese Chinese citizens. Referred to as the Mukden Incident, this provided the excuse for a full-scale Japanese invasion of Manchuria.

Japanese forces mobilised, and over the next six months took control over the whole of Manchuria, establishing the **puppet state** of Manchukuo in its place. In a blatant attempt to legitimise its actions, Japan installed the former Chinese Emperor Pu Yi as head of state in Manchukuo in March 1932. Two years later, he was formally declared Emperor of Manchukuo.

KEY TERM

Puppet state: a state that is nominally independent but actually under the control of another state.

ACTIVITY 4.8

a Look carefully at the Chinese government's statement regarding the Japanese invasion of Manchuria. In pairs, decide which of the following statements are true and which are false. In each case, explain how you reached your answer.
- Under the terms of various treaties, Japan had the right to take control of Manchuria.
- The League of Nations had done nothing to stop Japan's takeover of Manchuria.
- The statement uses emotive language in an attempt to gain the League's support.
- China is prepared to take military action against Japan.

b Look carefully at the letter written by a Chinese resident in Manchuria.
- What opinions do you think the writer had about the League of Nations?
- What did the writer think Japan would do once their takeover of Manchuria was complete?

Japan has consistently ignored treaties and insisted on having special rights in China, especially in Manchuria. Showing contempt for world opinion, Japan has carried military action into the heart of China. Japanese forces have killed large numbers of unarmed and peaceable Chinese men, women and children. They have imprisoned, maltreated and executed many more. Japan has rejected every avenue to peace, leaving China no alternative but to adopt measures for self-defence. China has endured humiliation in the hope that the League of Nations might halt Japan's reckless course. Despite the League's failure, China maintains its faith in world justice, but it cannot passively submit to Japan's invasion of China's territory and slaughter of its people. Since September 1931, the sky has been red with the glare of burning cities and villages. The tramp of Japan's armies and the thunder of its guns have been heard throughout Manchuria and elsewhere in China.

A statement made by China's KMT government in February 1932

I realise that China has already asked for the support of the League of Nations to regain our rights here in Manchuria – or should I say Manchukuo – but I fear that the Japanese are too strong to bow down to a couple of disapproving officials and impractical sanctions. Even worse, I have noticed that lately the size of the Japanese army has increased. To me, Manchuria is only the first step for the ambitious Japanese, and with their increasing army size and prospering industry, I fear that it is only a matter of time before they continue on their path to conquer China and eventually all of Asia.

A letter written by Po-Yu Yen, a Chinese resident of Manchuria, July 1932

Confronted by a Japanese invasion of part of its territory, China appealed for assistance from the League of Nations, which instructed Japan to withdraw its forces and established a commission to investigate the contrasting claims of China and Japan. However, the League took no action when the Japanese government simply ignored the instruction for an immediate withdrawal of its troops from Manchuria.

Japan's refusal to comply with the League's instructions was interpreted with a mixture of anger and fear in China. To many Chinese it seemed a clear indication that Japan intended to extend its territory in China beyond Manchuria, and that the League would be powerless to stop it. For example, in a private letter to his brother, a Chinese resident of Manchuria wrote in July 1932:

Fears of further Japanese inroads into China were heightened following the publication of the report by the League's commission of enquiry in which they decided that Manchuria should be restored to China. The Japanese government refused to accept the decision, withdrew from the League and continued to establish the state of Manchukuo, exploiting its resources for the benefit of Japan's economy. A new government, composed entirely of Japanese officials, was established. Pu Yi was simply a convenient figurehead, lacking any power. The League's failure to take action against Japan exposed China to further Japanese intimidation and aggression throughout the 1930s. Denied international support, China had no option but to confront the Japanese threat alone.

Chiang decided to adopt a policy of non-resistance to the Japanese. There were two main reasons for this.

1   The KMT's control of China was far from complete. Large parts of the country, mainly in the north-west, remained under the control of warlords, while Mao's CCP had gained a strong foothold in many rural areas, particularly in Shensi Province, where its army was based.

2   Weak, divided and lacking a large navy to defend its long coastline, China could not hope to win a war against Japan.

Chiang's policy was to concentrate his resources on the internal reconstruction of China, and in particular, on defeating the challenge of communism. Chiang's priority was to destroy the CCP rather than to defend China against Japanese aggression. At a time when there was considerable unrest throughout the country

as a result of Japan's actions, leading to an increase in Chinese nationalist sentiments, many members of the KMT believed that Chiang's priorities were wrong. They were particularly concerned that failure to confront the Japanese would lead to a decline in popular support for the KMT government.

Chang Hseuh-liang (Zhang Xueliang) and Yang Hu-ch'eng (Yang Hucheng), generals in the KMT army, had been appointed by Chiang to lead attacks against the CCP stronghold in Yenan. They came to the conclusion that fighting against the communists was less important than forming a united front against the Japanese. Indeed, Zhang had a personal reason for feeling that priority should be given to resisting Japanese aggression – his father, a Manchurian warlord, had been murdered by the Japanese in 1928. Accordingly, they urged Chiang to change policy and form an alliance with the CCP.

Chiang totally rejected this suggestion, and sent troops under his direct command to ensure that Zhang and Yang continued to carry out their orders to attack CCP strongholds. On 4 December 1936, Chiang arrived in Xi'an to personally supervise affairs.

On 12 December 1936, Zhang and Yang took action that began what has become known as the Xi'an Incident. Fearing that he would be punished for his reluctance to fight against the communists, Zhang ordered 150 of his soldiers to storm Chiang's quarters. Chiang, dressed in pyjamas, briefly escaped and hid in a nearby cave, but subsequently surrendered.

Chiang and some of his leading supporters were placed under arrest. Zhang and Yang sent a telegram to the KMT government in Nanking demanding an end to the war against the CCP and the immediate adoption of a campaign to oppose Japanese aggression against China.

Confronted with a situation in which their leader had effectively been arrested by his own men, senior members of the KMT government were divided over what action to take. Some recommended an immediate military attack on Xi'an to secure Chiang's release. Others felt that this would put Chiang's life in danger, and argued in favour of seeking to negotiate a settlement. Among those who recommended military action were Wang Jingwei and He Yingqin (Ho Ying-chin), both of whom favoured compromise with the Japanese and viewed the situation as an opportunity to enhance their own power within the KMT at the expense of Chiang.

157

If the KMT government was divided over what action to take, so too were the supporters of Zhang and Yang. Many of them were Manchurians, particularly angered by Japanese aggression, and they were strongly in favour of executing Chiang. Others felt that this would simply strengthen divisions within the KMT, and argued in favour of negotiations to ensure that Chiang was prepared to work with the CCP to form a united front against the Japanese.

The CCP was to play a vital role in resolving the problems created by the Xi'an Incident. Senior members of the CCP had been in negotiation with Zhang and Yang since mid June, and were not only aware of, but fully supported, their plan to force Chiang to change his policy towards the Japanese. They had played a major role in persuading Zhang and Yang that it was in China's interest for the CCP and the KMT to work in partnership in an effort to resist ongoing Japanese aggression. In this, the CCP's leadership was acting on the instructions of their Russian advisers. Deeply concerned about the threat that Japanese aggression posed to its own interests in China, the USSR was keen to ensure that the Chinese mounted a united resistance to Japan. This could only be achieved if the CCP and the KMT collaborated.

In 1936, the USSR had a vested interest in keeping Chiang alive. Under his leadership, the KMT had been internationally recognised as being the legitimate government of China following the success of the Northern Expedition by 1928. Therefore, any alternative Chinese government would lack legitimacy within the international community. With the CCP still relatively weak and isolated, both domestically and internationally, the USSR viewed Chiang as the only realistic leader of China. The Russian aim, therefore, was to change Chiang's policies rather than to remove him as head of government. With this in mind, the USSR instructed a senior member of the CCP, Chou En-lai, to conduct negotiations in Xi'an.

As a result of these negotiations, the Xi'an Incident was settled peacefully. On 24 December, Chiang agreed to cease his campaigns against the CCP and to collaborate with it in mounting resistance against the Japanese. This became known as the Second United Front. Chiang also agreed to the release of a number of CCP prisoners. In return, Chiang was himself released the following day. This was a compromise arrangement that appeared to suit all parties concerned.

- It enabled Chiang to regain his freedom and resume his positions as leader of the KMT and head of China's only internationally recognised government.

- Zhang and Yang were relieved of the immediate threat of attack by KMT forces seeking to secure Chiang's release. They had also achieved their aim of forcing Chiang to end his policies of non-resistance to Japanese aggression and attacking the CCP.
- The USSR achieved a more unified Chinese approach to the task of fighting the Japanese.
- The CCP was relieved from the constant KMT campaigns that had threatened its survival, giving it time to develop and establish itself with the Chinese people as the party most committed to the national unity and defence of China.

However, there were ways in which not everyone was content with the outcome.

- It ended the hopes of those members of the KMT, such as Wang Jingwei, who had expected the Xi'an Incident would enhance their own power.
- Yang was soon arrested by Chiang, imprisoned and then in 1949 executed to prevent him being released by advancing CCP forces.
- Zhang was also arrested and spent the next 40 years under house arrest. When fleeing a victorious CCP advance, the KMT even moved him to Taiwan in order to maintain his imprisonment. He was released following Chiang's death in 1975.

The Xi'an incident resulted in a truce between the KMT and the CCP, and a renewal of the collaboration between them that had characterised the 1920s before Chiang began the Purification Movement. It did not take long before the effectiveness of this collaboration, the Second United Front, was tested. In 1937 full-scale war broke out between China and Japan.

ACTIVITY 4.9

Discuss the following questions in pairs or small groups.
- **a** Why did Chiang adopt a policy of non-resistance to Japanese aggression?
- **b** Why do you think this policy was unpopular with many members of the KMT?
- **c** Why do you think the CCP was prepared to renew its collaboration with the KMT despite the problems it had faced due to Chiang's Purification Movement?
- **d** How significant do you feel the USSR was to the development of both the KMT and the CCP in the period from 1920 to 1936?

Attempts at modernisation and reform

Sun Yat-sen's dream had been the creation of a strong, unified and democratic China, free from foreign interference and the chaos caused by the warlords. By the conclusion of the Northern Expedition in 1928, the KMT under Chiang's leadership had gone a long way towards achieving the unification of China. While some parts of the country, primarily in northern and western areas, remained under the influence of warlords and the CCP continued to pose a potential threat, the KMT had achieved effective control over most of China. Announcing that its intention was to modernise China through a series of political, social and economic reforms, the KMT established the Nationalist Government of the Republic of China, based in Nanking (Nanjing). This rapidly gained international recognition as the sole legitimate government of China, with Chiang as head of state.

Politically, the Nationalist government declared its commitment to developing democracy in China by following proposals made by Sun Yat-sen in 'A Programme of National Reconstruction', published in 1918. In this document, Sun had identified what he called 'the three stages of revolution'. These were:

1 the unification of China through military action

2 a transitional period, in which the government would educate the Chinese people in preparation for democracy – Sun believed that this stage would last about six years, during which China would need to be governed by an authoritarian, military government

3 the establishment of a constitutional democracy that gave the Chinese people the right to elect their own leaders.

In 1928, Chiang announced that the Northern Expedition had successfully completed the first stage and that China was now entering the transitional period. The Chinese people, he declared, would be prepared for democracy through an educational programme directed by the KMT. At the same time, the Nationalist government outlined its intention to introduce a number of ambitious plans designed to enhance China's economy, increase its agricultural and industrial output, end the unwanted influence of foreigners and improve the conditions of factory workers and peasants.

The Nanking Decade: KMT successes

The period between the ending of the Northern Expedition in 1928 and the formal outbreak of war between China and Japan in 1937 is generally referred to as the 'Nanking Decade'. It was during these years that Chiang's Nationalist government based in Nanking developed a number of policies and reforms in support of its aim to modernise China. Chinese historians who supported Chiang's KMT in its subsequent civil war against the CCP call it the 'Golden Decade'. They argue that it was in this period that the foundations of the modern state of China were laid. There is some justification for this view. It is certainly possible to see how, over time, the measures instigated by the Nationalist government could have been of great benefit to China and its people. These measures included: attempts to stimulate economic growth, industrialisation and investment; economic reconstruction; improvements to public health; reforms to the **penal system**; reforms to land use and agriculture; and reforms to the education system.

KEY TERM

Penal system: the punishments which people receive for breaking the law as defined in the legal system.

The Nationalist government made attempts to stimulate economic growth, industrialisation and investment. Following the establishment of the Central Bank of China in 1928, a national currency was introduced with the aim of overcoming regional variations. Through diplomatic negotiations with other countries, the Nationalist government was able to reduce foreign influence over China's trade and gain access to foreign loans, particularly from the USA.

Through a programme of economic reconstruction, the Nationalist government began the process of improving China's transport and communication systems, both of which had been neglected and severely damaged by the warlords and their activities. This led to the construction of highways and railways, together with improvements in postal and telegraph systems. The programme was also designed to increase regional access to electricity. These plans had the potential to significantly improve China's industry and trade, both domestic and international.

Efforts to improve public health led to more efficient methods of water storage and the construction of sewers and the introduction of street lighting in major cities. The Nationalist government also announced a crackdown on opium trafficking.

With the aim of standardising practice across the whole country, the government introduced reforms designed to modernise the legal and penal systems. The intention

159

was to adopt Western-style legal systems and, with this in mind, China's first Supreme Court was established in 1931.

Under a Land Law passed in 1930, the government outlined its plans to improve China's agricultural output. These plans included deforestation and wasteland reclamation projects to increase the amount of land under cultivation, irrigation and flood prevention schemes, together with reforms relating to land ownership laws. Tenancy agreements, by which farmers rented their land from wealthy landowners, were to run for a minimum of five years with fixed rents. This was intended to ensure that tenant farmers took good care of the land on which they farmed, and to prevent landowners increasing rents unfairly.

The government announced its intention to greatly enhance China's education programme, which it saw as a way of encouraging national integration. A centralised educational administration was established with the task of determining standards and programmes of study for all levels of schooling. It also made efforts to popularise the national language in a further attempt to unify the country and help overcome the problems caused by regional and local languages.

A number of social reforms were put in place. For example, it was intended to protect factory workers by restricting their hours of employment and improving their working conditions. Similarly, the government brought in measures designed to enhance the status of women and restrict the traditional practice of arranged marriages.

That these reforms had some positive effects is suggested by the report of a US research team, which was published in 1944. The report provided statistics intended to show how China had progressed under Chiang's Nationalist government. For example:

Infrastructure		
Highways	1927	28 000 km
	1936	109 747 km
Factories	1927	1 347
	1936	2 695
Education		
Number of elementary schools	1912	86 000
	1936	261 000
Number of high schools	1912	373
	1936	1 911

These figures should, however, be treated with great caution. By 1944, Chiang's Nationalist government

was involved in a civil war against Mao's CCP. The USA supported Chiang, and clearly had a vested interest in praising the achievements of his government in China. Moreover, the evidence quoted in the report is highly misleading. For example, the statistics given for the number of schools in China compare 1912 with 1936, making it impossible to determine how much of the growth occurred after Chiang's KMT formed the Nationalist government in 1928. The report does, however, indicate that the number of Chinese factories in 1913 was 245. That this had increased to 1 347 by 1927 clearly suggests that industrialisation had been occurring in China even before Chiang came to power.

THINK LIKE A HISTORIAN

Governments often use statistics and other similar evidence to demonstrate the positive impact of their policies. This type of evidence can be interpreted in a number of different ways and be, at times, misleading.

Think of some current or recent examples of governments making use of such evidence in order to maintain or increase public support for their policies.

The Nanking Decade: failures and limits to success

Whatever good intentions the Nationalist government may have had, its attempted reforms had made little impact on China by 1936. There were several reasons for this.

Although Chiang had hailed the Northern Expedition as a total success, the KMT had achieved only limited control in many of the northern provinces, and this was only by enlisting the support of powerful warlords such as Feng Yu-hsiang (Feng Yuxiang) and Zhang Xueliang – KMT control over many northern provinces and Manchuria depended on a series of agreements with these warlords. Disagreeing with the KMT's plans regarding the political and military control of China, several of these warlords joined together in 1930 demanding Chiang's resignation as leader of China.

In May 1930, Chiang sent a 600 000-strong KMT army against these warlords in what became known as the Central Plains War. Well equipped with aircraft and artillery, supplied by the Western powers, Chiang's forces were able to defeat the warlord armies in a six-month campaign. However, the Central Plains War proved an expensive drain on the Nationalist government's money and resources.

Throughout the period from 1928 to 1936, the Nationalist government was continuing its campaign against the CCP.

This was expensive in terms of time and money, and deflected the focus away from pursuing its package of reforms.

The Nationalist government lacked the political will and authority to enforce its intended reforms. It had little control over many of the more remote rural and mountainous regions of China, where traditional ideas remained strong and prevented the implementation of government plans to modernise the legal system and improve the status of women. Elementary and secondary education remained under the control of local authorities, which resisted government attempts to develop a national system based on a four-year compulsory education programme. Educational facilities remained extremely limited, especially in rural areas. In 1934, for example, secondary education was available to 213 of every 10 000 people in Shanghai, but to only 4 of every 10 000 people in provinces such as Shensi. In 1935, the government launched a programme designed to provide one year's primary education to a greater proportion of school-age children over the next five years. School enrolment did increase from 13 million to 23 million over the next two years. However, the quality of education remained low, and the programme ended with the outbreak of war against Japan in 1937.

Moreover, leading members of the KMT were far from united over how the country should be governed. Many were deeply opposed to any kind of social reform or the adoption of practices that they considered were opposed to traditional Chinese methods. For example, the Nationalist government refused to implement the kind of taxation system that was common practice in Western countries. As a result, it lacked the financial resources that might have been derived from income tax and taxes on businesses. Moreover, the government's improvements to China's transport and communication systems were motivated by military, rather than economic, factors. They were designed to help the KMT maintain its control over China, rather than to enhance the country's industrial infrastructure.

Japanese aggression further undermined Chiang's attempts to establish himself as leader of China and the KMT as its government. The Japanese takeover of Manchuria, for example, robbed the Nationalist government of resources, such as iron ore and coal, which were vital to its proposals for economic development.

The Great Depression, which followed the Wall Street Crash in 1929, adversely affected China in a number of ways. For example, it prevented the acquisition of foreign loans on which much of the proposed industrial and economic development depended. Moreover, it reduced the potential domestic and international market for Chinese products, which, in turn, led to a decline in investment.

As a result of these factors, the reforms proposed by the Nationalist government were never fully enforced or, in some cases, never implemented at all. Evidence suggests that, by the mid-1930s, 47% of the government's income was used to supply the military, while less than 5% was spent on education and almost nothing on social welfare schemes.

By 1936, therefore, Chiang's Nationalist government had achieved little progress in its attempts to unify and modernise China. Its attempted reforms had produced only limited effects, and large parts of the country remained outside its authority. Warlord armies continued to cause chaos and distress in many northern provinces, while Japanese forces had taken control of Manchuria and were posing an increasing threat to other parts of China. Perhaps most significantly, the CCP had survived the relentless and expensive campaigns which Chiang had mounted against it.

161

ACTIVITY 4.10

Divide into four groups. Each group should take one of the following questions, discuss it and prepare a short presentation on their discussion and conclusions.

a   What were the aims of the reforms proposed by Chiang's Nationalist government?

b   In what ways would the people of China have benefitted from these reforms if they had been fully implemented?

c   Identify the reasons why the proposed reforms were never fully implemented. Place them in what you consider to be an order of significance, with the most important at the top and the least important at the bottom.

d   How far did the aims and achievements of the Nationalist government during the Nanking Decade reflect the Three Principles established by Sun Yat-sen when he was leader of the KMT?

Reflection: In what ways are the four questions in Activity 4.10 different from one another? How possible is it in each case to answer them? What do you think the most significant point made in response to each question was and why?

4.3 Why did the Chinese Communist Party (CCP) gain support up to 1945?

Results of the Long March and the leadership of Mao Zedong

By 1936, with the Long March completed, the surviving members of the CCP had established a safe base in Shensi Province, relatively secure from KMT campaigns. Moreover, in theory if not always in practice, the Xi'an Incident had led to a truce between the CCP and the KMT, a truce that would enable the CCP to rebuild and establish its own claim to the political leadership of China.

In many ways, the Long March should be seen as a defeat for the CCP. It was, after all, a military retreat from KMT forces with little or no forward planning, a retreat that resulted in the loss of up to 90% of the CCP's Red Army. Fully aware of the importance of propaganda, Mao transformed this defeat into a perceived victory for the CCP. Under Mao's direction, the official CCP accounts of the Long March stress the courage and resilience of the Red Army soldiers, describing them as heroes and martyrs willing to die for the cause of Chinese nationalism. Although it is not always easy to prove in the absence of reliable eye witness accounts, there seems little doubt that the hardships encountered by the marchers were exaggerated and distorted. This is certainly the case in one particular incident. CCP histories claim that, in May 1935, the Red Army defeated a large and well-equipped KMT force at Luding Bridge over the Dadu River near the town of Yenan (Yan'an). Reliable evidence suggests a rather different version of events – the bridge was guarded by a small group of warlord soldiers who simply ran away at first sight of the approaching Red Army.

Regardless of modern debates regarding the severity of the hardships encountered by those involved in the Long March, Mao's propaganda unquestionably served its purpose at the time. It earned the CCP the respect, and subsequently, the support of large sections of the Chinese population, particularly the peasants. Mao was fully aware that the future growth of the CCP would depend largely on support from China's large peasant population. In his 'Eight Points For Attention', a list of rules laid down for the marchers, Mao had instructed his soldiers to avoid harming the peasants or their livelihood, even when the marchers were in dire need of food.

Mao claimed that the conclusion of the Long March marked the beginning of a new phase in the history of the CCP – a phase that would lead to the full unification of China under a communist government.

ACTIVITY 4.11

Discuss the following in pairs:

a What motives would the CCP have for deliberately exaggerating the hardships encountered by those taking part in the Long March?

b Mao claimed that the Long March was important for three reasons – what were they?

c Mao argued that, for the people of China, 'The Red Army is their only hope of liberation'. What did he mean by this?

What is the significance of the Long March? We answer that the Long March is the first of its kind in the annals of history, that it is a manifesto, a propaganda force, a seeding machine.

It is a manifesto. It has proclaimed to the world that the Red Army is an army of heroes, while Chiang Kai-shek and his like are powerless. It has shown their utter failure to encircle, pursue, obstruct and intercept us.

It is a propaganda force. It has announced to some 200 million people in China that the Red Army is their only hope of liberation.

It is a seeding machine. It has sown many seeds which will sprout, leaf, blossom and bear fruit, and will yield a harvest in the future.

Mao Tse-tung, 'On Tactics Against Japanese Imperialism', December 1935

The Long March also secured Mao's undisputed leadership of the Red Army. He was hailed as a great military leader, whose tactical brilliance had enabled the marchers to reach their objective against all odds. However, Mao was not yet guaranteed leadership over the CCP as a whole. In this, he faced rivals from two main factions within the CCP:

1 those who believed in the ideas which had led to the May the Fourth Movement – their long-term aim was to establish a Western-style democracy in China

2 those who wanted China to experience a revolution similar to that which had occurred in Russia in 1917.

The latter group posed the greatest threat to Mao's overall leadership of the CCP. Their leaders, the main one of whom was Wang Ming, became known as the '28 Bolsheviks'. They had all studied at the Sun Yat-sen University in Moscow, and were under instructions from the USSR to encourage a Chinese **proletarian** revolution – a revolution spearheaded by the working class.

KEY TERM

Proletariat: a term used to describe the urban working class – people working in factories and other industrial activities in cities.

Mao clearly wanted to instigate a revolution, but argued that copying the Russian experience was inappropriate given the situation in China. With only limited industrialisation, China lacked a large working class population.

Mao believed that a Chinese revolution would have to be driven by the peasantry, by far the largest section of the population. As he wrote in *Problems of Strategy in Guerrilla War*, published in 1938:

> China's revolutionary war is waged in the specific environment of China and so it has its own specific circumstances and nature. There are many factors specific to the Chinese Revolution and the Chinese Red Army.

With this in mind, Mao instigated policies designed to address two key issues:

1. continuing the process of gaining support from China's peasant population – he stressed that the CCP should 'listen attentively to the voice of the masses' in an attempt to win over 'their hearts and minds'.

2. establishing himself as undisputed leader of the CCP.

ACTIVITY 4.12

Chiang Kai-shek and Mao Tse-tung experienced similar problems in achieving and maintaining control over their respective parties. In small groups, identify as many reasons as you can to explain this. Which was the most significant?

The establishment of the Yenan Soviet, land reform and Mao's Rectification Campaign (1941–44)

Relatively secure in Shensi Province, the CCP established the town of Yenan (Yan'an) as their headquarters. It was to remain so throughout the period from 1936

to 1948. In the surrounding area, the CCP established what became known as the Yenan Soviet. Mao insisted that CCP members, including its leaders, live and work amongst the local peasant population, helping them to farm the land and generally treating them with respect. This, together with the provision of health care and education, enhanced the CCP's popularity within the peasant community. Local people were given advice on personal hygiene and access to traditional Chinese remedies and, when resources allowed, modern medicines. Medical assistance was made available to women during pregnancy and childbirth, while operating theatres, capable of dealing with minor surgery, were established. Schools were provided to ensure that local people gained basic literacy skills.

Perhaps most significant in gaining local support for the CCP was its policy of land redistribution.

In November 1931, the CCP Committee in Shensi Province issued its policy on land reform. The opening section of the policy stated:

> The peasant struggle continues to develop. Despite the violent resistance of the imperialists and militarists, the Soviet movement grows and expands. In one area after another, the Chinese peasantry, armed and organised in the ranks of the Red Army, casts off the centuries-old chains of landlords. It confiscates and redistributes the land of these oppressors. It destroys the power of the Kuomintang and builds up the workers' and peasants' Soviet regime. In order to establish uniform regulations for the confiscation and distribution of land, the CCP has passed the following agrarian law, which will best secure the solution of the agrarian question.
>
> Article 1 – All the lands of the landlords and other big private landowners shall be subject to confiscation without any compensation whatever. The Soviets will distribute the confiscated lands among the peasants.
>
> Article 2 – The Red Army is the front rank fighter in the defence of the Soviet government and in the overthrow of the rule of imperialism and the government of landlords. Therefore, each Red Army man must be given a plot of land.

In line with this policy, and organised by associations of peasants supported by Red Army soldiers, land was taken from landlords and distributed to poorer peasants who previously had either:

- no land on which to farm, and had been forced to seek employment as landless labourers at low wages

or

- been forced to pay high rents for small plots of infertile land, incapable of producing sufficient food for them to feed their families.

Under Mao's direction, CCP propaganda portrayed the Yenan Soviet as providing an idyllic social and economic system, totally suited to the needs of the Chinese people. This positive view of what the CCP was achieving in Yenan was shared by a number of foreign visitors who spent time in the area. For example, Edgar Snow, an American journalist, spent four months in Yenan in 1936, interviewing Mao and studying life under CCP control at first hand. His book *Red Star over China*, published in 1937, was full of praise for the communists' accomplishments.

At least 15 other foreigners visited Yenan in the period from 1936 to 1940, and all shared Snow's positive impression. One of them, the Canadian surgeon Norman Bethune, assisted with the provision of healthcare by establishing mobile operating theatres. In 1944, with the USA still involved in its war against Japan, President Franklin D. Roosevelt sent a number of diplomatic and military observers to Yenan. Referred to as the Dixie Mission, their task was to evaluate the CCP's social, economic and military achievements in comparison with those of Chiang's Nationalist government. As with earlier foreign visitors, these observers returned with glowing reports of the work undertaken by the CCP in Yenan.

All was not quite as it seemed in Yenan, however. Restricted by their inability to speak Chinese, the foreign visitors had been allowed to see only what the CCP leadership wanted them to see. That schools were being used as a vehicle for pro-CCP and anti-KMT propaganda went unnoticed. The darker side of events in Yenan, such as the extreme force often used to take land away from wealthier peasants and landlords, was well hidden. So too were the measures taken by Mao to secure his own position as leader of the CCP.

Mao spent much of his time in Yenan writing and developing his political ideas. In 1940 he wrote *On*

New Democracy, in which he outlined plans for what he termed 'democratic dictatorship'. He argued that, through revolution, the CCP should form a single-party government of China, with complete and uncontested control over its affairs. At the same time, the CCP should listen and respond to the needs and desires of the Chinese population, and particularly the peasants who compromised by far the largest proportion.

Mao's vision of a revolution instigated by the peasantry was not shared by many other members of the CCP's leadership group. Wang Ming and the '28 Bolsheviks', for example, still argued that China's revolution should begin with the urban working class. In order to confront this opposition to his plans, Mao began what he termed a 'Rectification Movement' in 1941.

In its initial stages, the Rectification Movement comprised a series of study and discussion sessions for the thousands of new recruits arriving in Yenan to join the CCP. By 1942, all members of the CCP were required to read and make comments on Mao's writings. They were encouraged to criticise Mao's political views and CCP policies, and to make suggestions for improvements. Those who did so were arrested and accused of 'individualism', putting themselves above the needs of the CCP and the people of China. Wang Ming, Mao's leading rival for leadership of the CCP, was publicly humiliated.

The Rectification Movement developed into a terror campaign under the leadership of Kang Sheng, Mao's chief of security. Those who disagreed with Mao's ideas were accused of being spies, arrested and tortured. CCP members were encouraged to identify and expose those, including members of their own families, who disagreed with CCP policies. Many leading members of the CCP were removed from office, and it is estimated that at least 60 of them were forced to commit suicide. It is impossible to be certain about how many people died as a result of the Rectification Movement, but some historians claim that it was up to 10 000.

In 1944, Mao brought the Rectification Movement to an end, claiming that the terror tactics associated with it had been the result of the excessive actions of local CCP officials rather than his official policy. By then, however, it had served its purpose. Mao had secured his position as undisputed leader of the CCP and removed potential opposition for his plans for a revolution in China instigated by the peasantry.

ACTIVITY 4.13

a Look carefully at Edgar Snow's account of his visit to the communist base in Yenan. What reasons does he give to explain why peasants supported the CCP?

b How reliable do you think Edgar Snow's account of life in the Yenan Soviet is? Explain your answer.

c Why do you think the CCP was keen to give a positive impression to foreign visitors of life in the Yenan Soviet?

d It could be argued that the primary purpose of the Rectification Movement was to secure Mao's leadership of the CCP. Look back over Mao's earlier political career, identifying other examples of his determination to maintain and enhance his own power by methods which were often violent.

e Make two lists in your notes, outlining -

   i the reasons Mao gave for establishing the Rectification Movement

   ii other possible motives Mao may have had for establishing the Movement

> I must admit that most of the peasants to whom I talked seemed to support the communists and the Red Army … To understand the peasant support for the communist movement, it is necessary to keep in mind its economic basis … the burden borne by the peasantry under the KMT regime. Now, wherever the Reds went, there was no doubt that they radically changed the situation for the tenant farmer and all the 'have-not' elements. All forms of taxation were abolished in the new districts for the first year, to give the farmers a breathing space … Secondly, they gave land to the land-hungry peasants … Thirdly, they took land and livestock from the wealthy classes and redistributed them among the poor … Landlords and peasants were each allowed as much land as they could farm with their own labour.
>
> **Edgar Snow, *Red Star Over China* (1938 edition), pp. 237, 238.**

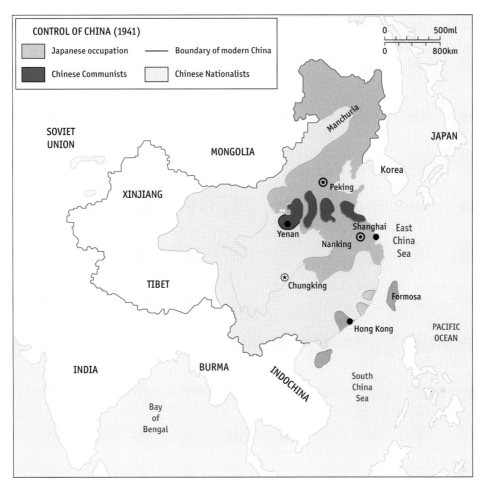

Figure 4.4: The situation in China by 1941

Impact of war with Japan after 1937

With communist propaganda highlighting the positive aspects of the Yenan Soviet, and the negative aspects well hidden from public view, support for the CCP appeared to increase. In what Mao referred to as the 'Organisation Phase', CCP leaders were sent to other villages and rural areas to repeat the process that had led to the establishment of the Yenan Soviet. Mao's intention was to gradually take control of the countryside, thereby isolating the towns and cities that were dominated by the KMT. The CCP's appeal, however, was not entirely confined to rural areas. Some urban factory workers, angered by the KMT government's failure to implement reform of their living and working conditions, adopted CCP methods in seeking to establish worker cooperatives. Similarly, some small businessmen, wearied by the heavy taxation burden imposed by the Nationalist government, were attracted to some aspects of the CCP's policies. The outbreak of full-scale war between China and Japan in 1937 was to strengthen the CCP's popularity still further.

Following its invasion of Manchuria in 1931, Japan had taken full control, renaming it Manchukuo. Chiang's Nationalist government had formally recognised Japanese ownership of the area by signing the Tanggu Truce in May 1933. This did not, however, prevent further Japanese raids into Chinese territory over the next four years. In 1933, for example, Japanese forces attacked the Great Wall region near Peking. This led to the establishment of a demilitarised zone protecting Japan's puppet-state of Manchukuo from any attack by KMT forces. A series of subsequent agreements with local warlords willing to collaborate enabled Japan to enhance its influence over northern provinces, such as Chihli, Shani and Shantung. Chiang's government had effectively abandoned northern China.

In July 1937, Japan launched a full-scale invasion of China, beginning the Second Sino-Japanese War. Seven months earlier, following the Xi'an Incident, the Nationalist government and the CCP had formed the Second United Front, by which they agreed to collaborate in resisting Japanese aggression. With the CCP's Red Army still isolated in Shensi Province, the initial resistance to Japan's invasion came from Chiang's Nationalist forces.

Chiang's armies were no match for well-prepared Japanese forces equipped with modern weaponry, such as tanks and aircraft. Major cities along China's east coast quickly fell to a fast-moving army of almost half a million Japanese soldiers. By the end of 1937, the Nationalist government was forced to retreat from its headquarters in Nanking to a safer base in western China. Unprotected, many Chinese cities fell victim to brutal treatment by the Japanese. Some estimates suggest that as many as 300 000 people were massacred in Nanking alone. There is considerable evidence to suggest that Japanese troops were responsible for countless atrocities, including the use of chemical and biological warfare. Practising a 'scorched earth' policy, the Japanese destroyed factories, crops and infrastructure as they continued their relentless progress, leaving millions of Chinese homeless and without food.

In June 1938, desperate to prevent further Japanese inroads into western China, Chiang ordered the destruction of dikes on the Yellow River Dam. The resulting floods served their purpose in delaying the Japanese advance. However, they also resulted in the deaths of between 500 000 and one million Chinese, rendered millions more homeless and destroyed vast amounts of good farming land leading to a long-term problem of starvation. Unable to progress further, Japan consolidated its control over the areas it had taken in the early stages of the war.

The inability of the Nationalist government to protect the Chinese people from Japanese aggression was keenly exploited by the CCP. Although the CCP's Red Army carried out some guerrilla warfare campaigns against Japanese troops, in truth it had taken little part in the war. Japan had no real interest in taking control of the isolated and mountainous regions where the CCP had its headquarters. Moreover, CCP activity was largely focused on seizing areas which the Japanese were already vacating. Nevertheless, CCP propaganda gave the impression that the Red Army had been considerably more successful than the National government's forces in defending China against the Japanese invasion. Claiming that its actions against the hated Japanese enemy were 'heroic' enabled the CCP to recruit more young men and women to its cause by appealing to their nationalistic sentiments. The CCP portrayed itself as the true party of Chinese nationalism and as providing a viable alternative government of China.

ACTIVITY 4.14

Divide into four groups. Each group should take one of the following questions, discuss it and prepare a short presentation on their discussion and conclusions.

a Compare and contrast the ways in which the KMT and the CCP reacted to the Japanese invasion of China after 1937.

b What problems were Japanese troops likely to face in their attempts to conquer the whole of China?

c Chiang claimed that China's resistance to Japan was 'a united effort of government and people'. How true do you think this was?

d How significant do you think the use of propaganda was in the development of the CCP?

Use the following table to help you.

KMT	CCP

China cannot be defeated. We are fighting this war against Japan for our own national existence and for freedom to follow the course of national revolution laid down for us in the Three Principles. The morale of our people is excellent. Our resistance is a united effort of government and people.

Speech to KMT leadership by Chiang Kai-shek, January 1939

Unpopularity of Chiang Kai-shek and the Kuomintang

Support for Chiang's KMT Nationalist government had been declining amongst many sections of the Chinese population well before the outbreak of war against Japan in 1937. There were a number of reasons for this.

Much of the early support for the KMT had resulted from its collaboration with the CCP prior to 1927. Peasants and factory workers welcomed Chiang's forces enthusiastically during the Northern Expedition in the belief that a future KMT government would carry out CCP-inspired social and economic reforms, such as land redistribution and improvements in factory conditions. When Chiang began the Purification Movement in 1927, removing communist influence from the KMT, hopes began to fade that such policies would be carried out.

While Chiang's government did establish a number of social and economic reforms, these were largely ineffective and, indeed, often not fully implemented. For example, some laws were passed banning child labour in textile factories, but these were never enforced. As a result, conditions in factories and other industrial establishments remained poor.

The large peasant population saw no improvement in their living and working conditions, and the promised land redistribution never took place. Concerned that small plots of land led to inefficient farming, the KMT aimed to increase the size of land holdings. Land ownership became increasingly confined to a group of relatively wealthy landlords. As a result, it is estimated that more than 60 million Chinese peasants were both landless and unemployed by 1934. While peasants suffered terrible hardships as a result of droughts and bad harvests in the early 1930s, landowners and profiteering merchants charged high prices for wheat and rice stockpiled in the cities.

To the vast majority of the Chinese population, it appeared that Chiang's government was concerned only with protecting the interests of the wealthy – the businessmen, bankers, factory owners and land owners. The government itself did little to challenge this perception. Whereas the CCP was developing highly effective propaganda in an attempt to gain popular support, the KMT did nothing to explain and justify its policies to the people of China.

The Nationalist government was increasingly accused of being corrupt. This was unquestionably true of its dealings with China's massive opium trade. Outwardly, the government was committed to ending the opium trade in China; it carried out a number of raids on opium farms and arrested many opium traders. Rather than ending opium trading, however, this simply enabled the government to take control of, and gain increasing income from, it – income that it desperately needed to fund its ongoing battles against the CCP and northern warlords.

By 1937, no progress had been made towards establishing Sun Yat-sen's third stage of revolution – the adoption of a democratic constitution in China. It became clear that, partly as a result of Chiang's increasing fascination with European fascism, the Nationalist government had no intention of relinquishing its power to any form of democracy. In 1934, the government introduced censorship of the press, films and books. Civil liberties were curtailed and any criticism of Chiang or his government led to imprisonment or, as in the case of two newspaper editors, death. The KMT justified these extreme measures by stating that the development of the Chinese nation was more important than the rights of individuals.

At the same time, Chiang introduced what he called the 'New Life Movement'. Outwardly, this was an attempt to revive traditional Chinese values, such as morality, responsibility and honesty in the interests of China's future.

> In a speech delivered in 1934 and entitled 'Essentials of the New Life Movement', Chiang argued that, by observing these traditional virtues:
>
>> it is hoped that social disorder and individual weakness will be remedied and that people will become military minded. If our country cannot defend itself, it has every chance of losing its existence. Therefore our people must have military training. We must preserve order, emphasise organisation, responsibility and discipline, and be ready to die for our country at any moment.
>>
>> **Chiang Kai-shek, speech in Nanchang, September 1934**

The similarity of this statement to those made by fascist leaders in Europe, such as Hitler and Mussolini, makes it clear that the primary purpose of the New Life Movement was to reinforce Chiang's own power by encouraging loyalty and obedience to a single leader.

Increasingly militaristic in outlook, and determined to eradicate all potential opposition, Chiang was attempting to ensure that the KMT's Nationalist government retained its position as the internationally recognised legitimate government of China. Whereas Mao's CCP sought power by enlisting mass support through carefully devised propaganda, Chiang's KMT aimed to retain it through military power, censorship and the denial of civil liberties.

The KMT's perceived failures in defending the Chinese people from Japanese aggression after 1937 simply increased its growing unpopularity, and provided Mao's CCP with further propaganda opportunities. Japanese troops were finally forced to withdraw from China in 1945 following Japan's defeat in the Second World War. Devastated by years of unimaginable human suffering and economically exhausted, China was about to experience further hardship – a full-scale civil war

between the rival factions of Chiang's KMT Nationalist government and Mao's CCP.

ACTIVITY 4.15

Do you think that the increasing unpopularity of the KMT during the 1930s was due to its inability to protect China from Japanese aggression?

Completing a table, such as the one below, will help you to ensure that you reach a reasoned and balanced judgement.

AGREE	DISAGREE

Reflection: Swap tables with another student. Read through each other's tables and conclusions, writing comments where appropriate. In particular, make sure that the conclusion contains *both* a balanced assessment of appropriate evidence *and* a supported judgement which addresses the requirements of the actual question.

Discuss your findings in pairs – in particular, discuss ways in which you feel the answers could be improved.

4.4 Why did Japan become a military dictatorship in the 1930s and with what consequences?

Japan's international status in 1919 and its reactions to the Paris peace settlements

Japan emerged from the First World War in a strong position. It was now a wealthy nation with an efficient, modern industrial sector, a powerful navy and increased influence over China. It had developed a form of constitutional democracy, and its government was determined to follow a pro-Western foreign policy as a means of assuring the major powers that Japan posed no threat to their interests in China and the Far East. The Japanese policy of expansionism in the Far East, which had characterised the pre-war period, was abandoned. At the Paris Peace Conference in 1919, Japan was recognised as one of the five great powers; its chief delegate, Saionji Kinmochi, sat with Wilson,

Lloyd George, Clemenceau and Orlando around the negotiating table. In the settlement that emerged from the Conference, Japan was awarded control over Germany's former possessions in China's Shantung Province and a permanent seat on the Council of the League of Nations.

Despite this, however, tensions emerged at the Paris Peace Conference that were to have a major impact on future relations between Japan and the Western powers. As the only non-Western great power at the Conference, Japan was determined to ensure that Western notions of racial superiority would not undermine its position and influence as a great power in its own right.

> Japan proposed that a 'racial equality clause' be included in the Covenant of the League of Nations.
>
> > The equality of nations being a basic principle of the League of Nations, the High Contracting Parties agree to accord as soon as possible to all alien nationals of states, members of the League, equal and just treatment in every respect making no distinction, either in law or in fact, on account of their race or nationality.

The proposal was supported by the Conference delegates of a number of nations, including France, Italy, Brazil, China, Greece and Czechoslovakia. However, it was totally opposed by most. Britain, for example, was deeply concerned about the implications that accepting the principle of racial equality might have for its authority over an empire compromising largely non-white populations. Several countries, such as the USA, Canada, New Zealand and Australia had already adopted policies of banning Japanese immigration, the legality of which would clearly be called into question if they accepted the racial equality proposal. Billy Hughes, the Prime Minister of Australia, pointed out that the Australian people, fearful of their employment prospects if faced with large-scale immigration from Asia, 'rejected the very idea of equality'. He continued, 'no government could live for a day in Australia if it tampered with a White Australia'. More significantly, President Wilson realised that it would be difficult enough to persuade the American people to accept the idea of participation in a League of Nations, without also expecting them to accept the concept of racial equality and the threat of large-scale Asian immigration.

Despite the fact that the Japanese proposal had gained significant support amongst the delegates at the Paris

Peace Conference, it was finally rejected as a result of Wilson's insistence that such an issue could only be accepted by unanimous agreement. The Japanese delegation was incensed. Having played a significant role in helping the Allies to win the First World War, Japan had expected greater respect.

> **ACTIVITY 4.16**
>
> **a** Why did Japan want a 'race equality clause' included in the Covenant of the League of Nations?
>
> **b** Identify as many reasons as you can to explain why this proposal was rejected.

Public opinion in Japan had already been deeply divided over the issue of their country's involvement in the proposed League of Nations. Many Japanese were deeply opposed to membership of an organisation that they saw as Western-dominated. Such views became more popular with the rejection of the race equality clause proposal and the continuation of policies banning Asian immigration into many Western countries. The impression that Japan was not being treated as a true equal by its Western allies, and the USA in particular, was popularised in Japanese newspapers and radio broadcasts.

Japanese anger and resentment grew still deeper when, following representations from the Chinese government, the Paris Peace Conference reversed its original decision regarding control over Germany's former possessions in Shantung Province. Originally granted to Japan, control was now awarded to China. Despite the fact that deals with regional Chinese warlords enabled Japan to maintain considerable power and influence within the province, the Conference's decision was interpreted by many Japanese as yet another example of the Western powers exerting their dominance over Japan.

The Japanese government decided to continue with its pro-Western foreign policy despite increasing public opinion opposition to it. At the Washington Naval Conference (1921–22), it agreed to limit the size of the Japanese navy to three-fifths the size of the US and British fleets (see Chapter 2.2). Historians disagree about the reasons why Japan was prepared to abandon its earlier expansionist policy and accept the international agreements reached in Washington. Some claim that, confronted by the combined power of Britain and the USA, the Japanese government realised that it had little choice but to reach agreement. In particular, there was simply no way that Japan could win a naval arms race against the USA. However, the opposing

169

view is that, rather than being forced into it, Japan reached agreement because it genuinely wanted to. Many Japanese politicians, such as Kijuro Shidehara (Japanese Ambassador in the USA), realised that such multinational cooperation would not only guarantee Japan's security but also enable it to continue its economic expansion in China. Whatever the government's reasons, its policies were increasingly at odds with public opinion in Japan.

ACTIVITY 4.17

Prepare a response to one of these two questions:

a Explain why many Japanese people were disappointed and angered by the decisions made at the Paris Peace Conference. Remember to include the following points in your notes:

- identify as many reasons as you can rather than simply stating a single factor
- explain **why** they were angry and disappointed, rather than simply describing **what** they were angry and disappointed about.

b Summarise the problems of Chinese and Japanese expectations of the Paris Peace Conference. How justified do you think the expectations of the two countries were? How possible would it be to reach a decision that would satisfy both – or either – of them? Remember to provide a balanced account.

KEY CONCEPT

Interpretation

Look at the alternative ways in which historians have interpreted the Japanese government's willingness to make concessions at the Washington Naval Conference. Which interpretation do you find most convincing, and why?

Political and economic factors in the failure of democracy

Japan had adopted a form of constitutional democracy in 1889, prior to which the emperor had supreme power. A **Diet** was established, and by 1925 all adult Japanese males were afforded the right to vote. The emperor retained enormous power – he alone could make decisions about war and peace, he remained commander of the armed forces and he had the right to dismiss the Diet if he so wished. Nevertheless, Japan was moving towards a political system similar to those in the Western democracies. New political parties emerged, most of

which were more concerned with promoting domestic reform than in pursuing a militaristic foreign policy. However, just as in Italy, Germany and Spain, social, economic and political problems began to emerge during the 1920s and early 1930s – problems that democratically elected governments seemed incapable of overcoming.

KEY TERM

Diet: a national assembly, the lower house of the Japanese parliament, which first sat in 1890.

As disputes raged both between and within political parties, military leaders grew increasingly powerful. Secret military groups, such as the Sakurakai (Cherry Blossom Society) established in 1930, were organised. Their aim was to end party politics and restore the emperor as head of state in a military dictatorship. Concerned that politicians were dividing rather than uniting their country, many people in Japan grew increasingly supportive of the aims of such groups. By the early 1930s, Japan's experiment with democracy was coming to an end for a variety of reasons, both political and economic.

Political factors in the decline of Japanese democracy

Used to a situation in which the emperor held total power, the concept of democracy was still relatively new to the Japanese people. The large number of political parties appeared to make decision making slow and often ineffective. Governments could only be formed as a result of unstable alliances between political parties that held different, and often contradictory, views. As government minsters argued amongst themselves, little progress was made in addressing key issues, such as dealing with Japan's post-First World War economic problems and the need for reform of the education system. The Japanese people's respect for parliamentary democracy declined quickly when it became evident that many politicians were corrupt and open to bribery. The main political parties were heavily funded by large industrial companies, such as Mitsui and Mitsubishi, and their policies often reflected the needs of those companies rather than the best interests of Japan and its people. The elected government appeared to have been humiliated at the Paris Peace Conference, with the failure to gain acceptance of its race equality proposals and the revised decision to award control of Shantung Province to China. Moreover, the agreements Japan signed at the Washington Naval Conference were not widely popular.

Most Japanese citizens were heavily nationalistic and held anti-Western opinions, which did not fit well with their government's willingness to compromise and cooperate with the USA and the major European nations. These opinions were enhanced when the USA passed the Japanese Exclusion Act in 1924, which effectively ended further Japanese immigration to the USA. This was extremely unpopular in Japan, leading to mass protests. Moreover, public opinion tended to agree with the army and navy leaders who felt that the Japanese government should be exploiting China's weakness as an opportunity for Japanese expansion.

As ultra-nationalist sentiments continued to develop in Japan, so the influence of the secret societies was enhanced. In a series of incidents, most notably in March and October 1931 and February 1932, secret society supporters attempted to undermine the authority of the constitutional government by assassinating leading politicians. These incidents culminated in the May 15th Incident in 1932, when the prime minister, Inukai Tsuyoshi, was assassinated by a group of 11 young naval officers. At their subsequent trial, the naval officers stressed their loyalty to the emperor and exploited the opportunity to criticise the government's failings. They were given very lenient prison sentences, a factor that further eroded the government's credibility.

The military's increasing influence over Japan's decision-making process is also reflected in the fact that it was a requirement for the government ministers responsible for the army and navy to be serving military officers. As a result, governments found it increasingly difficult to control the activities of the Japanese military.

Economic factors in the decline of Japanese democracy

The economic boom that Japan had experienced during the First World War ended by 1920, by which time European industry had revived and was beginning to recover lost markets. The war had artificially boosted the demand for, and the price of, Japanese exports, encouraging a rapid expansion of industrial output. Once the war ended, it was clear that Japanese manufactured products were not internationally competitive in terms of both quality and price. Unable to maintain its export markets, Japan was significantly over-producing, leading to a significant fall in prices. For example, between January and December 1920, the price of Japanese cotton yarn fell by 60% and that of silk by 70%. Many companies went out of business, while others were forced to reduce their workforce. Unemployment

began to rise in Japan's industrial cities. At the same time, farmers were hit by falling prices. Attempts by industrial workers and farmers to form political organisations were systematically suppressed by the government.

In an attempt to prevent further bankruptcies and unemployment, the Japanese government provided extensive loans to banks and industries. This enabled Japan's economy to recover gradually during the 1920s, but it was a short-term solution that simply disguised underlying problems – problems that re-emerged during the worldwide economic crisis following the Wall Street Crash in 1929. Japan entered a steep economic depression in 1930, which led to rural areas becoming impoverished and increasingly susceptible to periods of famine. Japan's economy was heavily reliant on the export of textiles, mainly cotton and silk. International demand for these products fell dramatically during the Great Depression, with the result that the value of Japan's textile exports fell by over 50% between 1929 and 1931. Unemployment rose, and as poverty spread across much of the country, most Japanese people blamed the government for their misfortunes.

By the early 1930s, therefore, the idea of democracy had become increasingly unpopular in Japan, and the government it created was being subjected to intense criticism. In 1931, the government's inability to command widespread respect and enforce its authority was fatally exposed.

Manchuria

It was events in Manchuria, a large province of China, which led to the final collapse of Japanese democracy. As a result of its increasing influence over China following the Russo-Japanese War (1904-05) and the Twenty-One Demands during the First World War, Japan had developed extensive trade and investment interests in Manchuria, protected by a military force known as the **Kwantung Army**. In September 1931, the Kwantung Army mobilised, and over the next six months took control of the whole of Manchuria establishing the puppet state of Manchukuo. This action had been taken without the permission of the Japanese government, and it was Prime Minister Inukai Tsuyoshi's criticism of it that led to his assassination. **Emperor Hirohito** deplored the attack on Manchuria, but steadfastly refused to order the Kwantung Army to withdraw. He was afraid that his prestige among the population would be damaged if his order was ignored by the army – which it was likely to be.

KEY TERM

Kwantung Army: Japanese army units deployed in the Japanese-controlled areas of Manchuria to protect Japan's interests within the province. The Kwantung Army damaged a Japanese railway line near Mukden and blamed it on the Chinese. This provided the pretext for the full-scale invasion of Manchuria. (Not to be confused with Kwangtung Province.)

Hirohito was emperor of Japan from December 1926 until his death in January 1989. In the interwar years, he presided over Japan's period of militarisation and expansion, and he brought Japan into the Second World War. In 1945, Hirohito escaped prosecution for war crimes even though many other Japanese leaders were put on trial.

172

Historians disagree about the reasons why the Kwantung Army officers took the decision to invade Manchuria in open defiance of their own democratically elected government. Several possible explanations have been put forward.

- Since 1928, Chiang's KMT Chinese government had claimed that various treaties between China and Japan were invalid. In some parts of China, Japanese settlers were expelled without compensation. Moreover, the Manchurian warlord Chang Tso-lin (Zhang Xuolin) was threatening Japanese interests in Manchuria itself. Chang was assassinated by a Kwantung Army officer in 1928, a factor that increased the anti-Japanese sentiments of his son, Zhang Xueliang, one of the main instigators of the Xi'an Incident. To the leaders of the Kwantung Army, it seemed clear that the Chinese were trying to reduce Japanese influence over trade and business within Manchuria. This would have been a serious blow to the Japanese economy, already suffering as a result of the worldwide depression.

- Manchuria was rich in iron ore and coal deposits. To a small resource-poor island nation such as Japan, these were prize assets.

- Many army officers were concerned about Japan's vulnerability in the event of any future war. As a small nation dependent on trade, Japan could easily be blockaded into submission. Potential enemies, such as the USA and the USSR, would find it relatively easy to prevent essential supplies reaching Japan in the event of war. Therefore, it was vital for Japan to achieve economic self-sufficiency, and this could only be done by acquiring new territory.

- The events of 1931 seemed to present the ideal opportunity to invade Manchuria. China was distracted by terrible floods and the ongoing civil war between the KMT and the CCP. At the same time, Europe and the USA were busy dealing with their own problems brought on by the world-wide economic depression.

- Japanese army officers were dismayed by their government's determination to press ahead with cuts to Japan's army and navy. The conquest of Manchuria would demonstrate just how important the army was to Japan's future.

- Public opinion in Japan was largely supportive of the Manchurian campaign. As in Italy and Germany, the Great Depression led to a rise in ultranationalist sentiments. To most Japanese, the conquest of Manchuria would provide an economic solution to the Depression – a new market for trade and investment.

The invasion of Manchuria was to have profound effects in Japan. It was abundantly clear that the already unpopular constitutional government of Japan had lost control of its own armed forces. The emperor's advisers came to the conclusion that a democratically elected government could no longer provide stability in Japan. Following this advice, Emperor Hirohito appointed a National Unity government under Admiral Makoto Saitō. In effect, the armed forces assumed control of Japan. Japan had become a military dictatorship.

ACTIVITY 4.18

a What does the Japanese invasion of Manchuria in 1931 tell us about:

i nationalism in Japan in 1931

ii the power of the Japanese emperor in 1931

iii Japanese opinions about China in 1931.

b In groups of four, hold a debate on the following statement – two of you support the statement, the other two oppose it.

Democracy failed in Japan during the 1930s for economic rather than political reasons.

Implications of military rule for Japanese expansionism

Following China's appeal for international assistance, the new Japanese government justified the invasion of Manchuria in the following statement at the League of Nations in December 1932:

ACTIVITY 4.19

a In the statement to the League of Nations (below), how did Yōsuke Matsuoka justify the Japanese takeover of Manchuria?

b Look carefully at the American cartoon published in 1931 (Figure 4.5). What point do you think the cartoonist is trying to make?

c Compare and contrast the opinions expressed about Japan's takeover of Manchuria in these two sources.

d Compare and contrast the statements of the Chinese and Japanese governments regarding the invasion of Manchuria.

Japan seeks in Manchuria only the observance of our treaty rights and the safety of the lives of our people. We wanted from China the right to trade, according to the existing treaties, free from unwarranted interference and molestation … Chinese propaganda has been used to shape world opinion against Japan. Japan has acted in self-defence against a Chinese government which aims to terminate our interests and treaties in Manchuria … The fundamental principle of the League is to promote international cooperation and achieve international peace and security … Japan, for her part, is ready to do all in her power to cooperate with the League in helping China to attain progress … The spirit of the League coincides with the fundamental policy of Japan, which is to consolidate peace in the Far East and to contribute to the maintenance of peace throughout the world … It is true that voices have been raised in some quarters criticising the efficiency of the League. But the fact that the Manchurian affair has not led to open war between China and Japan … is assuredly due to actions of the League.

Statement by Yōsuke Matsuoka, Japanese delegate, to the Assembly of the League of Nations, 6 December 1932

173

Figure 4.5: A 1931 American cartoon comments on Japan's failure to abide by treaties following its invasion of Manchuria

In open defiance of the League of Nation's instruction to Japan to withdraw its troops from Manchuria pending the outcome of its enquiry, the Lytton Commission, into the situation, the Japanese government poured further military resources into the invasion. By the time the League concluded its enquiry with the publication of the Lytton Report, and decided that Manchuria should be returned to China, Japan had already established full control over the region, which it renamed Manchukuo. In anger at the League's decision, the Japanese delegation stormed out of the Council and never returned to the League of Nations. Japan was now an isolated country, lacking in allies and acting in defiance of international opinion, as indicated by an American cartoon, published in c.1931 (Figure 4.5).

However, the League of Nations took no action to force Japan to relinquish its control over Manchukuo. This weak international response to such blatant aggression in defiance of international agreements led some of Japan's military leaders to call for further inroads into China. Others were less convinced, arguing that the first priority was to develop the Japanese armed forces in preparation for a possible attack by the USSR, which was showing its own interest in Manchuria. As this debate continued, Japan withdrew from the League of Nations in March 1933 and rejected arms control. The agreements made at the Washington Conference were no longer valid. In November 1936, Japan signed the Anti-Comintern Pact with Germany – this provided a guarantee that the USSR would receive no German assistance if it went to war with Japan. The Pact was subsequently joined by Italy in 1937.

Outbreak of the Second Sino-Japanese War

In the period from 1931 to 1937, relations between Japan and China remained strained. Under the Boxer Protocol of 1901, Japan and other countries had been allowed to station troops near Peking to guard important railway lines and other communications systems. It was clear, however, that the number of Japanese troops stationed in China far exceeded that allowed under the terms of the Boxer Protocol. Japan's efforts to extend its economic interests within China resulted in a number of skirmishes between Chinese and Japanese troops, but these were relatively minor affairs which were settled relatively quickly. In July 1937,

however, one such incident resulted in the outbreak of full-scale war between Japan and China, a war which was to last until 1945.

Precise details of the incident at the Marco Polo Bridge near Peking are unconfirmed, but it would appear that a Japanese training exercise was misinterpreted by Chinese troops as genuine military action. The Chinese fired on the Japanese. Immediately realising its mistake, China issued an apology, but the Japanese government used the incident to declare war on China.

KEY CONCEPT

Cause and consequence

The incident at the Marco Polo Bridge is described in some books as the cause of what became known as the Second Sino-Japanese War (1937–45).

a   Research the incident at the Marco Polo Bridge.

b   How far do you agree that it was this incident that caused the Second Sino-Japanese War? Explain your answer.

Make sure that your answer is balanced – to achieve this, you need to identify and consider other factors which might be seen as causes of the Second Sino-Japanese War.

Well equipped and well organised, Japanese troops poured into China, initially with great success. Major cities, such as Shanghai, were quickly taken, and China's Nationalist government was forced to relocate from Nanking to a more secure base in western China. By 1939, however, the war had reached a stalemate. Renewed unity between Chiang's KMT and Mao's CCP following the Xi'an Incident meant that the Japanese were confronted by much sterner opposition than anticipated. As Japanese troops moved further into the Chinese interior, their vital supply and communications lines became increasingly stretched and a target for sabotage conducted as part of the CCP's guerrilla tactics. In the west of China, Japanese troops faced major counter-offensives from KMT soldiers equipped with modern Russian-supplied weapons. Japan controlled many of China's major cities, where countless atrocities were unquestionably committed against the Chinese population. However, China's vast size made it virtually impossible for Japanese troops to retain control over the countryside.

There was renewed concern amongst the Western powers, particularly the USA and Britain, about Japanese aggression, and some considered imposing economic sanctions against Japan. By 1939, however, Britain was heavily involved in fighting its own war against Nazi Germany and the USA was still pursuing an isolationist policy. Under these circumstances, there was little possibility of China receiving any direct help from the West.

The dilemma facing Japan

Japan's military leaders were divided over what action to take next. Most of them were of the opinion that the outbreak of the Second World War in Europe in 1939 offered an opportunity similar to that which Japan had successfully exploited during the First World War. They argued that Japan should continue its aggressive policy and seize Dutch, British and French possessions in the Far East. Success against Indo-China, Thailand, Burma, Malaya and the Dutch East Indies would provide Japan with new sources of tin, oil and rubber. However, others – including Prime Minister Prince Konoye – argued for a more cautious approach. They were concerned about the possibility of attack by the USSR and felt that it was more important to safeguard against this than to risk further military engagements, especially with so many Japanese troops engaged in China.

This dilemma was ended in June 1941 when Germany invaded the USSR, eliminating the threat to Japan. There now seemed to be nothing to prevent Japan taking more territory. A new prime minister, **General Hideki Tojo**, was appointed. Japan's descent into military dictatorship was now complete. This had major implications for Japan's foreign policy. The military-dominated Japanese government was now committed to the extension of Japanese territory by military force. Its main objectives were to complete the conquest of China and to expand southwards by seizing the wealth and resources available in the South East Asian possessions of Britain, France and the Netherlands.

ACTIVITY 4.20

Discuss the following questions in pairs.

a Identify as many reasons as you can to explain why Japan was not able to conquer the whole of China following its invasion in 1937.

b Why were Japanese military leaders divided over what action to take following the invasion of China?

c What was the significance for Japan's foreign policy of Germany's invasion of the USSR in June 1941?

HIDEKI TOJO (1884–1948)

Tojo was prime minister (and effectively military dictator) of Japan during the Second World War. He was a great admirer of Hitler, believing that Japan's future would be best served by adopting the type of government that the Nazis had imposed on Germany. Tojo was subsequently found guilty of war crimes by an international tribunal and was sentenced to death. He was hanged on 23 December 1948.

Reasons for Japanese involvement in the Second World War

With the major European nations fully occupied in fighting the Second World War, and the threat of attack by the USSR now removed, Tojo's government embarked on a programme of territorial expansion. This was to bring it into conflict with the USA, which was concerned about the effects of Japanese expansionism on its own interests in the Far East and the Pacific Ocean. This was a conflict that was to lead to Japan's own catastrophic involvement in the Second World War.

175

The USA had been increasingly concerned about Japanese expansion since the invasion of Manchuria in 1931. However, with its policies still largely dictated by the isolationist determination to avoid direct involvement in international affairs, it had done little more than express criticism of Japanese actions. In 1940, when Japan invaded Indo-China, the USA had imposed some economic sanctions, but these were restricted to military equipment such as aeroplanes. The USA's attitude began to change when Japan extended its control over French Indo-China in 1941. Tojo claimed that this action posed no threat to the USA and that Japan was keen to maintain peace with USA. However, the American intelligence services had broken the Japanese diplomatic code, and President Roosevelt was fully aware of Japan's plans for further territorial acquisitions in the Pacific region and the threat which this posed to American interests.

In response, Roosevelt increased the USA's military presence in the Philippines, and in July 1941, ended American oil exports to Japan. Given the vital importance of American oil to Japan's military capabilities, Roosevelt believed that economic sanctions would be enough to force the Japanese to back down. This belief was based on two assumptions. First, that Japan was militarily weak, as demonstrated by its failure to force a quick defeat on China. Second, that the presence of British and American forces in the Pacific region would be sufficient to deter Japanese aggression. Both assumptions were wrong.

Denied vital American oil imports, Japan faced a stark choice – either reach a diplomatic settlement with the USA or continue seizing raw materials from the South-East Asia region, including the oil of the Dutch East Indies. Japan pursued both options. Just as Hitler had disguised his aggressive intentions behind constant claims that his only desire was for peace, so Tojo pursued negotiations with American diplomats while, at the same time, preparing his armed forces for war.

It was not until 26 November 1941, when Roosevelt demanded that Japan cease its military build-up in the Pacific region, that Tojo finally broke off diplomatic relations with the USA.

ACTIVITY 4.21

Look carefully at the statement issued by the Japanese government on 7 December 1941.

a How did the Japanese government justify its decision to end diplomatic relations with the USA?

b What were the implications of this statement for the USA?

> The earnest hope of the Japanese government to adjust Japanese-American relations and to preserve and promote the peace of the Pacific through cooperation with the American Government has finally been lost.
>
> The Japanese Government regrets to have to notify the American Government that in view of the attitude of the American Government it cannot but consider that it is impossible to reach an agreement through further negotiations.

By then, a fleet of Japanese ships was already three weeks into its journey towards the American naval base at Pearl Harbor in the Hawaiian Islands. On board six aircraft carriers, protected by two battleships, two cruisers and over 50 other vessels, were 453 Japanese fighter planes armed with bombs and torpedoes. Their aim was to destroy the American Pacific fleet in line with a plan that had been devised by Admiral Isoroku Yamamoto. Surprisingly, these Japanese ships went undetected either by American patrol vessels or radar. Despite the obvious threat posed by Japan's warlike preparations, the American base seemed totally unprepared for a possible attack. At 8 a.m. on Sunday 7 December 1941, the first wave of 183 Japanese aircraft attacked. By 1.30 p.m., when the attack finished, the USA had suffered the loss of 2 402 men and almost 190 aircraft, together with major damage to eight ships. The attack had come as such a surprise that, during the first wave of bombing by Japanese fighter planes, only four US aircraft were able to get airborne to offer any defence.

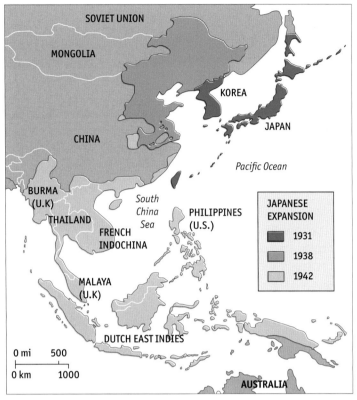

Figure 4.6: The Pacific region, showing Japanese expansion during the 1930s and early 1940s

177

Later on 7 December, the nature of the attack and its implications were described in a BBC radio broadcast in Britain:

Japan has launched a surprise attack on the American naval base at Pearl Harbor in Hawaii and has declared war on Britain and the United States. News of the daring raid has shocked members of the American Congress at a time when Japanese officials in Washington were still negotiating on lifting US sanctions imposed after continuing Japanese aggression against China. President Roosevelt is working on a message to Congress tomorrow, in which he is expected to ask for a declaration of war with Japan. The US government expects Germany and Italy to declare war on the USA within hours. Although the attack has shocked the American people, there is little doubt that it has been brewing for some years. Relations between Japan and the USA have deteriorated since 1931 when Japan occupied Manchuria in Northern China. Last year, the US imposed trade sanctions on Japan. In September 1940, Japan signed a Pact with Germany and Italy. It became a formal member of the Axis alliance fighting the European war but continued to negotiate with America for trade concessions.

ACTIVITY 4.22

Discuss the following questions in pairs:

a Why would the Japanese attack on Pearl Harbor have been of great interest to the people of Britain?

b What implications do you think the Japanese attack on Pearl Harbor would have on public opinion in the USA?

Make sure that your notes contain a list of all the possible reasons why the Japanese government made the decision to attack Pearl Harbor.

The Japanese attack on Pearl Harbor poses two key questions for historians. First, why did Japan's military leaders order such an attack when it would almost certainly lead to war against the powerful USA? Second, when the USA was aware of Japanese intentions to continue an expansionist policy in the Pacific region and the threat that this posed to American interests, why was the naval base at Pearl Harbor totally unprepared for an attack?

Japan's motives for mounting the attack on Pearl Harbor can be explained in a number of ways.

- Japanese military leaders were already convinced that war with the USA was inevitable. They interpreted the increased American military presence in the Philippines as a prelude to a US attack on Japan. The fact that both the USA and Britain had enhanced their naval deployment in the Pacific Ocean reinforced this opinion. Rather than wait for such an attack to occur, the Japanese came to the conclusion that it was logical to mount a **pre-emptive strike**.

- Japanese victory in the Russo-Japanese War of 1904-05 had been largely secured by the destruction of the Russian fleet in Port Arthur. Japan's military leaders believed that, in much the same way, the attack on Pearl Harbor would seriously undermine the USA's ability to fight a naval war in the Pacific.

- Destroying much of the USA's Pacific fleet would enable Japan to continue its expansionist policy without interference from the USA. In particular, it would hinder the USA's ability to mobilise its military forces in the Pacific.

- The Japanese government also believed that a devastating attack on Pearl Harbor would seriously undermine the morale of the American people and encourage the USA to seek a peaceful settlement with Japan.

KEY TERM

Pre-emptive strike: an attack designed to destroy an enemy's ability to respond. It is based on the assumption that the enemy is itself planning an imminent attack.

The reasons why the American base at Pearl Harbor was so unprepared for the attack have become a topic for great debate amongst historians. Some have argued that, since American intelligence services had cracked the Japanese diplomatic code, it should have been obvious that Japan was planning such an attack. They suggest that Roosevelt and his government were fully aware that an attack was imminent, but failed to do anything about it. Roosevelt had long argued that it was in the USA's best interests to become involved in the Second World War. Indeed, when war broke out in 1939, he advocated US entry into the war in support of Britain in order to protect American interests in Europe.

Such views were extremely unpopular in the USA, where public opinion remained steadfastly isolationist. Even members of Roosevelt's own Democratic Party had labelled him a warmonger. This has led to the accusation that Roosevelt did nothing to prevent the attack on Pearl Harbor because it would force the American people to accept that he had been right all along, and that the USA had no choice but to enter the Second World War.

These controversial views are rejected by most historians, who argue that there are more logical explanations for Pearl Harbor's lack of preparation for a Japanese attack.

They point out that the US intelligence services had intercepted such a vast amount of Japanese material that it would have been impossible to identify Japan's plans for an attack on Pearl Harbor. As an example, they claim that, due to a decoding delay, the full implications of Japan's announcement that it was breaking off diplomatic relations with the USA did not become clear in Washington until six hours before the attack on Pearl Harbor on 7 December. There is considerable evidence to suggest that the US government had been anticipating a Japanese attack, and had placed American military personnel on high alert. However, it was assumed that such an attack would be launched against the Dutch East Indies or the American bases in the Philippines. Pearl Harbor had not been identified as a possible target.

Figure 4.7: President Roosevelt signing the official declaration of war against Japan on 8 December 1941.

The Japanese attack on Pearl Harbor had a profound and lasting effect on US foreign policy. It completely ended the USA's commitment to isolationism. Americans could no longer claim that events in the wider world did not affect or concern them, and the Second World War was clearly no longer an exclusively European affair. The USA formally declared war on Japan. Hitler greeted the news of Japan's attack on Pearl Harbor with jubilation. With Japan as an ally, he believed Germany would be invincible.

Consequently, Germany declared war on the USA – a decision that guaranteed American involvement on the battlefields of Europe.

For Japan, too, the attack on Pearl Harbor had major implications. Devastating as it was, the attack had failed in its key objectives. A number of American ships, including three aircraft carriers (*Enterprise, Lexington* and *Saratoga*) were at sea at the time, and therefore escaped undamaged. The ships anchored in Pearl Harbor were in shallow water, making it relatively easy for some of them to be salvaged and repaired. The number of American deaths was far lower than Japan had envisaged, because most crew members were on shore leave at the time. Moreover, the attack had failed to destroy large supplies of oil that were to prove vital in supplying the USA's subsequent war effort. Though seriously damaged, the American Pacific fleet was far from destroyed.

The descent into military dictatorship had led to fundamental changes in Japan's foreign policy and its relations with the international community. It had acted in open defiance of various treaties to which it had been a signatory. It had blatantly ignored, and subsequently withdrawn from, the League of Nations, of which it had been a founder member. It had allied itself with the aggressive fascist regimes of Germany and Italy, adopting similar methods of territorial expansion though military power. Japan's attempt to increase its power and influence in the Far East was to bring destruction upon itself.

The Japanese had become involved in a war against an increasingly united China from which it derived no benefit. Japan's close links with Hitler's Germany had simply brought it into conflict with Western democratic nations such as Britain. And, in December 1941, Japan had made an enemy of the most powerful nation on earth.

ACTIVITY 4.23

a   Analyse the reasons why Japan attacked the US naval base at Pearl Harbor in December 1941.

b   Analyse the reasons why the US naval base at Pearl Harbor was unprepared for such an attack.

c   Do you think that the Japanese attack on Pearl Harbor ended in failure?

Drawing up a table, such as the one below, will help with your answer.

AGREE	DISAGREE

Reflection: Discuss your answers in pairs or small groups. Have you included different types of historical evidence to support your reasons? How would you adapt your answer following your discussion with your partner or group?

179

Exam-style questions

Source analysis questions

Read all four sources and then answer both parts of question 1.

The Japanese attack on Pearl Harbor, 1941

SOURCE A

Japan hereby declares war on the USA and Britain. We have followed the far-sighted policy of seeking the stability of East Asia and contributing to world peace. To cultivate friendship among nations and to enjoy prosperity in common with all nations has always been the guiding principles of our foreign policy. It has been truly unavoidable and far from our wishes that Japan has now been brought to cross swords with the USA and Britain. More than four years have passed since China, failing to comprehend Japan's true intentions and recklessly courting trouble, disturbed the peace of East Asia and compelled us to take up arms. Eager to dominate Asia, both the USA and Britain have increased disturbances by supporting China. Moreover, these two powers have increased military preparations to challenge Japan. They have obstructed our peaceful commerce and resorted to ending economic relations. They have shown no willingness to compromise. If left unchecked, their policies would damage our efforts for peace in East Asia and endanger our very existence. Japan, for its existence and self-defence, has no alternative but to go to war and crush every obstacle in its path.

Japan's declaration of war against the USA and Britain, 8 December 1941

SOURCE B

Yesterday, December 7th, 1941, the USA was suddenly and deliberately attacked by naval and air forces of the Empire of Japan. The USA was at peace with Japan and was still in conversation with its government looking toward the maintenance of peace in the Pacific. The distance of Hawaii from Japan makes it obvious that the attack was deliberately planned many days or even weeks ago. During the intervening time, the Japanese government has deliberately sought to deceive the United States by false statements and expressions of hope for continued peace. The attack yesterday on the Hawaiian Islands has caused severe damage to American naval and military forces. I regret to tell you that very many American lives have been lost. No matter how long it may take us to overcome this premeditated invasion, the American people in their righteous might will win through to absolute victory. Since the unprovoked attack by Japan on Sunday, December 7th, 1941, a state of war has existed between the USA and Japan.

President Roosevelt addressing the people of the USA, 8 December 1941

SOURCE C

With a promptness and unanimity that left no possible room for doubt, the USA yesterday answered with decisive action Japan's bloody, treacherous challenge. Hardly 30 minutes after President Roosevelt appeared before the historic joint session of Congress to ask for a declaration of war, both the House of Representatives and the Senate had passed a resolution formalising the conflict which began with the dastardly attack on Hawaii at dawn on Sunday. We are in this thing now, all the way – and we are in to win. We have answered the defiance of a cowardly, back-stabbing enemy who talked peace even while plotting undeclared war.

From an article in the St Petersburg Times, *an American newspaper, 9 December 1941*

SOURCE D

The main American naval force was shifted to the Pacific region and Britain declared its intention to join the fight on the side of the USA within 24 hours should war break out between Japan and the USA.

Japan therefore faced considerable military threats. Japan attempted to overcome these dangerous circumstances by diplomatic negotiation and was willing to make concessions in the hope of finding a solution through mutual compromise. There was no progress because the USA would not retreat from its original position. The USA repeated demands that, under the circumstances, Japan could not accept. At this point, Japan lost all hope of reaching a solution through diplomatic negotiation. In order to protect itself, Japan decided to prepare for war on 1 December 1941. However, even during the preparations for war, we laid our plans in such a manner that, should there be progress through diplomatic negotiation, we would be well prepared to cancel operations.

Hideki Tojo, writing while in prison in 1947

1 a Compare and contrast the views expressed in Sources A and B regarding which country was most responsible for the outbreak of war between Japan and the USA.

b How far do Sources A to D support the view that Japan attacked Pearl Harbor as a means of self-defence?

Essay based questions

Answer both parts of the questions below.

2 a Explain why students protested on the streets of Peking on 4 May 1919.

b 'Communist support was the most important factor in the success of the Kuomintang's Northern Expedition.' How far do you agree?

3 a Explain why the Xi'an Incident (1936) led to renewed collaboration between the Kuomintang and the Chinese Communist Party.

b To what extent was the growth in popularity of the Chinese Communist Party in the 1930s due to the failings of the Kuomintang?

Sample answers

Here are two sample answers to Question 1(b) above.

ANSWER 1

Source A is Japan's declaration of war against Britain and the USA on 8 December 1941. It says that Japan had always wanted to cultivate friendship and peace among nations,

but that Britain and the USA clearly wanted war and had shown no willingness to compromise.

Source B is the USA's declaration of war against Japan. It says that Japan had deliberately deceived the USA by claiming it wanted peace while preparing for war at the same time. It mentions the damage done to American people and equipment by the Japanese attack on Hawaii.

Source C is an extract from an American newspaper shortly after the Japanese attack on Hawaii. It shows how the American House of Representatives and Senate both agreed to support President Roosevelt's intention to declare war on Japan.

181

Source D was written by Hideki Tojo when he was in prison six years after the Japanese attack on Hawaii. It says that the USA had increased its naval force in the Pacific and that Britain was willing to join the USA in a war against Japan. Japan tried to negotiate in order to maintain peace, but the USA refused to compromise. This led to war.

> Taking each source in turn, this answer simply:
> - explains what the source is
> - repeats what the source says, at times using the same words (e.g. 'cultivate friendship').
>
> There is no attempt to analyse source content, and the answer does not actually address the question. This is, therefore, a weak answer.

ANSWER 2

By 1941, Japan was committed to a policy of expansionism in Asia. Heavily involved in an invasion of China since 1937, the Japanese government intended to expand further into areas such as the Dutch East Indies. With the danger of an attack on Japan by the USSR removed with the German invasion of the USSR in June 1941, the biggest threat to Japanese expansionism came from the USA, which was deeply concerned about the impact of Japanese actions on its own interests in the region.

In December 1941, Japan attacked the US naval base at Pearl Harbor, Hawaii. Historians have long debated Japan's motives for launching this attack – was it a defensive move to prevent an imminent attack by the USA? Or, was it an aggressive act designed to prevent US interference in Japanese plans for further expansion? The four sources reflect this debate.

Sources A and D, both of Japanese origin, support the view that Japan's motives were in self-defence. Source A, Japan's declaration of war against the USA and Britain, stresses that Japan wanted peace and stability in East Asia, but that this was threatened by the military build-up conducted by both the USA and Britain and their lack of willingness to compromise. Not only did this threaten to adversely affect Japan's 'peaceful commerce', but it also posed a threat to the very 'existence' of Japan. As a result, Japan had 'no alternative but' to go to war in self-defence. This interpretation is shared by Source D, in which Tojo argues that Japan was threatened by the military preparations of both the USA and Britain. Japan's attempts to negotiate a peaceful solution, he claims, were thwarted by the USA's steadfast refusal to compromise. Tojo argues that Japan was willing to negotiate right up to the moment of the attack on Pearl Harbor, but the USA continued to resist diplomatic negotiations and continued to prepare for war.

Sources B and C, both of American origin, clearly disagree with this interpretation. In Source B, US President Roosevelt describes the attack on Pearl Harbor as 'unprovoked', and claims that Japan had deliberately set out to deceive the USA by pretending to engage in peaceful negotiations while, at the same time, preparing the attack. He points out that, at the time of the attack, Japan had not yet formally declared war against the USA. Source C, an extract from an American newspaper two days after the attack on Pearl Harbor, makes the same point, describing the attack as a 'dastardly' action by a 'cowardly, back-stabbing enemy who talked peace even while plotting undeclared war'. According to Sources B and C, the Japanese attack on Pearl Harbor was not a defensive action, but an aggressive act designed to prevent the USA from interfering in Japan's plans for further expansionism in Asia.

All four sources are, of course, biased and interpret events from their own viewpoints only. It is not surprising that Sources A and D are in agreement – Tojo was, after all, the prime minister of Japan at the time of the attack on Pearl Harbor. Source A's claim that China was entirely responsible for causing the Second Sino-Japanese War in 1937 because of its failure to 'comprehend Japan's true intentions' is difficult to justify given the constant Japanese aggression against China following the invasion of Manchuria in 1931. Tojo's claim that Japan was still willing to negotiate a peaceful settlement right up until the attack on Pearl Harbor seems equally unlikely.

In Source B, President Roosevelt is addressing the American people. Public opinion in the USA, still largely isolationist in character, had opposed Roosevelt's long-held view that the USA should enter World War 2. Roosevelt therefore needed to stress the unprovoked nature of the Japanese attack and the devious nature of Japanese involvement in negotiations, to ensure public support for the USA's declaration of war against Japan. Source C makes it clear that Roosevelt now had this support, as shown by the speed with which Congress agreed to the declaration of war. Source C reflects the anger of the American people following the attack on Pearl Harbor.

On balance, and taking contextual knowledge into account, the sources do not support the view that Japan attacked Pearl Harbor as a means of self-defence. A more logical explanation is that the Japanese government was determined to remove the USA as a potential obstacle to its plans for further expansion within Asia.

This is an impressive answer because:

- It is characterised by good contextual knowledge. For example, the opening paragraph puts the Japanese attack on Pearl Harbor into its historical context. This is necessary in order to demonstrate full understanding of the question.
- Contextual knowledge is used to good effect in a number of places. For example, the answer states 'It is not surprising that Sources A and D are in agreement – Tojo was, after all, the prime minister of Japan at the time of the attack on Pearl Harbor.' This is important because it demonstrates understanding that Tojo, who wrote Source D, would also have had a major input into the writing of Source A.
- The answer does not simply deal with each source in turn in the order in which they appear in the question. It is clear that the student read all four sources carefully and developed an outline before starting to write a response.
- The answer correctly groups the sources into those which support the statement in the question, and those which challenge it.
- The key support and challenge points are identified and explained – appropriate quotations are taken from the sources to highlight key points.
- The sources are analysed in two ways:
  o by cross-referencing between the sources – for example, showing how Sources A and D say much the same things
  o by evaluating source reliability – rather than simply asserting that the sources are biased, the answer seeks to explain how and why they are biased.
- The answer is fully focused on the requirements of the question throughout, demonstrating understanding of the arguments which both support and challenge the statement in the question.

However, this answer does have one significant weakness. It reaches the conclusion that, on balance, the sources do not support the statement in the question. In effect, this implies that Sources B and C are seen as more convincing than Sources A and D. The reasons for this are not explained. The answer reaches a conclusion, but does not fully explain how this conclusion was reached.

ACTIVITY 4.24

a How would you rewrite the concluding paragraph of Sample Answer 2?

b In its 8 December 1941 edition, the *New York Daily News* newspaper quoted these comments made by Cordell Hull, the US Secretary of State, the previous evening:

> Japan has made a treacherous attack upon the United States, and its action in making unprovoked war while talking peace is infamous conduct. Japan is guilty of falsehoods and distortions on a scale so huge that I never imagined until today that any government on this planet was capable of uttering them.

With which of the four sources, A to D, were Hull's comments most in agreement?

Explain how you reached your decision.

Explain why these two sources are in agreement.

Imagine you are Hideki Tojo on 8 December 1941. How would you respond to Cordell Hull's comments?

Summary

After working through this chapter, make sure you understand the following key points:

- the impact of Chinese nationalism in general and the May Fourth Movement in particular on the development of the Kuomintang and the Chinese Communist Party

- the similarities and differences between the political ideologies of the Kuomintang and the Chinese Communist Party

- the reasons why during the 1930s the popularity of the Kuomintang declined while that of the Chinese Communist Party increased

- the reasons why Japan embarked on a policy of territorial expansionism during the 1930s, and the impact which this had on international relations.

Further reading

Barnhart, M. (1988). *Japan Prepares For Total War: The Search for Economic Security 1919-41*. **Cornell University Press.** Chapter 11 is particularly good for explaining the dilemma facing the Japanese government in the late 1930s – whether to continue expansionism or prepare for a possible attack by the USSR.

Beasley, W. E. (1987). *Japanese Imperialism, 1894–1945*. **Clarendon Press.** Chapters 12 and 13 provide relatively detailed accounts of Japanese aggression against China during the 1930s, and the impact this had on international relations.

Clements, J. (2017). *A Brief History of Japan*. **Tuttle.** Chapter 7 provides a useful overview of Japan's modernisation and rise to world-power status, while Chapter 8 covers the Japanese attack on Pearl Harbor.

Fenby, J. (2011). *Chiang Kai-shek and the China He Lost*. **Harvard University Press.** Chiang Kai-shek is generally portrayed as corrupt and incompetent, a man more concerned with maintaining his own power than in the well-being of China and its people. This book attempts to paint a rather more positive image of Chiang. Chapter 1 Parts 2 and 3 are useful for studying Chiang's role in the Northern Expedition and the 'Nanking Decade'.

Huffman, J. (2010). *Japan in World History*. **Oxford University Press.** Chapter 6 provides a detailed analysis of Japan's rise to world-power status and its increasingly aggressive foreign policy in the period from 1919 to 1945.

Ienaga, S. (2012). *Pacific War 1931–45: A Critical Perspective on Japan's Role in World War Two*. **Presidio Press.** A book that looks at the build-up to the Second World War from the Japanese perspective. Chapters 4 and 5 deal with Japan's aggression towards China, while Chapter 7 explains how Japan became involved in the Second World War.

Iriye, A. (1987). *The Origins of the Second World War in Asia and the Pacific*. **Routledge.** Chapter 1 and the first part of Chapter 2 analyse the reasons why Japan began to adopt an aggressive foreign policy in the 1930s. Chapter 5 explains Japan's decision to go to war with the USA, and the conclusion contains an account of the attack on Pearl Harbor.

Kobayashi, A. (2016). *Japan's Pacific War*. **Createspace.** An easy to read book that, in Chapters 1, 2 and 3, seeks to analyse Japanese motivation for expansionism within Asia and the ways in which this led to Japan's involvement in the Second World War.

Lynch, M. (2016). *China 1839–1997*. **Hodder.** Chapter 3 deals with China in the period from 1901–25, explaining the warlord problem and the early years of the KMT and the CCP. Chapter 4 outlines the growing rivalry between the KMT and the CCP between 1925 and 1945. Chapter 5 outlines the impact of Japanese aggression against China in the 1930s.

Snow, E. (1973 edition). *Red Star Over China*. **Penguin.** This book, first published in 1937, was written by an American who spent time at the CCP base in Shensi Province and paints a glowing picture of CCP achievements there. It is well worth reading Snow's account of the Long March (Part 5) and the Yenan Soviet (Part 6), and comparing his views with your own contextual knowledge.

Walker, B. (2015). *Concise History of Japan*. **Cambridge University Press.** Chapters 12 and 13 cover the reasons for the failure of democracy in Japan, its descent into military dictatorship and its adoption of an aggressive/ expansionist foreign policy in the 1930s.

Chapter 5
Preparing for assessment

Learning Objectives:

In this chapter, you will:

- learn about the skills that you will develop by studying AS Level History
- find out what types of question will test your skills and learn what other skills you will need in order to answer them
- understand how your skills and work might be assessed and how you can study and revise most effectively.

5.1 Introduction

In order to achieve success at AS Level History, you will need to develop skills that, perhaps, were less important in courses you might have taken in the past. Generally, pre-AS Level assessments require you to demonstrate your knowledge and understanding of certain historical events. Now you will be required to analyse and interpret your knowledge in much greater depth.

This has implications for the way you study History at a higher level. Your teacher will provide the essential background knowledge, help you to develop the various skills you need in order to do well, and suggest the resources that you will need to work with.

It is essential at AS Level, however, that you are prepared to work and research independently and participate in

discussion, which is essential for developing your own ideas and judgement. Your teacher cannot tell you what to think or what opinions to have, although they can help you learn how to think and how to form opinions. At AS Level, you will have far more responsibility for developing your own ideas, views and judgments. If you wish to aim for high-level grades at AS Level, you will have to put forward your own views on a subject and explain your reasons for coming to those views. To do this effectively, you need to acquire independent learning skills. In particular, this means reading as widely as possible around a topic so you can gain access to different interpretations of the same issues and events.

History is not a series of universally accepted facts, which once learned, will provide you with a detailed and accurate understanding of the past. Just as historical events were perceived in many different (and often contradictory) ways by people who experienced them at the time, so they have been interpreted in many different (and often contradictory) ways by historians who have studied them subsequently. Historical debates rage all the time, which make it very clear that historians often disagree fundamentally about the reasons for, or the significance of, certain key events.

You need to understand, for example, that there is no right answer to why the Japanese government made the decision to attack Pearl Harbor in 1941. Many great historians have researched this topic in great depth, and come to very different conclusions. You will need to learn to reflect on those conclusions, and come to your own judgement. This process of reflection will also give you an insight into the methods historians use to put across their ideas; you will be able to adapt these methods for your own use when answering historical questions.

History may seem to deal primarily with facts, but it is equally about opinions, perceptions, judgements, interpretations and prejudices. Take, for example, the question of whether Hitler's foreign policy was based on a calculated long-term plan of territorial expansion, or whether he was simply an opportunist, exploiting advantageous circumstances as they arose. There are many diverse opinions from historians on this issue.

You will be asked for your opinion or judgement on an issue like this, and will have to make up your own mind. You need to study the evidence, reflect on what kind of evidence it is and then analyse what it proves. This then allows you to form an opinion. When asked for an opinion or judgement, you will need to back up what you offer with reasons and evidence. In this way, historians are like lawyers in court. You are making a case and then proving it. Sometimes your fellow learners and teachers might disagree with your opinion and be able to provide compelling evidence to demonstrate why. Sometimes they might convince you to change your mind. Sometimes you will be able to convince them to change or refine their opinions. Sometimes you might just agree to differ. It is this ability to see things in different ways, and to have the confidence to use your own knowledge and understanding to make judgements, form opinions and develop arguments, that makes history so interesting and challenging.

5.2 What skills will I develop as I study AS Level History?

It is worth stressing that, alongside your historical knowledge and understanding, a wide range of skills will be assessed in the course of your studies. Most of these will be invaluable to you in both higher education and your working life. They include the ability to:

- acquire in-depth subject knowledge
- learn how to select and use knowledge effectively
- use independent research skills, which are critical for success, at AS Level and beyond
- develop independent thinking skills
- apply knowledge and understanding to new as well as familiar situations
- handle and evaluate different types of information source
- think logically and present ordered and coherent arguments
- make judgements, recommendations and decisions
- present reasoned explanations and understand implications and communicate them early and logically
- work effectively under pressure
- communicate well in English
- understand that information learned in one context can be usefully deployed in another.

All of these will be tested in some way in your History assessments. Merely learning a large number of facts will not enable you to achieve your best at AS Level History: you have to demonstrate a range of skills as well. Work on the principle that roughly half the marks awarded are going for knowledge and understanding, and half the marks are awarded for your use of the skills listed above.

How can I acquire and demonstrate the most important skills?

It is worth stressing that these skills will form an essential part of the assessment process at AS Level. AS Level studies are not just about learning facts: you have to develop the skills to use them properly.

Acquiring in-depth subject knowledge

You need to find the most suitable way for you to acquire the knowledge you need and the most effective way of remembering it so that you can use it when necessary. Often, it is a combination of reading, noting, listening, writing and discussing that helps to retain knowledge.

Selecting and using that knowledge effectively

Once you have acquired the right amount of subject knowledge, you must learn how to use it effectively. If you are asked a question on 'To what extent was appeasement responsible for the outbreak of the Second World War?' you should not only focus on appeasement, but also the other vital factors which led to the outbreak of war.

Using independent research skills

The ability to research for yourself is vital. It would be virtually impossible for any teacher to give you all the information you need. You must be able to use, effectively, a library and other research sources and tools, such as the internet, to find out things for yourself.

Developing independent thinking skills

You must learn how to think for yourself and be able to challenge ideas. You will be asked for your view on a subject, for example whether the outcome of the Russo-Japanese War of 1904-05 was due to Japanese strengths or Russian weaknesses. Both have a strong claim here, but which do you think played the greater role and why?

Handling and evaluating different types of information

You need to look at different types of information and assess how accurate and useful they might be. For example, you may need to put yourself in the position of a historian who is analysing the reasons for, and impact of, Mussolini's decision to invade Abyssinia. We are confronted by the different, and often contradictory, views expressed in a wide range of sources. Some are obviously from biased writers or cartoonists; others might have benefited or lost by the decision. Which is the most reliable and useful? Why? This is the sort of skill which might help you to make up your mind today, in an election, for example, when you are presented with many different reasons for voting one way or another.

Analysing and making judgements

This combination is a vital skill. You will be asked for a judgement on, for example, whether the Long March should be seen as a success or a failure for the CCP. First, you will have to work out for yourself what the criteria for success is in this context. Then you will need to consider the grounds on which it might be seen as a success – in the role of defence counsel, if you like. Next, you should consider the grounds on which it might not be seen as a

success. Finally, in the most difficult part, you will have to weigh up the two sides and come to a conclusion. You must be prepared to give clear reasons to defend your decision.

Explaining

You will need to explain quite complex issues clearly. For example, you could be asked to explain why the Dawes Plan was so essential for the reduction of international tension during the 1920s and have ten minutes in which to do it. You will have to briefly explain what the Dawes Plan involved, and then in three or four sentences explain why this was essential to the process. Note that you will need to give sufficient focus to the 'so' word in the question.

5.3 What types of question will test my skills?

There are three broad types of question at AS Level. They will assess your:

- knowledge and understanding and skills in communicating them
- analytical, evaluative and communication skills
- ability to read a range of sources, under pressure of time, grasp the essential points they make, contrast and evaluate those sources and reach a judgement on them, demonstrating a range of skills as well as historical knowledge and understanding.

Understanding what a question is asking you to do

There are certain key words that appear in many AS Level History questions. These 'command words' are the instructions that specify what you need to do. Accompanied by other key words, they make it clear what is expected from a response in terms of skills, knowledge and understanding.

Source-based questions

Questions based on source extracts might ask, for example:

To what extent do Sources A and C agree *on the reasons why France took no effective action in response to Germany's remilitarisation of the Rhineland in 1936?*

This type of question is looking for a firm *judgement* on the **extent** to which the sources **agree** (and disagree) on the reasons for French inaction. It is your *understanding* of those two sources that is looked for and your ability to *identify the key points showing agreement and disagreement*. The question is also looking for *source analysis* and *contextual knowledge*.

Note that, in this instance, only the two sources specified should be used.

Compare and contrast *the views in Sources B and D regarding the likely impact of the Kellogg-Briand Pact on international relations.*

This type of question is looking for your ability to *identify the similarities and differences* of the views expressed in the two sources about the ways in which the Pact might affect international relations. A good response will comment on whether there are more similarities than differences, and why. *Contextual knowledge* and *source evaluation* will also be expected.

Again, only the two sources specified should be used.

'The Locarno Treaties of 1925 greatly eased French fears of Germany.' **How far do Sources A to D** *support this view?*

What this task is looking for is a clear *judgement* of **how far** all four sources (not just the two specified in the first type of question) do, or do not, support the given view that France was less concerned about the threat posed by Germany as a result of the agreements reached at Locarno. You might find that a useful way of dealing with this response is by using the structure outlined below for questions that highlight knowledge and understanding. You need to offer a *balanced argument* in addition to your judgement, and you must make careful use of all four sources and demonstrate contextual knowledge as well. The supporting paragraphs after your judgement are a good place to do this. Demonstration of *source evaluation* skills will also be required.

To what extent *do Sources A to D support the view that the League of Nations' decision in 1921 to allow Finland to retain possession of the Aaland Islands was unjustified?*

You can take a similar approach to this type of question as you did with the 'How far …' question above. There needs to be a firm *judgement* made on *how far* the sources back up the claim (not just a vague 'to some extent'). There also needs to be a good case for your argument.

It is important to use all four sources and contextual knowledge when backing up your points. It is appropriate to quote the occasional phrase if you feel it is important to your argument, but avoid copying out large sections of the documents. Demonstration of *source evaluation skills* will be crucial here.

Other questions that assess knowledge, understanding and analytical skills

Command terms and key words in non-source-based questions might include:

Explain why *Britain and Japan formed an alliance in 1902.*

This type of question clearly requires an *explanation of why* both Britain and Japan signed the Anglo-Japanese Alliance in 1902. It is therefore your *ability to explain something clearly* that is being assessed, as well as your *knowledge and understanding of the British and Japanese motives*. It is assessing your ability to *select and apply your in-depth knowledge effectively*.

'The Kuomintang's failure to establish effective government in China during the 1930s was caused by poor leadership.' **How far do you agree?**

This type of question requires *analytical* skills as well as your *knowledge and understanding of the reasons* for the failures of the KMT government during the 1930s. You need to consider whether it was just leadership factors which led to the failure, or whether there were other, more important, factors. You need to make a *judgement* based on the *evidence* you have learned.

Your ability to analyse a topic you know a lot about is being assessed, as well as your ability to come to a judgement on **how far** (based on a scale from, for example, 'not at all' to 'completely') you agree that poor leadership was, or was not, responsible.

To what extent *was Hitler responsible for the outbreak of the Second World War?*

This type of question is also assessing your *analytical* skills and needs a similar approach to a 'How far' question. There has to be a firm *judgement* on the issue of **extent**. There also has to be evidence in the response to show that you have analysed the implications of Hitler's actions, and the extent to which other factors played an important part in leading to war. Then you need to come to a *conclusion* based on the evidence.

How successful *was the Japanese attack on Pearl Harbor in December 1941?*

This type of question assesses your *analytical* skills as well as your *knowledge and understanding* of the attack on Pearl Harbor. It requires a firm *judgement* on the *degrees* of success, or otherwise, that should be attributed to the attack. Again, there needs to be some *reflection* on what the *criteria for success* might be. There needs to be evidence of your knowledge and understanding of what the attack involved and what impact it had.

An examination of the nature and extent of the success achieved should then lead to a judgement on the degree of success attained.

How effective *were attempts to improve international relations during the 1920s?*

A similar approach can be used here to the 'how successful' type of question. Some *reflection* on what **effective** attempts might imply is expected. Easing tensions between France and Germany? Reducing the Western Powers' concerns regarding Japanese intentions in the Far East? Establishing an organisation designed to prevent future wars? The question requires an *examination of evidence* of the impact which the various attempts to improve international relations, such as the conferences in Genoa (1922) and Locarno (1925) had looked for. A good response will come to a *firm judgement based on the evidence*. Avoid vague responses such as 'It had some effect'. Argue your case strongly.

Questions that highlight knowledge and understanding

This type of question assesses your ability to:

- understand a question and its requirements and keep a firm focus on that question alone
- recall and select relevant and appropriate factual material and demonstrate your understanding of a possibly complex topic
- communicate your knowledge and understanding in a clear and effective manner.

An example of a 'knowledge and understanding' question might be: 'Explain why Britain pursued a policy of appeasement towards Nazi Germany during the 1930s.'

A good-quality answer to this type of question will:

- be entirely focused on this question. It should only be related to the reasons *why* Britain pursued a policy of appeasement towards Nazi Germany in the 1930s and no reference to other important factors is expected.
- identify three or four relevant points and develop them with supporting detail.
- indicate which of those points you feel are the most important, and why. This is vital in an 'explain why' type of question to demonstrate that you have thought about the relative importance of the points you are writing about.
- be written in as clear English as possible.

When answering, remember:

- Explain why.
- Answer the question that was asked and do not spend much time on other factors.
- Do more than merely list facts which might or might not be linked to the question.
- Make specific points and back them up with relevant and accurate detail.

This type of question is testing understanding as well as knowledge. It is not just a case of remembering one relevant point. It is also very important to show that you understand its significance in context.

Questions that highlight analysis and evaluation

This type of question assesses your ability to:

- understand the question and its requirements and keep a firm focus on that question alone
- recall and select relevant and appropriate factual material
- analyse and evaluate this material in order to reach a focused, balanced and substantiated judgement
- communicate your knowledge and understanding in a clear and effective manner.

Examples of these questions are:

- 'How Far do you agree with the view that Japan's motives for invading Manchuria in 1931 were economic rather than political?'
- 'How effective was the League of Nations during the 1920s?'

Your answer to the first question, on the Japanese invasion of Manchuria, should contain a clear judgement or argument.

- It should be entirely focused on this question. It is not asking how successful the invasion was. It is asking whether you think economic factors were more important than political factors in explaining why Japanese troops took possession of Manchuria in 1931. Be careful not to write a narrative history of the invasion itself or spend time on the background history of relations between China and Japan unless you can show how it is directly linked to the question set.

189

- Demonstrate that you have thought about causative factors in general. You need to demonstrate an understanding of Japan's economic and political circumstances in 1931, and how they impacted on its foreign policy. For example, the growing unpopularity of Japan's democratically elected government, and the country's desperate need for new sources of raw materials at a time when it was confronted with major economic problems.

- Be balanced: show that you have considered the ways in which both economic and political factors can be used to explain why Japan invaded Manchuria.

- Demonstrate that you have thought about a wide range of issues, weighed them all up and come to your own conclusion.

- Offer knowledge and understanding by backing up the various points you make with accurate and relevant detail.

- Include careful analysis: demonstrate that you have weighed up both the case for and the case against and come to a reasoned judgement. (See the box opposite.) Your response should not simply lay out the case for and against and then leave it to the reader to come to a decision.

Remember:

- Avoid simply stating a case for and against and leaving it to the reader to decide what the answer is. This is a very common error.

- Give a clear and developed answer. Make sure that your case is clearly laid out and developed carefully. You have made it quite clear why you think economic factors were more important than political considerations (or not) and given clear reasons for that. Those reasons should then be followed up in subsequent paragraphs which contain the factual details to back up those points. Good responses usually contain an opening paragraph which sets out the answer clearly and gives the reasoning behind it. Later paragraphs – perhaps three or four of them – deal with the development of the case. Then there is scope for looking at the case against, and indicating why you do not think it valid, and so demonstrating you are aware of alternative views.

Tips for answering questions that ask 'How far do you agree?'

How far do you agree with the view that 'Japan's motives for invading Manchuria in 1931 were economic rather than political'.

Try thinking about this in terms of a scale, with 'I completely agree because …' at one end and 'I completely disagree because …' at the other, with 'somewhat' in between:

Completely agree Somewhat agree Somewhat disagree Completely disagree

Depending on where you are on the scale, responses could be similar to the ones below:

1 Economic factors were the principal motivations for Japan's invasion of Manchuria in 1931, this can be evidenced by… While there were other causative factors, such as ….. and …., they did not play nearly such an important part as the economic factors.

2 While political factors did play an important role in Japan's motivations for invading Manchuria in 1931, for the following reasons … it was the economic factors that were more important. Economic factors were more important because …

3 Economic factors cannot be seen to have played anything other than a minor role in Japan's motivations for invading Manchuria in 1931. The principal causes were political, which can be seen by the growing unpopularity of Japan's democratically elected government, and the country's desperate need for new sources of raw materials…

4 Economic factors did not play a significant role as motivation for Japan's invasion of Manchuria in 1931. Much more important were … and … as it was these two factors which …

Opening sections like these demonstrate thinking about the relative importance of causes and not just trying to remember what all the causes were. It shows analytical skills and understanding, not just knowledge. Remember that all three are being assessed at AS Level.

A response to the second question, on the effectiveness of the League of Nations during the 1920s, should show the following:

- It should be entirely focused on the League's effectiveness during the 1920s. The question is not asking about how the League came to be established, or why it failed to maintain international peace and security in the 1930s. It needs to be just about how *effective* it was during the 1920s, on a scale from very effective to very ineffective.

- It should demonstrate evidence of thinking about how effectiveness might be shown in the very challenging circumstances confronting the League in the 1920s. Did the League maintain international peace? Did it uphold the Paris peace settlement, facilitating peaceful resolutions to border disputes and encouraging international disarmament? Did it have the support of all the major powers? It is important to show that you are thinking analytically.

- It should demonstrate knowledge and understanding by identifying the League's aims and the various ways in which the League influenced international relations during the 1920s.

- It should show analytical ability by weighing up the League's stated aims, commenting on the extent to which you consider its actions during the 1920s to be effective or not. The focus should be on the effectiveness of each action, but there should also be comment on the overall effectiveness.

Another example of a timed essay-type question might be: *'How far does an analysis of Hitler's foreign policy in the period from 1933 to 1939 support this view?'* Different students will take different approaches to this type of question, and you will find your own. While you are developing your techniques, you might find the following structure helpful. Even if you choose to organise your essay differently, it is important to note the strengths of this one and apply the same principles in your own writing.

Paragraph	Content
1	This needs to contain a succinct, clear answer to the question. Did Hitler intend to cause a major war or not? An answer might be, for example: *Some historians have argued that Hitler did indeed intend to cause a major war, and that he actively planned and prepared for it throughout the period from 1933 to 1939. However, careful analysis suggests that such long-term planning would have been impossible and that, in reality, Hitler wanted to avoid involving Germany in a major war - particularly a war against Britain and France. Evidence in support of this view includes:* *(a) …* *(b) …* *(c) …* This paragraph does not need not to contain much detail, just broad reasons, and should demonstrate that you are focusing on the question and thinking analytically. Avoid vague introductions or trying to 'set the scene'.
2	This could take point (a) and develop it in detail. Make sure that the objective of the paragraph is made clear from the start, for example: *The principal reason for suggesting that Hitler did not intend to cause a major war was …* And then bring in three or four accurate and relevant facts to back up your point: the evidence. This section might also explain why you feel this particular issue was the most important point, highlighting an analytical approach.
3	Point (b) could be developed here in a similar way. Again, take care to ensure that the objective of the paragraph is made clear: that you are relating what you write very obviously to your answer that Hitler did not intend to cause a major war. There is often a tendency to forget the purpose of the paragraph and simply list the facts. This often leaves the reader asking, 'So…?'
4	Make the objective clear and add as much commentary as you can to explain why this point is of less importance than (a).
5	This is a good place to develop the case 'against' in points (d) and (e), to demonstrate the balance required in this type of response. There is nothing wrong with strong arguments, however, and if you feel there is no case 'against', say so and why. It might nonetheless be a good idea to start this paragraph with, for example: *Those who support the view that Hitler did intend to cause a major war might argue that…* and bring out a possible defence of his work, however weak you might think it is.

→

6	If you have developed your response as suggested above, this can be quite brief. Avoid repetition, and keep an analytical focus, perhaps emphasising the reasons behind your thinking.
	It is important to have included an introduction as suggested in paragraph 1, not just indicate a case each way and leave all the analysis and answer to the 'conclusion'. That type of response is likely to have insufficient time and to contain facts and no analysis or judgement. It merely presents the cases each way.
	Another failing might be that the case for is very long and detailed, while the case against is much briefer and undeveloped, and yet the brief conclusion is that the case against wins even though all the facts presented point the other way. In this case, there is just not enough analysis to fully answer the question asked.

Another type of analysis and evaluation question might be: ***Evaluate the reasons for the success of the Kuomintang's Northern Expedition.***

One way of approaching this type of question is:

Paragraph	Content
1	Identify the principal reasons for the success of the Northern Expedition, such as the support it received from various sections of the Chinese population, and the importance of the KMT's collaboration with the CCP. Emphasise your response to the 'so' word in the question. It demonstrates that you are thinking analytically from the start. Including between three and five reasons shows good knowledge and understanding.
2	Take what you think was the most important reason for the Northern Expedition's success – for example the well-organised and well-equipped nature of the KMT's National Revolutionary Army, and develop this this point in detail. Make it very clear *why* you think this was the most important factor, demonstrating your analytical skills.
3, 4 and 5	Continue to develop in depth the reasons you have set out in your first paragraph, again making sure that your analytical thinking is clear and you are not merely listing reasons.
6	Avoid repetition. Focus on why you prioritised in the way you did, and show that you have thought very carefully about the 'so successful' aspect of the question.

Questions that highlight your ability to read, contrast, evaluate and judge a range of sources

Source-based questions are testing your ability to:

- understand a question and its requirements
- understand the content of a source in its historical setting
- analyse and evaluate source content and the sources themselves
- reach a focused and balanced judgement based on evidence
- communicate your argument in a clear and effective manner.

A source-based question might contain, for example, four sources on the League of Nations' response to the Italian invasion of Abyssinia.

SOURCE A

I write to inform you, very confidentially, of the government's present position regarding the Abyssinian issue. Public opinion is greatly hardening against Italy. The people regard the League of Nations as an instrument of collective security, and are determined to stick with the League's Covenant, yet are anxious to keep out of war. These points are self-contradictory, but at present the country believes that they can be reconciled. It is essential that we are seen to support the League. It must be the League, and not the British government, which is seen to declare sanctions against Italy impracticable. The blame should be placed on League members who will not play their full part or non-members

→

whose absence would make the application of sanctions futile. Treat this letter as entirely between you and me.

From a confidential letter by Samuel Hoare (British Foreign Secretary), to the British Ambassador in Paris, 24 August 1935.

SOURCE B

In conformity with its obligations, the League stands, and my country stands with it, for the collective maintenance of the Covenant in its entirety, and particularly for collective resistance to all acts of unprovoked aggression. The attitude of the British nation in the last few weeks has clearly demonstrated the fact that this is no variable and unreliable sentiment, but a principle of international conduct to which they and their government hold with firm, enduring and universal persistence. The British people have clung to their ideal of collective security and are not prepared to abandon it. Britain will be second to none in its intention to fulfil, within measure of its capacity, the obligations which the Covenant lays upon it. However, the lack of agreement within the League itself has created uncertainty.

From a speech by Samuel Hoare (British Foreign Secretary) to the League of Nations Assembly in Geneva, 11 September 1935.

SOURCE C

There is no sign of any weakening in overwhelming support for the Covenant, nor any sign that members of the League would be unwilling to shoulder their obligations should the situation demand it. The only nation which has shown a marked lack of enthusiasm for effective action against Italy is France. The French are concerned about Germany and cannot bring themselves to take

→

any step which could weaken a united front against the German peril. Britain's view that the failure of the League to act firmly against Italy at this time would fatally weaken it in any future crisis does not appeal with equal force to the French. French support of the League does not rest on a conception of international law. They regard it mainly as an instrument of French policy, to be used when it is convenient to France. Their aim is not to antagonise Italy while keeping the League alive for another crisis when it may be of value to them.

Telegram to the British government from the British Minister for League of Nations' Affairs in Geneva, September 1935.

SOURCE D

Mr Baldwin assured us that Britain held faithfully to all its pledges with regard to the League. However, he said that taking action against Italy raised extremely difficult questions. He explained the great gravity of the European situation, including the danger that Mussolini might make a 'mad dog' attack on the British fleet. Though this would, in the long run, lead to the defeat of Italy, the war might last a long time and produce both losses and serious diplomatic complications. He added that Britain could not rely on effective support from any other member of the League. With the exception of Britain (and its own preparations had fallen far into arrears) none of the members of the League seemed in a position to take decisive action against Italy. As to France, the whole French nation had a horror of war and could hardly be mobilised by any provocation short of actual invasion.

Report of a League of Nations delegation following a meeting with Stanley Baldwin, the British Prime Minister, December 1935.

1   Compare and contrast Sources C and D as evidence of how far member states of the League of Nations were prepared to take effective action against Italy in 1935.

2   'In 1935 the British government was willing to support any action which the League of Nations proposed to take in response to the Italian invasion of Abyssinia.' How far do Sources A to D support this view?

A response to a question such as number 1 should contain:

- evidence that you have really understood the points made in both sources and grasped their overall argument
- evidence that you have identified areas of both difference and similarity between the two sources
- contextual awareness, showing that you have background knowledge on the topic
- evaluation of both sources and consideration of their validity and provenance. Which would you trust most and why?

When answering, remember:

- You do not need to provide a summary of the sources, or copy out large parts of them. You might need, however, to quote just a phrase or two to back up your points.
- Evaluate the sources. You must show clearly that you have really thought about their provenance and validity.
- Include relevant contextual knowledge.

A response to a question such as number 2 above should contain:

- Evidence that you have fully understood all four sources (not just the two specified in the first question!) and grasped their overall arguments. Demonstration of clear comprehension is vital for a high-quality answer.
- Evidence that you have clearly identified the extent to which each of the four sources does, or does not, suggest that the British government was willing to support any action which the League proposed to take against Italy.
- A focused and balanced judgement on the issue of the British government's willingness, of otherwise, to fully support the League over the Abyssinian issue.
- Contextual awareness – that you have background historical knowledge and understanding and that you are not just relying on the sources for information.

- Evaluation of all four sources in this specific context (which is likely to differ from that of the first question) and consideration of their validity and provenance.
- A firm, specific judgement. Avoid merely saying, for example, 'The government showed some willingness.'

Further guidance on source-based questions

In order to make judgement and form opinions about past events, historians need to gather as much information and evidence as possible. They use a wide variety of sources for this, including written extracts, speeches, photographs, cartoons, posters, film footage, oral records and archaeological finds. Much of the evidence historians use is contradictory, reflecting the many different perspectives and opinions of the people who produced the sources. Documents and photographs, for example, can be altered by those wishing to create a more favourable view of themselves. Historians, therefore, need to analyse their sources very carefully in order to form their own opinions and judgements about the past while avoiding a one-sided or very biased study of an event or person.

Learning how to reflect on and evaluate the information you receive before you make up your own mind on a subject – whether this is who you might vote for or which mobile phone you might buy – is an important skill to acquire. The feature 'Think like a historian' used throughout this book should give you an idea about how the skills you develop in this course are useful in other areas of your life.

In much the same way, you will be faced with a variety of different historical sources during your course. You will need to be able to analyse those sources in the light of your own subject knowledge. The key word here is *analyse*. This means going far beyond just a basic *comprehension* of what a source is saying or showing. A mistake to avoid in answering source-based questions is just describing or summarising the source. You need to ask yourself questions about how reliable the source is and why it appears to contradict what some other sources seem to suggest.

Primary sources

A primary source is one that was, for example, written, spoken, drawn or photographed at, or very near, the time. It could also be a recollection some years later of an event or person. It is usually the product of someone who was directly involved in the event, or who was, in some sense, an eyewitness to it.

It needs to be stressed that primary sources tend to reflect the customs and beliefs of the creator and the time and place from which they come. You should not be critical of the contents of a primary source just because, for example, they so not share your values. Opinions today about equal rights, for instance, are very different from those held by many people 150 years ago.

A primary source has many advantages to a historian:

- It provides a first-hand, contemporary account.
- It can offer an insight into the author's perceptions and emotions at the time.
- A source created by someone directly involved in an event might give detailed 'inside information' that other people could not possibly know.

Disadvantages of a primary source might be:

- The source only gives the reader the opinions of the person who created it, which might not be typical of opinions at the time.
- A source created by someone directly involved might contain bias, for example in trying to convince an audience to agree with a particular line of argument.
- Eyewitnesses might not always be completely reliable. They might not have access to the full details of an event, or they might be trying to impose their own opinions on the audience.
- The source might be based on the memory of an event or meeting which happened many years before, or could be over-reliant on the recollections of another person.

Different types of primary source you might be asked to use include:

- a speech
- a private letter
- a diary
- an official document, such as an Act of Parliament, an order from a minister to a civil servant, a report from an ambassador to his foreign secretary, a secret memorandum by an official, a legal judgement
- an autobiography
- a cartoon
- a photograph
- a newspaper report
- an interview.

A note on bias

The word 'bias' is often misused in history essays. A dictionary definition of bias is 'the action of supporting a particular person or thing in an unfair way by allowing personal opinions to influence your judgement'. Bias can be explicit and conscious, for example, politicians seeking election will naturally emphasise the good points about their record, and emphasise the bad points about their opponents. It can also be implicit and unconscious.

A note on hindsight

Hindsight is the ability to look back at an event some time after it has occurred, with a fuller appreciation of the facts, implications and effects. With hindsight, it is easier to understand the reasons why an event took place, its significance and the impact it had. It is vital to remember that people living at the time of the event did not have the advantage of hindsight!

Assessing the reliability of sources

It should now be clear that historians have to be extremely careful when using sources. They cannot afford to accept that everything a source tells them is completely reliable or true. People exaggerate. People tell lies. People might not have seen everything there was to see People have opinions that others do not share. People simply make mistakes.

Imagine you were out walking, lost in your own thoughts, when you suddenly hear a screeching of brakes and a thud behind you. As you turn in the direction of the sounds, you see a pedestrian fall to the ground, clearly having been hit by the car, which you see driving quickly away. You are the only other person around. Your first priority would be to try to assist the pedestrian and call the emergency services. When the police arrive, they see you as a vital eyewitness to the accident, and they naturally want to take a statement from you.

But were you really an eyewitness? Did you see the accident, or just hear it and see the result? You saw the car drive quickly away, but does that mean the driver was speeding or driving dangerously at the time? How might your sense of pity for the pedestrian affect your idea of what actually happened? Could you be certain the pedestrian was not to blame for the accident? Could the pedestrian have stumbled into the path of the car? Deliberately jumped? Could you describe the car in detail, or the driver? How far might your recollection of the event be influenced by your own shock? How and why might the statements of the car driver and the pedestrian differ from your own?

So, what can we do, as historians, to minimise the risk of drawing inaccurate conclusions from sources? There are a number of questions that need to be asked in order to determine how reliable a source is and to evaluate its provenance. These apply to all types of source, not just written ones: spoken, recorded, drawn, photographed and so on.

- Who wrote it?
- When was it written?
- What is the context?
- Who was the intended audience?
- Why was it written? What was the author's motive?
- What does it actually say?
- How does it compare with your own subject knowledge and with what other sources say?
- What do you think the author might have left out?

Suppose, for example, that this is the statement given to the police later in the day by the driver of the car involved in the accident: 'I was driving carefully along the road well within the speed limit. Suddenly and without warning, a pedestrian jumped out in front of me from behind a parked lorry. I did not see him until it was far too late and it was impossible for me to stop in time and avoid hitting the pedestrian. In a state of panic, I did not stop. I drove away, in shock, but within minutes I calmed down and realised that I had to go and report the issue to the police. I had my children in the car, so once I had taken them home, I reported the incident to the police.'

- **Who wrote the source?** The driver of the car involved in the accident. Naturally, the driver would clearly not wish to be blamed for the accident, and therefore might have a very good reason for being less than honest.
- **When was it written?** Later on the same day as the accident. By this time, the driver would have recovered from the initial shock and understood that there was probably no option but to report the incident to the police. The driver might well have seen the witness and believed that the witness had the car's details and description. However, there would have been time for the driver to reflect on the incident and develop

a version of events so that the responsibility for the incident can be placed on the pedestrian. Given the shock and what might have happened since, would the driver's memory be accurate?

- **What is the context?** The driver reporting to the police to admit involvement in the accident. The police would have to take such statements, as they might be needed if there was a prosecution in a court.
- **Who was the intended audience?** Initially the police, but also possibly a counsel who might have to decide whether or not to prosecute the driver, and therefore, a judge and a jury.
- **Why was it written? What was the author's motive?** The statement had to be written as it was the law. It is possible that the driver accepted the need to report involvement in the accident. It is also possible that the driver, realising that the police would most likely catch up with him, was anxious to report the incident in order to clear his name by laying blame on the pedestrian.
- **What does it actually say?** The driver argues that he was not driving too fast or dangerously and that the accident was entirely the pedestrian's fault for jumping out suddenly into the road from behind a lorry, without checking for traffic. He admits to leaving the scene of the accident out of panic.
- **How might it compare with what other sources say?** The police are in a difficult position here. The driver might well be telling the whole truth and giving a perfectly accurate description. The driver might also have made up the entire story as he was driving too fast and using his phone. Other witnesses might be able to comment on how fast the car was going at the time. There might be some CCTV footage of the accident of variable quality. Mobile phone records can be checked. Marks on the road can be assessed. The driver mentions 'children' in the car. Would they be able to give a version of events, but, if so, would they just support their parent? If the parked lorry which hid the pedestrian from view had been moved, can an accurate picture of the whole event be made? The pedestrian might be concussed and not have an accurate recollection of events. If the police discover that the pedestrian had a long record of depression, might that not reinforce the possibility that he had 'jumped out' as the driver's statement alleges?

Finding the truth can be a very challenging task.

The following source is an extract from a speech by Francisco Franco from 17 July 1936.

> Spaniards! The situation in Spain grows more critical every day. Anarchy reigns in most of the countryside and towns, while the government fails to impose law and order. Murderers use pistols and machine guns to settle their differences and to kill innocent people. Revolutionary strikes paralyse the nation, destroying its wealth and creating hunger, forcing working men to the point of desperation. Serious crimes are committed, yet the government refuses to allow the armed forces to defend public order.
>
> Source: http://spartacuseducational.com

All sources need to be viewed critically, not just accepted at face value. To analyse this source effectively, you need to consider the same questions.

- **Who wrote (spoke) it?** Francisco Franco, a general in the Spanish army.
- **When was it written?** On 17 July 1936.
- **What is the context?** Spain was in turmoil, its elected government unable to provide solutions to the country's social and economic problems, or even maintain public order. On 17 July 1936, the date on which Franco made this speech, a group of army generals, working in collaboration with the right-wing Falange, began a revolt. Franco was flown in from the Canary Islands to assume leadership of the revolt.
- **Who was the intended audience?** The people of Spain.
- **Why was it written?** What was the author's motive? To encourage support for, and reduce opposition to, the army's attempt to take control of Spain.
- **What does the speech actually say?** That Spain had descended into anarchy and was facing the prospect of revolution. The democratically elected government had lost control, and no longer had the power of authority to govern the country. By implication, the army needed to take control in order to restore order and prevent further violence and catastrophic strikes.
- **How does it compare with other sources?** There was clearly considerable opposition to the army's attempt to take control of Spain - as evidenced by the fact that the Spanish Civil War lasted so long. Spain was divided into those who supported the army's revolt and those who strongly opposed it. Sources reflect this division.
- **How reliable is it likely to be?** It is a biased speech, seeking to justify a military takeover of Spain in defiance

of the country's constitution and against the wishes of many Spaniards.

Questions that ask you to compare and contrast sources

One type of question you might face is 'compare and contrast'. Whenever you compare two or more things, you should draw attention to the similarities and what they have in common. When contrasting, you should draw attention to the differences and points where they disagree.

A high-quality answer will show examples of the following skills:

- *Makes a developed comparison between the two sources, recognising points of similarity and difference.*
- *Uses knowledge to evaluate the sources and shows good contextual awareness.*

You are expected to do a great deal more than just give a summary of the two sources. You have to show that you have reviewed the content of the sources and that you fully comprehend them and can use your knowledge and understanding of them to answer the question. You also have to demonstrate contextual knowledge and show that you are fully aware of the sources' provenance. You must evaluate them very carefully.

SOURCE A

> The Republicans are trying to defeat the plan for a League of Nations, which, if organised, will reduce military armament among all the great powers, and make war almost, if not, impossible. If the Senate destroys the League of Nations, then the USA must begin at once to arm on a greater scale than any other nation in the world, because we must be strong enough to beat all comers. This means a navy in the Atlantic big enough to overcome the combined navies of at least three European powers. It means a navy in the Pacific bigger than Japan. It means the greatest standing army we have ever had. If we want to promote human slaughter and increase taxation, we should defeat the League of Nations. If we must abandon the glorious ideas of peace for which this nation has always stood, we must do so with full knowledge that the alternative is wholesale preparation for war.
>
> *From a public speech by Senator William G. McAdoo (Democrat), 1919*

SOURCE B

Can any American be willing to merge our nationality into internationality? We do not mean to live within and for ourselves alone, but we do mean to hold our ideals safe from foreign interference. Americans will not fail civilization in the advancement of peace. We are willing to give, but we resent demand. We desire a world relationship which will maintain peace through justice rather than force, yet still hold us free from menacing involvement. It is better to be the free agents of international justice than to be shackled by a written compact which surrenders our freedom of action and gives the League the right to proclaim America's duty to the world. No surrender of rights to a world council should ever summon Americans to war. There is sanctity in that right which we will not surrender.

From a public speech by Senator Warren G. Harding (Republican), 1919

In order to look at the similarities and differences between the two sources, there has to be some analysis.

- **What information does the source contain?** The two sources present different views on the debate which took place in the USA during 1919 regarding whether or not the country should join the proposed League of Nations. The sources are both extracts from speeches. Source A argues that the USA should join, while Source B argues that it would be against American interests to do so.
- **Who made these speeches?** Two American Senators, William McAdoo and Warren Harding.
- **When were these speeches made?** 1919.
- **Context?** Democratic President Woodrow Wilson returned to the USA in 1919 with details of the proposals, agreed at the Paris Peace Conference, for the establishment of a League of Nations. He actively sought political and public support for these proposals. These speeches were made during the heated debate which then took place, both within the Senate and across the country as a whole, regarding whether the USA should become a member of the League of Nations.

- **Audience?** Since these were both public speeches, the Senators were addressing the American people.
- **Motive?** To sway American public opinion on the issue of whether or not the USA should become a member of the League of Nations.
- **Context?** In 1919, the US Senate was split largely along party lines. Most Democrats supported Wilson's proposals - they favoured *internationalism*, the USA working closely with other nations to develop a League of Nations which would reduce the risk of future wars. Republicans, who now held a majority in the Senate, supported *isolationism* - they argued that membership of the League would undermine American independence, and force the USA to become involved in wars in support of the League's decisions. With a presidential election due In 1920 both Democrats and Republicans tried to sway public opinion to support their contrasting views.
- **Validity? Provenance?** These were politically motivated speeches, reflecting the personal views of the speakers and the parties they represented.

A good way of comparing the views contained in these two sources is to devise a simple plan once you have read them carefully, keeping the focus strictly on the issue of whether or not the USA should join the League of Nations. For example, Source A:

- Argues that the League of Nations would lead to disarmament and make future wars 'almost, if not, impossible'.
- If the USA did not join the League, it would need to increase its armed forces in order to protect its interests and ensure its national security.
- Enhancing the USA's armed forces would require an increase in taxation.
- Joining the League was the best way to ensure future peace – not becoming a member of the League would lead to the USA's involvement in wars.
- McAdoo, a Democratic Senator, is heavily critical of the Republican Party's attempts to defeat the proposals for US membership of the League of Nations.

Source B shows that:

- Harding supports the basic aim of the League (maintaining 'peace through justice rather than force'), but argues that membership of the League would undermine the USA's independence.
- Membership of the League would lead to foreign interference in American affairs.

- It could also lead to the USA's involvement in wars in support of decisions made by the League.
- The USA should be free to make its own decisions on issues such as whether or not to go to war – it should not be compelled to do so because of its commitments to a League of Nations.
- Harding was a Republican Senator who strongly opposed Wilson's vision of a League of Nations, and was to be victorious in the presidential election of 1920.

From this plan it is easy to see where the authors agree and disagree. They both want international peace and the avoidance of the USA's involvement in any future war. However, they disagree about the best way of achieving these aims, and the possible implications if the USA decided to become a member of the League of Nations.

Visual sources: posters

Visual sources should be analysed and evaluated in much the same way. Look carefully at Figure 5.1 and the caption details below:

Figure 5.1: Republican poster published c.1937. It shows Republican supporters fighting a defensive battle against Franco's Nationalist forces during the Spanish Civil War. The slogan reads 'They shall not pass'.

- **What is its message?** The Republicans are fighting a determined war against the military Nationalist forces of General Franco. The Republican fighters are totally committed to the task of preventing Spain falling under military control. They are well-organised (e.g. they all appear to be wearing similar uniforms), and, as such, have every chance of winning the war.
- **Who is providing the information?** The Republican side in the Spanish Civil War.
- **Context?** In 1936, a group of army generals, in collaboration with the right-wing Falange Party, began a revolt designed to remove the democratically elected government of Spain and take control of the country. Known as the Nationalists and led by General Franco, they were opposed by the Republicans in a civil war which lasted until Franco finally gained victory in 1939. Those who fought on the Republican side were mainly civilian volunteers, supported by foreigners who had gone to Spain after joining the International Brigades.
- **Audience?** The people of Spain. It is possible that the poster was also distributed in other countries.
- **Motives?** To encourage more people to join the Republican fighters in the war against the Nationalists.
- **Contextual knowledge?** Unlike the professional soldiers under Franco's command, the Republicans were largely armed workers who lacked military experience, organisation and discipline. Moreover, while Franco had maintained the unity of the various right-wing groups that made up the Nationalists (e.g. the army, the Church, monarchists, Falangists), the Republicans were far less unified, comprising various left-wing groups with their own, often contradictory, aims (e.g. communists, socialists, anarchists). A considerable amount of evidence suggest that, in reality, Republican fighters were not as well-organised and well-equipped as the poster implies.

Visual sources: photographs

Photographs also need careful analysis and evaluation.

- **What does the image tell us?** Like those depicted in Figure 5.1, the Republican supporters in Figure 5.2 are fighting with courage and dedication for a cause they obviously believe in strongly. However, the impression given here is very different from that of the poster. The Republican fighters here are far less numerous than those shown in the poster. They seem less well-organised (they are not all wearing similar uniforms, and some are clearly in civilian clothing). They seem less well

199

Figure 5.2: Republican fighters defending an unidentified road against Nationalist forces during the Spanish Civil War (photo taken by an unknown press photographer in c.1937)

equipped (they are firing different types of weapons, including handguns which would be relatively inefficient in such a battle).

- **Who is providing the information?** A press photographer covering the Spanish Civil War.
- **When was it taken?** C.1937 - as with the poster, the exact date is uncertain.
- **Context?** During the Spanish Civil War. The context is the same as that of the poster.
- **Audience?** Readers of the newspaper(s) in which the photograph was published.
- **Motives of the photographer?** The press photographer would make money by selling pictures of the war to newspapers. The photograph would be used to illustrate written coverage of the Spanish Civil War. In order to speculate further about motives, we would need to know something about the photographer, such as his nationality and whether there were reasons to suspect that he favoured either the Republicans or the Nationalists in the Spanish Civil War.

- **Subject knowledge?** This photographs fits more logically than the poster with the mass of evidence regarding the nature of the Republican resistance to Franco's forces in the Spanish Civil War. However, we need to remember that it is simply a single photograph of one particular incident in the war, which may or may not be typical.

Like all sources, photographs can be of tremendous value to a historian, but they need to be used with care. Photographs can easily be stage-managed. For example, there is a well-known photograph of Hitler being enthusiastically welcomed into Vienna by large numbers of Austrians following Anschluss in 1938. The impression is that the Austrian people were delighted that their country had been united with Germany. Can we be certain, however, that their delight was genuine? Could they have been acting in response to guns trained on them by German soldiers strategically positioned out of camera shot? We should also remember that, using techniques such as air brushing, photographs can easily be altered to give a totally different impression to that originally intended.

Visual sources: cartoons

Cartoons can be difficult to analyse. In most cases they are drawn and published for two reasons:

- to amuse and entertain
- to make a point and send a message.

To achieve either, or both, of these, cartoons might employ symbolism and a subtle form of humour which might be easily understandable to people at the time, but which is less obvious to us.

RENDEZVOUS

Figure 5.3: This cartoon was published in a British newspaper on 29 September 1939. The image text reads: [Hitler] 'The scum of the Earth I believe?' [Stalin] 'The bloody assassin of the workers, I presume?'

Hitler (left) and Stalin (right) are drawn as clearly recognisable figures. They look smug and pleased with themselves. They are greeting each other with exaggerated politeness (doffing caps, bowing, hands on hearts), yet their verbal greetings imply mutual dislike. Hitler greets Stalin with the words 'The scum of the earth, I believe', while Stalin is depicted saying 'The bloody assassin of the workers, I presume'. Both are drawn carrying guns, symbols of their warlike and aggressive tendencies. They are shown as meeting over the prostrate body of a soldier, representing Poland. Debris and rubble convey the destruction of war and the aggressive nature of Germany's invasion of Poland. The background could be interpreted as smoke rising from bombs, or as storm clouds gathering to represent future conflicts. Either way, a bird – possibly the dove of peace – flies low to avoid it.

- **Who is providing the information?** The cartoonist and the British newspaper which published the cartoon. The easily-recognisable signature at the bottom right tells us that the cartoonist was David Low, who worked in Britain and was well-known for his politically-inspired cartoons.
- **When was it published?** 29 September 1939.
- **Context?** Germany's invasion of Poland, commencing on 1 September 1939, finally led to the end of appeasement. Britain and France declared war on Germany on 3 September 1939. However, it took time for these countries to mobilise their troops and they were able to offer little support to Poland, which fell by 29 September 1939. As agreed in the Nazi-Soviet Pact, Germany and the USSR divided the spoils between them.
- **What is the message?** Hitler and Stalin are portrayed as deceitful, evil, selfish and aggressive. Their plan to conquer Poland and divide the spoils between them has been successful - they are proud of what they have achieved and show no remorse. The Nazi-Soviet Pact is depicted as a treaty between enemies, prepared to ignore their mutual hatred in order to further their desire for territorial conquest. The policy of appeasement had clearly failed - it had not stopped Hitler from continuing with an aggressive foreign policy, leading to the destruction of Poland. It is likely that Hitler will continue to seek further conquests.
- **Readership?** The cartoon was published in a British newspaper and was intended for a British audience - an audience that was now involved in a war against Hitler's Germany.
- **Motives of the cartoonist and the editors of the newspaper?** Britain's declaration of war on Germany obviously caused great concern to the British people. Fear of involvement in another major war had been a key reason why British public opinion had largely supported Britain's appeasement policy during the 1930s. Some people doubted the wisdom of going to war in defence of a country situated far away in Central Europe. The cartoon was intended to address these concerns by stressing that Britain's decision to declare war on Germany was justified - the people of Britain were involved in a just and honourable war against evil and unprovoked aggression.

When you study a cartoon like this, you need to reflect carefully how far your own subject knowledge supports or challenges the views represented.

201

Cross-referencing between sources

A source should never be used in isolation. It needs to be interpreted in the light of information obtained from other sources, as well as your own knowledge. There are three main reasons why cross-referencing between sources is so important.

- We can only judge how useful and reliable a source is by comparing it with what we already know and what other sources say.
- Reading several sources can help us deal with apparent contradictions and other concerns we might have about the source.
- By using a combination of sources, we can often deduce things that none of the individual sources would lead us to by themselves.

Look at the three sources below.

SOURCE A

The settlement of the Czechoslovakian problem, which has now been achieved, is, in my view, only the prelude to a larger settlement in which all of Europe may find peace. This morning I had another talk with the German Chancellor, Herr Hitler, and here is the paper which bears his name upon it as well as mine. I would just like to read it to you –

'We are agreed in recognising that the question of Anglo-German relations is of the first importance for the two countries and for Europe. We regard this agreement as symbolic of the desire of our two peoples never to go to war with one another again'.

Source: Extract from a public speech by the British prime minister, Neville Chamberlain, on his return to Britain following the Munich Agreement, 30 September 1938

SOURCE B

I prayed that the responsibility might not fall upon me to ask this country to accept the awful fact of war. I fear that I may not be able to avoid that responsibility. Responsibility for this terrible catastrophe lies on the shoulders of one man, the German Chancellor, who has not hesitated to plunge the world into misery in order to serve his own senseless ambitions.

Source: Extract from a parliamentary speech by the British prime minister, Neville Chamberlain, 1 September 1939

SOURCE C

I did not think it possible that Czechoslovakia would be virtually served up to me on a plate by her friends.

Source: The German Chancellor, Adolf Hitler, addressing his senior generals following the Munich Agreement, September 1938

There seems to be a contradiction between Sources A and B. In Source A, Chamberlain claims that, at Munich, he had reached an agreement with Hitler – an agreement which would lead to peace in Europe; a commitment that Britain and Germany would 'never go to war with one another again'. However, in Source B, Chamberlain is informing parliament that Britain is about to go to war against Germany, and that Hitler is entirely to blame for this 'terrible catastrophe'. How can we explain this apparent contradiction?

- The first thing to note is that Source A is dated September 1938, while Source B comes from a year later - September 1939. The conclusion we can draw from this is that, at some point in the intervening year, Chamberlain changed his assessment both of Hitler and of the significance of the agreement signed at Munich.

- This raises a new question: why did Chamberlain change his mind about the agreement? Source C can help us answer this. It is clear from Source C that Hitler's interpretation of the Munich Agreement was very different from Chamberlain's. Hitler believed that by signing the agreement, Britain was effectively giving its approval for the German takeover of Czechoslovakia - a clear sign of weakness that Hitler had every intention of exploiting.

- Desperate to avoid involving Britain in a costly and unpopular war, Chamberlain had chosen to believe Hitler's claims at Munich that he wanted only what rightfully belonged to Germany and that he had no more territorial ambitions in Europe. By September 1939, it was obvious that Hitler had been lying to Chamberlain during their meeting in Munich. It would have been impossible for Chamberlain to deny this fact – after all, on 1 September 1939, the date of Source B, German troops began the invasion of Poland and, later that same day, Britain would declare war against Germany.

- By linking these three sources with our own subject knowledge, we can also reach another conclusion. When he returned to Britain from the Munich Conference in September 1938, Chamberlain proudly waved the piece of paper outlining the agreement he had made with Hitler. He boasted that the agreement removed the terrifying threat of war, and was keen to take the credit for getting Hitler to make such peaceful commitments. By September 1939, however, it was clear that these were hollow boasts – the truth was that Hitler had deceived Chamberlain at Munich. Rather than admitting that he had made an error of judgement, Chamberlain chose to lay all the blame for the outbreak of the Second World War on Hitler. This was a way of deflecting attention and criticism from his own errors, particularly his long-term support for the policy of appeasement, which had been exposed as a blatant failure.

A summary on dealing with source-based questions

- Show that you have fully grasped what the source is saying. Try highlighting the key points. Remember that the key point can often be in the last sentence.

- Demonstrate that you have thought about its provenance and reliability. You must not just accept what the source is saying. Think about what the author might have left out. You need to test a source's reliability by:

  - comparing what it says with what other sources say and with your own subject knowledge
  - looking carefully at who created it, when, why and for what purpose or audience
  - establishing if there are any reasons to doubt the reliability of the source.

- Interpret. What can be learned from the source, taking into account your judgement on how reliable the source is?

- Keep objective. Always look at a source objectively and with an open mind.

- Never make assumptions. For example, don't assume that a source must be biased because it was written by a certain person from a certain place at a certain time. These points might establish a motive for bias, but do not necessarily prove that a text is biased.

- Never make sweeping or unsupported assertions. A statement such as 'Source A is biased...' *must* be accompanied by evidence that you know exactly what bias is as well as evidence and examples to demonstrate in what way it is biased, together with reasons to explain why it is biased.

- Compare sources. If you are asked to compare and contrast two sources, make sure you analyse both sources carefully before you start to write your answer. Draw up a simple plan.

- Evaluate the sources clearly.

- Draw conclusions: what can you learn from your analysis of the sources? How does it enhance your knowledge and understanding of a topic or event?

- Include contextual knowledge.

5.4 How might my skills and work be assessed?

Revision techniques

Too often, students can think that the purpose of revision is to get information into your brain in preparation for an assessment. It is seen as a process where facts are learned. If you have followed the course appropriately, however, and made sensibly laid-out notes as you have gone along, all the information you need is already there. The human brain, like a computer, does not forget what it has experienced. The key purpose of revision is not to put information into the brain, but to ensure that you can retrieve it when it is required.

Revision needs to be an ongoing process throughout the course, not just in the days or weeks before an exam.

The focus of your revision should be identifying the key points, on, for example, why there was international tension in the period from 1919 to 1923. Once you have those key points clear, the supporting detail will come back to you. The notes you make during the course therefore are very important, and it is vital that they are presented effectively.

Copying lists of facts from a book can be a pointless exercise. You need to think about what you are writing, comprehend it and learn to analyse it. Make your notes in such a way that you are answering a simple question. For example: 'What were the most important causes of the 'Scramble for Africa?' Don't just write a list of the causes. Prioritise them with reasons. This will prompt you to study all the various events that happened in those days. You will think about which were the most important and why. Once you have identified the key points, make sure there are two or three relevant factors which show you understand why they were key points. Doing this will then help you deal with a variety of question such as: 'Explain why the Genoa Conference of 1922 failed to reach an agreement,' and 'To what extent was the Treaty of Versailles based on Woodrow Wilson's Fourteen Points?'

Quality revision and plenty of practice in attempting questions under timed conditions is vital. If you feel you have not done enough at school, you could ask your teacher to provide some questions you can practise on your own under timed conditions.

Exam preparation

This section offers a few general points about how you could approach an examination. Some might seem obvious, but it is worth remembering that, under pressure, we are all capable of making mistakes. It is useful to be aware of potential pitfalls.

The syllabus will include details of what you need to know during your course and for the exams. You should be aware of:

- What topics the questions can be about. This will be covered during your course.
- What form the questions can take. Your teacher can help you understand the types of task you are likely to face, and the syllabus will give details of wording. The different types of question in this book should also help you become more familiar with exam-style questions.
- How long you will have to answer an assessment paper.

- Which parts of a question paper you can ignore. Some question papers might have separate sections for those who have studied European History or those who have studied US History.
- The equipment you will need for writing and what you may or may not bring into an exam room. There are very strict rules on mobile phones, for example, and smart watches. Check if you are allowed to bring water in.

Rubric

All examination papers contain **rubric**. This provides you with essential information about how long a timed assessment will last, how many questions you have to answer and from what sections, and so on. It is surprising how many students make rubric errors each year, by doing too many questions for example, or questions from inappropriate sections of the paper. These basic errors can really damage your chances of success.

KEY TERM

Rubric: This is the set of rules and instructions you must follow in an exam. They will usually tell you how long the exam will last, where to put your answers, how many questions to answer and from which sections.

Question selection

Sometimes, you will be required to answer all the questions in a paper. However, if you have an opportunity to choose, for example, two out of three questions, this advice might be useful:

- Read all parts of all questions before you make your selection.
- Avoid choosing a question just because it is about a *topic* you feel confident about. This is not necessarily a guarantee that you understand what the question is asking and you can answer it effectively.
- Select by task – what the question is asking you to do – rather than by the basic subject matter.
- If questions consist of more than one part, make sure that you can answer all of the parts. Avoid attempting a question because you are confident about the topic in part (a) if you know very little about part (b).
- Decide the order in which you are going to attempt the questions. Perhaps you should not leave the question you feel most confident about until last if you are worried about running out of time.

Timing

It is a very good idea to work out well in advance how long you have to complete each question or part of a question. Make a note of it and make every effort to keep to that timing.

Practising answering questions under timed conditions is something you can do on your own as part of your revision. Take care not to make the mistake of spending too much time on a question which you know a great deal about and leave yourself insufficient time for a question which might carry twice as many marks.

If you run out of time, you will not be able to answer all of the questions fully. If you have spent too long on your first question with its two parts, there might be a case for attempting the second part of the next question if it carries more marks.

Planning

There is nearly always the temptation in an exam to avoid spending time on planning and instead just get started. Without planning, however, there is very real risk of including irrelevant information, or not fully explaining the relevance of information, when answering questions.

A useful plan for an 'Explain why ...' question might be three or four bullet points identifying the main reasons for the event, in order of importance, with a couple of supporting facts for each. Effective plans for the longer essay-type questions, such as 'To what extent ...', could be set out in 'case for' and 'case against' columns or as a mind - map, which has a focus on thinking out an answer. A plain list of facts will not be much help as a plan. Use the plan to clarify your ideas on what the question is asking.

How much information should be included in a response?

This is not a straightforward question to answer. An important factor to remember at AS Level is that about 50% of marks are allocated to your knowledge and understanding of a topic, and about 50% to the skills used in applying them. In the source-based sample questions provided in this book, you can see that it is important to bring in contextual knowledge to back up your source evaluation and the points you are making. A couple of factual points such as *'Chamberlain said this on 1 September 1939, the day on which German troops began the invasion of Poland, in an attempt to justify Britain's*

declaration of War against Germany', is a suitable approach for the first part of a source-based question. For a second part, where you should develop a case, the points you make need to be backed up by clear references to the sources, and then by at least two factual points.

For questions in papers where there are no sources, the factual information plays a more significant role. However, see it as providing support to your explanations or arguments, and do not let it dominate. In an 'explain why' type of question, it is most important to identify the reasons why something happened, and then back up each of those reasons with two or three items of information. In essay-type questions, you should think in terms of bringing three or four factual items to support your points. Look on facts as support for your ideas; the evidence of your knowledge and understanding.

How much should I write?

There is no requirement to write a specific number of words in a response, nor to fill a certain number of pages. Aim to keep your focus on writing a relevant response to the question set and making sure that you are aware of the assessment criteria for the type of question you are dealing with. Don't worry if another student seems to be writing more than you are.

Past papers

Previous exam papers can be very helpful to all learners and teachers. They will give an idea of what types of question have been assessed in the past and provide plenty of opportunities for practise. If you use past papers, it is important to attempt the questions under the appropriate timed conditions. It should be stressed, however, that, while tackling past papers is very good practice, attempting to memorise answers is very poor preparation. Students who produce ready-made answers are likely to be answering a question they might have expected, and not the one they are actually being asked.

The syllabus

The syllabus provides:

- details of the options to be studied at AS level
- how many options have to be taken
- how long each examination is
- what proportion of the overall marks are allocated to each paper

- the assessment objectives and the relationship between them and the different papers you take. It might say, for example, that:
  - 30% of the total marks at AS Level are awarded for Assessment Objective (AO) 1(a), which is knowledge and understanding in Paper 2
  - 30% of the marks are awarded for AO2(a), which is analysis and evaluation in Paper 2

Details of each of the papers, what form the questions take and how many questions there are in each paper; if there are sources, it will be clear how many there will be, what type of sources might be used and the maximum number of words in an extract, so you will know how much you will have to read

The key questions; these indicate broad areas of history for study; all questions set in the exam will fit into one of the key questions. To use the International syllabus as an example, if a key question is 'Why was there a rapid growth of industrialisation after 1780?' then one of the AS Level exam questions might be something like, 'To what extent was improved transport the principal cause of the rapid industrialisation in the late 18th century?'

Key content; this suggests some of the areas which should be studied, but these are not all the areas to study for a key question; the fact that you are studying something which is not specified in the key content does not mean it will not be examined.

There are decisions to be made by your teachers when it comes to AS Level History. There might be a choice of areas of study – for example, between European history and American history. The choice might depend on the teachers' expertise and the range of resources available in your school. There may also be a choice of how many topics to study. Your teachers will decide whether to study all three topics, in order to give you a choice of question in the exam, or just study two, in order to focus on them and so build up additional knowledge and understanding.

There are real benefits to having the syllabus available in helping you know what to expect during your course and in the assessments.

Mark schemes

Mark schemes accompany the question papers and make it clear how your work will be assessed. They are in two parts. The first is a generic mark scheme, which lays out what is required from a response in general terms. This will specify the elements that make up a high-quality work, such as developed analysis, balance or source evaluation. The second part indicates the type of factual support expected and the principal points in a 'compare and contrast' question.

The mark scheme helps you to see what a good-quality answer looks like and you can use this to reflect on your own work and consider how it might be improved. The mark scheme makes it clear that just learning facts is not enough, you need to demonstrate a range of skills as well.

Assessment objectives

Assessment objectives cover the skills to be tested in the exams. The assessment objectives (AO) for AS Level History are:

- AO1: Recall, select and deploy historical knowledge appropriately and effectively.
- AO2: Demonstrate an understanding of the past through explanation, analysis and a substantiated judgement of: key concepts causation, consequence, continuity, change and significance within an historical context, the relationships between key features and characteristics of the periods studied.
- AO3: Analyse, evaluate and interpret a range of appropriate source material.
- AO4: Analyse and evaluate how aspects of the past have been interpreted and represented.

Index